THE COSTS AND RESOURCES OF LEGAL EDUCATION

A Study in the Management of Educational Resources

THE COSTS AND RESOURCES OF LEGAL EDUCATION

A Study in the Management of Educational Resources

PETER deL. SWORDS

FRANK K. WALWER

Published by
COUNCIL ON LEGAL EDUCATION FOR PROFESSIONAL RESPONSIBILITY
New York   1974

Distributed by
COLUMBIA UNIVERSITY PRESS
New York   •   London   1974

Copyright © 1974 Council on Legal Education for Professional Responsibility

Distributed by the Columbia University Press

Council on Legal Education for Professional Responsibility, Inc.
280 Park Ave., New York, N.Y. 10017

Columbia University Press
562 W. 113 Street, New York, N.Y. 10025

Library of Congress Cataloging in Publication Data

Swords, Peter deL   1935-
   The costs and resources of legal education.

   Includes bibliographical references.
    1. Law — Study and teaching — United States — Costs.
I. Walwer, Frank K., 1930-   joint author.
II. Council on Legal Education for Professional
Responsibility. III. Title.
KF272.S9   340'.07'1173   74-22459
ISBN 0-915120-00-3

Printed in the United States of America

To Janet and Deirdre, MaryAnn and Gregory

Contents

Acknowledgments

To begin, we are delighted to acknowledge our great debt to William Pincus, President of the Council on Legal Education for Professional Responsibility. His recognition of the need for all concerned to have a general understanding of the financial underpinnings of legal education gave birth to this study; the foundation of which he is President provided indispensable financial support; and his warm encouragement during the long course of our efforts sustained us often and made it immeasurably easier for our work to proceed.

We are particularly grateful for the assistance and information provided, in the process of gathering our data, by Millard H. Ruud (currently Executive Director of the Association of American Law Schools), formerly Consultant on Legal Education to the American Bar Association, and his successor, James P. White. Their cooperation throughout the study was essential to the successful completion of our task. We further acknowledge the generous and gracious cooperation of the personnel at the several case-study law schools with whom we worked closely in the tedious gathering and categorization of data. In this effort, E. Gordon Gee, then a doctoral candidate at Teachers College, Columbia University, was responsible for liaison with the case-study schools and over-all direction of the initial data gathering. His energetic and skillful efforts, in these early stages, prior to his appointment as Assistant Dean of the University of Utah College of Law, were extremely helpful.

We owe a special debt to the following who provided us with technical assistance. William Benton Schrader, formerly Director, Statistical Analysis, and currently Senior Research Psychologist, Educational Testing Service (ETS), was of particular assistance in reviewing and contributing to the formulation of several of our statistical methods and procedures. For their assistance in this area, we want also to acknowledge our appreciation of Barbara Pitcher, Senior Statistical Associate (ETS), and Jean-Claude Chetrit, then a student in the Department of Mathematical Statistics, Columbia University. For information and advice regarding our discussion of student financial aid, we are grateful to James L. Bowman, Director, Financial Aid Studies and Programs, (ETS), and Dwight H. Horch, Director, Graduate and Professional School Financial Aid Service, (ETS).

A major debt of gratitude goes to Ann M. Stark for her invaluable assistance in the enormous job of assembling, processing and tabulating the data for chapters 2, 3, 4, section 2 of chapter 6, and Appendices B through H. She worked painstakingly and long, and with great care and accuracy. In addition, Ms. Stark did all the graphic work that appears in this book. Indeed, the dedication and competence with which she carried through the aforementioned tasks was extraordinary. We wish to thank for their helpfulness Glenn A. Grossman, then a student at the Graduate School of Business, Columbia University, who primarily assisted by collating case-study materials for chapter 5, and Donald C. Skemer, then a student at the School of Library Service, Columbia University, who assisted by doing basic research for chapter 4. We acknowledge with appreciation the copy editing of Victory Pomeranz, and the proofreading of Dorothy M. Kane.

Throughout the study, we received the encouragement and advice of many. We would like to note our appreciation for the gracious support and suggestions of Morris L. Cohen, Maximilian W. Kempner, A. Leo Levin, Joseph H. Smith, Joseph T. Sneed, and Michael I. Sovern.

In closing, we want to express a special word of gratitude to our colleague and friend, Professor Harvey J. Goldschmid of the Faculty of Law, Columbia University. We have profited enormously from his insight and comprehensive understanding of legal education. Throughout the length of the study he gave generously of his time and made many invaluable suggestions concerning the manuscript. His support has been inestimable.

Peter deL. Swords
Frank K. Walwer

New York, New York
August 1974

Introduction and Summary

Introduction

This study finds its origin in the interest of the Council on Legal Education for Professional Responsibility in the fiscal aspects of legal education.[1] Over a period of years, the Council has been making grants to numerous law schools in support of clinical programs. Since it was a substantial benefactor, the Council was concerned not only with clinical programs but with the fiscal welfare of legal education generally. In furtherance of this interest, the Council's President invited a small group of law school deans to a meeting in June 1971 designed to develop some common insight into the fiscal state of legal education. Although only a handful met, the deans expressed widely held sentiments regarding "the new depression" in higher education and its implications for legal education. An extremely broad range of matters was discussed, including rapidly rising tuition charges, faculty salary pressures, rising library costs, the difficulty in maintaining adequate supporting services, and fiscal relations between law schools and central administrations as universities found themselves under increasing fiscal stress. In addition, such program-related topics as enrollment pressures, and the traditional concerns over high student/faculty ratios, large classes, and "education on the cheap" were discussed. But, if any particular theme was dominant, it was concern about the pervasive lack of knowledge regarding the fiscal underpinnings of legal education. It was apparent that this paucity of information—in a time of fiscal tensions—would serve only to exacerbate the growing stress over the costs and resources of legal education. Prompted by these concerns, a grant was made by the Council to Columbia University in the fall of 1971 to support a fiscal study of legal education.

1. The Council on Legal Education for Professional Responsibility is a specialized philanthropy established under a grant from the Ford Foundation to support experiments in clinical legal education.

At the outset it was determined that two objectives would be sought: first, to develop a descriptive framework and the means for analyzing and interpreting data concerning costs and resources; and second, to conduct a retrospective examination of the fiscal aspects of legal education between 1955 and 1970. To begin, precise data and program information were elicited from a small group consisting of six private schools and three public schools, referred to in this study as the "case-study schools." A questionnaire (reproduced in Appendix A) was prepared and issued in order to obtain information from the case-study schools for the academic years 1955-56, 1960-61, 1965-66, and 1970-71. Because of the complex and confidential nature of the information that was sought, the data were supplemented by close communication and, in most instances, personal visits to the schools. The case-study schools were selected to represent the private and public sectors, different geographic regions, and varying degrees of educational resources. The detailed and intimate fiscal and program data furnished by the case-study schools were used in an effort to acquire a comprehensive and informed understanding of the management of resources and the fiscal operations of law schools in a university setting. In reporting the findings, the case-study schools are referred to by code. Code designations for a single school vary throughout in order to maintain confidentiality. It should be noted that, in view of the diversity of legal education, the case-study schools should not be taken as representative of law schools generally.

In addition, to provide information with respect to law schools generally, certain data regarding a large number of law schools were examined. Information regarding faculty salaries, inspection reports, and other important data were made available by the Consultant on Legal Education to the American Bar Association (A.B.A.). Other sources of information included editions of the A.B.A.'s annual *Review of Legal Education* which contain extensive data regarding law school enrollments, faculty size, and tuition.

Examination of the data provided by the case-study schools and law schools generally required the development of new analytical approaches and methods. Such methods emerged during the course of our early efforts to make intelligible the welter of fiscal and program data involved in the several components of legal education. The study explains the use of these methods and also employs these tools in analyzing cost and resource trends during the fifteen-year period, 1955-1970.[2] It is hoped that such methods will be used by others for planning purposes, and as tools for interpreting how changes in costs and resources affect individual institutions or disciplines.

A brief outline of the study follows. To provide perspective and a general background, a history of legal education from a fiscal standpoint is set forth in chapter 1. The following areas are then examined: instructional costs (chapters 2 and 3), library costs (chapter 4), supporting services (chapter 5), and resources, including tuition and financial aid (chapter 6). Certain aspects of the costs and resources of legal education are not, however, covered. No investigation, for

---

2.   References in the study to the years 1955 and 1970 generally refer to the academic years 1955-56 and 1970-71.

example, has been made of the capital costs of legal education. Part-time and graduate legal education are not examined as such.[3] Relatively few comparisons are made between the costs of legal education and those of other disciplines. Finally, this is not an economic study in the sense of examining the value of legal education to a student or to society. All these subjects are important, and certainly warrant additional study in the future.[4]

Overview

Our study is divided between the two broad categories of costs and resources. The examination of costs is, in turn, divided into three major areas: Instructional, Library, and Supporting Services.

In the Instructional area, we define "instructional cost" to consist solely of amounts paid to the law school instructional staff as salaries. Funds made available for other activities related to the instructional program, such as secretarial assistance or allocations for faculty research, fall within the Supporting Services area under the category of instructional support.

Our examination of Instructional cost is twofold. First, through the use of a formula, an examination is made of changes in total and per-student instructional cost in terms of change in enrollment, student/faculty ratio, and faculty salary level. Second, an examination is made of how changes in the underlying structure of instructional cost are reflected in changes in the educational program of law schools, in terms of both curriculum and class size.

Library costs are deemed to consist of all dollars expended for library operations. Library costs are examined in two categories: expenditures for books and expenditures for personnel.

Supporting Services, by definition, is a "catch-all" category comprising all costs relating to activities other than Instructional and Library. Examples include dean's office administration, student activities, and maintenance. It is in this area that the distinction between "direct costs" and "indirect costs" is most pronounced. Thus, our examination of Supporting Services is broadly divided into two parts. The first part considers those costs which are incurred by law schools for supporting-service functions and defrayed by direct dollar allocations made explicitly available to law schools. Such costs are labeled "direct costs." The second part considers those costs which are incurred by universities on behalf of the supporting services for the law schools but defrayed by dollar allocations made available to various university activities (for example, plant operations) for the benefit of several departments. In this case, such costs are

---

3.   For a comprehensive study of part-time legal education, see Charles D. Kelso, "The AALS Study of Part Time Legal Education," *1972 Annual Meeting Proceeding*, Part One, Section 11 (Washington, D.C.: Association of American Law Schools, 1972).

4.   For recent discussions of legal education, see Herbert L. Packer and Thomas Ehrlich, "New Directions in Legal Education" (New York: McGraw-Hill, 1972), a report prepared for the Carnegie Commission on Higher Education, which also contains Paul D. Carrington, "Training for the Public Professions of the Law: 1971." Also, see Boyer and Cramton, *American Legal Education: An Agenda for Research and Reform*, 59 Cornell L. Rev. 221 (1974).

paid for out of the budget of a central university office. Such costs are labeled "indirect costs." The "full costs" of Supporting Services comprise both direct and indirect costs. The examination of Supporting Services is cumbersome due to this duality, and further complexities result from inevitable functional disparities that exist among diverse institutions. In order to modify the difficulties such disparities create and to provide a basis for developing greater information regarding the full costs of legal education, we set forth a matrix as a method through which direct and indirect costs relating to a particular institutional function can be combined.

Resources are deemed to consist of the following major categories: tuition, income from endowments, gifts, grants, receipts, and public support. These items are broadly considered in relation to each other, and an examination is made of tuition increases at law schools between 1955 and 1970. The relationship between increases in per-student instructional cost and tuition is shown. We also examine the area of financial aid in the form of grants and loans since both forms are used to offset the tuition and living expenses of the student. Since tuition funds available to meet the costs of legal education are often offset by scholarship grants our inquiry is directed toward the relationship between tuition income and financial aid, enrollment patterns, and the resources available to students to meet tuition and living expenses. In addition, a formula is provided as a means for projecting tuition increments according to program objectives including financial-aid considerations.

Resource Index

In order to develop some idea of the relative educational resources of law schools, a resource index was developed which was broadly construed to incorporate some measure of the quality of the faculty, student body, and library. A preponderance of the schools that existed during the period of the study were ranked in accordance with the resource index. In developing the resource index three criteria were used: (1) Law School Admission Test (LSAT) median score for the entering class in 1963,[5] (2) the number of library volumes held in 1970, and (3) the median faculty salary in 1970. Each school was given a rank, highest to lowest, on each criterion, the LSAT score, library volumes, and faculty salaries. The sum of these three ranks was used to determine the over-all ranking. The schools were then divided into quartiles. See Appendix B. It should be noted that the classification is quite gross and presents no more than an approximation of the relative position of the various schools. It is interesting, however, that the results of the classification in most cases are extremely similar to the classifications in Charles D. Kelso's study of part-time legal education.[6]

5. 1963 was the only year available to us which had the scores for all the schools. See Appendix B, footnote 1.
6. See Kelso, op. cit.

Note on Conversion of Current to Constant Dollars

Throughout this study comparisons are made among various cost, salary, tuition and similar figures. Frequently, these comparisons involve figures for different years. In order to make comparisons with figures of similar purchasing power, pre-1970 dollars have been converted to the worth that they would have in 1970 so that one such dollar would approximate the number of 1970 dollars required to purchase what one dollar would have purchased in 1955 or any subsequent year. The year 1970 is used since it is the last year of the period studied.[7] Roughly speaking, because of rises in the general price level, earlier-year dollars have been increased to reflect their 1970 purchasing power. These adjusted dollars are called "constant dollars" or sometimes "constant 1970 dollars." It should be noted that the figures given in chapter 1, which examines the history of legal education from a fiscal standpoint, have not been adjusted. Virtually every other pre-1970 figure has been adjusted to constant 1970 dollars.

Pre-1970 dollars were converted into constant 1970 dollars through the use of the Consumer Price Index (CPI). The CPI is a commonly used figure by which dollars are adjusted to reflect their increased or decreased purchasing power. The Index is a statistical measure which at the present time is based on changes in the retail prices of a specified mix of goods and services bought by urban wage earners and clerical workers. The Index is computed by the federal government (Bureau of Labor Statistics) and currently has 1967 as the base year. Once the Index figure is obtained, however, it can be manipulated so that any year can be used as the base year and any preceding or following year can be compared with that base year. The procedure used for deriving constant dollars in this study is as follows. The value of the dollar in February 1971 (roughly the midpoint of the 1970-71 academic year), as measured by the U.S. Average Consumer Price Index, is used as the base. The dollar figures for the three fiscal years studied (1955-56, 1960-61, 1965-66) are then adjusted to reflect their 1970 purchasing power. Specifically, the CPI for February 1956 is 80.3; for February 1961, 89.3; for February 1966, 96.0; and for February 1971, 119.4. Thus, using 119.4 as the base, 1955-56 current dollars are divided by .673, 1960-61 current dollars are divided by .748, and 1965-66 current dollars are divided by .804.

Throughout the study many computations are made and tables presented which, for purposes of arithmetic simplicity, use figures that have been "rounded." Accordingly, due to such "rounding," some computations produce results which, although sufficiently exact for the purposes intended, are not strictly precise.

---

7. In a few instances, years after 1970 are examined and some figures for these years are not adjusted. There are a few instances, in addition, where pre-1970 figures have not been adjusted. When figures are not adjusted they are said to be given in "current dollars." As indicated below all the figures in chapter 1, History, are in current dollars.

Summary

The fifteen-year period examined, 1955-1970, was one of enormous growth in the law school world, and, consequently, one of fundamental change. Indeed, although the law school world of 1955 was similar in important quantitative respects to what it had been for at least 30 years before, by 1970, a very different entity had evolved. Total law school enrollment was 44,289 in 1925 and 40,437 in 1955. During the intervening years, law school enrollment maintained a level of about 40,000 with a dip in enrollment during the depression and a sharp drop during World War II. By 1970, however, enrollment had grown to 86,028.

Faculty growth roughly paralleled the large enrollment increase that occurred between 1955 and 1970. This change, coupled with salary increases, produced a substantial increase in instructional cost. Similarly, enormous increases in the number of books acquired each year, and in total holdings, were accompanied by large increases in library personnel. These changes, coupled with the sharp increase in the price of books and in salaries paid to library personnel, produced a considerable increase in library costs. Finally, growth in supporting-service personnel, coupled with increases in the cost of materials and services, resulted in substantial increases in supporting-service costs. Revenues increased to meet these costs, and law school budgets grew tremendously.

We summarize these developments by considering first increases in instructional cost, and then library and supporting-service costs. We conclude by briefly considering changes in law school resources between 1955 and 1970.

Instructional Costs

In 1955, as had been true since at least the turn of the century, there were roughly speaking two kinds of law schools—large schools and small schools.[8] Large schools enrolled a substantial number of students and had faculties of appreciable size. As might be expected, small schools enrolled relatively few students and had small faculties. Small schools offered minimum curricula usually involving barely enough courses to satisfy bar admission requirements and few, if any, electives. Indeed, because of the small size of the faculties of many small schools, faculty members had to carry high teaching loads in order to meet minimum course requirements. All courses were necessarily given in small classes as a result of low enrollments.[9]

In contrast, large schools offered extensive curricula providing their students with a wide range of electives. Faculty at these schools tended to carry

---

8.   See chapter 1. The conclusions drawn in this part of the Summary are largely derived from the larger sample of schools. Where conclusions are drawn from the case-study schools this fact is expressly noted. In chapter 2 the schools we examined are divided into three groups—large, middle-sized and small. For present purposes, however, this kind of classification precision is unnecessary and the small and middle-sized schools are considered as one group.

9.   See chapter 3, section 3.

somewhat lighter teaching loads than those at the small schools. Differing also from small schools, large schools usually offered a mix of classes of various sizes. First-year classes were likely to be in large sections, and second- and third-year classes ranged from large to small.[10]

In 1955 small schools constituted about two-thirds of all schools and contained one-third of all students; and, accordingly, large schools constituted about one-third of all schools and contained about two-thirds of all students. Enrollments at small schools ranged from below 50 to 250 students, with the average small school enrolling about 140 students and engaging between 8 and 10 faculty members. Large schools, as we have defined them, ranged between 250 and 1,500 students in 1955. The average large school enrolled about 490 students and engaged on the average about 20 faculty members. These figures indicate that small schools had much lower student/faculty ratios than large schools. In fact, the average student/faculty ratio for the small school was 16/1 as compared to 25/1 for the large school.[11]

Normally, a low student/faculty ratio suggests a rich educational program; and, in contrast, a high student/faculty ratio, a lean one. As the description above indicates, however, this was not the case in 1955. Low student/faculty ratios for schools with low enrollments did not mean that they were able to offer extensive educational programs. In 1955, the number of faculty members needed to furnish a minimum program of about 90 semester hours was large enough to produce a low student/faculty ratio for the small law school but that's about all. In contrast, the large schools with high enrollments and large faculties had high student/faculty ratios, but, because of their large faculties, were able to offer far wider curricula.[12] Thus, the difference in student/faculty ratios between these two groups of schools did not result in the kind of program differences that might have been expected. However, certain cost differences did pertain and these were in line with what might have been expected. The small schools had a substantially higher per-student instructional cost than the larger schools. The average per-student cost of the small school in 1955 was about $720 as compared to $627 for the large, a difference of about 15%.[13] This difference would have been greater except that the salary levels were higher at the large schools than at the small schools.[14] This is explained in part by the fact that nearly all the schools in the top Quartile of the Resource Index were large schools.[15]

Between 1955 and 1970, many of the distinctions between large and small schools abated considerably or substantially disappeared. As mentioned, in

---

10.   Ibid.
11.   See chapter 2, section 1.
12.   See chapter 3, section 3.
13.   These figures have been converted into 1970 dollars.
14.   See chapter 2, section 4.
15.   As explained above, salary level is one of the measures used in constructing the Resource Index, so that there is a certain circularity to this proposition. The other measures are library volumes held and median LSAT scores. However, the Resource Index does at least roughly indicate how well supported various schools have been, and it is not surprising that those schools which have been best supported should pay the highest salaries to their faculty.

1955, about two-thirds of the schools examined were small schools; by 1970, less than one-fifth of such schools had enrollments under 250. By 1970, the average small school had grown to an enrollment of 425 (as opposed to 140 in 1955) and engaged 18 faculty members. Small schools became large schools as both faculties and enrollments grew. Although at many of these schools faculty increased appreciably in absolute terms, it did not increase as much as enrollment, and, as a result, student/faculty ratios increased. However, because their faculties did increase appreciably in absolute terms, their curricula broadened considerably. Generally, we estimate that in terms of new subject-matter offerings the curricula of these schools doubled. Large first-year sections became the usual pattern. Electives were made available to second- and third-year students, and a mix of class sizes in the upperclass years developed. Finally, with appreciably larger faculties, the average faculty teaching load was reduced somewhat. In general terms, by 1970 the small schools had reached a position similar to that of the large schools in 1955.[16]

During this period changes also occurred at the large schools. Both their enrollments and faculties increased. By 1970, the average large school had grown to an enrollment of 785 (as opposed to 490 in 1955) and engaged about 35 faculty members. However, unlike the small schools, faculties at large schools increased at a faster rate than enrollments. Accordingly, their student/faculty ratios lowered. As a result of these changes, the large schools' curricula expanded and the average size of their classes dropped. As faculties increased, and the number of courses correspondingly increased, nearly all of the curricular expansion took place in the second and third years.[17]

Generally, we have found that like the small schools, the large schools' upperclass curricula, in terms of new subject matter, doubled between 1955 and 1970. Of course, as large schools' curricula were substantially larger than those of the small schools in 1955 (very roughly twice as large), significant differences continued to exist between the breadth of the curricula of these two groups. Most of the curricular expansion of the large schools consisted of the addition of courses in the following subject areas: corporations, jurisprudence,[18] international law, criminal law, and urban affairs. Little expansion took place in the subject areas of commercial transactions, procedure, property, and taxation. For purposes of our study, courses under the subject areas of corporations, commercial transactions, procedure, property, and taxation comprise one over-all group, and those under the subject areas of jurisprudence, international law, criminal law, labor law, law and the person, administrative law, constitutional law, and a catch-all called "general" comprise the second. In 1955, generally speaking, 70% of law schools' upperclass curricula consisted of courses in the first group, and 30% of courses in the second. By 1970, the proportions had changed to 50/50, since most of the additional courses offered to the upperclasses as a result of faculty expansion were in the second group.[19]

---

16.   See chapter 2, section 1, and chapter 3, section 3.
17.   Ibid.
18.   For present purposes, we have defined jurisprudence broadly to include legal history, ethics, and a number of law and sociology offerings.
19.   See chapter 3, section 3.

Another result of the increase in the upperclass curricula was the development of an appreciable small-class program. This phenomenon reflects the lowering of average class sizes as a result of reductions in the schools' student/faculty ratios. Many of these small classes involved courses which were in the second group. Indeed, although curricula came by 1970 to be divided evenly between the first and second groups, students, as had been the case in 1955, continued to enroll most heavily in courses in the first group. As a result, the average class size of courses in the first group became larger and that of courses in the second group smaller.[20]

As indicated, student/faculty ratios of small schools increased and those of large schools decreased. The average student/faculty ratio of small schools increased from about 16/1 to 23/1 between 1955 and 1970 while the ratio of large schools decreased from about 25/1 to 22½/1. Why have these student/faculty ratios moved in opposite directions? We can only speculate, but there are a number of possible explanations. As an historical matter, many of the schools widely regarded as leading schools had been large schools. Among these schools a pattern of high student/faculty ratios and large classes had long prevailed. Thus, as enrollments increased at small schools, it is likely that few small schools perceived the need to have faculties expand at a rate that would enable these schools to continue to provide instruction in the same small-size classes, as had been the case when they had small enrollments. As explained, the original low student/faculty ratios of these small schools resulted from the need to have faculties sufficiently large to provide a minimum number of subjects. As enrollments grew, faculties also increased, although not nearly as rapidly as enrollments. With larger faculties in absolute terms, however, the curricula of these schools expanded to approximate those of the larger and more prestigious schools. Thus, little pressure was felt to further expand faculties in order to provide even broader curricula. Furthermore, it appears that a number of these smaller schools were running operating deficits in 1955. This resulted from high per-student instructional cost.[21] These deficits were small in absolute terms and probably did not impose too great a strain upon the universities of which these small schools were a part. However, if faculty growth had kept pace with enrollment, the operating deficits would have become quite substantial.

Unlike the student/faculty ratios of the small schools, those of the large law schools decreased. In sharp contrast to the small schools, many of the large schools began the period with the extremely high student/faculty ratios of 30/1 and higher. It is not surprising that between 1955 and 1970, an era of general expansion in higher education, faculties should grow and student/faculty ratios should lower. It should also be noted that some large schools began the 1955-1970 period with fairly low student/faculty ratios and managed to have them decrease to even lower levels by 1970. These schools are all included within the top Quartile of the Resource Index and are widely regarded as leading schools. It is not surprising that schools with appreciable resources would be able to decrease even relatively low student/faculty ratios during a period of

---

20. Ibid.
21. See chapter 6, section 2.

expansion. The reduction in their student/faculty ratios was not, however, as sharp as the reduction in the student/faculty ratios of the more representative large schools.

So far, we have considered changes in the instructional programs of law schools only from the standpoint of what might be called increases in "real" resources, that is, more students and more teachers. We are now in a position to consider these changes in dollar terms.[22] For purposes of this study, the category "instructional cost" includes only salaries paid to faculty members. It follows from this definition that changes in instructional cost are a function of changes in the size of a school's faculty (discussed above) and changes in salary level. As an average matter, we found that between 1955 and 1970 law school faculty salaries increased about 65%. Such increases were similar to salary increases received during the same period by faculty members of similar rank in other divisions of higher education and to increases in compensation received by members of the legal profession.[23] Contrary to what might be expected, the geographical location of a law school made very little difference in the level of faculty salaries, and the use of part-time faculty members did not result in significant reductions in instructional cost.[24]

Combining our findings with regard to increases in the size of faculties during the period examined (viz., that as an average matter faculties increased about 100%) with those involving increases in faculty salaries (viz., that as an average matter faculty salaries increased 65%) produces an estimate that the total instructional cost of law schools increased on the average about 230%. In fact, the average increase in total instructional cost between 1955 and 1970 among the law schools examined was about 210%.[25] The magnitude of these increases is emphasized when it is recalled that these changes are in constant dollars.

It should be understood, however, that there prevailed among the schools examined wide differences in such increases. They ranged from a low of 50% to a high of 680%, with the rest of the schools distributed fairly evenly between these extremes. These differences occurred, of course, because faculty size and faculty salary level increased at different rates.[26] Of these two factors,

---

22.   In reading the following analysis, it is important to keep in mind that all figures are in constant dollars (i.e., 1955 dollar figures have been increased to 1970 dollars), and thus, in interpreting increases in instructional cost, it should be recognized that adjustments have been made for inflation.
23.   Indeed, law professors appear to have done less well than those in similar positions in the legal profession.
24.   See chapter 2, section 2.
25.   The difference between the 210% increase and the 230% increase is explained by the arithmetical difference between dividing the sum of each school's total instructional cost figures by the number of schools examined and multiplying the percent increases of the average underlying factors. The median increase in total instructional cost was 230%. See chapter 2, section 4.
26.   Chapter 2 presents a method for analyzing dollar increases in instructional cost between two years in terms of changes in enrollment, student/faculty ratio, and level of faculty salaries. Through a formula called the Instructional Cost Equation, it is shown how the total increase in instructional cost can be broken down into parts attributable to the effect of changes in these three variables. This method may be generally applied in the management of educational resources.

differences in the rate of increase of faculty size was predominant in accounting for differences in increase in total instructional cost. This appears to have been so because the range of the differences in increase in faculty size was much wider than the range of differences in increase in salary level. In any event, ranking schools on the basis of increase in total instructional cost, we have found that increase in faculty growth tends to parallel this ranking, but increase in faculty salaries does not. Thus, differences in faculty growth have been the predominant factor underlying differences in increase in total instructional cost. And differences in faculty growth, in turn, may be related to differences in enrollment increase and variations in student/faculty ratio. Of these two variables, we believe that variations in student/faculty ratio have been the predominant factor in accounting for differences in increase in the size of faculties.[27]

Between 1955 and 1970, per-student instructional cost increased 33% on the average, i.e., average per-student instructional cost increased annually at a compound rate of about 2.0% in excess of the general rate of inflation. This figure might be compared with that set forth for higher education generally during the 1960's in the final report of the Carnegie Commission of Higher Education.[28] The Commission found that during the 1960's the annual increase in cost per student rose from the historical rate of cost of living plus 2.5% to a new rate of cost of living plus 3.4% (5.0% for private institutions).[29] If the Commission's figures, which refer to total costs of education and not merely to instructional cost,[30] are assumed to be representative of instructional cost alone, it appears that legal education—in terms of the richness of the educational experience created by dollars spent on individual students—has not fared as well as other branches of higher education in recent times.

Marked differences existed in per-student instructional cost between the small and large schools.[31] Between 1955 and 1970 the small schools' per-student instructional cost increased a relatively small amount. During this period faculty salary increases of these schools were offset in many cases by substantial increases in their student/faculty ratios. The average per-student instructional cost of a small school was $720 in 1955 and $847 in 1970, an increase of about 17%. In annual terms, the average per-student instructional cost at the small schools increased at a compound rate of 1.1% in excess of the general rate of inflation. In contrast, at the large schools the average per-student instructional cost increased substantially, from $627 in 1955 to $1,066 in 1970, or 70%. In annual terms, the average per-student instructional cost at these schools

27. See chapter 2, section 4.
28. *Priorities for Action: Fiscal Report of the Carnegie Commission on Higher Education* (New York: McGraw-Hill, 1973).
29. Ibid, p. 63.
30. It is unclear from the text whether total cost includes just direct costs or a combination of direct costs and indirect costs. In any event, expenditures made for research have been omitted from these calculations. Ibid.
31. As increases in per-student instructional cost are a function of student/faculty ratio changes and faculty increases, differences in per-student instructional-cost increases between the two groups of schools are not surprising when one recalls the differences in the pattern of the student/faculty ratio changes between them.

increased at a compound rate of 3.5% in excess of the general rate of inflation. These schools' student/faculty ratios decreased during the period studied and these decreases combined with faculty salary increases to produce enormous increases in per-student instructional cost.[32] It will be noted that the average per-student instructional-cost increase for the large schools on an annual basis, 3.5%, is very similar to the annual increase of 3.4%, given by the Carnegie Commission for the per-student cost of all higher education during the 1960's. In contrast, per-student instructional costs of the small schools increased at rates considerably lower than those of higher education generally.

Wide variations occurred in increases in per-student instructional cost. They ranged from about a 30% decrease to a 150% increase. As was the case for differences in total instructional cost, differences in student/faculty ratio changes rather than in faculty salary increases have been the most predominant factor in accounting for these variations in per-student instructional-cost increases. In view of such wide variations, we have found that it is not meaningful to analyze instructional cost in terms of average increases.[33] For similar reasons we have also found it meaningless to analyze the cost of educating law students in average terms. In 1970 the per-student cost of all the schools examined ranged from about $300 to $2,000, with most schools being distributed evenly between $400 and $1,300. Here also such differences are related to differences in the schools' student/faculty ratios and average faculty salaries, and of these two variables, differences in student/faculty ratios are the predominant factor in accounting for per-student instructional-cost variations.[34]

To briefly demonstrate these differences in per-student costs, a school with per-student instructional cost of $400 in 1970 might have had a student/faculty ratio of about 35/1 and an average faculty salary of about $16,000; a school with per-student instructional cost of $750[35] might have had a student/faculty

32. Nearly 40% of the large-enrollment schools had per-student cost increases of over 100%. See chapter 2, section 4.
33. Differences in increases of total instructional cost might be explained by differences in enrollment. This aspect has, of course, been eliminated when we compare per-student cost increases.
34. See chapter 2, section 4. A pamphlet recently published by the Committee on the Financing of Medical Education of the Association of American Medical Colleges examined the current costs of undergraduate medical education at twelve medical schools. The year examined appears to have been 1970/71. This study found that the annual per-student cost of undergraduate medical instruction at the twelve schools in 1972 dollars ranged between $5,700 and $10,200 with the remaining schools being distributed fairly evenly between these extremes. The Committee was quite concerned about the spread in cost figures.
   The per-student costs at most law schools range between $400 and $1,300, a difference of over 200%, as contrasted to the medical school range of slightly under 80%. Of course, the medical school sample (12 schools) was much smaller than the law school sample (115 schools); so it is likely that if a large number of medical schools were included in the sample the medical school range would be much wider and more closely approximate the law school range. In any event, the Committee felt constrained to observe that a range of per-student costs presumably reflects a "variety of approaches to the content and structure of the educational curriculum and the variety of educational objectives of the institution studied." See *Undergraduate Medical Education: Elements, Objectives, Costs,* Report of the Committee on the Financing of Medical Education (Washington, D.C.: Association of American Medical Colleges, 1973).
35. While the schools examined were distributed fairly evenly between $400 and $1,300, there was a slight clustering of schools with per-student costs around $750.

ratio of about 24/1 and an average faculty salary of about $17,500; and a school with per-student instructional cost of $1,300 might have had a student/faculty ratio of about 17/1 and an average faculty salary of about $22,500.[36] Below we show the highly significant programmatic differences that result when a school lowers its student/faculty ratio.

As faculties increase, the number of courses or sections offered by a law school also increases.[37] Considerable differences exist, however, between the manner in which courses are added to the first-year program on the one hand and the second- and third-year program on the other. Expansion of the first-year curriculum in most cases merely involves the addition of sections to existing first-year courses. This results because of the generally fixed nature of the first-year curriculum, which for the most part consists of required courses.[38] Such additions to the first year usually occur as enrollments increase by substantial amounts, and their purpose, of course, is to hold down the size of first-year sections. Among the nine schools we examined closely, wide differences existed in the size of first-year sections. It is our impression that as schools grow in size, the size of first-year sections also grow. Expansion of the upperclass curriculum usually follows an entirely different pattern, involving the addition of new courses rather than of sections to existing courses. This follows in large measure from the fact that the upperclass curriculum of most schools is predominantly elective.[39]

As a result of these differences between the first-year and the upperclass curriculum, we have found that faculty expansion tends to benefit the upperclass program to a far greater degree than the first-year program. Because of the first-year curriculum's fixed nature, unless first year courses are sectionalized, all the additional courses offered as a result of increases in faculty are usually given in the second-and-third-year curriculum. Thus, faculty increases, in conjunction with decreases in a school's student/faculty ratio, tend to benefit the school's upperclass curriculum almost exclusively. Furthermore, as faculties grow when enrollment increases occur without changes in a school's student/faculty ratio, in many cases the upperclass program will be expanded while the first-year curriculum remains fixed. Between 1955 and 1970, nearly all of the significant expansion of educational programs at law schools took place in the upperclass curriculum. In brief, as faculties have expanded and instructional cost has increased, the cost of the upperclass program relative to the first-year program has become far more expensive.[40]

Because of the differences in the manner by which curriculum expansion occurs between the first and upperclass years, there develops a significant

36. These figures, although hypothetical, were computed after examining the figures for actual schools with per-student costs near to that of the amounts supposed.
37. This would necessarily be so if faculties maintained a constant teaching load from one year to the next. "Teaching load" refers in terms of teaching hours to the number of courses each faculty member teaches each year. Our conclusions regarding teaching loads are discussed below.
38. Recently, however, a number of schools have added small sections to their first-year programs, and some offer a small number of electives to their first-year students.
39. See chapter 3, sections 1 and 2.
40. Ibid.

difference between these two programs when they are analyzed in terms of class size. Since first-year expansion involves, for the most part, only the addition of sections to required courses, first-year classes tend to remain all the same size. This is not the case in the upperclass years. As pointed out, most additions to the upperclass curriculum involve new courses or electives from which the second- and third-year students can choose. Some courses are more sought after than others. Classes of different sizes result since students do not distribute themselves evenly among the available electives. In addition, a number of upperclass offerings, such as seminars or clinical programs, have enrollment limits. A mix of class sizes develops. These typically involve large classes of 100 or more students, medium-size classes of between 40 and 70 students, and small classes, or seminars, of between 15 and 20 students. In cost terms there develops in the upperclass curriculum (at least for purposes of analysis) classes of variable expense; the small classes, of course, cost the most, and the large classes, the least. We estimate that small classes are about 230% more expensive than medium-size classes and about 500% more expensive than large classses and that medium-size classes are about 80% more expensive than large classes.[41]

Quite obviously, as a school's student/faculty ratio lowers, it is able to offer a larger number of upperclass courses in medium and small classes and a more extensive upperclass curriculum. Broadly speaking, a school with a student/faculty ratio of 35/1 is able to offer very few small classes and relatively few medium-size classes to its upperclass students. Most of a student's experience (we estimate 60%) in the upperclass years will be in large classes.[42] A school with a student/faculty ratio of 25/1 is able to provide its upperclass students with only a moderate small-class program, somewhat less than half of its upperclass courses in medium-size classes, and about 35% in large classes. On the other hand, a school with a student/faculty ratio of 16/1 is able to offer about 50% of its upperclass courses in small classes and few, if any, of its upperclass courses need be in large classes. Assuming these three schools have about the same enrollment, offer identical first-year programs, and do not sectionalize their upperclass courses, the school with a student/faculty ratio of 16/1 will offer to its upper classes about 80% more courses than the school with a student/faculty ratio of 25/1 and about 200% more courses than the school with a 35/1 student/faculty ratio. The school with a student/faculty ratio of 25/1 will in turn be able to offer about 70% more courses than the school with a 35/1 student/faculty ratio.[43]

It is asserted above that curriculum expansion follows faculty expansion. This proposition necessarily assumed that faculty teaching load remained fairly constant. We have found that among the many variables which may be considered when making a quantitative analysis of legal education—such as enrollment, faculty size, student/faculty ratio, or class size—faculty teaching load tends to be one of the more constant.[44] It may change from year to year

41. See chapter 3, sections 2 and 3.
42. All of the estimates made in this paragraph assume an average teaching load of 11 hours.
43. See chapter 3, section 2.
44. This is particularly so when compared to the other variables mentioned above.

but not by a great deal.[45] Among the nine case-study schools, over the years examined, the average faculty teaching load tended to decrease as their faculties increased in size. We have also noted that as a school's student/faculty ratio lowers its average teaching load tends to decrease. This results, of course, in a reduction in the number of courses that would otherwise have been provided had the teaching load remained constant. Nevertheless, in such cases, there is usually a net increase in the number of courses offered.[46]

In summary, a law school's instructional program is largely influenced by its student/faculty ratio. Our findings suggest that, as the small law schools of 1955 increased in enrollment to become schools of appreciable size by 1970, their student/faculty ratios increased. However, once a school attained a certain size, there developed a tendency for its student/faculty ratio to lower. It might be assumed that, as nearly all law schools today are of appreciable size, this tendency persists and may continue into the future. Such a phenomenon goes counter to what might be expected in a time of fiscal restraint. It is important to remember, however, that law school student/faculty ratios remain among the highest in higher education. The average law school student/faculty ratio in 1970 was 23/1. In contrast, Seymour E. Harris has recently suggested that the over-all student/faculty ratio in higher education for all types of undergraduate, graduate, and professional schools during 1969-70 was 15.75/1.[47] Student/faculty ratios at medical schools are much lower than this figure; Harris believes that a ratio of 3/1 is not uncommon for medical schools.[48] To get a sense of the situation at another type of professional school, we surveyed the student/faculty ratios of seven leading business schools for the academic year 1973-74 and found that their average student/faculty ratio was 10.4/1.[49] Of course, as these schools are among the nation's leading business schools they might be expected to have a lower than average student/faculty ratio. However, these statistics suggest that business schools generally have far lower student/faculty ratios than law schools. We know of no law school that has a student/faculty ratio as low as 10.4/1 today. These examples have been merely illustrative, but we believe they demonstrate that law schools have extremely high student/faculty ratios in comparison with other university divisions.

Library Costs

Library costs at law schools increased enormously between 1955 and 1970.

However, there are some important variables which tend to be more constant than teaching load, e.g., the number of credit hours students must successfully complete for graduation.
45.   We are referring here to a school's average teaching load.
46.   See chapter 3, section 2.
47.   Seymour E. Harris, *A Statistical Portrait of Higher Education* (New York: McGraw-Hill, 1972), p. 915.
48.   Ibid., p. 916.
49.   The Schools were: Dartmouth (Tuck), Harvard, M.I.T. (Sloan), Pennsylvania (Wharton), Carnegie-Mellon, Chicago, and Stanford. After examining the bulletins of these schools, letters were sent to each asking for verification of student enrollment and faculty-size figures. Faculty members listed who were on leave were excluded; those teaching part-time were not counted as full-time teachers, and undergraduate students were

This came about because holdings at most libraries grew exponentially and the cost of law books soared. Growth in library personnel paralleled library holdings and this, coupled with substantial increases in salaries and wages, produced tremendous increases in personnel costs. We will now briefly examine these developments.

Although wide variations existed, the average number of volumes held in 1954 by the libraries examined was 57,200. By 1970, this figure had increased to 118,900, a 108% increase or a compound increase of nearly 5% a year. During this period 70% of these libraries more than doubled their holdings. These increases are attributable to a number of factors, the most important of which is the position of law school libraries as research libraries; for, as new books and materials are published, many must be acquired if these libraries are to remain serviceable. A second factor contributing to growth in acquisitions relates to the type of books law libraries acquire. Perhaps more than any other kind of research library, they acquire serials, and serials produce inevitable growth in acquisitions. The continuations for each new serial purchased which must be acquired in subsequent years constitute, in effect, a fixed cost for future acquisition budgets. Roughly speaking, serials make up at least 70% of the typical law school library's total acquisition budget, and monographs, accordingly, 30% or less. Furthermore, as libraries grow, serials tend to make up an increasingly larger portion of total book expenditures. In addition, as law schools have broadened their curricula to include more courses oriented to the social sciences and interdisciplinary fields, the demand for monographs has grown. Finally, mention should be made of the revision in the late 1960's of the Library Standards of the Association of American Law Schools (A.A.L.S.) requiring every member school to have at least 60,000 volumes by 1975. This change has undoubtedly influenced the acquisition policy of smaller libraries. (In 1955, nearly 80% of the libraries examined held less than 60,000 volumes; in 1970, the comparable figure was 30%.)[50]

While exponential growth characterized library acquisitions between 1955 and 1970, a caveat must be stated for large libraries, those, for example, which hold over 200,000 volumes and may be acquiring 10,000 volumes or more each year. They tended to have their acquisitions level off and, by the end of the period examined, were acquiring about the same number of books each year. It may be that, as more and more law school libraries reach substantial size, library acquisitions will no longer increase exponentially. In any event, it should be noted that the change from an exponential rate of acquisition to a constant rate of acquisition occurs when the volume of books acquired reaches a very high level.[51]

The period of 1955-1970 witnessed not only large increases in acquisitions, but also enormous increases in the price of books. Very generally, we have found that the price of law books in constant dollars increased over 80%. Combining this figure with the figure for average increase in acquisition, we estimate that,

---

converted to full-time equivalents; doctoral candidates were included as full-time students in the ratios.
50.   See chapter 4, section 1.
51.   Ibid.

between 1955 and 1970, average expenditures for books at law school libraries increased well over 250%.[52]

Expenditures for library personnel increased at an even greater rate. With more books to process and maintain, and more students and larger faculties to serve, library staffs grew enormously. The revision of Library Standards by the A.A.L.S. doubtless caused many libraries to increase their professional staffs. Increases in professional staff have been paralleled by increases in nonprofessional staff. At the start of the period examined, library personnel tended to be among the lowest paid employees in law schools. Between 1955 and 1970, they received substantial increases in compensation. This, coupled with personnel increases, produced enormous increases in the amounts expended on library personnel. Among the schools studied, in 1955 total library expenditures were divided fairly evenly between book expenditures and expenditures for personnel. By 1970, personnel expenditures had become predominant.[53]

By the end of the period examined, substantial changes in library operations appeared in the works. Technological innovations involving various kinds of microforms and computer usage were being experimented with and ventures involving cooperative library arrangements had evolved. These developments were a response, at least in part, to the increasing fiscal pressures felt by libraries. As indicated, library costs have skyrocketed, and there appears to be a built-in dynamic which inevitably produces pressures for continuing increases. As fiscal stringency descended on universities at the end of the period, law libraries found themselves in positions increasingly difficult to maintain, and technological changes were sought to provide a solution to their problems.[54]

Supporting Services

The analysis of supporting services is divided into two main categories: (1) direct costs, which are defrayed by dollar allocations made explicitly available to the law school for supporting services, and (2) indirect costs, which are also incurred for law school supporting services but which are paid for out of the budget of a central university office. Examples of direct costs would generally include dean's office administration, secretarial assistance for the faculty and student activities; whereas examples of indirect costs might include such items as university security officers, janitorial personnel, and utilities. Many supporting services consist of functions that are often shared by both the law school and a central university office, and, thus, are accounted for by both direct and indirect costs. For example, alumni relations may be conducted by both law school personnel and central university officers.

The distinction between direct and indirect costs is important because those funds which are explicitly made available for law school instructional, library, and supporting services can more easily be managed and reallocated to serve

52. Ibid.
53. Ibid., section 2.
54. Ibid., section 3.

changing needs. Indirect-cost expenditures, on the other hand, are not as susceptible to law school influence. This is so since such expenditures are not, by their nature, easily ascertainable; are not the budgetary responsibility of the law school, and may involve a number of fixed cost items (e.g., heat and light).

Relationship among Supporting Service, Instructional, and Library Direct Costs

As has been noted, the three major cost categories are Instructional, Library, and Supporting Services. For purposes of this study, supporting services accounted for by direct costs consist of a "catch-all" category of all activities supported by direct-cost allocations other than instructional and library functions. For 1955 to 1970, case-study school data indicate that among the three categories there was a slight over-all increase in the proportion of funds available for library functions. A broad law school model, based on 1970-71 case-study and inspected school data, would apportion direct costs at somewhat less than 30 percent for supporting services, about 50 percent for the instructional program, and somewhat more than 20 percent for the library.[55] Such percentages are not, the reader should note, a standard, but a basis for examining trends. In order to ascertain whether a drain is being made on dollars available for instructional and library purposes to accommodate apparent needs in the supporting-services area, changes in the proportion of dollars allocated among supporting services, instructional, and library functions must be examined. A classification and allocation system for eliciting greater information regarding such a "mix" is developed in chapter 5.[56] Using median figures derived from the case-study schools, direct costs on a per-student basis during 1970-71 approximated $900 for instructional purposes, $400 for library functions, and $500 for supporting services.[57]

To begin to understand whether expenditures for supporting services can be reduced, we have further divided supporting services into several components. In examining the components it should be noted that direct costs for particular components of supporting services are likely to vary widely, due to distinctions in the level of personnel handling similar functions at different schools and due to operational variations. Keeping these differences in mind, our figures indicate that a prototype law school would expend the following for the direct costs of supporting services: (1) somewhat more than one-third for instructional support; (2) somewhat less than one-third for general administration; (3) about one-tenth each for admissions and student activities, and (4) about one-twentieth for placement, counseling, and alumni programs. For instructional support (secretaries, duplicating, equipment, etc.) salaries would constitute about 60 percent; this proportion remained relatively static over the period 1955 to 1970.[58] It may be because of the essential need for a number of

---

55.   See chapter 5, section 1.
56.   Ibid., section 4.
57.   Ibid., Table 5.
58.   Ibid., section 1.

supporting-service functions, that the expansion of funds available for instructional and library purposes cannot be met through a proportionate reduction in supporting services. In this connection, we have found that the costs for supporting services are more likely to be related to the size of the faculty and median instructional salaries than to the size of the student body.[59] Thus, increases in instructional cost are apt to be accompanied by correlative increases in the cost of supporting services.

Indirect Costs

"Full costs" of legal education consist of a combination of "direct" and "indirect" costs.[60] Thus, any study of the full costs of legal education will necessarily be limited to the extent that access to indirect-cost data is limited. The importance of such access rests on the fact that the amount of dollars available for direct costs, at least to some meaningful degree, may be a function of the amount of dollars required for indirect-cost items. Although both the instructional and library areas will also involve indirect costs, for many law schools the principal concern with indirect costs is apt to be centered on supporting services. Certain supporting-service functions accounted for as direct costs at some institutions may at other institutions be accounted for as indirect costs to the extent that a central university office performs such functions in whole or part. Although indirect-cost data do not readily lend themselves to comparative analysis because of a substantial lack of uniformity in treatment and categorization, a basic classification system can be devised which would broadly permit analysis of the costs of supporting services regardless of university/law school structural differences and variations in the treatment of direct and indirect cost items.[61] This is crucial if schools are ever to know where they stand on a comparative basis.

Although the indirect costs of supporting services are those which are *actually* incurred to sustain such services, an alternative approach to indirect costs stems from a law school perspective directed exclusively to the amount of law school resources, if any, which are devoted to all non-direct-cost items. This amount is ascertained by calculating the total amount of resources generated by the law school and deducting the sum of law school direct costs from the total. The difference, if positive, is often perceived to be "overhead" or "indirect costs" and may, as indicated, be the amount which influences the funds available for direct costs. If the difference is negative then, to that extent, the direct costs are being met through resources not generated directly by the law school. The problem with this approach is that it does not provide information as to what actual indirect costs are.[62]

In 1955, the direct costs of many schools exceeded the resources that they generated. Thus, in the mid-fifties there was minimal concern regarding the

---

59.   Ibid.
60.   Ibid., section 2.
61.   Ibid., section 4.
62.   Ibid., section 3.

"overhead differential," and actual indirect costs were being absorbed by resources not directly related to law schools. By 1970, however, the situation had changed substantially and, at many schools, appreciable dollar resources were going to the university as opposed to being allocated for direct costs.[63] The percentage of total resources generated by law schools—but retained by universities—varied considerably. The percentage is, of course, influenced by the relationships that exist between the two entities. Such relationships, in turn, often rest on the fiscal condition of the university and its law school. The financial strength and weakness of each can be measured by the difference between the resources available to each and the costs that must be absorbed. For example, if the law school is operating from a position of strength (i.e., its resources are rising at a faster rate than its costs) and the university is operating from a position of weakness (i.e., the costs which it is forced to absorb are rising at a faster rate than its resources), the latter will be tempted to retain a larger proportion of the law school's "surplus." Obviously, variations exist. We believe, however, that the "law school surplus" example became applicable to an ever increasing number of institutions during the period covered by the study. By 1970, the tuition income of law schools was rising far more rapidly than their costs, while universities were beginning to sustain a variety of new and expensive supporting services. In view of their tradition of large classes, many law schools were able to increase their enrollment, and thus tuition income, without a correlative increase in instructional cost. To the extent that universities had to rely on the resources of their better endowed divisions to sustain their central operating costs, the amount of funds available for the direct costs of a law school's program was determined by the amount of funds which had to be made available for indirect costs. Variations among law schools in the extent of their indirect costs determined, in part, variations in their educational programs. This is so since the level of a school's educational program is a function of the amount of income available to support it, and the amount of such income is, in part, a function of the amount it has to pay, in effect, for indirect costs. In these circumstances, many law schools will seek a more definitive and reasonable basis for allocating resources within a university system. A.B.A. and A.A.L.S. standards also support this trend. Systems for providing law schools with more sufficient data are needed to meet these concerns and standards.

Classification and Allocation Systems

Since variations in classifying and allocating indirect costs are likely to depend on the purposes to be achieved through the use of indirect-cost data (for example, government contract negotiations), universities will develop such systems in light of their distinct objectives. Nevertheless, regardless of such distinctions, law schools as a whole can create an elementary classification system that would be able to generate the basic data for developing comparative information regarding the costs of legal education. Such a system would embrace conventional law school functions, would enable law schools to provide and

---

63. Ibid.

interpret data with facility, and would provide compatibility with other systems. The National Center for Higher Education Management Systems (NCHEMS) provides useful guidelines to a program classification system. Various techniques exist for the allocation of indirect costs. Ideally, allocations of indirect costs should closely approximate actual usage and "parameters" should be developed which seem the most relevant and expedient.[64]

A broad classification system embracing contemporary law school supporting services would include: general administration, admissions, placement, development and alumni, student services, instructional support, and an unassigned category. University support activities would include: academic support (consisting of libraries, computing centers, academic administration and personnel); student services; institutional support (consisting of executive management, fiscal operations, general administrative services, logistical services, physical plant operations, faculty and staff services); and community relations (which includes alumni and development activities). Based on both the law school and university supporting services, a matrix can be developed which would provide considerable insight into the full costs of a law school program and realistic comparative studies can be undertaken.[65]

Increasing Costs of University Supporting Services

Through an examination of a variety of universitywide support services we have reached conclusions about their impact on the fiscal state of legal education. Various classes of supporting services exist. One class consists of conventional university activities, viz., executive management, personnel affairs, and operational functions involving the physical plant, fiscal control, student records, and computer systems. Another class includes activities such as audio-visual services, intra-mural athletics, and other functions which may not be conducted by all universities; but which, if conducted, would affect the indirect costs of a law school. Another class includes a range of auxiliary services, such as food, housing, etc., which generate income and contribute to indirect costs if expenditures exceed income. A final class includes activities which in kind or degree are truly unique to a particular institution, for example, the upkeep of an historic monument.[66]

Since 1955, federalization, automation, unionization, specialization, and the need for greater protection of plant and personnel have all contributed to an increasing variety of university supporting services and increased costs affecting each class of activity. These developments, in turn, have contributed to substantial increases in over-all indirect costs. Affirmative-action programs, government contract negotiations, health and safety regulations, governmental loan programs, computer technology, collective bargaining, automation, fancier buildings with more elaborate maintenance, and significant changes in campus security devices and arrangements, are examples of support functions which have absorbed considerable dollars and augmented the indirect costs of legal

64. Ibid., section 4.
65. Ibid.
66. Ibid., section 5.

education. Furthermore, to the extent that the resources of some divisions are insufficient to meet increases in their full costs, the resources of other divisions will be more severely affected by the increasing costs of university supporting services.[67]

Resources

The fiscal resources for legal education consist of tuition, endowment income, gifts, grants, receipts, and public support. Data from the schools examined indicate that, for private schools, tuition income is by far the predominant resource, and for public schools, tuition income, together with public support, are the predominant resources. Income from other sources was nonexistent or relatively minimal.[68]

Trends in Tuition Income

Tuition increases between 1955 and 1970 were substantial at both private and public schools. Although among individual schools examined wide variations occurred in tuition increases, the average increase, in constant dollars, was somewhat over 120% for private schools and about 130% for public schools.

In 1955, roughly speaking, tuition at private schools ranged between $500 and $1,000. By 1970, this range had increased to between $1,500 to $2,500. In 1955, resident tuition at public schools ranged between $0 and $400 with nonresident tuition ranging between $400 and $800. By 1970 the resident tuition ranged between $300 and $750 and nonresident tuition between $900 and $1,900. Tuition at private schools generally exceeds tuition at public schools. At public schools nonresident tuition exceeded resident tuition by about 135% in both 1955 and 1970 and, generally speaking, for both years private school tuition was about three times higher than tuition charged to resident students by public schools and about one-third higher than tuition charged to nonresident students.

At private schools average tuition between 1955 and 1970 increased substantially more than average per-student instructional cost. (Public schools are not considered here because subvention contributions made up a relatively significant proportion of their operating budget.) Contrasts between 1955 and 1970 are striking. In 1955, the per-student instructional cost of many small private schools exceeded the tuition charged individual students. This phenomenon was related to the high per-student instructional cost these schools sustained because of their low student/faculty ratios. Consequently, total per-student direct costs exceeded individual tuition charges by appreciable amounts. In addition, because little, if any, endowment or gift income was generated by these schools in 1955, a part of their direct costs was presumably subsidized by their universities, and none of the income they generated was used for indirect costs or other university purposes. These subsidies in absolute terms

---

67. Ibid.
68. See chapter 6, section 1.

must have been relatively small since the total budgets of these small schools in 1955 in absolute terms were insubstantial. Furthermore, at some of the larger schools in 1955, tuition exceeded per-student instructional cost by no more than 50%. Consequently, if it is assumed that instructional cost roughly makes up 50% of total direct costs, even at some of these schools there must have been university support in meeting both their direct and indirect costs. By 1970, the situation had changed dramatically and the tuition charged individual students at most law schools exceeded per-student instructional cost by large amounts. Indeed, the data suggest that the total tuition generated by many schools exceeded their direct costs and, in some cases, both their direct and indirect costs.[69]

Caveats in Calculating Tuition Income: Tuition–Scholarship–Loan Interrelations

In examining tuition income, financial-aid factors must be taken into account. Financial aid is considered here to be those scholarship (including fellowship) and loan funds which go toward meeting the tuition and living expenses of the student. Significant increases have taken place in the amount of scholarship awards to law students over the period covered by the study. At many of the schools examined the percent of students who could have been supported by "full tuition" scholarships tripled despite the fact that enrollments and tuition were substantially increasing during the same period.[70] For example, a school whose enrollment increased by two-thirds (from 600 to 1,000), whose tuition increased from $500 ($742 in constant dollars) to $2,000, and which almost tripled the percent of students who received full tuition scholarships (from 7% to 20%) would have increased its scholarship funds from about $31,000 to $400,000 (in constant dollars), an increase close to 1,200%.[71] Since scholarship funds are generally applied first as a credit toward tuition, to the extent that a scholarship program is not supported by endowment or gift income, the actual cash tuition income of the institution is the net amount available after credits for unsupported scholarships have been deducted. From 1955 to 1970 an increasing percentage of gross tuition income at the schools examined was represented by unsupported scholarship awards.[72]

By increasing tuition, a school generally seeks to produce more funds for its operating needs while, at the same time, providing for a scholarship program that will enable a given number of students to enroll without having to pay the full amount of the revised tuition charge. In chapter 6, a method is set forth for determining the amount by which each student's tuition must be increased in order to provide for the same number or additional scholarships and, at the same

---

69. Ibid., section 2.
70. Since the amount of individual scholarship awards will often vary, for comparative purposes the total amount of all scholarship awards was determined and then converted into the number of full tuition scholarships represented by the total. Thus we speak of the percent of students who "could have" been supported by "full tuition" scholarships.
71. See chapter 6, Table 8.
72. Ibid., section 3.

time, generate additional resources.[73] Since tuition income is the principal resource for private schools and since tuition increases create pressures for expanded scholarship resources, this method provides a basis on which to project future income after a realistic account is taken of the amount of scholarship that must be offered as a consequence of increasing tuition. There is some flexibility. If, for example, in order to generate enough funds to maintain average scholarship awards at a certain level, too high a tuition charge would be required, the average scholarship award can be reduced by converting to a greater dependence on loan funds.

Indeed, the schools examined show enormous increases in the amount of loan funds made available to law students over the period of the study.[74] Loan funds as such form an extremely significant base for enabling many students to obtain a legal education. Undoubtedly, the enormous expansion in loan funds has been a major factor in the expansion of law school resources and, thus, law school programs. The extent, therefore, to which students are willing to borrow, and to borrow more, is a significant factor in governing the amount of resources available to a law school. From the student's standpoint the type of loan plan, amount of personal indebtedness, and terms of repayment may influence a basic career choice or selection of a law school. Various categories of loan plans exist. There are those plans which originate with, and are supported by, the capital of the institution, and there are those in which the capital is provided by private lenders, most often with governmental guarantees. Furthermore, a combination of these two approaches can be developed when loan servicing is undertaken by a non-university party, which, unlike the university, is not concerned with building up favorable alumni relations. Other kinds of loan plans involve contingent and graduated repayment schemes.[75] Regardless of the particular loan source and terms of the loan, by 1970 it appeared that legal education was steadily moving to the brink of a period when loan funds would become the prevailing factor in meeting the costs of legal education.

The extent to which students will be willing to go into debt and the amount of tuition that the "traffic will bear" may be largely influenced by the demand for legal education. During the years 1955 to 1970, the number of students seeking admission to law schools far outstripped the spaces available. Thus, scholarship programs have become less a recruitment device and more a means of lessening the actual financial strain of needy students. When the ratio of applicants to spaces continues to be large, a financial-aid program can be developed which seeks to enhance the over-all quality of the student body by drawing funds from well qualified students who can meet higher tuition charges in order to defray the costs of students with less adequate resources.

For the student, total expenses comprise tuition and living expenses. Since 1955 the proportionate share of student resources that have been allocated between tuition and living expenses has changed substantially. In 1955, tuition was about one-third to one-half more than living expenses. By 1970, the

---

73.   Ibid., section 4.
74.   Ibid., section 5.
75.   Ibid.

educational investment for most students was equivalent to or exceeded living expenses, and, as in the case of extraordinary expenses generally, significant increases in student indebtedness have taken place to meet such exceptional expenses relative to basic living expenses.[76]

Three basic kinds of resources other than financial aid are potentially available to the law student: those provided by the student, those provided by the spouse, and those provided by parents. Based on data recently supplied by students applying for financial aid, the median amount of funds provided by students who reported that they would have cash resources was about $750. The median contribution of parents was about $800 based on income alone, and about $1,000 based on a combination of income and assets.[77] About 30% of the students indicated they would be married at the time law school commenced. Somewhat over a third of the spouses indicated they would also be students. Median earnings for working spouses were expected to be $3,400. Thus, at median levels for private schools, a single student applying for financial aid would have had $1,750 in resources and total living and tuition expenses of $4,550.[78] Similar figures for married students with working spouses would have been $5,150 and $5,400.[79] Taking into account median undergraduate loan indebtedness when beginning law school, single students who had to borrow the difference between resources and expenses would accrue a total indebtedness exceeding $10,000 by graduation.[80]

---

76. Ibid., section 7.
77. Ibid.
78. Based on a "moderate" budget standard for living expenses of $2,450 and a median tuition level of $2,100. Ibid.
79. Based on a "moderate" budget standard for living expenses of $3,300 and a median tuition level of $2,100. Ibid.
80. Ibid.

Chapter 1
History

This chapter provides a brief account of the history of legal education in America.[1] Emphasis is placed on the fiscal aspects of this development and on certain organizational and program characteristics of early law schools that may have had particular influence on their financial evolution.

Until near the end of the nineteenth century, the principal method of legal education in the United States was by apprenticeship and self-directed reading.[2] A small number of law schools, however, did exist during the early years of our country's development.[3] They are classifiable into three types. First there were

---

1. For a comprehensive and important summary of the history of legal education see Robert B. Stevens, "Two Cheers for 1870: The American Law School" in *Perspectives in American History*, v. 5, Donald Fleming and Bernard Bailyn, eds. (Cambridge, Mass.: Harvard, 1971), p. 405.
2. James Willard Hurst, *The Growth of American Law: The Law Makers* (Boston: Little, Brown, 1950), p. 256.
3. Information presented in this chapter regarding the founding of law schools up until the mid-1920's has been largely derived from Appendices to Alfred Zantzinger Reed, *Training for the Public Profession of Law* (New York: Carnegie Foundation, 1921) [hereafter: *Training for the Public Profession*] and *Present-day Law Schools in the United States and Canada* (New York: Carnegie Foundation, 1928) [hereafter: *Present-day Law Schools*]. These two books were done by Reed for the Carnegie Foundation for the Advancement of Teaching. In 1913, a Study of Legal Education was inaugurated by the Foundation at the request of the Committee on Legal Education and Admissions to the Bar of the A.B.A. This study was carried out over a twenty-year period during most of which Reed served as staff member in charge of the study. In addition to these two books, Reed produced most of the early editions of the *Annual Review of Legal Education*. In 1935 the *Review* was taken over by the Section of Legal Education and Admissions to the Bar. See 1931 and 1935 *Annual Review of Legal Education*.

those schools which were modeled somewhat after the Continental schools of the time, pursuant to which the law "school" was an integral department within a college or university. These schools appear to have provided instruction in legal education conceived as part of a liberal education.[4] Subjects such as jurisprudence, law of the nations, and constitutional law were emphasized.[5] The first of these schools to be established was William and Mary (1779-1861; 1920-   ) in Virginia, followed by Transylvania University (1799-1861; 1865-79; 1892-95; 1905-12) in Kentucky, the University of Maryland (1823-32; 1870-   ), and the University of Virginia (1826-   ).[6] Instruction in each of these schools was given by a single teacher who appears to have been supported out of general university funds.

The second type of early school was purely proprietary and professional, wholly without connections to any university or other officially organized institute of higher education. This type of school is exemplified by Connecticut's Litchfield Law School (1784-1833), the most famous of the early proprietary law schools. These schools were located for the most part on the East Coast and reached their peak during the first quarter of the nineteenth century. They usually evolved from the success of individual practitioners in attracting apprentices and offered strictly practitioner training through a systematic course of lectures.[7] Nearly all these schools had ceased to operate by 1850 although one lasted until 1878.[8] In accord with their independent nature these schools were self-supporting and any income in excess of expenses accrued to their proprietor instructors.[9]

The third type of early law school is exemplified by Harvard (1817-   ) and Yale (1824-   ). These schools were parts of universities, but their educational programs were similar to the Litchfield type of school. In fact, when Harvard reorganized under Story in 1829, John Ashmun was brought from Judge Howe's Litchfield-type school in Northhampton to provide much of the routine instruction.[10] The Yale Law School came into being through the university attaching to itself a Litchfield-type school that had been conducted for some time in New Haven as an activity of the firm of Stapels and Hitchcock.[11]

---

4.   Hurst, op. cit., p. 258.
5.   Ibid.
6.   In addition to the activity at these schools, James Kent delivered lectures in law at Columbia for the years 1794-1798 and 1824-1826 (Reed, *Training for the Public Profession*, pp. 120-121) and James Wilson delivered some lectures at the University of Pennsylvania in 1790 (Ibid., p. 122).
7.   Hurst has described them as follows: "These schools were little more than an extension of the office-apprenticeship type of training, more systematized and made available to more men by virtue of lectures." op. cit., p. 258.
8.   Reed, *Training for the Public Profession*, pp. 132-133.
9.   For a description of the Litchfield School and its imitators, see ibid., pp. 128-133 and Hurst, op. cit., p. 31.
10. Reed, *Training for the Public Profession*, p. 142.
11. Ibid., p. 140. Hurst has described the early efforts of these schools in the following manner: ". . . [L]aw instruction at both Cambridge and New Haven was dominated by the desire to meet the most immediate demands of the would-be lawyer. Thus, though the instruction was on a college campus, it was, like that at Litchfield, little more than an

By 1840, seven degree-conferring law schools existed in the United States.[12] Between 1840 and 1860, the number of degree-conferring law schools increased to 21. A number of schools were organized in the South during the 1840's,[13] and in the middle Atlantic and mid-West states in the 1850's.[14] During the next decade ten more schools were established,[15] and in 1870 there were 31 law schools.

By the end of the Civil War, the distinction between the Continental-influenced model (Virginia) and the Litchfield-influenced model (Harvard) had ceased, and, generally speaking, American law schools followed Harvard's strictly professional approach.[16] Hurst has said of this early period of legal education in America:

> In terms of what was accomplished, until the 1870's legal education in the colleges and universities was part of the era of apprentice training and proprietary schools. And, taking the bar as a whole, all types of schools contributed but a trickle of men.[17]

Indeed, the 1891 Report of the Committee on Legal Education of the American Bar Association, approximating the number admitted to the bar during the 1880's, concluded that little more than one-fifth of the total number of applicants admitted to the bar each year were law school graduates.[18]

It is important to recognize that none of these schools were graduate schools. In its early days the requirements for admission to the Harvard Law School were lower than those for admission to the college.[19] In a paper read before the Section of Legal Education of the American Bar Association in 1894, it was asserted:

> The majority of lawyers receive their preliminary education at public schools, and then study in private offices or the law schools, one or both, until they can pass the examination that will admit them to the bar. Of those who attend law schools, it has been computed that no more than one-fifth have a collegiate education.[20]

---

expanded form of office apprenticeship training. But it did eliminate the more rote, time-wasting clerical features of office learning." Op. cit., pp. 259-260.

12.   William and Mary, Transylvania, Harvard, Yale, Virginia, Dickinson (1834-1850; 1852-82; 1890-   ), and Cincinnati (1835-41; 1842-   ).

13.   Georgia (1843-61; 1865-   ), North Carolina (1845-68; 1877-   ), Alabama (1845-46; 1873-   ), Louisville (1846-   ), Tulane (1847-62; 1865-   ), and Cumberland (1847-61; 1866-1961). The Indiana University Law School (1842-77; 1889-   ) in Bloomington was also organized about this time.

14.   They include: Albany Law School (1851-   ), Columbia (reorganized 1858-   ), New York University (reorganized 1858-   ), Northwestern University (1859-   ), and the University of Michigan (1859-   ).

15.   They include: Washington and Lee University (1866-   ), Washington University, St. Louis (1867-   ), University of Wisconsin (1868-   ), Trinity College (Duke) (1868-81; 1890-94; 1904-   ), and Notre Dame (1869-   ).

16.   Reed, *Training for the Public Profession*, pp. 154-155. Hurst has said: "The wholly 'practical' curriculum of the Litchfield School was the highest response to this climate of opinion; the programs of the university and college law schools in mid-century, after proprietary schools had declined, were in essence no different." op. cit., p. 267.

17.   Hurst, op. cit., p. 260.

18.   14 A.B.A. Rep. 318 (1891).

19.   Reed, *Training for the Public Profession*, p. 145. The first law school to require a college degree was Harvard in 1909. Stevens, op. cit., p. 427.

20.   17 A.B.A. Rep. 462-463 (1894).

The structural relationship that these early law schools shared with their university is of particular significance from a fiscal standpoint. It appears that a number of colleges sought law schools in order to expand themselves into up-to-date universities.[21] Reed has described the relationship of these early law schools to the universities in the following manner:

> As regards the organic relationship of the law faculty to the university at large, the principal distinction during the early years was between Harvard and Virginia, on the one side, where the law school received effective financial support, and all other schools, where it did not. Whether, following the model of Yale, these other schools were adopted children, or were ostensibly founded by the university, their practitioner teachers were in all cases left to fend almost entirely for themselves. Even when the school had no existence prior to the appointment of a practitioner as Professor of "Jurisprudence" or "Law," the initiative came quite as often from the practitioner as from the college. A lawyer member of the board of trustees was peculiarly in a position to put through a friendly arrangement whereby a proprietary law class might advertise itself as a university school, conferring upon its graduates an academic degree, and often also given at least the use of rooms in the college building. Greater financial assistance than this, a weak denominational college was usually unable to provide. Nor, in the case of a state university, was the legislature disposed to expend public money for any such purpose as legal education. Lawyer members were satisfied with the office training that they had themselves received; lay members were not interested in helping an unpopular profession. Under such circumstances it was eminently proper that the practitioner teachers, who assumed all the risks, should collect all the fees. Not every financial fact is known in regard to every school. Certainly, however, the overwhelming majority of schools prior to the Civil War were conducted thus by educational promoters rather than by a salaried staff. Effective control can be secured only through the power of the purse. While, in a purely formal sense, the contribution of the mid-century may be summed up as the definite assumption of the burden of legal education by the American college, the burden must be confessed to have sat lightly upon it for the time. For all practical purposes, these were independent schools masquerading in university guise. In varying measure they doubtless did meritorious work along the lines of the original Yale school, relatively untouched either by the idealistic breadth of Virginia or by the scholarly traditions of Harvard.[22]

Between 1870 and 1890 appreciable growth in the number of law schools occurred, the amount nearly doubling from 31 to 61.[23] Not revealed in these

---

21.   Reed, *Training for the Public Profession*, p. 152.
22.   Ibid., pp. 183-184.
23.   For the rest of this chapter, growth in the number of law schools is described by noting the increases in law schools in 5 twenty-year periods, viz., 1870-1890, 1890-1910, 1910-1930, 1930-1950, and 1950-1970. Schools included as new schools in any period are those which were established between the first year of the period and the year before the first year of the next period, viz., 1870-1889, 1890-1909, etc. Information regarding the growth of law schools between 1870 and 1930 has been largely derived from a comparative analysis of Appendix § 1.A to Reed's *Training for the Public Profession* and a section

figures are about twelve schools that opened and closed between these dates.[24]
Nearly all the schools which were organized during this period were located in
the South and the West. A sizable number of schools were started in the states of
Ohio, Illinois, Indiana, and Iowa. Three were started in New York and one in
Pennsylvania.[25] No law schools were started in New England. This period saw a
large expansion in the number of state universities offering legal education,[26]
and a beginning of the growth of night law schools.[27] Seven black schools were
also founded between 1870 and 1890, but only three of the black schools
started during this period survived past 1890 and these closed down by 1920.
Finally, five of the new law schools were schools started by private normal
schools attempting to develop into universities. Of the 25 schools that were
established during this period and were still in existence in 1921 when Reed
published his first report, 21 were parts of universities (6 of state universities, 14
of private universities, 1 of a Catholic university), 1 was part of an aggregate of
professional and vocational schools, and 3 were independent.

Between 1890 and 1910, the number of law schools once more roughly
doubled, growing from 61 in 1890 to 124 in 1910. Not revealed in these figures
are about seventeen schools that opened and closed between these dates. Again a
large expansion in the number of state law schools occurred.[28] In addition, a
large number of law schools were started in major cities.[29] In connection with
this growth of metropolitan schools the number of night or mixed law schools

entitled "Description of Individual Law Schools by States and Provinces" in *Present-day
Law Schools*.
24.   Considering the increases over a twenty-year period, it should be recognized that a
number of schools established *before* the start of the period may have closed during the
period. Thus, one cannot determine the number of schools on hand at the end of the period
by merely adding the net number of schools (all those which started within the period less
those which started and closed within the period) that were established during the period to
the schools on hand at the outset.
25.   Cornell (1887-), Buffalo (1887-), and Lehigh (1878-89).
26.   Missouri (1872-), Kansas (1878-), California: Hastings College of Law (1878-),
West Virginia (1878-), Texas (1883-), Oregon: Northwestern College of Law (1884-),
South Carolina (reorganized 1884-), Minnesota (1888-), and Tennessee (1889-).
27.   Georgetown (1870-), National (1870–merged with George Washington University
in 1954), Metropolis (1888–merged with New York University in 1895), Chicago-Kent
College of Law (1888-), and Baltimore Law School (1889-). Minnesota and Oregon
opened as night schools.
28.   Ohio State (1891-), Nebraska (1891-), Colorado (1892-), Illinois (1897-),
Washington (1899-), North Dakota (1900-), California, Berkeley (1901-), South
Dakota (1901-), Louisiana State University (1906-), Kentucky (1908-), Oklahoma
(1909-), Idaho (1909-), Florida (1909-).
29.   The following schools were formed in major cities during this period: Detroit College
of Law (1891-), New York Law School (1891-), Franklin T. Backus Law School,
Western Reserve University (1892-), Temple (1895-), Kansas City (1895–closing date
unknown), Catholic University of America (1895-), Chicago Law School (1896–closing
date unknown), De Paul (1896-), Cleveland Law School (1897-), University of
Southern California (1898-), Cincinnati YMCA Night Law School (1900–closing date
unknown), Brooklyn Law School (1903-), Metropolitan Business College (1903-04),
Northeastern College (1904-), Potomac University (1904-07), Fordham University
(1905-), San Francisco Law School (1907-), Marquette University (1908-), Oriental
University (1908-17), Loyola University, Chicago (1908-), Northwestern College of Law,
Minneapolis (1909-27), Minneapolis College of Law (1909–closing date unknown).

increased markedly from 10 to 45.[30] Law school expansion continued to occur in the Midwest, particularly in Illinois, Indiana, Ohio, and Kansas, and also in the South. No less than 7 schools were started in Tennessee in this period.

Of the 48 schools established during this period and still in existence in 1921 when Reed published his first report, 31 were parts of universities (11 of state universities, 15 of private universities—3 of which began originally as independents—, 5 of Catholic universities), 5 were parts of an aggregate of professional and vocational schools (3 of YMCA systems), and 12 were independent.[31]

How can we account for this remarkable growth in law schools? Surely, the country's increasing population was a major factor.[32] And we have seen that the development of state universities, no doubt prompted by post-Civil War federal legislation, was another significant factor. It has been shown that during the 1880's, it was thought that only about one-fifth of those who were admitted to the bar graduated from law schools. In view of this, it cannot be said that a general shift from apprenticeship to law school instruction was a major factor in the growth of law schools from 1870 to 1890. It may be, however, that toward the end of this period a greater number of applicants to the bar had formalized instruction at law schools. The relationship between law school and apprenticeship education appears, however, to have changed dramatically between 1890 and 1910. The growth in total law school enrollment was enormous during these twenty years, increasing over 300% from 4,518 to 19,567.[33] If we take the Committee on Education's 1891 rule of thumb that one-tenth of the practicing bar is constituted by those who have been recently admitted,[34] it would appear that about 80% of the applicants for admission were law school graduates in 1910 while only one-quarter were so in 1890.[35] A number of reasons may be suggested for the displacement of apprenticeship training by law schools. The invention of the typewriter toward the end of the nineteenth century produced a small revolution in law offices by substituting the

---

30.   Hurst, op. cit., p. 273.
31.   Between 1890 and 1910, 26 schools were established that are not included in the above sample. Seventeen of these schools closed before 1910 and 9 more before 1920. Lack of information regarding these schools prevents their inclusion in the above classification.
32.   In 1870, the country's population was 38,558,371. By 1890, it had grown to 62,947,714, slightly over a 60% increase. Between 1890 and 1910, it grew to 91,972,266, an increase of almost 50%. Source: *Historical Statistics of the United States, 1789-1945*, A Supplement to the Statistical Abstract of the United States, U.S. Department of Commerce, Bureau of the Census (Washington, D.C.: U.S. Government Printing Office), 1949, p. 25.
33.   Throughout this chapter, various statistics are given regarding the number of law schools existing in any one year, and the number of students enrolled in them. They have been derived from Reed's two books and various editions of the *Annual Review of Legal Education*. There are discrepancies in data for similar periods among these sources so none of the figures should be taken as more than approximate.
34.   See footnote 18.
35.   In 1890, there were 89,630 lawyers; and in 1910, there were 122,149. Another estimate has been given by Jerold Auerbach who notes: "In 1870 one quarter of those admitted to the Bar were law school graduates; by 1910 two thirds would be." Jerold S. Auerbach, "Enmity and Amity: Law Teachers and Practioners, 1900-1922" in *Perspectives in American History*, v. 5, Donald Fleming and Bernard Bailyn, eds. (Cambridge, Mass.: Harvard, 1971), p. 573.

stenographer for the longhand copyist.[36] One of the main underpinnings of the
apprenticeship system was thus removed by a technological development. In
addition, it appears that the apprenticeship system had come to be increasingly
criticized. In the second year of its existence, the A.B.A. received a report from
its Committee on Legal Education which stated:

> There is little if any dispute now as to the relative merit of
> education by means of law schools, and that to be got by mere
> practical training or apprenticeship as an attorney's clerk. Without
> disparagement of mere practical advantages, the verdict of the best
> informed is in favor of the schools.[37]

Writing in 1928, Reed refers to the "admitted decadence of the American law
office as an effective educational instrument" and the "conceded inefficiency of
the law office method of preparation."[38] One may suppose that between these
two periods the popularity of the apprenticeship method steadily diminished. It
also seems safe to assume that the growing complexity of the law during this
period made systematic law school training more desirable than learning by
apprenticeship.[39] The wide acceptance of Harvard and Langdell's case method,
initiated in 1870, which with the passage of time became the primary way of
teaching law,[40] might also have been significant in law schools taking the field
from the apprenticeship method. Moreover, as the quotations above suggest, the
A.B.A. and local Bar Associations devoted time and energy to promoting
attendance at law schools as a superior method of legal education. Finally, the
growth of law schools may have been promoted by the revival in the late
nineteenth century and early twentieth century of state requirements for
prescribed periods of formal training as a condition for admission to the bar.
Earlier requirements of a similar nature had been largely eliminated during the
era of Jacksonian democracy.[41] Although it was not until the late 1920's that
any state stipulated law school attendance as necessary for formal training, the
reasons adduced above suggest that it was natural that applicants to the bar
would satisfy their formal training requirements at law school.

We have noted that a large increase in the number of metropolitan night or
mixed law schools occurred, particularly between 1890 and 1910. Indeed,
during this period the number of day schools increased from 51 to 79, a 57%
increase, while the night schools increased from 10 to 45, a 350% increase.[42] It

36.   Hurst, op. cit., p. 273.
37.   2 A.B.A. Rep. 216 (1879). In a report of the Committee on Admission to the Bar of
the Association of the Bar of the City of New York made in 1875, it was said: " . . . [W]e
wish to bear our testimony to the advantages which the student may gain in a well
conducted law school, and to say that, if practicable, we would require that all candidates
for the Bar be trained at such schools." Rep. of the Comm. on Admission to the Bar of the
N.Y.C.B.A. 12 (1876).
38.   Reed, *Present-day Law Schools*, p. 57.
39.   Reed, *Present-day Law Schools*, p. 210.
40.   Reed, *Training for the Public Profession*, pp. 380-81, 392.
41.   As Stevens, in discussing the expansion of formal training, has pointed out: "In 1860
only nine out of thirty-nine jurisdictions required it. In 1890, the number had risen to
twenty-three out of forty-nine. By 1917, the requirement had reached thirty-six out of
forty-nine, with twenty-eight demanding a three-year period." op. cit., p. 459.
42.   Hurst, op. cit., p. 273.

has been suggested that this development of part-time schools is directly related to the great European immigrations which occurred between 1880 and 1920.[43] As an alternative for the penurious student, part-time legal education may have developed as a compromise between the old apprentice system and the new institutional system of legal training by offering an opportunity for students to serve as assistants to lawyers while attending school. It is shown below that night schools continued to be organized in large numbers during the next twenty years.

Between 1910 and 1930, the number of law schools increased from 124 to 180 with total law school enrollment growing from 19,498 to 46,751. Approximately 83 schools opened during this period, 15 of which had closed by its end. An overwhelming majority of these schools were located in the Midwest[44] (21), the South[45] (25), and the West[46] (25). Only eight schools were organized in the East[47] and seven in the District of Columbia. Of these 83 new schools, 6 were parts of state university systems, 7 were parts of private universities (three of which were black), 11 were parts of Catholic universities, 10 were parts of aggregates of commercial and vocational schools, 14 were parts of YMCA systems, and 24 were independent. Eleven schools cannot be accounted for in terms of these categories, but as nine of them closed down after only a few years, the majority of them can be presumed to have been independent. Most of these schools were night schools.[48] By 1930 only eight of these 83 schools had managed to secure approval by the A.B.A.[49] and six of these were state law schools. Few of these schools exist today.[50]

From a fiscal standpoint, there are several aspects about these late nineteenth and early twentieth century law schools that are of particular significance.

---

43.   Auerbach, op. cit., p. 566.
44.   The "Midwest" includes the following states: Illinois, Iowa, Michigan, Minnesota, Pennsylvania, Ohio, and Indiana.
45.   The "South" includes the following states: Alabama, Arkansas, Florida, Kentucky, Louisiana, Maryland, Missouri, North Carolina, South Carolina, Tennessee, Texas, and Virginia.
46.   The "West" includes the following states: Utah, Montana, Oregon, California, Colorado, Oklahoma, and Washington.
47.   The "East" includes the following states: New York, New Jersey, Massachusetts, Connecticut, and Delaware.
48.   Writing in the 1930 *Annual Review of Legal Education*, in commenting upon a table setting forth the number of full-time and part-time schools in ten-year intervals from 1890 to 1930, Reed summed up the relative situation of full-time and part-time schools (part-time schools included "mixed" schools that maintained separate full-time and part-time divisions) in this manner:

> It will be observed that while the number of schools offering exclusively full-time work has doubled during this period of forty years, the number offering part-time work, either exclusively or in connection with full-time divisions, has approximately quadrupled. On the average, one new full-time law school has been added every year, as against two schools of the part-time or mixed type. The proportion of schools that offer only full-time work has shown a steady decrease, from over two-thirds of the total, in 1889-90, to well under one-half at present (p. 25).

49.   The significance of the A.B.A.'s accreditation system is explained below.
50.   Including the schools that had secured A.B.A. approval by 1930, it is estimated that no more than fifteen have survived.

Following the Civil War, it appears that many law schools which organized or reorganized themselves as university divisions adopted the structural relationship described above. Discussing this period, Reed states:

> The movement to multiply law schools coincided with a movement to multiply universities. The trustees of colleges or other institutions which possessed or might acquire the power to confer university degrees of every sort were only too willing to grant the use of it on easy terms. This would have been the golden age of law schools if 'academic freedom' were all that is necessary for educational salvation. Law school faculties in general were allowed to do about as they pleased, and with few exceptions were already, to all intents and purposes, proprietors of the school, assuming the risks and pocketing the profits, if any.[51]

During the last twenty years of the nineteenth century, however, a number of universities moved to make their law schools regular university divisions. Referring to these universities, Reed describes the situation this way:

> Some ... as their resources have permitted, have centralized the financial administration of their law department, collecting the fees and defraying the expenses, including salaries to the instructors. A condition of virtual independence, during which schools were transferred from one college to another or were even run under the auspices of two colleges simultaneously and sometimes took out separate charters of incorporation, has tended to be converted into a situation more resembling 'home rule'—a type of university organization in which a strong tradition of local self-government survives under a theoretically absolute control possessed by the university authorities. So Columbia, in 1878, ended Dwight's large profits from his successful law school by putting him on salary. The Cornell school prided itself upon being, from its beginning in 1887, 'coordinate in all respects with other university departments.' Other important universities that soon adopted the policy of collecting the tuition fees and defraying the expenses of their law departments were the University of Pennsylvania in 1888, New York University in 1889, and Northwestern University in 1891, upon the death of Henry Booth, the original dean and proprietor of the law school.[52]

In a footnote Reed points out that North Carolina did not assume the budget of its law school until 1899, and Yale did not until 1904.

During this period, roughly 1880-1920, most law schools were attached to universities with colleges at their cores.[53] It is not clear, however, how many of these law schools benefitted financially from a university connection. It is suspected that relatively few did.[54] In the 1907 Report of the Committee on Legal Education and Admissions to the Bar, the Committee noted that " ... in the United States, ninety-three of the existing law schools are in some way connected with a university, but in too many instances the connection is probably only nominal."[55] The Committee's notion of a nominal connection is

---

51.   Reed, *Training for the Public Profession*, p. 192.
52.   Reed, *Training for the Public Profession*, pp. 184-185.
53.   Reed, *Training for the Public Profession*, p. 187.
54.   See footnote 22.
55.   30 A.B.A. Rep. 537 (1907).

suggested in its observations that immediately preceded this conclusion. The Report stated:

> But if a professional school needs to be connected with a university, this connection needs to be not nominal but real, and university presidents and university corporations need to rid themselves of the heresy that the funds of a university are to be administered simply for the benefit of the college of arts or science and the professional school left to its own financial devices. Universities which allow their professional schools to maintain low standards and which fail to give them their share of the common funds in order that they may do their work in a proper manner ought not to have any professional schools. They are unfit to administer them.[56]

In addition to the university law schools, a number of law schools were parts of aggregations of professional or vocational schools: law schools and medical schools, law schools and teachers colleges, and law schools as part of a YMCA general system of vocational training.[57] It is unlikely that these law schools received any income other than tuition. In some cases the only support these schools received as part of a larger aggregation was the provision of classroom space.[58]

Finally, during this period the phenomenon of independent law schools with the power to confer degrees took root and flourished. In 1880, there were 5 such schools out of 51, or one-tenth of the total. In 1920, there were 48 out of 143, or about one-third of the total. Of course, these schools were entirely self-supporting.

In examining the growth of law schools from 1870 to 1930, the manner in which these schools were organized has been described. They fall into three categories, viz., law schools as parts of universities, law schools as parts of aggregations of professional and vocational schools, and independent law schools. It is interesting to note that the number of schools in the latter two categories increased as a percent of the total number of schools established in each of the twenty-year periods considered. Thus, of the 25 schools examined by organizational structure that were established between 1870 and 1890, 4, or 16%, were in the latter two categories; of the 48 schools so examined that were established between 1890 and 1910, 17, or 35%, were in the latter two categories; and of the 83 schools so examined that were established between 1910 and 1930, nearly 60, or over 70%, were in the latter two categories.

Writing in 1932 about universities in general and professional schools in particular, Reed described the economic situation of professional schools in the following manner:

> A quarter of a century ago, when the Carnegie Foundation was started, higher education had developed a plant in excess of current educational needs. The meager endowment funds of numerous

---

56.   Ibid., pp. 536-537.
57.   Reed, *Training for the Public Profession*, pp. 187-189. Later on, many of these aggregations instituted colleges of their own. Reed, *Present-day Law Schools*, p. 84.
58.   Reed, *Present-day Law Schools*, p. 98.

competing institutions necessitated a recourse to tuition fees if these institutions were to be kept alive; and these fees would not be forthcoming in adequate amounts unless entrance requirements were kept low. This was especially true in the case of professional education, because preparation for occupations other than the ministry had been slow in establishing its claim to benevolent treatment at the hands of endowed institutions or the state. Prevailingly, the profession itself was, at first, expected to supply the demand, either through a system of more or less formal apprenticeships, or through independent institutions, conducted by practitioners giving part of their time to teaching and supported by the fees of students. Even when these independent institutions became affiliated with existing colleges or so-called universities, or were supplanted by departments similarly organized, the old tradition survived of looking to student tuition fees for financial support. Economies in overhead expenses accompanied the merger, but rarely was the college or university in a position to supplement the income in any substantial way. Indeed, in some cases, large profits were derived from professional departments, and either were absorbed by an enterprising promoter, in the guise of salary, or were diverted by the trustees to meet deficits in the other departments.[59]

While Reed was purporting to describe professional schools generally, it is clear that he had law schools in mind.[60]

In his second major report,[61] Reed discusses the 111 degree-conferring law schools that were parts of universities with liberal arts colleges in 1926-27 and notes that even though a school is technically a subordinate department of a university, it will often function virtually as an independent school. "The actual control that the parent institution exercises depends largely upon the financial assistance that it is in a position to give."[62] In this connection he groups 110 of these schools in categories based on the amount of annual income available to their universities, other than income derived from students for services

---

59.   *Annual Review of Legal Education, 1932*, pp. 3-4.
60.   Writing about the same time concerning the transition in law and legal education after World War I, Roscoe Pound made similar observations:
   Even our longest established and best equipped law schools are none too well prepared to adjust easily to such an era of transition. None of our law schools have endowments adequate to their tasks. Not so long ago instruction in other departments of universities was often parasitic upon the law school and, although this condition has been largely or even wholly remedied in most institutions, it still obtains in some quarters. In a few institutions, law schools receive support from general funds. For the most part, they are required to be self-sustaining and, without any such endowments as are behind other departments, are called on by strong academic opinion to develop research and adjust to the methods and find a place for the disciplines of the several social sciences, and by strong lay and to some extent professional feeling to take account of the modern development of business methods, while striving at the same time to make their strictly professional training more adequate to the variety of tasks of the lawyer of today, and to competent handling of an increasingly complex and unstable body of law. *Annual Review of Legal Education, 1935*, p. 1.
61.   Reed, *Present-day Law Schools*.
62.   Ibid., p. 89.

rendered.[63] After so doing, however, he warns the reader that the amount of independent income a university may generate does not indicate whether any of it is available for legal education.[64] Nevertheless he does assert that " ... the greater are the financial resources of a college or university, the greater is the likelihood that funds for the improvement of the relatively inexpensive law department are either available or can be secured."[65] He then points out that there are "tremendous differences" among universities in the amounts of non-tuition income which they generate, and warns the reader against assuming that "technical control by a college or university is itself a guarantee that" the law school is not being run as a commercial enterprise.[66] He continues:

> If in some cases much more is given to the law students than they themselves pay for, in other cases the college or university provides little more than the hospitality of its classrooms and of its catalog, and sometimes not even this. Admission requirements and rates of faculty compensation are not infrequently kept low for the purpose of enabling the law department to carry itself, or even to bring in revenue to the parent institution.[67]

Reed then goes on to make some interesting suggestions regarding the financial independence of law schools during the course of which he offers several significant observations about the fiscal status of law schools during the mid-1920's. He begins by noting that since 1918, the Association of American Law Schools has not had as a member any school that is not connected with a college or university.[68] He points out, however, that neither the A.A.L.S. nor the A.B.A. has ever required such a connection and warns that "unless precautions are taken that the connection is of a proper sort, a requirement of this nature would be of little value."[69] Reed then observes that the question of the kind of institution which ought to have "the responsibility of conducting a law school has been approached" by eschewing law schools that are conducted as commercial enterprises, merely for the purpose of pecuniary profits.[70] Such schools were thought to be run primarily for their teachers or other officers and not in the interest of their students. Reed observes, however, that this approach may miss the mark for

> ... it makes little difference whether the inordinate financial profits of the law school go to a private promoter or to a struggling college or Y.M.C.A. And if in the latter instances the operation of the law department yields only a small financial profit, or none at all, or

63.   Ibid., pp. 89-92.
64.   Ibid., p. 93.
65.   Ibid. After setting forth a number of caveats with regard to his classification, Reed concludes: "Finally, in most cases the greater part of the current income, other than from students, is legally dedicated to particular purposes; even when it is not so dedicated, an apparently wealthy university may have so far committed itself to other lines of work that little support can be given to the law school" (p. 93).
66.   Ibid., pp. 93-94.
67.   Ibid., p. 94.
68.   Ibid., p. 99.
69.   Ibid.
70.   Ibid., pp. 99-100.

even an annual deficit, this by no means indicates that it is being run with a single eye to the interest of its students. The proper development of a law department may be just as much stunted by efforts to prevent, or to keep within reasonable bounds, a deficit occasioned by small receipts from tuition fees, as by efforts to maintain a handsome surplus derived from a larger number of paying students.[71]

Reed concludes by suggesting that in order for a school to be approved by the A.B.A., or to be admitted as a member of the A.A.L.S., it should " . . . enjoy all the income derived from its own students, and also an additional income of a certain specified amount, derived from other sources."[72] He further suggests that a distinction should be made between those " . . . law schools that are in a position to give students substantially more than they pay for, from schools that of necessity must adjust their educational ideals to their financial need."[73]

In a final footnote, Reed divides law schools into five groups. The classification is made on the basis of "comprehensive and detailed financial figures" that were obtained before World War I "from almost every school then in existence."[74] Reed suggests that in addition to the historical interest, the value of such material is also " . . . methodological as an analysis of the many different ways in which different law schools are likely, in the future as in the past, to meet the economic problem."[75] The five groups are as follows:

1. Small departmental schools, enjoying the use of more or less commodious quarters and library equipment, and either possessing an independent endowment (whether arising from benevolence or from their own accumulated earnings), or receiving subsidies from their parent institutions, or both. The total, as supplemented by their relatively small receipts from students, constitutes an assured and fairly stable income, upon the basis of which the department determines the amount of instruction it is prepared to give, and the scale on which it can afford to pay its instructors.

2. Small departmental schools, provided with classroom facilities, etc., but otherwise expected to carry themselves out of their own income from tuition fees. Here, for the first time, the question of how central or 'overhead' charges shall be distributed among the various departments of the university becomes acute.

3. Small independent schools, which, in addition to their other expenses, must find money to pay rentals or interest on mortgage debt.

4. Large schools, in other respects like any of the foregoing, but deriving from their students an additional income which is either spent at once upon the school or is accumulated for its benefit.

71. Ibid., pp. 100-101.
72. Ibid., p. 101.
73. Ibid., pp. 101-102.
74. Ibid., p. 103.
75. Ibid.

5.   Large schools in which excess earnings are more or less clearly
      appropriated for the benefit either of individual promoters, or (so
      more commonly before the War) of other branches of the parent
      institution.[76]

Additional information regarding the financial condition of law schools in the
late 1920's is provided by the 1929 Report of the Council on Legal Education
and Admissions to the Bar to the A.B.A. Part of this report summarized the
results of a 1928 questionnaire, completed by all of the approved law schools
and by many unapproved schools. In reporting upon its attempt "to secure
information concerning the financial structure of the various schools," the
Council echoed Reed's suggestions, in finding that:

> Many are being conducted at a very considerable profit and whether
> such schools are to be considered as commercialized would seem to
> depend not so much upon whether the receipts go into the pocket of
> a private individual or to the benefit of another department of the
> university, as whether they are being applied for the advancement of
> legal education. It may be as unfair to the law student to make him
> contribute to the building up of a dental or medical school or other
> enterprise, as it is to make him swell the fortunes of the private
> owner of some proprietary school.[77]

In describing the growth of law schools during the period of 1910-1930,
mention was made of certain schools having received approval by the A.B.A.

Before continuing with a description of how law schools have evolved since
1930, brief consideration will be given to the appreciable influence which the
A.B.A.'s Section on Legal Education and Admissions to the Bar has had on the
development of legal education.[78] The American Bar Association was founded
on August 31, 1878, in Saratoga, New York. One of its original purposes was to
improve legal education, and its first constitution provided for a Committee on
Legal Education and Admissions to the Bar.[79] The Section was formed in 1893,
and in 1900 the Section organized the Association of American Law Schools.[80]

---

76.   Ibid., pp. 103-104.
77.   52 A.B.A. Rep. 685 (1929). In concluding this section of its report, the Council
stated: "Legal education may be carried on not only at a lower cost than any other
professional work but even at a less cost than many branches of collegiate study. During the
past year adjustments have been effected in a number of institutions where the tuitions have
been out of proportion to the support allowed by the university for the conduct of legal
education, and there is need for much work along this line in many of the law schools of
America." In another section of this report, the Council stated: "Because of the fact that
legal education may be carried on at such a low cost, in many institutions not only is the
law school denied needed support and required to pay its own way while hundreds of
dollars per student are being expended in other departments, but not infrequently it is
required that it be operated at a profit with the result that the law student in practical effect
is required to pay for the education of those studying in other fields. It is not unusual to
find the law school and the janitor occupying the basement of one of the college buildings
with equipment that has been discarded by other departments." Ibid., p. 680.
78.   See Sullivan, *The Professional Associations and Legal Education*, 4 J. Legal Ed. 401
(1952).
79.   Ibid., p. 401.
80.   Ibid., pp. 408-409.

In its early days a number of significant actions were taken by the A.B.A. at the behest of its members working on legal education matters,[81] but, for purposes of this discussion, the most significant was its adoption in 1921 of standards for admission to the bar. In brief, the A.B.A. urged, in part, that every candidate for admission be a graduate of a law school that requires two years of study in college as a condition for admission, and offers a three-year program for full-time students and a longer program for part-time students.[82] In 1923, the A.B.A. issued its first list of schools approved under these standards. Of the 149 schools in existence that year only 38 received full approval.[83] By 1923 the number of two-year schools was diminishing,[84] and failure to require two years of college work as a condition for admission was the primary reason for most schools' noncompliance with A.B.A. requirements. It has been thought that one of the purposes in adopting these standards was to inhibit the further proliferation of proprietary schools.[85] Persons interested in quality legal education had been impressed by the success that medical education had recently achieved in reducing the number of proprietary medical schools, and they hoped that similar developments might take place with respect to law schools.[86] Immediate results did not, however, materialize. Although the number of schools receiving A.B.A. approval increased each year, so did the number of schools which were not receiving such approval. Between 1923 and 1930, the number of approved schools almost doubled. However, the number of unapproved remained about the same. Thus, roughly speaking, for every school that changed its status from unapproved to approved a new unapproved school was established. In 1930, of the total of 180 degree-conferring schools, 75 were approved and 105 were unapproved.[87]

Between 1930 and 1950 new law schools continued to be established, but

---

81. In 1881 the Association adopted a resolution urging State Bar Associations to recommend a three-year course of formal education and recommending also that the time spent in any chartered and properly conducted law school be counted as the equivalent of the same time spent in an attorney's office in computing the period of study prescribed for applicants for admission. In 1903 the A.B.A.'s Committee on Legal Education recommended two years of pre-legal college work as a prerequisite for admission to law school. Ibid., pp. 404-405.

82. Paralleling the A.B.A.'s efforts to raise standards of legal education have been similar efforts by the A.A.L.S. While the A.A.L.S.'s standards have for the most part been somewhat higher than the A.B.A.'s, the schools that have achieved A.B.A. approval and those with A.A.L.S. membership have been almost the same. Ibid., pp. 411-426.

83. Ibid., p. 416. All but 4 of these 38 schools had been founded before 1910.

84. In the 1923 advance extract from the 18th annual report of the Carnegie Commission, it is shown that only 6 out of the 149 existing schools had short courses. *Annual Review of Legal Education, 1923*, p. 21. In an appendix to Reed's first report it is shown that in 1909, 40 out of the 124 existing schools, or 30%, had short courses; in 1916, 23 of the 140 schools, or 16%, had short courses; and in 1920 only 16 of 142 schools, or 11%, had short courses. Reed, *Training for the Public Profession*, p. 449.

85. Stevens, op. cit., pp. 453-464.

86. Stevens, op. cit., pp. 459-460.

87. All but 4 of the 38 schools approved between 1923 and 1930 were founded before 1910.

more schools were closed during this period than were opened.[88] The 1930 *Annual Review of Legal Education* lists 186 law schools.[89] The 1949 *Annual Review* lists 168. About 50 new schools were opened during this twenty-year period, some 30 of which were in the South. Only 11 of these 50 new schools had received A.B.A. approval or provisional approval by 1950, and 20 had closed down by that year. In addition, about 50 of the schools that were in existence in 1930 were closed by 1950. None of the early 70 schools that closed between 1930 and 1950, with the exception of Furman in South Carolina, was ever approved by the A.B.A. Many of them consisted of big city evening schools. While the total number of law schools decreased by about 20 schools between 1930 and 1950, the number of A.B.A. approved schools increased appreciably, from 75 in 1930 to 114 in 1950. Table 1 lists the number of approved and unapproved schools for most years between 1928 and 1949. The percentage figures in parenthesis next to the school figures indicate the percent of total students that attended each type of school. It will be noted that it was not until 1936 that more students attended approved schools than unapproved schools, and not until 1937 did more approved than unapproved schools exist. Thus, the apparent objective of educating the majority of students in schools approved by the A.B.A. was not satisfactorily achieved until after World War II.

A factor in the reduction of the number of unapproved schools was the raising of standards for admission to the bar by the various states. In 1930, 27 states and the District of Columbia had no pre-legal education requirements before an applicant began his period of law study. Eight states required a high school degree, one state required one year of college, eleven states required two years of college, and one required a college degree.[90] Eight states had no requirements regarding the duration or situs of law study, 39 states and the District of Columbia required either office study or law school study of various durations,[91] and one state (West Virginia) required that law study be exclusively in a law school. In 1950, only five states had no pre-legal education requirement, 36 states and the District of Columbia required two years of college, five states required three years of college, and two states required a college degree. Two states had no requirements regarding the duration or situs of law study, 20 states

---

88.   Information regarding the growth of law schools from 1950 to 1970 is derived from various editions of *Annual Review of Legal Education.*
89.   While the *Review* lists 186 schools in its principal section, summary tables providing comparative figures include only 180 schools. Later editions of the *Review* use the figure 180, and we have used this figure in Table 1. However, for purposes of this paragraph examining the period 1930-1950, the figure 186 has been used as the analysis was made by tracing the history of individual schools through various editions of the *Review.* The discrepancy most likely involves difficulties in accounting for unapproved schools. See note to Table 1. In the following examinations of the 2 twenty-year periods, 1930-1950 and 1950-1970, it should be recalled that the actual periods run from 1930 to 1949 and from 1950 to 1969. See footnote 23.
90.   *Annual Review of Legal Education, 1930.* Requirements for college experience in many instances could be satisfied by passing special examinations.
91.   Most states required three years of law study, but about seven required less time; nine required four years of law study if the situs of study was a law office.

Table 1

Number of Law Schools and Enrollments: 1928 to 1949

Year	Total Enrollment	Total Number of Law Schools	Approved Law Schools (% of en.)	Unapproved Law Schools (% of en.)
1928	48,942	173	66 (33.2%)	107 (66.8%)
1929	46,751	180	68	112
1930	44,015	180	75	105
1931	42,165	182	81 (44.4)	101 (55.6)
1932	41,153	185	82	104
1933	–	190	85	105
1934	–	193	85	108
1935	41,920	195	88 (48.8)	107 (51.2)
1936	40,218	190	94 (54.9)	96 (45.1)
1937	39,255	185	97 (61.2)	98 (38.8)
1938	37,539	180	101 (63.7)	79 (36.3)
1939	34,539	180	102	78
1940	–			
1941	–	176	108	68
1942	–			
1943	–			
1944	6,422	159	109 (74.7)	50 (25.3)
1945	–			
1946	–			
1947	51,015	158	111 (85.7)	47 (14.3)
1948	56,914	166	112 (82.0)	54 (18.0)
1949	57,759	168	114 (80.7)	54 (19.2)

Note: These figures are derived from the A.B.A.'s *Annual Review of Legal Education*. It was not published for several years during World War II and so no figures are available for those years. In addition, the percentage breakdown of enrollment between approved and unapproved schools was not available for every year, and total enrollment figures were not provided for the years 1933 and 1934. Data involving unapproved schools should not be regarded as firm since many of these schools failed to respond to requests for enrollment information and the A.B.A. may have been unaware of the existence of some unapproved schools. Enrollment figures consist of total enrollment and include part-time, graduate, and special students on the same basis as full-time students.

required either office study or law school study,[92] one state required two years of law school study, and 25 states and the District of Columbia required three years of law school study.[93]

Between 1930 and 1950 total law school enrollment grew from 44,015 to 57,759. See Table 1. Apparently responding to the effect of the depression, law

92. One state required either two years of office study or law school study. Nineteen states required three years of law school; ten states required three years of office study, and nine required four years. *Annual Review of Legal Education, 1950*.
93. *Annual Review of Legal Education, 1950*.

school enrollment decreased all through the 1930's reaching a level of 34,539 in 1939. World War II devastated law school enrollments. In 1944, only 6,422 students were enrolled in American law schools. However, when the war ended, law school enrollment swelled again as returning veterans took advantage of the G.I. Bill. In 1950, as indicated, total law school enrollment reached 57,759. After that year law school enrollment dropped, and it was not until 1964 that total law school enrollment exceeded this figure.

From the end of the 1920's to the late 1940's little fiscal information is available concerning law schools. Reed's last major report was published in 1928, and after 1929, the A.B.A.'s Section on Legal Education appears to have become inactive as a data-collecting group. In the late 1940's, however, a study of legal education was conducted by the Survey of the Legal Profession, and this study provides information regarding the fiscal status of law schools in 1948-49.[94] In the late 1940's law schools, by and large, appear to have been profitable enterprises. Nicholson found that of 121 schools (106 approved and 15 unapproved) 21 reported deficits, 32 reported that their figures balanced, and 68 reported surpluses.[95] These figures were based on total income and expenditures of all kinds. Expenditures were divided into three general categories: teaching salaries, administrative items, and rent, maintenance, etc.[96] As it appears that what we denote below as "indirect costs" or "overhead" expenses were included in the expenditure categories, it may be assumed that surpluses were actual surpluses available to the law school or the university for whatever purposes they might wish to apply them. From the figures collected, Nicholson concluded that these law schools made a net profit of over two million dollars in 1948-49.[97]

Between 1950 and 1970, the total number of law schools increased by only 5 schools. See Table 2. The number of approved and provisionally approved schools, however, increased by 25 schools, from 120 to 145, while at the same time, the number of unapproved schools decreased by 20, from 47 to 27. Most of the schools that were approved during this period had previously been listed as unapproved, so that, roughly speaking, the period of 1950 to 1970 saw a number of law schools change their status from unapproved to approved while

---

94. Lowell S. Nicholson, *The Law Schools of the United States*. (Baltimore, Md.: The Lord Baltimore Press, 1958).
95. Ibid., p. 81.
96. Expenditures for administrative items included in the case of some university-connected law schools " . . . the share of the law school in the cost of the general university administration." Ibid., p. 104. Expenditures for rent, maintenance, etc., included " . . . rent, taxes, insurance, heat, light, water, etc." It also included the "maintenance charge made by some universities upon the university law school either as an estimated lump sum or on some percentage basis, as the law school's share of the general university maintenance expenses." Ibid., p. 106.
97. In analyzing these schools in terms of different types, he found that large enrollment schools had a larger average surplus than average enrollment schools, and that average enrollment schools had a larger average surplus than small enrollment schools; that unapproved schools had a slightly larger surplus than approved schools; that private schools had a markedly larger surplus than public schools; and that schools unconnected to a university had a markedly larger surplus than schools that were university connected. Ibid., p. 82.

Table 2

Number of Law Schools and Enrollments: 1950 to 1969

Year	Total Enrollment	Total Number of Law Schools	Approved Law Schools (% of en.)		Unapproved Law Schools (% of en.)	
1950	53,025	167	120	(82.4%)	47	(17.6%)
1951	47,610	169	124	(83.2)	45	(16.8)
1952	41,278	169	124	(86.3)	45	(13.7)
1953	39,339	171	126	(87.5)	45	(12.5)
1954	39,565	166	127	(88.5)	39	(11.5)
1955	40,347	166	127	(88.7)	39	(11.3)
1956	41,888	166	128	(90.6)	38	(9.4)
1957	42,271	159	129	(91.9)	30	(8.1)
1958	42,646	159	129	(91.8)	30	(8.2)
1959	41,879	159	130	(91.4)	29	(8.6)
1960	43,695	159	132	(92.4)	27	(7.6)
1961	45,012	160	134	(92.2)	26	(7.8)
1962	48,663	161	135	(92.1)	26	(7.9)
1963	54,433	161	135	(91.1)	26	(8.9)
1964	59,813	162	135	(90.7)	27	(9.3)
1965	65,057	161	136	(91.8)	25	(8.2)
1966	68,121	166	135	(91.8)	31	(8.2)
1967	70,332	170	136	(91.6)	34	(8.4)
1968	68,562	171	138	(91.6)	33	(8.4)
1969	72,032	172	145	(94.9)	27	(5.1)

Note: See note to Table 1 regarding completeness of data.

the total number of law schools remained nearly the same. Although the number of law schools changed by only a small amount during this period, law school enrollment increased enormously, growing from 53,025 to 72,032.[98]

Two characteristics of law schools which have particular relevance for the remainder of this study and which have roots in the early development of legal education should be noted. The first characteristic involves the size of individual law schools' enrollments; the second, the large size of many law school classes. In terms of student enrollment, from near the beginning of the great development of formalized legal education in law schools after the Civil War until quite recently, the law school world has contained two distinct types of schools: the large school and the small school. There follows an examination of four years, 1895, 1930, 1940, and 1955, spanning this period, which shows how

98.   Between January 1, 1970 and January 1, 1971, law school enrollments increased from 72,032 to 86,028, and have continued to increase each year since. The growth in law school enrollments from 1955 to 1970 is examined in greater detail in chapter 2.

law schools have been divided between large and small schools. In 1895, 43 (about 70%) of the 63 schools for which information was available to the Committee on Legal Education had enrollments below 150 students.[99] The average enrollment for these schools was 61. Seven of the schools had enrollments between 151 and 249, with an average of 179, and thirteen had enrollments over 250,[100] with an average of 367. In 1930, 41 (about 55%) of the 75 schools approved by the A.B.A. had enrollments below 150. The average enrollment for these schools was 86. Twelve of these schools had enrollments between 151 and 249, averaging 189. Twenty-three had enrollments over 250, averaging 507. In the early 1940's a study was made of 99 law schools for the year 1940-41.[101] The study examined what it defined as the "smaller law school."[102] Of the 99 schools examined, 39 (about 40%) averaged 91 students, another 39 averaged 132 students, and 21 averaged 360 students.[103] An analysis

---

99.   18 A.B.A. Rep. 332 (1895).

100.   Schools have been divided by size into three groups rather than two because a similar division is made in an examination of instructional cost in chapter 2. Dividing schools here in a similar manner permits comparisons between the information set forth in this chapter and in chapter 2. For purposes of the general proposition—that there are two types of schools by size, large and small—it seems fair to characterize schools with below 150 students as small and schools with above 250 students as large. In this context schools with enrollments between 151 and 249 are in a middle ground. In any event, regarding only the largest and smallest groups, it seems entirely appropriate to assert, about the years examined, that there were two types of law schools by size since for each year a high preponderance of the total number of schools fell into the two extreme groups and the middle group invariably contained the smallest number of schools.

101.   Boyer, *The Law Schools: Factors Affecting Their Methods and Objectives*, 20 Ore. L. Rev. 281 (1941). This article was originally prepared for the Seminar in Legal Education conducted at Columbia University School of Law by Professor Elliot E. Cheatham.

102.   At the start, it is asserted: "The law schools of this country may be readily divided into two categories: the larger and the smaller law schools." Ibid., p. 284. Although the study seems to have made the number of full-time faculty members as significant a characteristic as enrollment in defining what a "smaller law school" is, nevertheless it appears that the smaller law schools, however defined, had the smallest enrollments.

103.   The following statistics were found for these three groups of schools:

	Group I	Group II	Group III
Number of schools	21	39	39
Number of teachers	10 or more	6 to 9	5 or less
Average number of teachers	14	6.87	4.15
Average teaching salary	$6,600	$4,200	$3,500
Teaching load	6.71 hrs.	7.65 hrs.	8.66 hrs.
Average enrollment	360	132	91
Average expenditure per student	$373.50	$300.87	$250.75
Average number of volumes in library	98,757	23,455	15,556
Hours of instruction offered	109.3	94.1	91.3
Percentage of income derived from tuition	65%	72%	83%

The Boyer study examined 99 of the 108 schools that were approved by the A.B.A. in 1940-41 (p. 284). The *Annual Review of Legal Education* did not publish for the year 1940-41. Accordingly, we are not able to provide a breakdown for that year similar to the ones given above for the years 1895 and 1930. The article does suggest, however, that most schools in the two smaller groups, which it regarded as "smaller law schools," enrolled between 50 and 150 students (p. 285). The nearest year for which figures were published was 1939-40, and for that year the statistics were as follows: of the 102 schools approved by the A.B.A., 55 had enrollments below 150, averaging 92; 20 had enrollments between

was made of the factors which influenced the attainment by smaller schools of their educational objectives. Among the factors considered were size of faculty, teaching load, faculty salary, curriculum, and library size. In brief, it was found that the smaller schools had small faculties[104] carrying high teaching loads[105] and paid at relatively low levels.[106] In addition, these schools offered limited curricula[107] and had libraries holding a relatively small number of volumes.[108] Interestingly, it was also found that the smaller law schools derived a higher percent of their income from tuition income than the larger schools. Apparently the larger schools were better endowed. Finally, it will be shown in chapter 2 that the law school world in 1955 was also divided between the small and large school, but by 1970, the small school had largely disappeared.[109]

The second characteristic of legal education to be examined is the large size of many law school classes and its corollary, the high student/faculty ratio of many schools. Robert Stevens has suggested that the large law school class may be traced to Langdell's Socratic method.

> It was the vast success of Langdell's method too, which established the large-size class. While numbers fluctuated, Langdell in general managed Harvard with one professor for every seventy-five students. The schools attempting to emulate Harvard could barely ask for a 'better' faculty-student ratio. What was more, any educational innovation which incidentally allowed one man to teach ever more students was not unwelcome to university administrators. Although the university-affiliated law schools were slowly put on a nonprofit basis, the 'Harvard method of instruction' meant that from the first they were expected to be self-supporting.[110]

151 and 249, averaging 191; and 27 had enrollments over 250, averaging 509 (*Annual Review of Legal Education, 1939*). The schools examined in the Boyer study generally had low enrollments. Their average enrollment was 164. In contrast, the average enrollment of the 102 approved schools for the year 1939-40 was 222.

104.   As indicated above, the small size of their faculties was a determining characteristic of "smaller schools." See footnote 102.

105.   Teaching loads were high both in the sense of the total number of hours taught and in the sense of the number of different subject matters taught. It was suggested that because of the number and variety of different subjects taught by faculties at the smaller schools they had little time to engage in sustained research or to specialize in one particular field. Ibid., pp. 287-289.

106.   Ibid., pp. 287-288.

107.   Ibid., pp. 289-291.

108.   Ibid., pp. 291-292.

109.   In chapter 2, 126 schools are examined. In 1955, 47 of them had enrollments below 150 averaging 100, 36 had enrollments between 151 and 249 averaging 194, and 43 had enrollments over 250 averaging 483. By 1970, none of these schools had enrollments below 150 and only 14 had enrollments below 250.

110.   Stevens, op. cit., pp. 444-445. Toward the end of his account of the history of legal education, Stevens returns to this theme. "In fact, over the last one hundred years, the inherent conflicts in the purposes of legal education have been heavily accentuated by its remarkable underfunding. Even the leading law schools have faculty-student ratios which are unheard of in any marginally acceptable college and unthinkable in any other graduate or other professional school. This underfunding of legal education is probably attributable to the Langdellian model—for the case method seemed to work as well with two hundred students as it did with twenty. Indeed, Langdell's greatest contribution to legal education is the highly dubious one of convincing all and sundry that law schools were cheap" (pp. 534-535).

It may be, however, that large classes were endemic to law schools before Langdell instituted his teaching revolution at Harvard, and that perhaps he evolved his system within a context which assumed large classes. Litchfield never had more than two instructors,[111] and Harvard and Yale started with two instructors.[112] Before Langdell, Timothy Dwight at Columbia was perhaps the leading figure in formal (i.e., law school) legal education. Reed has said that he conducted his school virtually singlehandedly until 1875.[113] According to statistics for 1895 set forth by the Committee on Legal Education, Harvard had a student/faculty ratio of 40/1 that year.[114] In 1925, Reed's statistics show Harvard with a ratio of students to full-time (carrying 10 or more hours) teachers of 78/1.[115] High student/faculty ratio as a characteristic of law schools has long been reflected in the standards set by the law schools' own association, the A.A.L.S. In 1924, the A.A.L.S. adopted as a standard that a school have at least one full-time teacher for every 100 students.[116] In the early 1950's, this was changed to provide for one full-time teacher for every 75 students,[117] and this is the standard which prevailed until quite recently. At the 1962 annual meeting of the A.A.L.S. the stated criteria for school membership in the Association were changed. Among the changes, specific numerical standards regarding faculty size were dropped for a requirement that prescribes that each member school maintain a faculty of a suitable size.[118] These changes were made, at least in part, in response to the criticism that previous criteria had been overly quantitative and specific.[119]

---

111.   Reed, *Training for the Public Profession*, p. 128.
112.   Ibid., p. 132.
113.   Ibid., p. 182.
114.   18 A.B.A. Rep. 332 (1895).
115.   Reed, *Training for the Public Profession*, p. 264.
116.   Sullivan, op. cit., p. 416.
117.   Stevens, op. cit., p. 507.
118.   Article 6, Sec. 6-1. (4) *A.A.L.S. Proceedings, 1962*, 236.
119.   See, Report of the Special Committee on Standards, *A.A.L.S. Proceedings, 1962*, 197-204.

C h a p t e r 2

Instructional Cost –
Factor Analysis

Introduction

The subject of instructional cost is divided into two general topics. This chapter, Factor Analysis, examines increases in instructional cost and some of the factors and reasons underlying these increases. It develops a method of analyzing and apportioning increases in instructional cost between two periods in terms of enrollment growth, changes in a school's student/faculty ratio, increases in faculty size, and increases in the average salary paid to faculty. The method enables one to determine both total increases in instructional cost and per-student increases in instructional cost and reveals the relationship between these two increases. Through use of this method an examination is made in this chapter of increases in instructional cost of legal education from 1955 to 1970. The chapter concludes with a demonstration of how the method might be used by an individual law school to help obtain a clearer understanding of changes in its instructional cost and to facilitate rational decision making regarding program priorities and the effective use of law school resources. In sum, this chapter illustrates how increases in instructional cost may be ascribed to changes in a school's enrollment, student/faculty ratio, and faculty size.

Chapter 3, Content Analysis, examines changes that occurred in educational programs at law schools as a result of the increases in instructional cost. It examines the impact of these changes on the development of a school's educational program in terms of extended curricula, increased small-class instruction, and other educational options.

Instructional cost for purposes of the following analysis consists solely of salaries paid to faculty members.[1] Wages paid to faculty secretaries, expenses

---

1. In the following examination, fringe benefits are not included in "salaries" since such information as is available regarding fringe benefits is often not reducible to strict dollar terms. For instance, such benefits might include the use of parking and recreational facilities. However, as explained in section 2 below, for purposes of the analyses developed

incurred in preparing teaching materials, and similar items that might for some purposes be classified as instructional cost are included under the supporting services category. Consequently, instructional cost is a function both of the number of faculty members engaged by a school and of the average salary paid to those faculty members, and changes in instructional cost are related directly to increases in one or both of these two factors.

Increases in faculty size are examined in terms of increases in student enrollment, or *scale*, and changes in the number of students per teacher, or *student/faculty ratio*. *Scale, student/faculty ratio*, and increases in average salary levels paid to faculty members, or *input cost*, combine to produce changes in instructional cost. The relationships between these three factors are analyzed in order to reveal the underlying reasons for increases in instructional cost.

Our initial focus will be on growth in the size of faculty in relation to enrollment increases. Before we examine any actual data, brief consideration is given to our analytical assumptions regarding scale and student/faculty ratio as these factors relate to faculty growth. Our primary assumption holds that changes in faculty size parallel changes in student enrollment (scale). In other words, between two periods of time it is assumed for analytical purposes that a school's student/faculty ratio remains constant. Thus, if a school has doubled both the size of its faculty and its enrollment between 1955 and 1970, by hypothesis the faculty increase is attributed to the enrollment increase. In most cases, however, faculty and enrollment do not increase at the same rate, thereby producing changes in the student/faculty ratio.

When a school increases its student enrollment but its faculty size remains constant, we make two suppositions to reconcile the fact that the faculty did not increase with our analytical hypothesis that faculty increases parallel enrollment increases. First, we assume a hypothetical increase in the number of faculty members attributed to the enrollment increase. Second, offsetting this increase, we assume a decrease in faculty attributable to the increased student/faculty ratio. (A school's student/faculty ratio will necessarily increase when its student enrollment increases and its faculty remains constant.) Both the original number of faculty members and the number of additional faculty members, attributed in our initial assumption to the enrollment increase, will decrease. In this case, where faculty size actually remains constant, the increase in faculty attributed to the enrollment increase is exactly equivalent to the

---

in this chapter it does not matter whether fringe benefits are included in instructional cost or not. Fringe benefits are an example of indirect costs. This chapter and the next consider only the direct costs of the instructional program and not its indirect costs. The distinction between direct and indirect costs is mentioned above in the Introduction and Summary and is explained in detail in chapter 5 below. The instruction provided law students who take courses in other divisions of the university is another example of an indirect cost component of instructional cost. Although a number of schools permit students to take courses (for credit toward their degree) in other university divisons under specified conditions, the extent to which students take advantage of these opportunities is uncertain. Although during the years 1955 to 1970 this type of indirect cost is believed, in most instances, to have been of very small fiscal consequence, its impact in the future will, of course, be greater if interest in interdisciplinary courses grows appreciably.

decrease in faculty attributed to the increase in the school's student/faculty ratio.

A common development for a number of law schools during the period examined (1955-1970) has been to have both their enrollment and their faculty increase, with enrollment increasing at a faster rate than faculty. In these cases we make similar assumptions to those described immediately above—an increase in the size of the faculty paralleling enrollment increases and an offsetting decrease in the size of the faculty attributed to the increased student/faculty ratio. In these instances the increase in faculty attributed to the enrollment increase is greater than the decrease in faculty corresponding to the increase in the school's student/faculty ratio.

There is, of course, an artificiality to this approach. Student enrollment may increase and the size of the faculty may increase, but there need not be any causal relationship between these two occurrences. Enrollment might increase because the actual number of students accepting admission offers was greater than anticipated. Faculty size might increase because of the desire to add instructors to teach in new fields of law that were not covered by the existing faculty. In any event, a variety of reasons may actually underlie increases in faculty size. Of course, in many cases there will in fact be a causal relationship between enrollment growth and faculty growth. Increases in faculty size between 1955 and 1970 are undoubtedly due in part to the enormous expansion of the student body that took place at so many schools during that period. Even where there exists a real nexus between enrollment and faculty increases, such changes are not necessarily the product of an explicit policy determination regarding the school's student/faculty ratio. However, by relating faculty increases to enrollment increases, we are able to distinguish that part of a faculty's growth which may be hypothetically attributed to an increase in the level of instructional resources allocated to each student from that part of a faculty's growth which may be hypothetically attributed to maintaining the original level of instructional resources.

Much of the analysis that follows is cast in terms which suggest that increases in instructional cost are *caused* by increases in the number of faculty members teaching at law schools. This approach may, however, be misleading. In many instances, it may be more accurate to assert that increases in faculty size result from increases in the level of resources allocated for instructional purposes. Decisions regarding the level of instructional cost may control the size of the faculty or decisions regarding the size of the faculty may control the level of instructional cost. Undoubtedly, increases in instructional cost are the result of a combination of both approaches. Pressures to increase the size of the faculty push instructional cost upward and pressures to keep instructional cost from rising tend to keep the size of the faculty constant.

The determination of the size of a school's faculty is, of course, of critical importance to our examination. In making such a determination the problem of part-time instructors arises. In analyzing the data collected from the nine case-study schools, we determined the number of full-time-equivalent faculty members to be derived from part-time instructors in the following manner. First, we isolated all those faculty members who were clearly full-time teachers. This was done by examining the number of hours they taught and the amount of salary they received. In cases where the status of an instructor was unclear, we consulted with the school in question to resolve the matter. Second, we calculated the average teaching load of all the full-time instructors.[2] Third, we summed all the hours taught by part-time instructors, and finally we divided this result by the average teaching load of the full-time faculty. The quotient was added to the number of full-time faculty members, and the sum was deemed to be the size of the school's faculty. Certain theoretical problems with this method are discussed below in chapter 3. With regard to the data derived from the A.B.A. *Review of Legal Education*, since full faculty profiles were not available, we divided the number of part-time instructors listed as teaching at each school by four and added the quotient to the number of full-time faculty members so listed.

The part-time student population also presents an adjustment problem. Since a part-time student customarily completes the required credits in four years and full-time students complete the required credits in three years, each part-time student is given a weight of .75 and each full-time student is given a weight of 1.00. Thus, four part-time students equal three full-time students. The "part-time" category includes part-time morning students and part-time evening students. No graduate students or "special" students are included in any of our figures.

Section 1 — Enrollment and Faculty Growth: 1955 to 1970

This section examines the increases in enrollment and faculty between 1955 and 1970 of all law schools which were approved by the A.B.A. in 1970 and were in existence in 1955.[3] There were 135 such schools and they are collectively referred to in this study as the Totality. As indicated in the Introduction and Summary, the data for our examination of this larger sample of schools, including information regarding enrollment and faculty size, have been obtained from the *Review of Legal Education* published each year by the A.B.A.[4] Total enrollment and faculty figures are not emphasized, since our

---

2.   This was done by merely summing the teaching hours of each individual instructor and dividing the result by the number of full-time teachers.

3. See Appendix C.

4.   It should be recognized that when figures regarding faculty size are provided, they include part-time instructors reduced to the equivalent number of full-time instructors in the manner explained in the *Introduction* to this chapter; and that when figures regarding enrollment are provided, they include part-time students reduced to the equivalent number of full-time students in the manner explained in the *Introduction*.

inquiry seeks to reveal trends by examining groups of similar schools and individual law schools rather than aggregate growth patterns.

Faculty figures reported in the *Review of Legal Education* include Deans, Associate and Assistant Deans, and Librarians who teach on a reduced load basis. In analyzing the data collected from the case-study schools we have characterized such personnel as part-time faculty. Unless an instructor devotes substantially all of his time to teaching, to include such individuals in the category of full-time faculty distorts the significance of student/faculty ratio statistics for purposes of determining the nature of a school's educational program. This will become evident in chapter 3. However, where *Review* figures were used, no such segregation of Deans and Librarians could be made. Accordingly, *Review* faculty figures, at least for our purposes, will in some cases be somewhat inflated. However, these figures are sufficiently certain to reveal general trends and to support the conclusions that we draw.[5]

Enormous growth in student enrollment and faculty size took place during the fifteen-year period from 1955 to 1970. In 1955, only 32% of the Totality had enrollments above 250 students. By 1970, 85% had enrollments in excess of 250 students. By rank, the median school in 1955 had 191 students; in 1970, 461 students. The average-size school in 1955 had 240 students; in 1970, 527 students. This period of enormous enrollment growth was accompanied by large faculty expansion, although, as will be shown below, faculties increased at different rates depending upon the size of the school in 1955. In 1955, the median faculty size was 9.5, and the average faculty size was 11.8 teachers; in 1970, the median faculty size was 20.3, and the average faculty size was 23.1.

In both 1955 and 1970, enrollments ranged from several[6] very small schools to one or two schools with over 1,400 students. The distribution of the schools between these extremes was uneven. In 1955, virtually two-thirds of the Totality had enrollments between 50 and 250; in 1970, two-thirds had enrollments between 300 and 700. Figure 1 presents graphs of law schools on the basis of enrollment for the years 1955 and 1970. A clustering of schools is evident between these two enrollment figures. The remaining schools are distributed fairly evenly and relatively thinly on the higher-enrollment side of the 1955 cluster and on either side of the 1970 cluster.

There were 47 schools in 1955 with enrollments between 50 and 150.[7] These

---

5.   The faculty number used in this study for the schools in the Totality as reported in the annual *Review* comprises the number of full-time teachers plus the number of part-time teachers divided by four. In analyzing the detailed data collected for our nine case-study schools, it was found that part-time faculty members carried a teaching load which approached one-third of full-time faculty teaching load. If the actual teaching load of the Totality's part-time teachers was closer to one-third than one-fourth of the full-time load, then any inflation determined by the *Review*'s procedure of not segregating Deans and Librarians would be offset and the faculty figures used in this study might not, in fact, be inflated.

6.   In 1955 there were five schools with enrollments below 30; in 1970 there was one school with an enrollment below 100 students.

7.   There was one school with exactly 150 students. This school was placed in the Middle Enrollment Group.

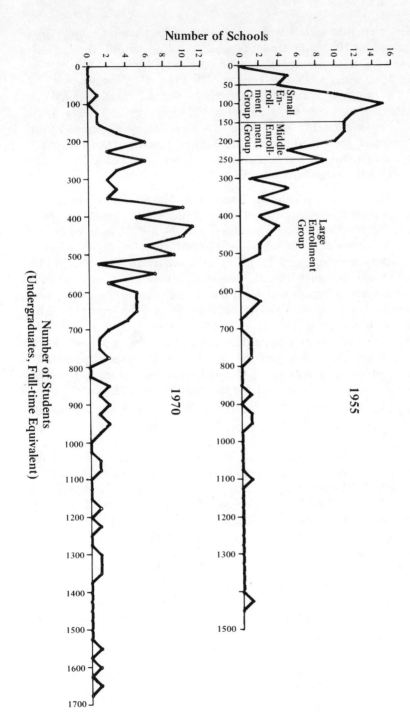

Figure 1
Enrollments of 135 Approved Law Schools Comprising the Totality
1955 and 1970

schools are referred to in this study as the "Small Enrollment Group." There were 36 schools in 1955 with enrollments between 150 and 250. These schools are referred to in this study as the "Middle Enrollment Group." There were 43 schools in 1955 with enrollments between 250 and 1,418. These schools are referred to in this study as the "Large Enrollment Group." It will be noted that the three Enrollment Groups contain 126 schools, 9 less than the Totality. These nine schools had enrollments below 50 in 1955, and because of their very small size and somewhat specialized nature, they have been omitted from inclusion in the Enrollment Groups. We will first examine the Small and Middle Enrollment Groups and then the Large Enrollment Group.

In 1955, many of the schools in the Small and Middle Enrollment Groups had extremely small faculties. Forty-two of the 47 schools in the Small Enrollment Group had 10 or fewer faculty members, and 29 had 8 or fewer faculty members. Twenty-one of the 36 schools in the Middle Enrollment Group had 10 or fewer faculty members, and 11 had 8 or fewer faculty members. In this connection it may be noted that faculties having between 6 and 8 teachers represent about the minimum size for a law school's faculty. Currently, most schools require students to complete between 80 and 90 credit hours for graduation, with an average requirement of 84 hours. A review of the 1955 catalogues of 83 law schools indicates that the average number of credit hours required by those schools that year for the LL.B. was 83.2. See Appendix D. Assuming an 84-hour requirement, 6 professors would have to teach an average load of about 14 hours a year just to cover the credit-hour requirements.[8]

Although the size of the faculties at schools in the Small and Middle Enrollment Groups was barely at a level sufficient to teach the minimum required curriculum, the enrollments were so low that many of these schools had extremely low student/faculty ratios by today's standards. Those Small Enrollment Group schools which had enrollments between 50 and 100 students had student/faculty ratios of approximately 11/1. The typical school in this group enrolled about 80 students and engaged 7 faculty members. Those which had enrollments between 100 and 150 students had student/faculty ratios of approximately 15/1. The typical school in this group enrolled about 125 students and engaged 8.5 faculty members.[9] Thus, many of the Small Enrollment Group schools had student/faculty ratios between 11/1 and 15/1. This range is markedly lower than the 17/1-24/1 range within which many of today's law schools lie. In contrast, in 1955, a good number of schools in the Middle Enrollment Group (between 150 and 250 students)[10] had

8. Seven teachers would have to teach 12+ hours, and eight would have to teach 10+ hours a year.
9. For instance, one case-study school enrolled 128 students in 1955 and engaged 8 faculty members, giving it a student/faculty ratio of 16/1.
10. Those Middle Enrollment Group schools which had enrollments between 150 and 200 had student/faculty ratios of approximately 18/1. The typical school in this group enrolled about 175 students and engaged 9.5 faculty members. Those which had enrollments between 200 and 250 had student/faculty ratios of approximately 22/1. The typical school in this group enrolled about 230 students and engaged 10.5 faculty members.

student/faculty ratios that fell approximately between 19/1 and 24/1. This range closely approximates the student/faculty ratio range existing today.

The enrollment growth of these law schools between 1955 and 1970 was tremendous. In 1955, the average enrollment of schools in the Small Enrollment Group was 101. In 1970, the average had increased to 354, a 251% increase. During the same period the average faculty size grew from about 7.7 to 15.8, a 105% increase. Consistent with these increases, the average student/faculty ratio of these schools increased from 13.1/1 in 1955 to 22.4/1 in 1970.

The Small Enrollment Group schools grew to a 1970 size that ranged between 155 and 643 students, with nearly all the 47 schools distributed quite evenly between enrollments of 155 and 500. Seventeen, or 36% of the total Group, clustered within a 155 to 283 enrollment range. The average faculty size of these schools was 12, and their average student/faculty ratio was 18.5/1. Twenty-six, or 55% of the total Group, clustered within a 323 and 490 enrollment range. The average faculty size of these schools was 18, and their average student/faculty ratio was 23.5/1.[11]

In 1955, the average enrollment of schools in the Middle Enrollment Group was 194. In 1970, this average had increased to 510, a 163% increase. During the same period the average faculty size grew from about 10 to 21, a 110% increase. Consistent with these increases, the average student/faculty ratio of these schools increased from 19.6/1 to 24.1/1. The Middle Enrollment schools grew to a 1970 size that ranged between 245 and 1541 students. Nearly all the 36 schools clustered into three groups. The first cluster contained 16 schools, or about 44% of the total Group, with enrollments ranging between 321 and 448. The average faculty size of these schools was 17 and the average student/faculty ratio was 22.5/1. The second cluster contained 6 schools, or about 17% of the total Group, with enrollments ranging between 486 and 582. The average faculty size of these schools was 27.5 and their average student/faculty ratio was 19/1. The third cluster contained 8 schools, or 22% of the total Group, with enrollments ranging between 602 and 661. The average faculty size of these schools was 24.5, and their average student/faculty ratio was 27.5/1.[12]

As seen, between the Small and Middle Enrollment Group schools wide variations existed in the extent of student/faculty ratio increases between 1955 and 1970. Schools in the Small Enrollment Group in 1955 had low enrollments and low student/faculty ratios. Substantial increases occurred in their student/faculty ratios as their enrollments increased. In contrast, the student/faculty ratios of schools in the Middle Enrollment Group increased, but at a substantially lower rate than the Small Enrollment Group schools. Indeed, seventeen, or almost half, had constant or decreasing student/faculty ratios. The variations in student/faculty ratio changes between the Small and Middle Enrollment Groups suggest that for schools that had attained enrollments of

---

11.   The four remaining schools had enrollments from 529 to 643 and an average faculty size of 17.
12.   Of the six remaining schools, three had enrollments lower than 321 and three had enrollments above 661.

about 200 or more in 1955, further enrollment increases tended to be matched by corresponding increases in faculty size. This conclusion is supported below by a comparison of enrollment and student/faculty ratio patterns between 1955 and 1970 of those schools with enrollments of higher than 250 in 1955.

Before examining the larger schools, brief consideration should be given to the high student/faculty ratio increases of many of the schools in the Small Enrollment Group. Low student/faculty ratios are generally regarded as desirable, and high student/faculty ratios as undesirable. However, as shown above, law schools with small enrollments and low student/faculty ratios may barely be able to provide the minimum curriculum. This was the case in 1955 for many of the schools in the Small Enrollment Group. On the other hand, by 1970, although student/faculty ratios of a number of these schools had increased markedly from 1955 (as their enrollments increased substantially), their faculties in absolute terms also increased. Thus, the same schools with higher student/faculty ratios in 1970 were able to offer far broader curricula than they offered with lower student/faculty ratios in 1955.[13] In short, increases in student/faculty ratios between 1955 and 1970 of schools in the Small Enrollment Group may not have been as undesirable as might be thought when considering student/faculty ratio figures alone.

We next examine the schools in the Large Enrollment Group. In 1955, they ranged in size from 253 to over 1400 students and were distributed fairly evenly throughout that range. Most of these schools' student/faculty ratios in 1955 were considerably higher than those of the schools in the Small and Middle Enrollment Groups. The average student/faculty ratio of schools in the Large Enrollment Group in 1955 was 25.1/1 as compared to 19.6/1 for the Middle Enrollment Group and 13.1/1 for the Small Enrollment Group. Of the 43 Large Enrollment Group schools, 16 had student/faculty ratios over 30/1, 8 between 25/1 and 30/1, 5 between 20/1 and 25/1, and 14 below 20/1. The average enrollment of the Large Enrollment Group schools grew from 483 in 1955 to 785 in 1970, a 62% increase. The rate of growth in enrollment of these schools was smaller than those of the Small and Middle Enrollment Groups largely because the smaller schools started with a smaller enrollment base and, accordingly, their rates of increase were substantially higher.

The average size of the faculty of Large Enrollment Group schools was 19.3 in 1955 and increased to 34.6 in 1970, an 80% increase. Consistent with this, the student/faculty ratios tended to decrease between 1955 and 1970 for this Group. The average student/faculty ratio decreased from 25.1/1 in 1955 to 22.7/1 in 1970. Of the 43 schools in this Group, 24, or 56%, had student/faculty ratios that decreased, 9, or 21%, had student/faculty ratios that remained about the same, and only 10, or 23%, had student/faculty ratios that increased. Wide variations existed among the first group of schools regarding the size of their student/faculty ratio decreases. Eight such schools demonstrated relatively small decreases, 10 schools demonstrated moderate decreases, and 6 schools

---

13.   See chapter 3, section 3.

experienced quite sharp decreases in their student/faculty ratios.

A striking feature of the 43 schools in the Large Enrollment Group is the substantial number (30 or 70%) that fell within the upper two Quartiles on the Resource Index.[14] In fact, 23, or 88% of the 26 law schools in the top Quartile, were in the Large Enrollment Group in 1955. Seven, or 27% of the 26 law schools in the Third Quartile, were in the Large Enrollment Group. In contrast, only 7, or 13% of the 53 schools in the Second and First Quartiles, were in the Large Enrollment Group.[15]

In summary, three general patterns emerge from an examination of the developments that occurred in the 135 law schools between 1955 and 1970. The first pattern involves the Small Enrollment Group. These schools, on the whole, experienced the largest rates of enrollment increase of all the schools examined. While the size of their faculties also grew, such growth was far less than their student growth. Consequently, for most of these schools the student/faculty ratios increased. The second pattern involves schools in the Middle Enrollment Group, which also increased their enrollments during the fifteen-year period. Since, in many instances, these schools' faculties grew at roughly the same rate as their enrollments, a number of these schools managed to hold their student/faculty ratios closer to a constant level. The third pattern involves the Large Enrollment Group. For most, enrollments increased, but faculties increased at a greater rate, and, thus, their student/faculty ratios decreased.

The implications of these three patterns in terms of cost due to faculty growth alone (and assuming no increases in average faculty salaries, or input cost) is obvious. For the schools in the first pattern, namely, those with substantial enrollment increases and small or virtually no increases in faculty size, total instructional cost remained the same or rose insubstantially, and per-student instructional cost decreased. For a number of schools in the second pattern, namely, those with parallel enrollment and faculty increases, total instructional cost increased and per-student instructional cost remained constant. Finally, for those schools in the third pattern, namely, those with larger faculty than enrollment increases, both total instructional cost and per-student instructional cost increased.

Table 1 sets out the total enrollment of each Enrollment Group for 1955 and 1970 with each Group being divided into publicly supported or state schools and privately supported schools. We will first examine the growth patterns of the three Enrollment Groups without regard to the distinction between public and private schools. The most notable change between 1955 and 1970 is the Large Enrollment Group's proportionate decrease in percent of total enrollment from 64% to 49% and the concomitant increases in percent of total enrollment for the Middle and Small Enrollment Groups. This increase was particularly marked for the Small Enrollment Group, increasing from 15% of the total to 24%. In

---

14.   See the Introduction and Summary, section 2, for explanation of the Resource Index.
15.   The remaining six schools in the Large Enrollment Group were not given a Quartile rank because of lack of data for one of the three criteria used for such ranking. See Appendix B.

Table 1

Enrollment of Small, Middle, and Large Enrollment Group Schools
in 1955 and 1970, by Public or Private Support

Group	Number of Schools	1955 Enrollment Total	Av.	% of 126 Schools	1970 Enrollment Total	Av.	% of 126 Schools
Small Enrollment Group							
Public law schools	19	2,086 (44%)	110		6,768 (41%)	356	
Private law schools	28	2,645 (56%)	94		9,885 (59%)	353	
Total	47	4,731 (100%)	101	15%	16,653 (100%)	354	24%
Middle Enrollment Group							
Public law schools	13	2,613 (37%)	201		6,917 (38%)	532	
Private law schools	23	4,384 (63%)	191		11,463 (62%)	498	
Total	36	6,997 (100%)	194	21%	18,380 (100%)	510	27%
Large Enrollment Group							
Public law schools	18	7,358 (35%)	409		14,414 (43%)	801	
Private law schools	25	13,426 (65%)	537		19,336 (57%)	773	
Total	43	20,784 (100%)	483	64%	33,750 (100%)	785	49%
Total (126 Schools)							
Public law schools	50	12,057 (37%)	241		28,099 (41%)	562	
Private law schools	76	20,455 (63%)	269		40,684 (59%)	535	
Total	126	32,512 (100%)	258	100%	68,783 (100%)	546	100%

absolute terms the schools in each Enrollment Group had quite similar growth patterns. The growth of the average school of the Small, Middle, and Large Enrollment Groups, respectively, was 253, 316, and 302 students. Because the smaller schools started with a smaller enrollment base than the larger schools, their percentage increases were considerably higher. The result of these changes was to bring the 126 schools' enrollments somewhat closer together. In 1955, the average Large Enrollment school was 378% larger than the average Small Enrollment school and 149% larger than the average Middle Enrollment school. In 1970, the average Large Enrollment school was only 121% larger than the average Small Enrollment school and only 54% larger than the average Middle Enrollment school. Size differences narrowed appreciably also between the Middle and Small Enrollment Groups. In 1955, the average Middle Enrollment school was 92% larger than the average Small Enrollment school. By 1970, this amount had shrunk to 44%.

Turning next to an examination of the growth patterns of public and private schools, between 1955 and 1970 total enrollment increased 133% at public schools and 99% at private schools. As a result, enrollment at public schools increased slightly as a percent of total enrollment, from 37% to 41%, and enrollment at private schools decreased slightly from 63% to 59%. Comparing the rates of enrollment growth between public and private schools within each Group, we note that, among schools in the Small Enrollment Group, private-school enrollment grew slightly faster than public-school enrollment, whereas enrollments at public and private schools in the Middle Enrollment Group grew at virtually the same rate. In marked contrast, in the Large Enrollment Group, enrollment at public schools grew at a considerably higher rate (96%) than at private schools (44%). Whereas, in 1955, enrollment at public schools constituted 35% of the Large Enrollment Group's total enrollment, by 1970, this amount had increased to 43%. Of the 126 schools examined, 50, or 40%, were public schools and 76, or 60%, were private schools. In 1955, the public schools enrolled 37%, and the private schools 63%, of the total enrollment. By 1970, the public schools enrolled 41%, and the private schools 59%, of the total enrollment. Thus, as an aggregate matter, there has been a close balance between public and private schools in terms of proportion of schools and proportion of students enrolled. Similar observations may be made when the schools are examined by Enrollment Group.

Section 2 — Increase in Salary Levels: 1955 to 1970

The second major factor causing increases in instructional cost is the increase in salaries paid to faculty members. Information regarding faculty salaries is limited to the median faculty salaries of 115 of the 135 schools included in the Totality.[16] Accordingly, for this section somewhat fewer schools are examined

---

16. Median rather than average salary figures were used. It is common statistical procedure when analyzing salaries to use median figures to prevent distortions that might be caused by a small number of abnormally high or low figures. However, in nearly every case examined the reported median and average salaries were almost identical.

than for section 1 regarding enrollment and faculty growth.[17] In the examination of increases in faculty salaries between the years 1955 and 1970, salaries paid in 1955 have been inflated so that all figures presented are in constant (1970) dollars.[18]

The data upon which the following analysis is based do not include fringe benefits because of the difficulty in assigning a cash value to many elements of the whole fringe package.[19] Schools, of course, differ widely in the amount of fringe benefits provided to their faculty and, assuming that accurate fringe-benefit figures were available, some of the differences in instructional cost increases mentioned below might be modified and some might be enlarged by the inclusion of fringe-benefit figures. However, we believe that the general trends discerned from the analysis of compensation figures ex-fringe are essentially sound. It should be clearly recognized, however, that the omission of fringe benefits from faculty compensation produces instructional cost figures lower than actual instructional cost.[20]

Variations among law schools in increases in salaries paid to faculty members between 1955 and 1970 are wide.[21] They range from one school which had a decrease in its average faculty salary to a school with an increase of 165%.[22] See Table 2. In 90 of the 115 schools, increases ranged from 30% to 100%. Between these limits the schools were quite evenly distributed. The average increase of the median faculty salaries of the 115 schools was 65%.[23] In terms of the annual average compound rate of growth this figure represents an increase of 3.4%.[24] The median increase was 68%, which represents an annual growth rate of 3.5%. Small Enrollment and Middle Enrollment schools had somewhat higher increases than Large Enrollment schools. Although the average increases of the three Enrollment Groups were roughly similar in absolute terms,[25] because the two

---

17.   By Enrollment Group, there are 43 schools in the Small Enrollment Group, 34 schools in the Middle Enrollment Group, and 38 schools in the Large Enrollment Group.

18.   See Note on Conversion of Current to Constant Dollars in the Introduction and Summary.

19.   Some examples of components of the fringe-benefit package to which exact cash values cannot be assigned are: medical benefits such as medical plans and services provided by the university health-care centers, some retirement plans, tuition-exemption arrangements, faculty housing, and the like.

20.   We believe that a detailed study of fringe benefits provided by American law schools would be extremely helpful for those concerned with the fiscal and management side of legal education. Within the limits of our study, such an investigation could not be made. Proper conduct of such an investigation would require the development of various accounting techniques and definitions and, we believe, in many instances, on-site inspections.

21.   Variations in salaries are not as wide, however, as the variations among these schools in increases in student enrollments and increases in the size of faculties. See below.

22.   The decrease is comprehensible when it is recognized that the changes in faculty salaries are in constant 1970 dollars. This, of course, makes the increase of 165% all the more extraordinary.

23.   In making this computation the salary figures were not weighted; so the average salary and average increase set forth in the text are not necessarily the same as the averages would be if the median faculty salary were weighted by the number of teachers in each school. The averages and increases used below are also unweighted.

24.   In current dollars, the annual average compound rate of growth was 6.2%.

25.   Actually, as will be shown below, the Large Enrollment schools had the largest increases in absolute terms.

smaller Groups started from substantially lower bases, i.e., lower 1955 salaries, they had higher percent increases.

Table 2

Distribution of Percent Increase in
Median Faculty Salaries for 115 Law Schools
1955 to 1970

Percent Increase in Input Cost	Number of Schools			
	Small Enrollment Group	Middle Enrollment Group	Large Enrollment Group	Total
below 20%*	0	2	1	3
20%-24%	0	0	2	2
25%-29%	0	0	1	1
30%-34%	3	2	3	8
35%-39%	2	2	1	5
40%-44%	1	0	4	5
45%-49%	2	1	1	4
50%-54%	2	1	5	8
55%-59%	4	3	1	8
60%-64%	0	1	2	3
65%-69%	5	5	2	12
70%-74%	6	4	4	14
75%-79%	1	2	1	4
80%-84%	4	0	2	6
85%-89%	2	4	0	6
90%-94%	4	2	0	6
95%-99%	0	1	0	1
100%-104%	1	0	2	3
105%-109%	1	2	2	5
110%-114%	0	0	2	2
115%-119%	2	0	2	4
120%-124%	0	0	0	0
125%-129%	1	1	0	2
130%-134%	1	0	0	1
135%-139%	1	0	0	1
above 140%	0	1	0	1
	43	34	38	115

*Two schools with an increase of 4% and one school with a decrease of 2%.

In 1955, about 70% of the schools in the Small and Middle Enrollment Groups had median faculty salaries of between \$8,000 and \$11,500.[26] The average faculty salary that year for schools in the Small and Middle Enrollment Groups was \$10,100 and \$11,300, respectively. In contrast, in 1955, only 26%

---

26.   Note that all 1955 salaries have been converted to 1970 dollars.

of the Large Enrollment Group had median salaries below $11,500, 32% had salaries between $11,500 and $13,000, and 42% between $13,000 and $24,000. The average faculty salary that year for schools in the Large Enrollment Group was $14,300. In 1970, about 52% of schools in the Small and Middle Enrollment Groups had faculty salaries of between $16,000 and $19,000, and about 53% of Large Enrollment schools had salaries between $20,000 and $25,000. The average faculty salary that year for schools in the Small and Middle Enrollment Groups was $17,500 and $18,700, respectively, and for schools in the Large Enrollment Group it was $22,400. An examination of increases in faculty salaries between 1955 and 1970 indicates that about 71 of the 115 schools examined had increases ranging between $5,000 and $9,000. A higher proportion of the Large Enrollment schools had increases above the $5,000 to $9,000 range than the schools in the other two Groups.

The above data demonstrate that schools in the Large Enrollment Group had average faculty salaries that were substantially higher than those of schools in the Small and Middle Enrollment Groups. This phenomenon is related to the fact that a high percent of the Large Enrollment schools (88%) were in the top Quartile of the Resource Index. In contrast, 4% of the schools in the Small Enrollment Group and 3% of the schools in the Middle Enrollment Group were in the top Quartile.[27] Median faculty salary is one of the three measures for the Resource Index. Thus, because most Large Enrollment schools had higher salaries than those in the other two Groups, a greater proportion of them tend to be in the top Quartile. One explanation for the concomitance of high enrollments in 1955 and Fourth Quartile status may be that in the early 1950s, when applicants for law schools were not as numerous as they are today, the Fourth Quartile schools with the largest amount of resources and more highly paid faculties attracted the most applicants and were able to have high enrollments while maintaining the quality of the entering class.

Effect of Geography on Salary Levels

We have examined salary levels by geographic area. To do this we have divided the country into the following five regions, each region containing the following states:

Northeast (28 law schools): Maine, New Hampshire, Vermont, Massachusetts, Connecticut, New York, New Jersey, Pennsylvania, Delaware, Maryland, District of Columbia.

Southeast (21 law schools): West Virginia, Virginia, Kentucky, Tennessee, North Carolina, South Carolina, Georgia, Alabama, Mississippi, Florida.

Southwest (24 law schools): Iowa, Nebraska, Missouri, Kansas, Arkansas, Oklahoma, Louisiana, Texas, Colorado, New Mexico.

---

27.   As only 99 schools of the 115 schools constituting the three Enrollment Groups were included in the Resource Index, these percentages are probably smaller in each instance than they would have been if all 115 schools had been included in the Resource Index.

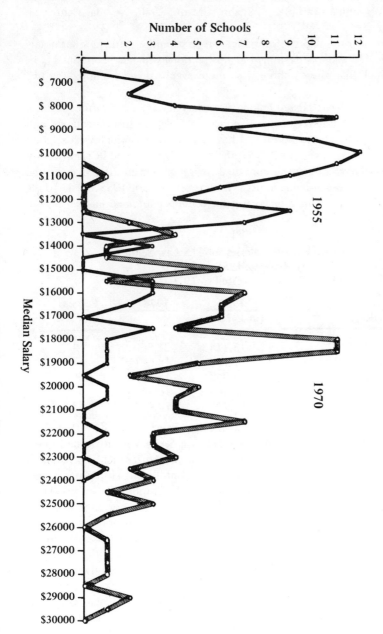

Figure 2

Distribution of Median Salaries of Full-time Law Teachers
(All Ranks) of 115 Law Schools, 1955 and 1970
(1955 figures converted to 1970 dollars)

Mid-North (24 law schools): Ohio, Indiana, Illinois, Michigan, Wisconsin, Minnesota.

Northwest & Pacific (18 law schools): North Dakota, South Dakota, Montana, Wyoming, Washington, Idaho, Oregon, Utah, Nevada, California, Arizona.

After the name of each region there is set out in parenthesis the number of law schools (of the 115 schools examined in this section) which are contained in it. It will be noted that these schools are quite evenly divided among the five regions.[28].

Some differences have existed among the salary levels of the various regions. Schools in the Northeast region have tended to have the highest salaries, and schools in the Southeast and Southwest have tended to have the lowest salaries. As indicated below, it is very likely that these differences would be significantly reduced if the salary figures were corrected for geographical differences by the use of comparative cost-of-living indices. Table 3 sets out for 1955 and 1970 the average of the median faculty salaries of the schools contained in each region.

Table 3

Average Faculty Salaries for 115 Law Schools
by Regions, 1955 and 1970
(1955 figures converted to 1970 dollars)

Region	1955 (in 1970 $)	1970	Percent Increase
Northeast (N=28)	$13,114	$21,569	64%
Southeast (N=21)	11,132	18,641	67%
Southwest (N=24)	9,068	18,655	106%
Mid-North (N=24)	12,306	18,549	51%
Northwest & Pacific (N=18)	11,946	19,462	63%

The third column represents the percent increase from 1955 to 1970 of these salary figures. These geographical differences in salaries may be attributed to the mix of schools by size in each region as well as to differences in cost of living. It was pointed out above that schools in the Large Enrollment Group had higher average salaries than schools in the Small and Middle Enrollment Groups. Thus, regions with a high proportion of Large Enrollment schools might be expected to have average faculty salaries on the high side, and regions with a low proportion of Large Enrollment schools to have average faculty salaries on the low side. Confirming these expectations, 57% of the schools in the Northeast region were Large Enrollment schools, whereas, of the schools in the Southeast and Southwest regions, only 14% and 17%, respectively, were Large Enrollment schools. Table 4 sets out the number of schools in each Enrollment Group by region. Next to each such number is placed the percent that it constitutes of all the schools in the region. To the right of this information is the percent of each Enrollment Group that is made up by the number of schools in each region.

---

28.   These regional divisions are the same as used in Lowell S. Nicholson, *Law Schools in the United States* (Baltimore: The Lord Baltimore Press, Inc., 1958), pp. 2-32.

Table 4

Regional Distribution of 115 Law Schools, by Small, Middle, and Large Enrollment Groups

Region	Small Enrollment Group		Middle Enrollment Group		Large Enrollment Group		Total		Enrollment Group		
	No.	%	No.	%	No.	%	No.	%	Small %	Middle %	Large %
Northeast	3	11%	9	32%	16	57%	28	100%	7%	26%	42%
Southeast	16	76%	2	10%	3	14%	21	100%	37%	6%	8%
Southwest	8	33%	12	50%	4	17%	24	100%	19%	35%	11%
Mid-North	7	29%	9	38%	8	33%	24	100%	16%	26%	21%
Northwest & Pacific	9	50%	2	11%	7	39%	18	100%	21%	7%	18%
									100%	100%	100%

Although regional differences exist in average salaries when all the schools in a region are considered, these differences are largely eliminated if schools in different regions are compared by Enrollment Groups. Table 5 sets out the average of the median faculty salaries of schools in each Enrollment Group according to the five regions.

Table 5

Average of Median Faculty Salaries for 115 Law Schools
by Regional Distribution and Enrollment Groups
(1955 figures converted to 1970 dollars)

Region	Small Enrollment Group			Middle Enrollment Group			Large Enrollment Group		
	1955	1970	Increase	1955	1970	Increase	1955	1970	Increase
Northeast	$11,640	$20,160	73%	$10,810	$19,480	80%	$14,690	$23,010	57%
Southeast	10,740	17,940	67%	12,020	19,500	62%	12,650	21,830	73%
Southwest	9,650	17,530	82%	10,820	18,740	73%	10,610	20,650	95%
Mid-North	9,240	15,750	70%	12,150	17,760	46%	15,160	21,890	44%
Northwest & Pacific	8,590	16,960	97%	11,440	18,430	61%	15,120	22,970	52%
Weighted Average	$10,120	$17,450	73%	$11,280	$18,700	66%	$14,270	$22,430	57%

It is apparent from Table 5 that regional salary differences by Enrollment Group are much smaller than such differences computed by considering each region as a whole. Schools in the Northeast region of each Enrollment Group have only slightly higher average salaries. Furthermore, Southeast and Southwest schools do not have the lowest salaries when schools are considered by Enrollment Groups. It is likely that whatever small differences exist between regions on this basis would be eliminated if all salary figures were corrected for geographical differences by use of comparative cost-of-living indices. On the basis of the above, it is our conclusion that differences in salary levels attributed to geographical differences are insignificant.

Section 4 will demonstrate that although increases in average faculty salaries (input cost) between 1955 and 1970 have been the least significant factor in explaining the differences between the various schools' increases in instructional cost, input cost increases have been a material factor in contributing to the substantial increases in instructional cost of legal education during this period. As indicated above, the median increase in input cost was 68% in constant dollars. This means that if input cost increases had been the only change, the instructional cost of half the law schools examined would have increased at least 68%. It is not at all surprising, of course, that input cost increases have been a significant factor in increased instructional cost. Labor cost is a major factor in the expenses of any enterprise, and in enterprises that are labor intensive, such as law schools, increases in the cost of labor are necessarily a predominant factor contributing to increases in total cost.

Comparison of Law Professors' Salaries with Those of Practicing Lawyers and Other University Teachers

In considering increases in law professors' salaries, it is instructive to compare these salaries with those of other professors and lawyers. The following table summarizes average increases in salaries for full-time teachers in higher education, medical school teachers, and law school teachers, between 1960 and 1970. These figures include the salaries of professors, associate professors, assistant professors, and instructors, gathered by the American Association of University Professors (AAUP) and the A.B.A. Salary figures for 1955 are not provided because the AAUP survey of college and university teachers in 1955 included too small a sample (35 institutions) to permit meaningful comparisons.

Table 6

Average Salary Levels for Three Categories
of College and University Teachers
(Converted to 1970 dollars, current dollars in parenthesis)

	Full-time College and University Teachers (All Ranks)	Full-time Medical School Teachers (All Ranks)	Full-time Law School Teachers (All Ranks)
		Salary + Fringe	
1960	$10,361 ($ 7,750)	$12,269 ($ 9,177)	$14,080 ($10,532)
1965	11,963 (9,618)	17,379 (13,973)	16,726 (13,448)
1970	13,284 (13,284)	17,910 (17,910)	18,919 (18,919)

Dollar and Percent Changes

1960-65	$1,602 = 15%	$5,110 = 42%	$2,646 = 19%
1965-70	1,321 = 11%	531 = 3%	2,193 = 13%
1960-70	2,923 = 28%	5,641 = 46%	4,839 = 34%

Note: The AAUP survey of college and university teachers encompassed 452 institutions in 1960, 822 in 1965, and 1,161 in 1970. Law school teachers' salaries are included within this category. The medical school teachers' data include salary plus fringe benefits. In 1970, fringe benefits were 11% of the figure presented. The A.B.A. survey of law school teachers encompassed 129 law schools in 1960, 130 in 1965, and 143 in 1970. For all years, the median faculty salary for each school is used, the figure shown here being the average of the medians. Unfortunately, the 1960 data include fringe benefits whereas the 1965 and 1970 data exclude fringe benefits. In 1965, fringe benefits for those schools which reported them equaled 9.2% of their average median salary; in 1970, 10.7%. There is no fringe figure for 1960. However, if it is assumed that fringe benefits were 8% of the average median salary in 1960, then the average median salary ex-fringe would be $13,037 ($9,752). In this case, the increase from 1960 to 1965 would be 28%, and from 1960 to 1970 it would be 45%, instead of the 19% and the 34% shown. In considering these figures, account should be given to the fact that law school faculties usually contain an appreciably higher proportion of tenured faculty members than the faculties of many other divisions. In addition, law faculties usually have a high ratio of professors to associate and assistant professors. Source: *American Association of University Professors Bulletin*, v. 47, no. 2 (June 1961), p. 109, 111; v. 52, no. 2 (June 1966), p. 141; v. 57, no. 2 (June 1971), p. 223. American Bar Association, confidential data.

Figures for average salaries of lawyers are not so easily available or comparable. Based on tax returns filed by single practitioners and active partnerships, income figures are available for these two groups for 1960 and 1965, with only an estimate for 1970.

Table 7

Average Salaries for Lawyers
(Converted to 1970 dollars,
current dollars in parenthesis)

	Sole Practitioners*	Partnerships
1960	$ 9,706 ($ 7,260)	$22,460 ($16,800)
1965	12,909 (10,379)	27,628 (22,213)
1970 (est.)	18,000 (18,000)	27,000 (27,000)

Dollar and Percent Changes

1960-65	$3,203 = 33%	$5,168 = 23%
1965-70	5,091 = 39%	−628 = −2%
1960-70	8,294 = 85%	4,540 = 20%

*The average income of sole practitioners includes part-time and semi-retired lawyers.
Source: *American Bar Association Journal*, v. 50 (May 1964), p. 457; v. 55 (June 1969), p. 563. Estimate from "The Gilt-Edged Profession," *Forbes* (Sept. 15, 1971).

It is apparent from the above figures that, for each year examined, law professors had higher average salaries than sole practitioners, teachers in colleges and universities, and medical school teachers, and lower average salaries than lawyers who were members of partnerships. For the period 1960-1970, the salaries of law professors increased at a higher rate than those of partners, at somewhat above the rate for college and university teachers, and at a lower rate than those of sole practitioners or medical school teachers. Moreover, law professors (who, on the basis of their academic records, appear headed for the top of their profession when graduated from law school) are well behind comparable lawyers in absolute terms. In this regard the partnership figures appearing in Table 7 may not be suitable for purposes of comparison with law professors. It has been observed that, as a rule, the larger the firm, the larger the amount of each partner's share. Thus, it is estimated that in a six-man firm the average salary in 1970 was $35,000, in a nine-man firm $45,000, and in the fifty largest firms, from $50,000 to $125,000 and above.[29] Top corporate counsel in 1970 has been estimated to have earned $33,000 and more.[30] Thus, the input cost increases examined above, while of considerable significance in accounting for instructional cost increases, have not been out of line when compared with salary increases paid to other professors in higher education and to members of the legal profession, and, when compared with those at the top of the legal profession, the increases appear moderate indeed.

Before leaving the subject of rising faculty salaries, a brief summary will be made of William J. Baumol and William G. Bowen's thesis regarding the special cost pressures that beset educational institutions arising from the nature of their

29.   *Forbes* (Sept. 15, 1971).
30.   Bureau of Labor Statistics, *Bulletin 1693* (1971), p. 16.

technology.[31] Bowen formulates the thesis as follows: "In every industry in which increases in productivity come more slowly than in the economy as a whole, cost per unit of product must be expected to increase relative to costs in general."[32] Applied to legal education, this means that per-student cost will rise faster than costs in the economy at large. Generally speaking, unlike other sectors of the economy, for example, manufacturing or agriculture, education is not able to increase its productivity through capital accumulation or technological innovations.[33] The essential input in the educational process remains the individual faculty member, and no significant ways have yet been devised for him to teach substantially larger numbers of students than he has in the past.[34] However, other industries in the economy do enjoy the benefit of capital accumulation and technological changes and, accordingly, are able to increase their output per worker. As a result, these industries can and do increase salaries and wages without increasing their per-unit labor costs. The thesis is completed by assuming that salary increases will have to be given to faculty members merely to keep their living standards at the same level as those people working in industries who enjoy productivity gains. The essential difference however, between educational enterprises and those that benefit from productivity gains is that educational institutions can not increase salaries without increasing their per-unit labor cost.

Part-time Faculty Members

Before we leave the topic of faculty salaries, brief consideration will be given to the use of part-time faculty personnel. Some of the analysis that follows does not relate directly to faculty salaries, but we believe it is desirable to consider the subject of part-time faculty in one place. From a historical standpoint, the subject has two main elements. First, we examine whether greater or lesser use of part-time faculty was made in 1970 as compared with 1955, and, second, we trace the extent of increases in the amounts paid to part-time faculty during the period examined.

From an examination of the A.B.A.'s 1955 and 1970 annual *Review of Legal Education*, we have determined for each school in the Totality the ratio of full-time faculty to the equivalent number of full-time faculty members made up by part-time faculty, for both 1955 and 1970. On an aggregate basis, in 1955, for every 4.7 full-time faculty members, one part-time faculty member was engaged. In 1970, there were appreciably more full-time faculty members than

31. Other commentators have made similar analyses, but none, in our estimation, have expressed it so clearly as Baumol and Bowen. See William G. Bowen, *The Economics of the Major Private Universities* (Berkeley: The Carnegie Commission on the Future of Higher Education, 1968), esp. pp. 12-16, and William J. Baumol and William G. Bowen, *Performing Arts: The Economic Dilemma* (New York: Twentieth Century Fund, 1966), esp. chap. 7.
32. Bowen, *The Economics of the Major Private Universities,* p. 16.
33. There have been some technological advances, such as the use of video equipment, but they have so far had a minimal effect on a law school's productivity.
34. This point is a particularly poignant one for legal education with its extraordinarily large classes as compared with most other branches of education.

part-time, the ratio for that year being 7.4 to 1.[35] In other words, between 1955 and 1970, the number of full-time faculty engaged by law schools increased a great deal more (107%) than the number of part-time faculty (32%).[36]

Information available to us regarding the amounts paid to part-time faculty has been limited to the case-study schools. To analyze changes in amounts paid to part-time faculty members at the case-study schools, we have determined the amounts paid to a full-time-equivalent faculty member.[37] In 1955, the average salary paid to a full-time equivalent (in 1970 dollars) was $11,295. In 1970, this amount had increased to $13,797, a 22% increase. It is of interest to compare these figures to the amounts paid to full-time faculty members. In 1955, the average salary of a full-time faculty member was $12,746. Comparing this figure to the average amount paid to a full-time equivalent that year ($11,295), we note that the average salary paid to a full-time equivalent was only 11% less than that paid to a full-time faculty member. In 1970, the average salary of a full-time faculty member was $20,936. Comparing this figure with the average amount paid to a full-time equivalent that year ($13,797), we note that the average salary paid was 34% less than that paid to a full-time faculty member. Thus, at the case-study schools the cost of part-time instruction relative to the cost of full-time instruction became less expensive between 1955 and 1970.[38]

If our conclusion regarding the decreased use of part-time instruction between 1955 and 1970 in the Totality is combined with our conclusion regarding the relative decrease in cost of part-time instruction at the case-study schools, we might speculate that part-time instruction during the period examined has come to have much less of a fiscal impact on instructional cost than in the past. In brief, in 1970, fewer part-time teachers were used, relative to the number of full-time teachers, than in 1955, and, in contrast to the earlier year, they were paid relatively less than full-time instructors. Wide differences existed in the amounts paid to full-time-equivalent instructors at the case-study

---

35.   These computations have been made on the assumption that part-timers teach at one-quarter the load of full-timers (i.e., that four part-timers are the equivalent of one full-timer). We have assumed this to be the case both for 1955 and 1970. In actuality it might, of course, have been otherwise. In fact, as pointed out in footnote 5, at the case-study schools, part-time instructors taught a load closer to one-third of the load of full-time instructors. Without more detailed information, some convention, such as the one we used, had to be employed, and we believe that the results obtained from it are accurate enough to demonstrate general trends. It might also have been the case that the teaching load of part-timers changed from 1955 to 1970. Here also, even if there had been such a change, in all probability, it would have been small and, thus, would not alter our general conclusions. An examination of the case-study schools reveals very little change in the teaching load of part-timers between 1955 and 1970.

36.   In 1955, as an aggregate matter, for every 7.1 full-time instructors engaged by the case-study schools, one part-time instructor was engaged, whereas, in 1970, for every 5.7 full-time instructors, one part-time instructor was engaged. Thus, the ratio at the case-study schools moved in the opposite direction. Between 1955 and 1970, the number of full-time instructors at the case-study schools increased 102% and the number of part-timers increased 155%.

37.   This was done by dividing the total amount of salaries paid to part-timers by the quotient of the sum of part-time teaching hours divided by the average teaching load of full-time instructors.

38.   The average salary of full-time instructors increased 64% as compared to 22% for part-time instructors.

schools. At some schools they were paid at levels near, or fairly near, those of full-time instructors,[39] and at other schools they were paid at substantially lower levels than full-time instructors. These differences are shown in Table 8.

Table 8

Faculty Salaries at Nine Case-study Schools
(1955 figures converted to 1970 dollars)

	1955					**1970**			
	Full-time Teachers		**Full-time-equivalent Teachers**			**Full-time Teachers**		**Full-time-equivalent Teachers**	
Teaching Load	**No.**	**Average Salary**	**No.**	**Average Salary**	**Teaching Load**	**No.**	**Average Salary**	**No.**	**Average Salary**
11.1	15	$ 8,892	.9	$ 3,137	11.7	21	$18,371	4.2	$ 5,512
14.1	8	$10,609	.4	$ 5,947	11.5	14	$21,910	1.1	$17,788
15.4	9	$11,945	3.4	$ 3,253	10.9	27	$21,307	5.8	$14,663
11.9	9	$13,951	1.1	$18,787	10.8	25	$20,202	2.2	$11,361
12.6	20	$12,667	2.1	$15,941	10.7	40	$23,044	2.0	$18,937
9.3	11	$15,230	1.7	$16,318	10.5	24	$20,512	4.4	$20,467
14.8	5	$11,620	1.7	$12,911	10.5	13	$18,546	4.5	$10,082
12.0	5	$13,195	3.1	$11,971	10.3	18	$19,933	3.2	$7,336
9.0	25	$16,601	1.1	$13,386	8.8	36	$24,590	11.6	$18,027
		Average					Average		
12.2	11.9	$12,746	1.7	$11,295	10.6	24	$20,936	4.3	$13,797

Section 3 — Explanation of Instructional Cost Equation

The preceding sections have shown the extent to which faculties have increased in size, how they have increased relative to enrollment growth, and how much faculty salaries have increased. Because we define instructional cost as consisting solely of salaries paid to faculty, we now have the information necessary to analyze increases in instructional cost.[40] To do this we have developed an Instructional Cost Equation ("I.C. Equation") which reveals in terms of three factors the underlying structure of increases in instructional cost between any two years.

The first factor, referred to as the Scale factor, is the increase in instructional cost attributable to increases in faculty size which in turn are attributable to

---

39. In 1955, at four of the case-study schools they were paid at higher levels than full-time faculty members.
40. As indicated above, fringe benefits are not included in our figures relating to actual law schools. For purposes of understanding the analysis developed in this section, a number of hypothetical examples are given. Because of the hypothetical nature of the examples, it does not matter whether fringe benefits are considered as included in input costs or not so long as it is assumed that the treatment of fringe is consistent.

increases in student enrollment.[41] The second factor, referred to as the Student/Faculty Ratio factor, is the change in instructional cost attributable to changes in the number of students per teacher.[42] The third factor, referred to as the Input Cost factor, is the increase in instructional cost attributable to the increase in the average salary paid to faculty members.[43] Arithmetic values equivalent to the change in each of the three factors between any two years are determined and are multiplied together in a double-product multiplication, the final product[44] of which, minus 1.00, times 100, constitutes the percent increase in instructional cost between the two years. The I.C. Equation is as follows:

> Scale factor × Student/Faculty Ratio factor
> × Input Cost factor = Instructional Cost factor.
> (Instructional Cost factor − 1.00) × 100
> = Percent increase in instructional cost.

There follows a brief explanation of the I.C. Equation. A more complete explanation is contained in Appendix E. The three factors are determined as follows.

The Scale factor is computed by dividing the enrollment in the later year (Year 2) by the enrollment in the earlier year (Year 1).

For example, if a school enrolled 200 students in 1955 and 450 students in 1970, the numerical value of 2.25 would be assigned to its Scale factor (450 ÷ 200 = 2.25). This is equivalent to a 125 percent increase in enrollment between such two years, and, more importantly for these purposes, it constitutes the percent increase in faculty size between 1955 and 1970 if the school had maintained a constant student/faculty ratio.[45]

The Student/Faculty Ratio factor is computed by dividing the Year 1 student/faculty ratio by the Year 2 student/faculty ratio.[46]

---

41.   Logically, instructional cost might decrease because of a decrease in the size of the faculty attributable to a decrease in enrollment. Accordingly, it might be more accurate to refer to "changes" in instructional cost attributable to "changes" in enrollment. As the actual experience of the overwhelming majority of law schools during the period studied has involved only increases in enrollment, the formulation is cast in terms of "increases."

42.   With regard to this factor, the formulation is cast in terms of "changes." As has been seen above, the student/faculty ratios of a number of law schools increased between 1955 and 1970 and a number decreased. Increases in enrollment (to which the Scale factor is related) and in faculty size (which combines with enrollment to produce the Student/Faculty Ratio factor) have been discussed in section 1.

43.   With regard to the Input Cost factor, the formulation is cast in terms of "increases," since the actual experience of virtually every law school during the period studied has involved only increases in average faculty salary. Increases in faculty salaries have been discussed in section 2.

44.   The final product of this double-product multiplication is referred to as the Instructional Cost factor ("I.C. factor") and when multiplied by the dollar value of the instructional cost of the earlier year (Year 1) gives the dollar value of the instructional cost of the later year (Year 2).

45.   It will be recalled that, in evaluating the effect of enrollment changes alone on changes in faculty size, we assume that student/faculty ratio remains constant.

46.   Note that Year 1 is divided by Year 2, which is the opposite of the procedure used

In the above example, if the school had a student/faculty ratio of 25/1 in 1955 and 20/1 in 1970, the numerical value of 1.25 would be assigned to its Student/Faculty Ratio factor (25 ÷ 20 = 1.25). This is equivalent to a 25 percent increase in the size of the school's faculty between 1955 and 1970 at a constant enrollment.[47] A negative value is produced when a school's student/faculty ratio increases. In such cases the Student/Faculty Ratio factor would have a value less than 1.00. In the above example, if the school had a student/faculty ratio of 20/1 in 1955 and 25/1 in 1970, the numerical value of .8 (20 ÷ 25 = .8) would be assigned to its Student/Faculty Ratio factor. If 1.00 is subtracted from the quotient, the result is a negative number, −.20, which constitutes the decrease of 20% in the size of the school's faculty between 1955 and 1970 at a constant enrollment.

The Input Cost factor is computed by dividing the average faculty salary in Year 2 by the average faculty salary in Year 1.

In the above example, if the average faculty salary was $10,000 in 1955 and $20,000 in 1970, the numerical value of 2.00 would be assigned to the Input Cost factor ($20,000 ÷ $10,000 = 2.00). This is equivalent to a 100 percent increase in the school's average faculty salary between 1955 and 1970.

In the above example we used a school having 200 students in 1955. With a student/faculty ratio of 25/1, such a school would engage 8 professors. At an average salary of $10,000 per professor, it would incur an instructional cost of $80,000. In 1970, the school had an enrollment of 450 students. With a student/faculty ratio of 20/1 it would engage 22½ professors. At an average salary of $20,000 per professor it would incur an instructional cost of $450,000. Thus, between 1955 and 1970, instructional cost increased $370,000 or 462.5%. The percent increase in instructional cost may also be derived, of course, by merely dividing 1970 instructional cost by 1955 instructional cost and converting the quotient to a percentage ($450,000 ÷ $80,000 = 5.625 − 1.00 = 4.625 = 462.5%). However, the percent increase in instructional cost does not reveal the relative importance of the three factors in producing the over-all increase in instructional cost. By applying the I.C. Equation, these relationships are made evident. Thus, in the foregoing example, the I.C. Equation is:

2.25 (Scale factor) × 1.25 (Student/Faculty Ratio factor)
× 2.00 (Input Cost factor)
= 5.625 (Instructional Cost factor).
(5.625 − 1.00) × 100 = 462.5% (Percent increase in
instructional cost).

Scale and Input Cost are the predominant factors, with the Scale factor having the most impact.

---

with the other factors. Mathematically this allows a decrease in a ratio to be reflected as a positive value.

47. Similar to the assumption made when evaluating the effect of enrollment changes above is the assumption made here in evaluating the effect of student/faculty ratio changes

Although the relative importance of the three factors is demonstrated by the I.C. Equation, the amount of increase in instructional cost cannot be broken down into three parts, each representing one of the factors. The compound nature of the equation precludes this kind of analysis. Thus, in the example above, it is not possible to assert that some part of the 462.5% total increase is attributable to scale alone, some part to student/faculty ratio alone, and some part to input cost alone, and that all these individual parts in percentage terms add up to 462.5%.[48] Arithmetically, the three factors must be considered together as a double-product multiplication rather than individually. While part of the total increase can be attributed to each of the factors alone, additional amounts of the increase are to be attributed to the joint effect of any two of the factors (Scale and Student/Faculty Ratio, Scale and Input Cost, Student/Faculty Ratio and Input Cost) and to the joint effect of all three factors. The multiplicative nature of the equation is reflected in these joint or compound effects. To illustrate the compound effect of the equation, an analysis will first be made of how faculty increases in the above example are accounted for, and then consideration will be given to the impact of input cost.

In brief, of the total number of new professors added to the faculty, some are deemed to have been added to provide the original number of students with a reduced student/faculty ratio, some are deemed to have been added to provide the additional students resulting from the enrollment increase with a student/faculty ratio identical to what was provided in 1955, and some are deemed to have been added to provide such additional students with the reduced student/faculty ratio. It will be recognized that the last-mentioned additional faculty members are attributable to both the enrollment increase and the decrease in student/faculty ratio or are attributable to the joint effect of changes in scale and student/faculty ratio. As indicated, faculty size increased by 14½ professors (from 8 to 22½), a 181% increase.[49] With respect to scale alone, 10 such additional professors may be attributed to the 250 increase in student enrollment on the assumption that 10 new professors would have been added to the faculty to maintain the school's original (Year 1) student/faculty ratio of 25/1 at the increased enrollment.[50] With respect to changes in student/faculty

---

alone on changes in faculty size, namely that enrollment remains constant.

48.   For example, it would be improper to assert that faculty increases attributable to enrollment increases (scale) account for 125% of the increase in instructional cost; that faculty increases attributable to a decrease in the student/faculty ratio account for 25% of the increase; and that increases in salary paid to faculty (input cost) account for 100% of the increase. Note that the addition of these three figures falls short of 462.5%. Nor can 462.5% be divided into three parts, each representing one of the factors.

49.   In addition to determining the total increase in instructional cost through the I.C. Equation, one may derive the increment in faculty size between two years by using two of its three factors. This is done by multiplying the Scale factor by the Student/Faculty Ratio factor and then converting the product to a percentage. Thus, in our example the Scale factor is 2.25 and the Student/Faculty Ratio factor is 1.25. These two figures multiplied together produce 2.81. This product is referred to in this study as the Faculty Growth factor. The Faculty Growth factor minus 1.00, times 100 equals the percent increase in faculty $((2.81 - 1.00) \times 100 = 181\%)$. In the I.C. Equation format: Scale Factor $\times$ Student/Faculty Ratio factor = Faculty Growth factor. Faculty Growth factor $\times$ Input Cost factor = Instructional Cost factor.

50. $250 \div 25 = 10$. If scale were the only change, one could derive the increase in faculty

ratio alone, 2 such additional professors may be attributed to the decrease in the school's student/faculty ratio on the assumption that, based on the original enrollment (Year 1) of 200 students, 2 professors would have been added to the faculty if the school had reduced its student/faculty ratio from 25/1 to 20/1.[51] Finally, 2½ such additional professors may be attributed to a combination of the increase in the school's student enrollment and the decrease in its student/faculty ratio, on the assumption that 2½ new professors would have been added to the faculty to provide the additional 250 students with the decreased student/faculty ratio of 20/1.[52] These increases in faculty size may be translated into increases in instructional cost by considering each additional professor to be equivalent to a $10,000 increase in instructional cost, since $10,000 was the average faculty salary of one professor in 1955. This is proper, since our analysis so far has not considered increased input cost. Thus, $145,000 of the total increase in instructional cost is attributable to increased faculty size without regard to salary increases (14½ X $10,000).

The same analysis applies when input cost is examined. Here, the introduction of a third factor once more involves the compound effect. If the only change between 1955 and 1970 had been the increase of $10,000 in the average salary paid to the original 8 faculty members, instructional cost would have risen only $80,000 (8 X $10,000). As indicated, however, the faculty increased in size. Thus, salary increases combine with faculty increases to produce the over-all instructional cost increase. As demonstrated above, part of the faculty increase is attributable to enrollment increase, and this increase combines with increased input cost to account for part of the total increase in instructional cost. Part of the faculty increase is attributable to a decrease in the school's student/faculty ratio, and this increase combines with increased input cost to account for part of the total increase in instructional cost. Finally, part of the faculty increase is attributable to the combined effect of increased enrollment and a decrease in the school's student/faculty ratio, and this increase combines with increased input cost to account for part of the total increase in instructional cost.

The various attributes of increases in instructional cost may be summarized as follows.

---

attributable to the increase in enrollment by multiplying the 1955 faculty of 8 professors by the Scale factor less one (8 X (2.25 − 1.00) = 10).

51. 200 ÷ 20 = 10, the number of professors that would have been engaged to teach the original enrollment at a student/faculty ratio of 20/1. As 8 were actually engaged to teach the original enrollment at a student/faculty ratio of 25/1 (200 ÷ 25 = 8), 2 of the additional 14½ professors are attributable to a student/faculty ratio change alone. If this were the only change, one could derive the increase in faculty attributable to the decrease in the school's student/faculty ratio by multiplying the 1955 faculty of 8 professors by the Student/Faculty Ratio factor alone less one (8 X (1.25 − 1.00) = 2).

52. 250 ÷ 20 = 12½, the number of professors that were needed to teach the additional enrollment at a student/faculty ratio of 20/1. As 10 of these professors were assumed above, in footnote 50, to have been added to teach the additional enrollment at a student/faculty ratio of 25/1, 2½ of the 14½ additional professors may be attributed to the joint effect of changes in scale and the student/faculty ratio. One can derive the joint effect of changes in scale and student/faculty ratio by multiplying the 1955 faculty of 8 professors by the Scale factor minus one and the Student/Faculty Ratio factor minus one (8 X 1.25 X .25 = 2.5).

1.	Scale (10 additional professors at Year 1 salary of $10,000)	$100,00
2.	Student/Faculty Ratio (2 additional professors at Year 1 salary of $10,000)	$ 20,000
3.	Joint Effect of Scale and Student/Faculty Ratio (2½ additional professors at Year 1 salary of $10,000)	$ 25,000
4.	Input Cost (8 original professors receiving an additional $10,000)	$ 80,000
5.	Joint Effect of Scale and Input Cost (10 additional professors receiving an additional $10,000)	$100,000
6.	Joint Effect of Student/Faculty Ratio and Input Cost (2 additional professors receiving an additional $10,000)	$ 20,000
7.	Joint Effect of Scale, Student/ Faculty Ratio, and Input Cost (2½ additional professors receiving an additional $10,000)	$ 25,000
		$370,000

It will be noted that items 3, 5, 6, and 7 totaling $170,000, or about 46% of the total increase in instructional cost, are to be attributed to the joint effect of two or three factors.

In addition to determining total increases in instructional cost through the I.C. Equation, one may derive the percent increase in instructional cost per student between two years by using two of its three factors.[53] This is done by multiplying the Student/Faculty Ratio factor by the Input Cost factor, subtracting 1 from the product, and multiplying by 100. Thus, in our example, the Student/Faculty Ratio factor is 1.25 and the Input Cost factor is 2.00. These two figures multiplied together and converted to a percentage produce 150%.[54] Here, also, the operation of the two factors involves a joint effect: part of the

---

53. This modified I.C. Equation is referred to as the Per-student Instructional Cost Equation or the Per-student Cost Equation.
54. 1.25 × 2.00 = (2.50 − 1.00) × 100 = 150%. In 1955, the school enrolled 200 students and its instructional cost was $80,000. Consequently, its instructional cost per student in 1955 was $400. In 1970, the school enrolled 450 students and its instructional cost was $450,000. Thus, its instructional cost per student in 1970 was $1,000, a 150% increase over 1955.

per-student cost increase is attributable to a reduction in student/faculty ratio, part to an increase in input cost, and part to the compound effect of both factors. In 1955, with a student/faculty ratio of 25/1, the per-student cost was the equivalent of 1/25th of the average faculty salary of $10,000, or $400. In 1970, with a student/faculty ratio of 20/1, the per-student cost was the equivalent of 1/20th of the average faculty salary of $20,000, or $1,000. Thus, per-student cost increased $600: $400 of this increase is attributable to the increase in input cost alone;[55] $100, to the decrease in student/faculty ratio alone;[56] and $100, to the joint effect of changes in input cost and student/faculty ratio.[57]

Section 4 — The Instructional Cost Equation
for 115 Law Schools and 9 Case-study Schools

The I.C. Equation may be used to interpret past trends in instructional cost between two points of time. On the basis of information contained in the A.B.A.'s annual *Review of Legal Education* and information from A.B.A. sources regarding median faculty salaries, I.C. Equations have been constructed for 115 law schools for the period 1955 to 1970.[58] From an analysis of these equations we derive a number of conclusions regarding the evolution of instructional cost at American law schools between 1955 and 1970. We believe that such information regarding the 115 schools, although not as precise as the data collected from the nine case-study schools,[59] is sufficient to support these conclusions. Paralleling our examination of the I.C. Equations of the larger sample of schools, we include an examination of the I.C. Equations of the nine case-study schools. The conclusions we draw from the case-study schools in every instance reflect the conclusions drawn from the larger sample of schools. Of course, a number of findings can be derived only from the larger sample of schools.

---

55. $10,000 (average increase in faculty compensation from 1955 to 1970) ÷ 25 (1955 student/faculty ratio) = $400 (amount of increase attributable to increased input cost alone).

56. $10,000 (1955 average faculty compensation) ÷ 20 (1970 student/faculty ratio) = $500 (per-student cost at 1970 student/faculty ratio and 1955 faculty compensation level) − $400 (1955 per-student cost) = $100 (amount of increase attributable to decreased student/faculty ratio alone).

57. $10,000 (average increase in faculty compensation from 1955 to 1970) ÷ 20 (1970 student/faculty ratio) = $500 (amount of increase in faculty compensation allocated by hypothesis to each student) − $400 (amount of such increase already allocated to each student in footnote 55) = $100 (amount of increase attributable to joint effect of increased input cost and decreased student/faculty ratio).

58.   It was not possible to construct I.C. Equations for all the schools included in the Totality because, as indicated in section 2, information regarding median salaries was available for only 115 of these 135 schools. Accordingly, for this section a slightly reduced larger sample of schools is used.

59.   See especially the discussion regarding number of faculty members in section 1 and faculty salaries in section 2.

Table 9 lists the I.C. Equations for the 115 law schools. As indicated in the Table, the average of the total increase in instructional cost for all these schools was 208% and the median increase was 233%. It should be recognized that these increases are computed on the basis of constant 1970 dollars. These figures are the equivalent of average and median annual compound growth rates of 7.8% and 8.3%, respectively. The average total increase in instructional cost of the nine case-study schools for the period studied was 230% and the median was 258%, or the equivalent of compound annual growth rates of 8.3% and 8.9%, respectively. In view of the fact that the I.C. Equations of the case-study schools

Table 9

Instructional Cost Equations for 115 Law Schools
1955 to 1970

Scale Factor $\times$	Student/ Faculty Ratio Factor $=$	(Faculty Growth Factor) $\times$	Input Cost Factor $=$	Total Instructional Cost Factor	Percent Increase in Instructional Cost
1.42	1.08	(1.54)	.98	1.51	51%
1.71	.48	(.83)	2.02	1.67	67%
1.54	.84	(1.30)	1.31	1.69	69%
1.45	.85	(1.23)	1.45	1.79	79%
1.11	.98	(1.08)	1.66	1.80	80%
2.27	.56	(1.28)	1.47	1.88	88%
1.18	.76	(.90)	2.15	1.94	94%
1.90	.65	(1.24)	1.58	1.97	97%
1.30	1.19	(1.55)	1.27	1.97	97%
2.80	.54	(1.51)	1.30	1.97	97%
2.58	.52	(1.33)	1.50	2.00	100%
2.07	.74	(1.54)	1.34	2.06	106%
1.50	1.12	(1.68)	1.23	2.07	107%
1.16	1.41	(1.63)	1.30	2.13	113%
1.46	.96	(1.41)	1.51	2.13	113%
3.98	.37	(1.48)	1.46	2.17	117%
1.65	.78	(1.29)	1.73	2.22	122%
3.24	.39	(1.26)	1.80	2.26	126%
2.02	.72	(1.45)	1.59	2.30	130%
2.57	.54	(1.39)	1.66	2.31	131%
3.21	.51	(1.63)	1.44	2.33	133%
1.14	1.26	(1.43)	1.65	2.36	136%
1.47	1.17	(1.72)	1.41	2.42	142%
1.30	1.35	(1.75)	1.40	2.46	146%
1.23	1.42	(1.75)	1.42	2.49	149%
3.69	.50	(1.84)	1.36	2.50	150%
1.73	.76	(1.31)	1.92	2.51	151%
1.33	1.05	(1.39)	1.81	2.52	152%
2.82	.53	(1.48)	1.71	2.53	153%

Table 9 (continued)

Instructional Cost Equations for 115 Law Schools
1955 to 1970

Scale Factor X	Student/ Faculty Ratio Factor =	(Faculty Growth Factor) X	Input Cost Factor =	Total Instructional Cost Factor	Percent Increase in Instructional Cost
2.15	.55	(1.18)	2.19	2.58	158%
2.28	.72	(1.63)	1.59	2.59	159%
2.70	.51	(1.38)	1.90	2.62	162%
2.16	.74	(1.61)	1.63	2.62	162%
1.78	.77	(1.38)	1.91	2.63	163%
2.87	.54	(1.54)	1.71	2.63	163%
3.79	.45	(1.69)	1.56	2.64	164%
1.54	1.09	(1.69)	1.56	2.64	164%
4.06	.63	(2.55)	1.04	2.64	164%
2.38	1.09	(2.58)	1.04	2.68	168%
4.60	.31	(1.44)	1.92	2.76	176%
2.76	.54	(1.50)	1.85	2.78	178%
1.84	.89	(1.65)	1.71	2.81	181%
2.92	.72	(2.09)	1.37	2.87	187%
1.28	1.39	(1.78)	1.63	2.89	189%
2.03	.85	(1.72)	1.68	2.90	190%
1.57	1.20	(1.90)	1.54	2.92	192%
2.96	.59	(1.74)	1.68	2.93	193%
1.46	1.15	(1.69)	1.76	2.97	197%
3.40	.58	(1.98)	1.51	2.99	199%
2.22	.81	(1.80)	1.71	3.08	208%
2.30	1.03	(2.37)	1.31	3.09	209%
4.05	.44	(.79)	1.72	3.09	209%
1.44	1.25	(1.80)	1.74	3.13	213%
3.62	.49	(1.78)	1.84	3.27	227%
2.98	.61	(1.81)	1.81	3.27	227%
1.66	1.31	(2.17)	1.51	3.29	229%
2.91	.48	(1.40)	2.37	3.32	232%
2.05	.88	(1.81)	1.84	3.33	233%
2.27	1.10	(2.50)	1.35	3.37	237%
2.12	1.06	(2.24)	1.50	3.37	237%
2.33	.90	(2.10)	1.66	3.48	248%
2.08	1.11	(2.32)	1.51	3.49	249%
2.70	.58	(1.56)	2.25	3.51	251%
2.66	.85	(2.26)	1.55	3.51	251%
2.09	1.03	(2.15)	1.63	3.52	252%
2.58	.79	(2.03)	1.73	3.52	252%
1.79	1.05	(1.88)	1.88	3.53	253%
3.13	.58	(1.81)	1.95	3.53	253%

Table 9 (continued)

Instructional Cost Equations for 115 Law Schools
1955 to 1970

Scale Factor ×	Student/ Faculty Ratio Factor =	(Faculty Growth Factor) ×	Input Cost Factor =	Total Instruc- tional Cost Factor	Percent Increase in Instruc- tional Cost
2.70	.95	(2.57)	1.39	3.56	256%
2.81	.76	(2.14)	1.68	3.61	261%
5.14	.46	(2.36)	1.53	3.63	263%
2.65	1.03	(2.74)	1.35	3.70	270%
4.53	.49	(2.22)	1.68	3.73	273%
7.41	.38	(2.80)	1.35	3.76	276%
1.60	1.15	(1.83)	2.06	3.78	278%
1.61	1.11	(1.78)	2.13	3.79	279%
3.47	.65	(2.26)	1.68	3.80	280%
2.52	.81	(2.03)	1.89	3.83	283%
3.99	.60	(2.40)	1.60	3.83	283%
2.75	.89	(2.45)	1.57	3.85	285%
3.42	.59	(2.00)	1.94	3.87	287%
1.58	1.51	(2.38)	1.63	3.87	287%
3.48	.64	(2.22)	1.79	3.97	297%
1.87	1.13	(2.11)	1.92	4.05	305%
3.40	.70	(2.37)	1.75	4.14	314%
2.07	1.42	(2.94)	1.42	4.17	317%
3.63	.62	(2.24)	1.86	4.17	317%
1.75	1.10	(1.92)	2.20	4.21	321%
3.07	.67	(2.05)	2.06	4.24	324%
2.66	.96	(2.56)	1.68	4.32	332%
5.51	.56	(3.09)	1.40	4.33	333%
1.61	1.53	(2.46)	1.79	4.40	340%
3.81	.63	(2.39)	1.85	4.41	341%
3.20	.82	(2.63)	1.74	4.58	358%
7.86	.36	(2.81)	1.69	4.71	371%
2.49	1.60	(4.00)	1.20	4.79	379%
3.63	1.01	(3.68)	1.32	4.84	384%
2.91	.85	(2.48)	1.96	4.86	386%
1.75	1.35	(2.36)	2.08	4.90	390%
2.39	1.33	(3.18)	1.55	4.91	391%
1.76	1.40	(2.46)	2.02	4.98	398%
5.24	.44	(2.29)	2.18	4.99	399%
3.98	.73	(2.90)	1.73	5.02	402%
1.59	1.77	(2.81)	1.81	5.10	410%
2.56	1.05	(2.68)	2.00	5.39	439%
2.22	1.50	(3.33)	1.71	5.69	469%
1.56	1.74	(2.71)	2.15	5.80	480%

Table 9 (continued)

Instructional Cost Equations for 115 Law Schools
1955 to 1970

Scale Factor	X	Student/ Faculty Ratio Factor	=	(Faculty Growth Factor)	X	Input Cost Factor	=	Total Instruc- tional Cost Factor	Percent Increase in Instruc- tional Cost
2.09		1.51		(3.14)		1.87		5.87	487%
3.96		.85		(2.36)		1.75		5.88	488%
7.32		.36		(2.64)		2.32		6.12	512%
4.68		.81		(3.78)		1.71		6.47	547%
2.23		1.43		(3.19)		2.06		6.56	556%
4.21		.71		(3.00)		2.29		6.87	587%
3.09		1.19		(3.69)		2.07		7.64	664%
4.12		.71		(2.93)		2.65		7.77	677%
Median 2.39		.81		(1.92)		1.68		3.33	233%
Average 2.13		.83		(1.93)		1.65		3.08	208%

Note: The average figures were obtained by dividing the 1970 total of the underlying data for each factor by the 1955 total. Thus, the total enrollment of the 115 schools was 63,364.5 in 1970 and 29,787.5 in 1955 (63,364.5 ÷ 29,787.5 = 2.13).

are based on data whose reliability is more certain, the fair similarity between the average and median percent increases of the schools included in the larger sample and the case-study schools lends some support to the accuracy of the percent increase figures for the larger sample of schools.[60] For the reasons outlined below, these average and median statistics have limited value. However, although the scope of this study is confined to legal education, such percent increases may have general significance for comparing the instructional cost of legal education with other branches of education or with cost increases in the economy as a whole. Furthermore, from the standpoint of legal education alone, a school might be interested to know how far above or below the average it fell.

Table 9 demonstrates wide differences among the individual schools in the amount of their total increase in instructional cost. They range from a low of 51% to a high of 677%, and, between these extremes, the remaining schools are fairly evenly distributed.[61] Accordingly, rates of increase in instructional cost differed very markedly among the various individual law schools, and the average figures have relatively little significance so far as indicating what may have been

60.   As stated in the text, 22 percentage points separate the average increases of the larger sample and case-study schools. It will be recognized, however, that the instructional cost of the average case-study school increased only 11% more than that of the average school of the larger sample.
61.   Similar differences existed among the case-study schools. Their increases ranged from a low of 155% to a high of 457%, and the remaining seven schools were distributed fairly evenly between these extremes. Because the case-study schools constitute a far smaller group than the larger sample of schools (9 vs. 115), it is understandable that wider extremes existed in the larger group.

the rate of increase at any one school. Thus, from the viewpoint of the law-school world as a self-contained entity, it is essentially meaningless to inquire about uniform rates of increase in the instructional cost of legal education. For similar reasons, questions regarding the instructional cost of educating law students are not susceptible to generalized answers.[62]

Despite these wide differences, however, certain uniform patterns may be discerned by dividing the 115 schools into the three Enrollment Groups discussed above. On this basis there are: 43 Small Enrollment Group schools (1955 enrollments between 50 and 150), 34 Middle Enrollment Group schools (1955 enrollments between 150 and 250), and 38 Large Enrollment Group schools (1955 enrollments over 250 students). Table 10 sets forth an I.C. Equation for each of these Enrollment Groups using the average of each factor for each such Group.

Table 10

Instructional Cost Equations Using Average of Instructional Cost Factors for 115 Schools in the Three Enrollment Groups
1955 to 1970

Schools Grouped by Enrollment	Scale Factor		Student/ Faculty Ratio Factor	(Faculty Growth Factor)		Input Cost Factor		Total Instruc- tional Cost Factor
Small Enroll- ment Group	3.36	X	.61	(= 1.95)	X	1.73	=	3.47
Middle Enroll- ment Group	2.68	X	.79	(= 2.12)	X	1.66	=	3.52
Large Enroll- ment Group	1.64	X	1.10	(= 1.83)	X	1.57	=	2.81
Percent Change								
Small Enroll- ment Group	236%		−39%	95%		73%		247%
Middle Enroll- ment Group	168%		−21%	112%		66%		252%
Large Enroll- ment Group	64%		10%	83%		57%		181%

Note: Each factor presented is the average for each Enrollment Group, computed in the same manner as in Table 9. The total Instructional Cost factor is also an average and, therefore, is not the exact product of these factors multiplied together. For explanation of the Faculty Growth factor, see footnote 49. The percent change is derived from a factor by subtracting 1.00 and multiplying by 100 (e.g., (3.36 − 1.00) × 100 = 236%).

---

62.   This will be discussed more fully below.

It is observable from Table 10 that average increases in faculty growth and input cost are rather similar for the three Enrollment Groups, that the average increases in total instructional cost of the Small and Middle Enrollment Groups are similar and the Large Enrollment Group's is somewhat lower, but that there are wide differences in average enrollment increase and in average student/faculty ratio change. In general terms, the average size of law schools' faculties increased by nearly 100% during the fifteen-year period. Salary increases averaged around 65%, and total instructional cost increased around 210%. Small Enrollment Group schools had an average enrollment increase of 236%, which far outpaced their average increase in faculty (somewhat under 100%), and, accordingly, their average student/faculty ratio increased substantially.[63] Middle Enrollment Group schools had an average enrollment increase of 168% that also outpaced their average increase in faculty (just over 100%), but not to the extent of the Small Enrollment schools. As a result, their average student/faculty ratio increased, but not as much as that of the Small Enrollment schools. Finally, those schools in the Large Enrollment Group had an average enrollment increase of 64%, which, in contrast to the first two Groups, was outpaced by their average faculty increase (about 83%). As a result, the average student/faculty ratio for these schools decreased. In sum, although the three Enrollment Groups had fairly similar increases in average input cost and faculty size and, thus, in total instructional cost, they differed markedly in their average enrollment increases and in their average student/faculty ratio changes.

The net result of these various changes over the fifteen-year period was the movement of a substantial number of the schools in each Enrollment Group toward a "middle" range of student/faculty ratios in 1970, namely, student/faculty ratios between 17/1 and 24/1, which will be referred to as the "1970 Standard Range." In 1955, 37 of the 43 Small Enrollment schools had student/faculty ratios below, and only 6 schools had student/faculty ratios within, the 1970 Standard Range. By 1970, 23 of the Small Enrollment schools had student/faculty ratios within the Range, with 8 below and 12 above. Consequently, during this period, student/faculty ratios for most Small Enrollment schools increased, most of them moving to a position within the 1970 Standard Range.

In contrast, in 1955, 10 of the 34 Middle Enrollment schools had student/faculty ratios below the 1970 Standard Range, 20 had student/faculty ratios within the Range, and 4 had student/faculty ratios above. By 1970, only 3 Middle Enrollment schools had student/faculty ratios below the 1970 Standard Range, 19 had student/faculty ratios within the Range, and 12 had student/faculty ratios above. Thus, student/faculty ratios increased somewhat within the Middle Enrollment Group but most of its schools remained within the 1970 Standard Range.

In 1955, of the 38 Large Enrollment Group schools, 4 had student/faculty ratios below the 1970 Standard Range, 14 had student/faculty ratios within the

---

63. The substantial increase in student/faculty ratio is reflected in the low Student/Faculty Ratio factor.

Range, and 20 had student/faculty ratios above the Range. By 1970, 4 such schools had student/faculty ratios below the 1970 Standard Range, 23 had student/faculty ratios within the Range, and only 11 schools had student/faculty ratios above the Range. Consequently, the student/faculty ratios decreased for most of the Large Enrollment schools, with many of them moving toward a position within the 1970 Standard Range.[64]

Table 11 sets forth the I.C. Equation for each of the case-study schools. In 1955, two schools were Small Enrollment schools, two were Middle Enrollment schools, and five were Large Enrollment schools. The average of each of the factors of the case-study schools included in each Enrollment Group is also

Table 11

Instructional Cost Equations for Nine Case-study Schools
1955 to 1970

Schools Listed by Enrollment Group	Scale Factor X	Student/ Faculty Ratio Factor =	(Faculty Growth Factor) X	Input Cost Factor =	Total Instructional Cost	Percent Increase in Instructional Cost
Small Enrollment						
	3.99	.65	(2.61)	1.37	3.58	258%
	3.40	.76	(2.57)	1.43	3.68	268%
Average	3.68	.70	(2.59)	1.40	3.64	264%
Middle Enrollment						
	2.18	1.25	(2.72)	1.34	3.64	264%
	2.44	.74	(1.80)	2.23	4.01	301%
Average	2.29	.95	(2.30)	1.71	3.77	277%
Large Enrollment						
	1.39	1.31	(1.82)	1.40	2.55	155%
	1.34	1.15	(1.53)	1.79	2.74	174%
	1.59	1.41	(2.24)	1.33	2.98	198%
	1.75	1.09	(1.90)	1.76	3.35	235%
	1.55	1.71	(2.65)	2.10	5.57	457%
Average	1.55	1.33	(1.97)	1.62	3.15	215%
Nine Schools						
Average	1.78	1.11	(2.09)	1.59	3.30	230%

---

64. It will be pointed out below that one effect of the movement between 1955 and 1970 of a large number of schools in each Enrollment Group toward the 1970 Standard Range has been the narrowing of the differences in the average per-student instructional cost of the three Enrollment Groups during the same period.

shown. It will be noted that these averages are fairly similar to the averages shown in Table 10 for the 115 schools. Although these averages (based upon the more certain data of the case-study schools) are derived from too small a sample to validate the averages derived from the larger sample of schools, the essential differences observed above among the larger sample's three Enrollment Groups are clearly reflected in these case-study schools. The two Small Enrollment case-study schools increased their student/faculty ratios from 1955 to 1970. Of the two Middle Enrollment schools, one increased its student/faculty ratio and one decreased its student/faculty ratio. All five of the Large Enrollment schools decreased their student/faculty ratios. In 1955, only four of the case-study schools had student/faculty ratios within the 1970 Standard Range. By 1970, five of these schools had student/faculty ratios within the Range.

Analysis of Variations in Instructional Cost and Student/Faculty Ratio

Since the I.C. Equations set forth in Table 10 are based on averages for each of the three Enrollment Groups, they fail to disclose the wide differences that exist among schools within each Group in the amount of increases in total

Table 12

Instructional Cost Equations for 115 Law Schools by Enrollment Groups, 1955 to 1970

	Scale Factor X	Student/ Faculty Ratio Factor =	(Faculty Growth Factor) X	Input Cost Factor =	Total Instruc- tional Cost Factor	Percent Increase in Instruc- tional Cost
SMALL ENROLLMENT GROUP						
Subgroup L	1.54	.84	(1.30)	1.31	1.69	69%
(Low increase	2.27	.56	(1.28)	1.47	1.88	88%
in instruc-	3.98	.37	(1.48)	1.46	2.17	117%
tional cost)	3.21	.51	(1.63)	1.44	2.33	133%
	2.82	.53	(1.48)	1.71	2.53	153%
	2.15	.55	(1.18)	2.19	2.58	158%
	2.28	.72	(1.63)	1.59	2.59	159%
	2.70	.51	(1.38)	1.90	2.62	162%
	1.78	.77	(1.38)	1.91	2.63	163%
	2.87	.54	(1.54)	1.71	2.63	163%
	3.79	.45	(1.69)	1.56	2.64	164%
	4.60	.31	(1.44)	1.92	2.76	176%
	2.76	.54	(1.50)	1.85	2.78	178%
	2.92	.72	(2.09)	1.37	2.87	187%
	2.96	.59	(1.74)	1.68	2.93	193%

Table 12 (continued)

**Instructional Cost Equations for 115 Law Schools
by Enrollment Groups, 1955 to 1970**

	Scale Factor X	Student/ Faculty Ratio Factor =	(Faculty Growth Factor) X	Input Cost Factor =	Total Instruc- tional Cost Factor	Percent Increase in Instruc- tional Cost
	3.40	.58	(1.98)	1.51	2.99	199%
	4.05	.44	(.79)	1.72	3.09	209%
Subgroup M	3.62	.49	(1.78)	1.84	3.27	227%
(Medium in-	2.98	.61	(1.81)	1.81	3.27	227%
crease in	2.91	.48	(1.40)	2.37	3.32	232%
instruc-	2.05	.88	(1.81)	1.84	3.33	233%
tional cost)	2.27	1.10	(2.50)	1.35	3.37	237%
	2.33	.90	(2.10)	1.66	3.48	248%
	2.66	.85	(2.26)	1.55	3.51	251%
	2.09	1.03	(2.15)	1.63	3.52	252%
	3.13	.58	(1.81)	1.95	3.53	253%
	2.81	.76	(2.14)	1.68	3.61	261%
	5.14	.46	(2.36)	1.53	3.63	263%
	4.53	.49	(2.22)	1.68	3.73	273%
	7.41	.38	(2.80)	1.35	3.76	276%
	3.99	.60	(2.40)	1.60	3.83	283%
	3.42	.59	(2.00)	1.94	3.87	287%
	3.48	.64	(2.22)	1.79	3.97	297%
Subgroup H	3.63	.62	(2.24)	1.86	4.17	317%
(High increase	3.07	.67	(2.05)	2.06	4.24	324%
in instruc-	5.51	.56	(3.09)	1.40	4.33	333%
tional cost)	5.24	.44	(2.29)	2.18	4.99	399%
	3.98	.73	(2.90)	1.73	5.02	402%
	2.56	1.05	(2.68)	2.00	5.39	439%
	3.96	.85	(2.36)	1.75	5.88	488%
	7.32	.36	(2.64)	2.32	6.12	512%
	4.68	.81	(3.78)	1.71	6.47	547%
	4.21	.71	(3.00)	2.29	6.87	587%

MIDDLE ENROLLMENT GROUP

	Scale Factor X	Student/ Faculty Ratio Factor =	(Faculty Growth Factor) X	Input Cost Factor =	Total Instruc- tional Cost Factor	Percent Increase in Instruc- tional Cost
Subgroup L	2.58	.52	(1.33)	1.50	2.00	100%
(Low increase	2.07	.74	(1.54)	1.34	2.06	106%
in instruc-	3.24	.39	(1.26)	1.80	2.26	126%
tional cost)	2.02	.72	(1.45)	1.59	2.30	130%
	2.57	.54	(1.39)	1.66	2.31	131%
	3.69	.50	(1.84)	1.36	2.50	150%

Table 12 (continued)

Instructional Cost Equations for 115 Law Schools by Enrollment Groups, 1955 to 1970

	Scale Factor X	Student/ Faculty Ratio Factor =	(Faculty Growth Factor) X	Input Cost Factor =	Total Instruc- tional Cost Factor	Percent Increase in Instruc- tional Cost
	1.73	.76	(1.31)	1.92	2.51	151%
	2.16	.74	(1.61)	1.63	2.62	162%
	1.54	1.09	(1.69)	1.56	2.64	164%
	4.06	.63	(2.55)	1.04	2.64	164%
	2.38	1.09	(2.58)	1.04	2.68	168%
	1.84	.89	(1.65)	1.71	2.81	181%
	2.03	.85	(1.72)	1.68	2.90	190%
	2.22	.81	(1.80)	1.71	3.08	208%
	2.30	1.03	(2.37)	1.31	3.09	209%
Subgroup M (Medium in- crease in instruc- tional cost)	2.12	1.06	(2.24)	1.50	3.37	237%
	2.70	.58	(1.56)	2.25	3.51	251%
	2.58	.79	(2.03)	1.73	3.52	252%
	1.79	1.05	(1.88)	1.88	3.53	253%
	2.70	.95	(2.57)	1.39	3.56	256%
	3.47	.65	(2.26)	1.68	3.80	280%
	2.52	.81	(2.03)	1.89	3.83	283%
	2.75	.89	(2.45)	1.57	3.85	285%
Subgroup H (High increase in instruc- tional cost)	1.87	1.13	(2.11)	1.92	4.05	305%
	2.66	.96	(2.56)	1.68	4.32	332%
	1.61	1.53	(2.46)	1.79	4.40	340%
	3.81	.63	(2.39)	1.85	4.41	341%
	7.86	.36	(2.81)	1.69	4.71	371%
	2.91	.85	(2.48)	1.96	4.86	386%
	2.22	1.50	(3.33)	1.71	5.69	469%
	2.09	1.51	(3.14)	1.87	5.87	487%
	2.23	1.43	(3.19)	2.06	6.56	556%
	3.09	1.19	(3.69)	2.07	7.64	664%
	4.12	.71	(2.93)	2.65	7.77	677%

LARGE ENROLLMENT GROUP

	Scale Factor X	Student/ Faculty Ratio Factor =	(Faculty Growth Factor) X	Input Cost Factor =	Total Instruc- tional Cost Factor	Percent Increase in Instruc- tional Cost
Subgroup L (Low increase in instruc- tional cost)	1.42	1.08	(1.54)	.98	1.51	51%
	1.71	.48	(.83)	2.02	1.67	67%
	1.45	.85	(1.23)	1.45	1.79	79%
	1.11	.98	(1.08)	1.66	1.80	80%
	1.18	.76	(.90)	2.15	1.94	94%
	1.90	.65	(1.24)	1.58	1.97	97%
	1.30	1.19	(1.55)	1.27	1.97	97%

Table 12 (continued)

Instructional Cost Equations for 115 Law Schools by Enrollment Groups, 1955 to 1970

	Scale Factor ×	Student/ Faculty Ratio Factor =	(Faculty Growth Factor) ×	Input Cost Factor =	Total Instruc- tional Cost Factor	Percent Increase in Instruc- tional Cost
	2.80	.54	(1.51)	1.30	1.97	97%
	1.50	1.12	(1.68)	1.23	2.07	107%
	1.16	1.41	(1.63)	1.30	2.13	113%
	1.46	.96	(1.41)	1.51	2.13	113%
	1.65	.78	(1.29)	1.73	2.22	122%
	1.14	1.26	(1.43)	1.65	2.36	136%
	1.47	1.17	(1.72)	1.41	2.42	142%
	1.30	1.35	(1.75)	1.40	2.46	146%
	1.23	1.42	(1.75)	1.42	2.49	149%
	1.33	1.05	(1.39)	1.81	2.52	152%
Subgroup M	1.28	1.39	(1.78)	1.63	2.89	189%
(Medium in-	1.57	1.20	(1.90)	1.54	2.92	192%
crease in	1.46	1.15	(1.69)	1.76	2.97	197%
instruc-	1.44	1.25	(1.80)	1.74	3.13	213%
tional cost)	1.66	1.31	(2.17)	1.51	3.29	229%
	2.08	1.11	(2.32)	1.51	3.49	249%
	2.65	1.03	(2.74)	1.35	3.70	270%
	1.60	1.15	(1.83)	2.06	3.78	278%
	1.61	1.11	(1.78)	2.13	3.79	279%
	1.58	1.51	(2.38)	1.63	3.87	287%
Subgroup H	3.40	.70	(2.37)	1.75	4.14	314%
(High increase	2.07	1.42	(2.94)	1.42	4.17	317%
in instruc-	1.75	1.10	(1.92)	2.20	4.21	321%
tional cost)	3.20	.82	(2.63)	1.74	4.58	358%
	2.49	1.60	(4.00)	1.20	4.79	379%
	3.63	1.01	(3.68)	1.32	4.84	384%
	1.75	1.35	(2.36)	2.08	4.90	390%
	2.39	1.33	(3.18)	1.55	4.91	391%
	1.76	1.40	(2.46)	2.02	4.98	398%
	1.59	1.77	(2.81)	1.81	5.10	410%
	1.56	1.74	(2.71)	2.15	5.80	480%

TOTAL 115 SCHOOLS

	Scale Factor ×	Student/ Faculty Ratio Factor =	(Faculty Growth Factor) ×	Input Cost Factor =	Total Instruc- tional Cost Factor	Percent Increase in Instruc- tional Cost
Median	2.39	.81	(1.92)	1.68	3.33	233%
Average	2.13	.83	(1.93)	1.65	3.08	208%

instructional cost.[65] Table 12 presents the I.C. Equation for all 115 schools by Enrollment Group.

The final column in Table 12 clearly reveals the wide differences that exist in instructional cost increases. Schools in the Small Enrollment Group range from an increase of 69% to 587%, a difference of 518%. Schools in the Middle Enrollment Group range from an increase of 100% to 487%, a difference of 387%,[66] and schools in the Large Enrollment Group range from an increase of 51% to 480%, a difference of 429%. Between these limits the schools included within each Group are evenly distributed.

We have attempted to account for these considerable variations in increase in instructional cost in terms of the three factors that make up the I.C. Equation. Our analysis is set out in detail in Appendix F. There follows a summary of our method and conclusions. We divided all the schools in each Enrollment Group into three subgroups. This was done on the basis of increases in instructional cost. Those schools with the lowest increases were put in subgroup L, those with medium increases in subgroup M, and those with the highest increases in subgroup H. We then sought to determine which factors, if any, were particularly significant in explaining the placement of schools in one subgroup or another. We found that each Enrollment Group manifested the same general pattern. First, we found that the predominant factor in producing differences in instructional cost increase was difference in faculty growth rather than difference in input cost increase. Second, we found that the predominant factor in producing differences in faculty growth was difference in change in student/faculty ratio rather than difference in enrollment increase. Thus, generally speaking, those schools whose student/faculty ratios changed in the most favorable way as compared with the other schools in their Enrollment Group had the highest faculty growth and the highest increase in instructional cost.[67]

An underlying trend that has emerged in the foregoing analyses is that as law schools developed between 1955 and 1970 they tended to move toward student/faculty ratios in the low 20/1s. Thus, those schools with low student/faculty ratios in 1955, such as many Small Enrollment schools, tended

---

65.   In this connection it should be noted that the conclusions mentioned above for all schools in the larger sample regarding the relative insignificance of average increase figures are equally applicable to the average figures derived for the three Enrollment Groups.

66.   Three schools in the Middle Enrollment Group had instructional cost increases in excess of 487%. These schools' increases were so much greater than the schools below them with the next largest increases that they have been omitted for purposes of demonstrating the range of increases within the Group.

67.   These were the schools in subgroup H. Strictly speaking, the proposition in the text is not accurate for subgroup H. Subgroup H schools had the highest enrollment growth, and they had student/faculty ratio changes which were as favorable as those of any other subgroup. It is assumed, however, that if they had had more normal enrollment increases, their student/faculty ratio changes would have been the most favorable of the three subgroups. The schools with the next most favorable student/faculty ratio changes were in subgroup M, and those with the least favorable student/faculty ratio changes were in subgroup L. "Favorable" student/faculty ratio changes meant quite different things depending on which Enrollment Group the schools were in. Thus, for the Large Enrollment Group, it meant rather sharp decreases in student/faculty ratios, but, for the Small Enrollment Group, it meant the smallest increases.

to have their student/faculty ratios increase and move up into the low 20/1s as their enrollments increased. On the other hand, schools with high student/faculty ratios in 1955, such as many of the Large Enrollment schools and some Middle Enrollment schools, tended to have their student/faculty ratios decrease and move down into the low 20/1s; and many of those schools with student/faculty ratios in the low 20/1s in 1955, such as a number of the Middle and Large Enrollment schools, tended to have their student/faculty ratios remain relatively constant.

It is understandable that schools with student/faculty ratios of 14/1 and below did not maintain constant student/faculty ratios as their enrollments grew. As explained above, most of the schools with low student/faculty ratios in 1955 had extremely low enrollments. Virtually no law school of any substantial size (as most law schools were by 1970) has ever operated with a student/faculty ratio lower than 14/1. It appears that the tradition among large schools of high student/faculty ratios and large classes was sufficiently entrenched during the period of 1955 to 1970 as to exert a force that moved student/faculty ratios of schools with increasing enrollments up to levels at least as high as the low 20/1s. However, it should be recalled that in the Introduction and Summary it was pointed out that student/faculty ratios about the level of 16/1 are not unusual for other university divisions. Chapter 3 will demonstrate that a great deal could be done to enrich the educational programs of law schools if they had student/faculty ratios this low.

It is interesting to consider those schools with high student/faculty ratios in 1955, i.e., student/faculty ratios of 30/1 and above, whose student/faculty ratios decreased between 1955 and 1970 while at the same time their enrollments increased. These schools might have maintained a constant student/faculty ratio. If they were operating successfully in 1955 with a high student/faculty ratio, there is nothing in the occurrence of increased enrollments that would have forced them to lower their student/faculty ratios. Of course, although a school with a high student/faculty ratio can provide a program offering minimum curriculum requirements with, presumably, reasonable effectiveness, it is, nevertheless, greatly limited in its ability to provide more. It is understandable, therefore, that, during a period of fiscal expansion in higher education, such as the period 1955 to 1970, a number of law schools with high student/faculty ratios would move in the direction of lowering their student/faculty ratios. In this connection it will be recalled that over half of the Middle and Large Enrollment schools with student/faculty ratios over 30/1 had their student/faculty ratios decrease into the low 20/1s by 1970.

Analysis of Instructional Cost Increases in Dollar Terms

Thus far our examination in this section has considered increases in total instructional cost largely in percentage terms, in order to demonstrate the factors underlying such increases, and to reveal the different patterns that evolved between 1955 and 1970 among different groups of schools. To further illustrate the impact of these changes, several analyses in dollar terms are given below, based on hypothetical models. The first group of models involves three hypothetical schools, one from each of the three Enrollment Groups. For convenience, we will refer to these as the "Small Enrollment School," the "Middle Enrollment School," and the "Large Enrollment School." In constructing these models, we have used figures that closely approximate the characteristics of schools whose Instructional Cost Equations are set forth above in Table 10, based on the average of each Enrollment Group. We have used the same average faculty salary for 1955 and the same salary increase for all three schools. It will be recalled that average input cost increases between the three Enrollment Groups were quite similar. For each of the hypothetical schools we assume the following data.

Table 13

Basic Data Assumed for Three Model Schools
Representing Typical Schools from Each Enrollment Group

	1955	1970
Small Enrollment School		
Enrollment	104	365
Faculty size	8	17.4
Student/Faculty ratio	13/1	21/1
Average faculty salary	$12,000	$20,400
Total instructional cost	$96,000	$354,240
Middle Enrollment School		
Enrollment	200	530
Faculty size	10	22
Student/Faculty ratio	20/1	24/1
Average faculty salary	$12,000	$20,400
Total instructional cost	$120,000	$448,800
Large Enrollment School		
Enrollment	490	835
Faculty size	19	36.5
Student/Faculty ratio	26/1	23/1
Average faculty salary	$12,000	$20,400
Total instructional cost	$228,000	$744,600

Note: These figures are very close to the average figures for the Small, Middle, and Large Enrollment Groups. Minor adjustments were made for arithmetic simplicity.

Based on the above data, the hypothetical schools' I.C. Equations are as follows.

Table 14

Instructional Cost Equations for Three Model Schools
Representing Typical Schools from Each Enrollment Group

Represent- ative Model School	Scale Factor		Student/ Faculty Ratio Factor		Input Cost Factor		Total Instruc- tional Cost Factor
Small Enrollment School	3.50	X	.62	X	1.70	=	3.69
Middle Enrollment School	2.65	X	.83	X	1.70	=	3.74
Large Enrollment School	1.70	X	1.13	X	1.70	=	3.27

Note: The data used in constructing these models were based on the factors set forth in Table 10, presenting actual I.C. Equations for each Enrollment Group of the 115 schools. They differ because minor adjustments to the data were made for arithmetic simplicity.

Table 15 presents an analysis of the data in Table 13 and the I.C. Equations of Table 14 in terms of seven coefficients. The total dollar increase in instructional cost is broken down into seven parts, representing the various impacts of the three factors and combinations of factors.

Table 15

Instructional Cost Increases for Three Model Schools
in Terms of Seven Coefficients

	Coefficient	Small Enrollment School	Middle Enrollment School	Large Enrollment School
1.	Scale	$240,000	$198,000	$159,600
2.	Student/Faculty Ratio	−36,500	−20,400	29,600
3.	Input Cost	67,200	84,000	159,600
4.	Scale & S/F Ratio	−91,200	−33,600	20,800
5.	Scale & Input Cost	168,000	138,600	111,700
6.	S/F Ratio & Input Cost	−25,500	−14,200	20,800
7.	Scale & S/F Ratio & Input Cost	−63,800	−23,600	14,500
	Total Increase in Instructional Cost	$258,200	$328,800	$516,600

Note: Figures are rounded. For detailed explanation of method used in deriving these figures, see section 5.

To demonstrate the pronounced effect of changes in a school's student/faculty ratio on its instructional cost, we next assume that the student/faculty ratio of each of the model schools remained constant between 1955 and 1970; that is, the Student/Faculty Ratio factor is 1.00, and the percent change is zero. In these circumstances, items 2, 4, 6, and 7 would be zero for each model school. Table 16 shows dollar amounts previously attributed to the increase in instructional cost by each of the four coefficients involving the Student/Faculty Ratio factor. These amounts would be eliminated if the student/faculty ratio remained constant. The bottom line shows the new increase in instructional cost.

Table 16

Instructional Cost Changes for Three Model Schools
for Four Coefficients Involving the Student/Faculty Ratio Factor

Coefficient	Small Enrollment School	Middle Enrollment School	Large Enrollment School
2. Student/Faculty Ratio	−$36,500	−$20,400	$29,600
4. Scale & S/F Ratio	−91,200	−33,600	20,800
6. S/F Ratio & Input Cost	−25,500	−14,200	20,800
7. Scale & S/F Ratio & Input Cost	−63,800	−23,600	14,500
Total amount contributed by four coefficients	−$217,000	−$ 91,800	$ 85,700
Total Increase in Instructional Cost with Change in Student/Faculty Ratio	$258,200	$328,800	$516,600
Total Increase in Instructional Cost with No Change in Student/Faculty Ratio	$475,200	$420,600	$430,900

This Table demonstrates the significantly different manner by which instructional cost would have changed at these three schools if the student/faculty ratio had remained constant between 1955 and 1970. The Small Enrollment School had considerably reduced instructional cost because of its substantial student/faculty ratio increase. If it had maintained a constant student/faculty ratio between 1955 and 1970, its instructional cost would have been $475,200, or 84% higher. The Middle Enrollment School also had lower total instructional cost by virtue of an increasing student/faculty ratio, but its "saving" in instructional cost was not as great as that of the Small Enrollment School because its student/faculty ratio increased less than that of the smaller school. If the Middle Enrollment School had maintained a constant student/faculty ratio between 1955 and 1970, its instructional cost would have been $420,600, or 28% higher. In contrast, the Large Enrollment School had a decrease in its student/faculty ratio from 1955 to 1970. This increased its instructional cost by $85,700. If its student/faculty ratio had remained constant, this increase would not have occurred and its instructional cost would have been $430,900, or 17% lower.

Per-student Instructional Cost

Thus far the examination has considered only increases in total instructional cost. Equally significant have been the increases in per-student instructional cost at these schools. Table 17 lists the Per-student Instructional Cost Equations for the 115 law schools. As indicated in the Table, the average of the per-student increases in instructional cost for all these schools was about 33%, and the median increase was 38%.[68] It should be recognized that these increases are computed on the basis of constant 1970 dollars. These figures are the equivalent of average annual compound growth rates of 2.0% and 2.2%, respectively. (The average increase in per-student instructional cost for the nine case-study schools was about 63%, or the equivalent of an average annual compound growth rate of 3.3%.) It will be observed from Table 17 that the individual schools differed widely in the amount of their per-student instructional cost increases. For this reason the significance of average cost-increase figures is limited. This aspect of these figures is further discussed below.

Table 17
Per-student Instructional Cost Equations
for 115 Law Schools, 1955 to 1970

	Student/ Faculty Ratio Factor	X Input Cost Factor =	Per-student Instructional Cost Factor	Percent Change in Per-student Instructional Cost
Small Enrollment Group	.38	1.35	.51	−49%
	.37	1.46	.54	−46%
	.31	1.92	.60	−40%
	.45	1.56	.70	−30%
	.46	1.53	.71	−29%
	.51	1.44	.73	−27%
	.44	1.72	.76	−24%
	.56	1.40	.79	−21%
	.49	1.68	.83	−17%
	.56	1.47	.83	−17%
	.36	2.32	.84	−16%
	.58	1.51	.88	−12%
	.53	1.71	.90	−10%
	.49	1.84	.90	−10%
	.54	1.71	.92	− 8%
	.44	2.18	.95	− 5%
	.60	1.60	.96	− 4%
	.51	1.90	.97	− 3%
	.72	1.37	.98	− 2%
	.59	1.68	.99	− 1%

68. The Per-student Instructional Cost factor minus 1.00, times 100 equals the percent increase.

Table 17 (continued)

Per-student Instructional Cost Equations
for 115 Law Schools, 1955 to 1970

Student/ Faculty Ratio Factor	×	Input Cost Factor	=	Per-student Instructional Cost Factor	Percent Change in Per-student Instructional Cost
.54		1.85		1.01	+ 1%
.61		1.81		1.10	10%
.84		1.31		1.10	10%
.58		1.95		1.13	13%
.59		1.94		1.13	13%
.72		1.59		1.14	14%
.48		2.37		1.14	14%
.64		1.79		1.14	14%
.62		1.86		1.15	15%
.55		2.19		1.20	20%
.73		1.73		1.26	26%
.76		1.68		1.28	28%
.85		1.55		1.32	32%
.67		2.06		1.38	38%
.81		1.71		1.38	38%
.77		1.91		1.47	47%
1.10		1.35		1.48	48%
.85		1.75		1.49	49%
.90		1.66		1.50	50%
.88		1.84		1.62	62%
.71		2.29		1.63	63%
1.03		1.63		1.68	68%
1.05		2.00		2.10	110%

Middle Enrollment Group

Student/ Faculty Ratio Factor	×	Input Cost Factor	=	Per-student Instructional Cost Factor	Percent Change in Per-student Instructional Cost
.36		1.68		.60	−40%
.63		1.04		.65	−35%
.50		1.36		.68	−32%
.39		1.80		.70	−30%
.52		1.50		.78	−22%
.54		1.66		.90	−10%
.74		1.34		.99	− 1%
.65		1.68		1.10	+10%
1.09		1.04		1.13	13%
.72		1.59		1.14	14%
.63		1.85		1.16	16%
.74		1.63		1.21	21%
.58		2.25		1.30	30%
.95		1.39		1.32	32%
1.03		1.31		1.35	35%
.79		1.73		1.37	37%
.81		1.71		1.38	38%
.89		1.57		1.40	40%

Table 17 (continued)
Per-student Instructional Cost Equations
for 115 Law Schools, 1955 to 1970

Student/ Faculty Ratio Factor	X	Input Cost Factor	=	Per-student Instructional Cost Factor	Percent Change in Per-student Instructional Cost
.85		1.68		1.43	43%
.76		1.92		1.45	45%
.81		1.89		1.52	52%
.89		1.71		1.53	53%
1.06		1.50		1.59	59%
.96		1.68		1.62	62%
.85		1.96		1.67	67%
1.09		1.56		1.71	71%
.71		2.65		1.89	89%
1.05		1.88		1.97	97%
1.13		1.92		2.17	117%
1.19		2.07		2.47	147%
1.50		1.71		2.57	157%
1.53		1.79		2.73	173%
1.51		1.87		2.82	182%
1.43		2.06		2.95	195%

Large Enrollment Group

Student/ Faculty Ratio Factor	X	Input Cost Factor	=	Per-student Instructional Cost Factor	Percent Change in Per-student Instructional Cost
.54		1.30		.71	−29%
.48		2.02		.98	− 2%
.65		1.58		1.04	+ 4%
1.08		.98		1.06	6%
.70		1.75		1.22	22%
.85		1.45		1.23	23%
1.01		1.32		1.33	33%
.78		1.73		1.35	35%
1.12		1.23		1.38	38%
1.03		1.35		1.39	39%
.82		1.74		1.43	43%
.96		1.51		1.46	46%
1.19		1.27		1.52	52%
.98		1.66		1.62	62%
.76		2.15		1.63	63%
1.17		1.41		1.64	64%
1.11		1.51		1.68	68%
1.41		1.30		1.84	84%
1.20		1.54		1.86	86%
1.05		1.81		1.90	90%
1.35		1.40		1.90	90%
1.60		1.20		1.92	92%
1.31		1.51		1.98	98%

Table 17 (continued)

Per-student Instructional Cost Equations for 115 Law Schools, 1955 to 1970

Student/ Faculty Ratio Factor	X	Input Cost Factor	=	Per-student Instructional Cost Factor	Percent Change in Per-student Instructional Cost
1.42		1.42		2.02	102%
1.42		1.42		2.03	103%
1.15		1.76		2.04	104%
1.33		1.55		2.06	106%
1.26		1.65		2.07	107%
1.25		1.74		2.17	117%
1.39		1.63		2.26	126%
1.11		2.13		2.36	136%
1.15		2.06		2.36	136%
1.10		2.20		2.41	141%
1.51		1.63		2.46	146%
1.35		2.08		2.80	180%
1.40		2.02		2.83	183%
1.77		1.81		3.20	220%
1.74		2.15		3.73	273%

Total 115 Schools

Median	.81	1.68		1.38	38%
Average	.83	1.65		1.33	33%

Table 18

Per-student Instructional Cost Equations for Nine Case-study Schools, 1955 to 1970

Schools Listed by Enrollment Group	Student/ Faculty Ratio Factor	X	Input Cost Factor	=	Per-student Instructional Cost Factor	Percent Increase in Per-student Instructional Cost
Small						
Enrollment	.65		1.37		.90	−10%
	.76		1.43		1.08	8%
Average	.70		1.40		0	0
Middle						
Enrollment	.74		2.23		1.64	64%
	1.25		1.34		1.67	67%
Average	.95		1.71		1.65	65%

Table 18 (continued)

Per-student Instructional Cost Equations
for Nine Case-study Schools, 1955 to 1970

Schools Listed by Enrollment Group	Student/ Faculty Ratio Factor	X	Input Cost Factor	=	Per-student Instructional Cost Factor	Percent Increase in Per-student Instructional Cost
Large Enrollment	1.31		1.40		1.83	83%
	1.41		1.33		1.88	88%
	1.09		1.76		1.92	92%
	1.15		1.79		2.05	105%
	1.71		2.10		3.59	259%
Average	1.33		1.62		2.06	106%
Nine Schools						
Average	1.11		1.59		1.63	63%

Differences in per-student instructional cost increases existed among the three Enrollment Groups. The 43 schools in the Small Enrollment Group had the lowest increases in per-student instructional cost.[69] In fact, in nearly half of these schools, per-student cost decreased even though substantial increases in input cost occurred between 1955 and 1970. This resulted, of course, from the enormous student/faculty ratio increases at many of these schools. As an average, the per-student cost of these schools increased only 5.3% over the fifteen-year period examined. (The average per-student cost of the two case-study schools included in the Small Enrollment Group remained constant.) Only 4 of the 43 schools in the Small Enrollment Group had per-student cost increases in excess of 50%.

The per-student cost of the 34 schools in the Middle Enrollment Group increased to a far greater extent than that of the Small Enrollment Group. This difference is attributable to the fact that the student/faculty ratio increases of the Middle Enrollment Group were considerably less than those of the Small Enrollment Group, although the input cost increases were similar in the two Groups. The average per-student cost at these schools increased 38.3% from 1955 to 1970. (The average per-student cost increase of the two case-study schools included in the Middle Enrollment Group was 65%.) Only 20% of the Middle Enrollment Group had per-student cost decreases during that period, and 40% of the schools had per-student cost increases in excess of 50%.

The highest increases in per-student cost occurred at the 38 schools of the Large Enrollment Group. In contrast to the Small and Middle Enrollment Groups, most of the Large Enrollment Group's student/faculty ratios decreased

---

69.   For the remainder of this section, per-student instructional cost will be referred to as per-student cost.

between 1955 and 1970.[70] The average per-student cost at these schools increased about 70% from 1955 to 1970. (The average per-student cost increase of the five case-study schools included in the Large Enrollment Group was 106%.[71]) These increases are truly extraordinary.[72] Only two of the schools in the Large Enrollment Group had per-student cost decreases, and only 30% of such schools had increases below 50%. On the other hand, 40% of the schools in the Group had per-student cost increases in excess of 100%.

The result of the different percent changes in per-student cost among the three Groups of schools[73] has been to bring their per-student cost closer together.[74] The mean per-student cost of the three Groups in dollar terms in 1955 and 1970 is as follows.[75]

Table 19

Average Per-student Instructional Cost
By Enrollment Group, 1955 and 1970
(in 1970 dollars)

	1955	1970
Small Enrollment Group	$810	$ 854
Middle Enrollment Group	$606	$ 838
Large Enrollment Group	$627	$1,066

It will be observed that in 1955 the average per-student cost of the Small Enrollment Group was substantially higher than that of the other two Groups (about 30%), and that the average per-student cost of the Middle and Large Enrollment Groups was nearly the same. Between 1955 and 1970, the Small Enrollment Group's average increased only a small amount; the Middle Enrollment Group's, a large amount; and the Large Enrollment Group's, an even larger amount. The result was that the average per-student cost in the three

---

70.   All but three of the Small Enrollment Group's student/faculty ratios increased between 1955 and 1970. About three-quarters of the Middle Enrollment Group's student/faculty ratios increased, and, in sharp contrast, only about one-fourth of the Large Enrollment Group's student/faculty ratios increased.
71.   If one school, which had an unusually high per-student cost increase, is eliminated, the average is brought down to 91%.
72.   Particularly so when it is remembered that they are in constant - dollar terms.
73.   The Small Enrollment Group increased 5.3%, the Middle Enrollment Group, 38.3%, and the Large Enrollment Group, 70.0%.
74.   Within each Group, however, per-student cost increases differed substantially. This aspect of the problem is discussed below.
75.   The per-student instructional cost is calculated by multiplying the median faculty salary by the number of full-time-equivalent faculty members engaged, and dividing that product by the number of students enrolled. Because of the uncertainty of the data on which it is based (see footnote 5 above), it is only an approximation. We feel certain, however, that these figures accurately reflect the actual range of differences in these costs.

Groups was closer together in 1970 than in 1955.

As indicated above, this phenomenon is explained in large part by the different manner in which the student/faculty ratios changed among the three Groups of schools. To review, the Small Enrollment Group had very low student/faculty ratios in 1955, and as their enrollments increased, their student/faculty ratios increased. Thus, increases in their per-student cost attributable to increased input cost were offset by increases in their student/faculty ratios. The Middle Enrollment Group had moderate student/faculty ratios in 1955, and as their enrollments increased, their student/faculty ratios also increased, but not as much as those of the Small Enrollment Group. Accordingly, while increases in the Middle Enrollment Group's per-student cost attributable to increased input cost were offset to some extent by increasing student/faculty ratios, the effect of student/faculty ratio increases in holding down per-student cost increases was of far less moment at these schools. In contrast to the Small and Middle Enrollment Groups, the student/faculty ratios of the Large Enrollment Group decreased between 1955 and 1970. Accordingly, increases in their per-student cost attributable to increased input cost were made even greater by the reduction in their student/faculty ratios. The narrowing of the differences in average per-student cost of the three Enrollment Groups between 1955 and 1970 has been ascribed in large part to changes in their student/faculty ratios. This recalls the phenomenon discussed above regarding the movement of a substantial number of schools in each Enrollment Group toward a "middle" range of student/faculty ratios (between 17/1 and 24/1) referred to as the 1970 Standard Range. In fact, such a phenomenon is directly related to the narrowing of the differences in per-student cost.

It has been demonstrated that the per-student cost changes of the three Enrollment Groups differed substantially. There were also wide differences in per-student cost changes among the schools in each Enrollment Group. Most of the Small Enrollment Group schools ranged from a 30% decrease in per-student cost to a 68% increase, a difference of 98%; most of the Middle Enrollment Group ranged from a 35% decrease to a 117% increase, a difference of 152%; and most of the Large Enrollment Group ranged from a 2% decrease to a 146% increase, a difference of 148%.[76] (Among the case-study schools, changes in per-student cost ranged from a 10% decrease to a 259% increase.)

As with increases in total instructional cost, definite patterns are evident among the three subgroups. Subgroup L schools tended to have the lowest per-student cost increases. It will be recalled that schools in this subgroup had the least favorable student/faculty ratio development.[77] Both subgroup M and H schools had more favorable student/faculty ratio changes than schools in subgroup L. Although schools in subgroups M and H had similar student/faculty

---

76.   As can be seen from an examination of Table 17, a small number of schools string out below and above these extremes, therefore, the text refers to "most" of the schools within each Group.

77.   See Appendix F. In the Small and Middle Enrollment Groups, the student/faculty ratios of subgroup L schools increased the most; in the Large Enrollment Group, subgroup L schools decreased the least.

ratio changes, subgroup M schools had lower per-student cost increases than schools in subgroup H. This can be attributed to the fact that subgroup H schools had higher input cost increases than subgroup M schools. Table 20 illustrates these relationships.

The wide range of differences in per-student cost increase again suggests that little can be meaningfully said about typical cost trends in legal education between 1955 and 1970.[78] Wide differences in increase in total instructional

Table 20

Average Per-student Instructional Cost by Subgroups
1955 to 1970

Groups and Subgroups	Student/ Faculty Ratio Factor	×	Input cost Factor	=	Per-student Instructional Cost Factor	% Change	Average Dollar Value 1955 (1970 $)	1970
Small Enroll- ment Group	.61		1.73		1.05	5%	$810	$ 854
Subgroup L	.58		1.64		.89	−11%	$915	$ 812
Subgroup M	.63		1.71		1.15	15%	$709	$ 813
Subgroup H	.65		1.90		1.24	24%	$795	$ 989
Middle Enroll- ment Group	.79		1.66		1.38	38%	$606	$ 838
Subgroup L	.72		1.48		1.08	8%	$729	$ 788
Subgroup M	.75		1.72		1.43	43%	$643	$ 917
Subgroup H	.90		1.91		2.06	106%	$411	$ 848
Large Enroll- ment Group	1.10		1.57		1.70	70%	$627	$1,066
Subgroup L	.95		1.46		1.43	43%	$758	$1,084
Subgroup M	1.22		1.65		1.96	96%	$600	$1,177
Subgroup H	1.25		1.70		2.08	108%	$451	$ 938
Total 115 Schools	.83		1.65		133	33%	689	$ 919

Note: All figures are averages.

cost were noted above. These differences were explained in part by differences in rates of enrollment increase. This variable enters only implicitly into calculations of per-student cost, which, therefore, are regarded as more meaningful for making comparisons between schools. Accordingly, the

78.   With regard to changes in total instructional cost, one could at least say that costs have increased, however significant or insignificant that proposition might be. For per-student cost, even this assertion cannot be made. Twenty-nine of the 115 schools examined had per-student cost decreases.

Figure 3

Per-student Instructional Cost in 1970
for 115 Law Schools

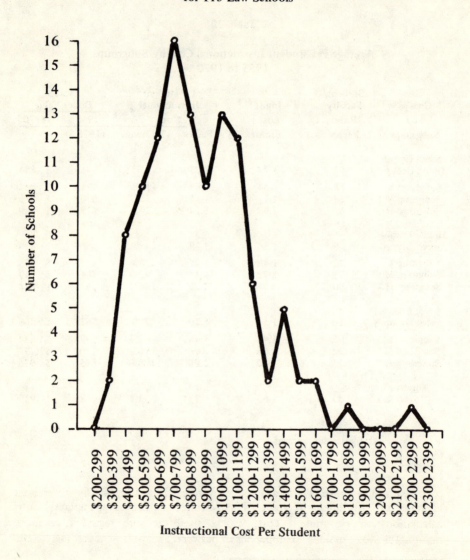

conclusion offered at the start of this section regarding the essentially inconsequential nature of inquiries about uniform rates of increase in instructional cost of legal education is reinforced by a consideration of the differences in per-student cost increase. The underlying significance of these wide variations is revealed when it is recalled that such variations are attributable in large part to differences in student/faculty ratio change (input cost increase being relatively uniform). It is well known that differences in schools' educational programs may be ascribed in part to differences in schools' student/faculty ratios. This aspect of instructional cost is dealt with in the next chapter. The variations in per-student cost increase over the fifteen-year period are reflected in variations in 1970 cost-per-student statistics which are shown in Figure 3.

At the close of our analysis of increases in total instructional cost, we set forth several examples of three hypothetical schools, each based on a representative school from one of the three Enrollment Groups. This was done to demonstrate the impact in dollar terms of the changes in the three key factors (Scale, Student/Faculty Ratio and Input Cost) on such increases. For like reasons, to complete our analysis of per-student instructional cost increases, we set forth in Table 21 the Per-student Instructional Cost Equations of these three representative model schools.

Table 21
Per-student Instructional Cost Equations
for Three Model Schools Representing
Typical Schools from Each Enrollment Group

Representative Model School	Student/ Faculty Ratio Factor		Input Cost Factor		Per-student Instructional Cost Factor
Small Enrollment School	.62	X	1.7	=	1.05
Middle Enrollment School	.83	X	1.7	=	1.41
Large Enrollment School	1.13	X	1.7	=	1.92

It will be recalled that the three schools had similar average faculty salaries in 1955, namely $12,000; and that the Small Enrollment School had a student/faculty ratio of 13/1; the Middle Enrollment School, 20/1; and the Large Enrollment School, 26/1. Accordingly, for purposes of Table 22, the Small Enrollment School had a per-student cost of $923, the Middle Enrollment School, $600; and the Large Enrollment School, $465. By 1970, it is assumed that all three schools' average faculty salaries had increased to $20,400. The Small Enrollment School's student/faculty ratio increased from 13/1 to 21/1, the Middle Enrollment School's student/faculty ratio increased from 20/1 to 24/1, and the Large Enrollment School's student/faculty ratio decreased from

26/1 to 23/1. Accordingly, the Small Enrollment School had a per-student cost of $971 in 1970; the Middle Enrollment School, $847; and the Large Enrollment School, $892.

Table 22 presents an analysis of the three Per-student Instructional Cost Equations of Table 21 in terms of three coefficients.[79] The dollar increase in per-student cost is broken down into three amounts representing the various impacts of the two factors and their combination.

Table 22

**Per-student Instructional Cost Increases for Three Model Schools
in Terms of Three Coefficients
1955 to 1970**

	Small Enrollment School	Middle Enrollment School	Large Enrollment School
1. Student/Faculty Ratio	−$352	−$102	$ 60
2. Input Cost	646	420	325
3. S/F Ratio & Input Cost	−246	−71	42
Total Increase in Per-student Instructional Cost	$ 48	$247	$427
1955 Per-student Cost	$923	$600	$465
1970 Per-student Cost	$971	$847	$892

Again, the dramatic impact of different student/faculty ratio changes is evident. If the student/faculty ratio had remained constant between 1955 and 1970, items 1 and 3 would be zero (a constant factor represents no change). In these circumstances, the Small Enrollment School's per-student cost would then be $1,569, or 61% higher ($923 + $646 = $1,569). If the student/faculty ratio had remained constant at the Middle Enrollment School, its per-student cost would be $1,020, or 20% higher ($600 + $420 = $1,020). The Large Enrollment School decreased its student/faculty ratio. If it had remained constant, its per-student cost would be $790, or 12% lower ($465 + $325 = $790). It will be observed that, as a result of the changes shown in Table 22, the 1970 per-student costs of the three model schools are closer together than they were in 1955.

Section 5 − Individual Application of Instructional Cost Equation

In this section we show the utility of the I.C. Equation in analyzing the increases in total instructional cost, and the per-student cost at any individual law school. Through the I.C. Equation, a school can develop an understanding of the factors contributing to increments in instructional cost (Scale,

---

79.   For the method used in deriving these figures, see section 5.

Student/Faculty Ratio, Input Cost) and the relationships between these factors. Additionally, by applying data from previous years, trends will be suggested and tentative projections can be made. To the extent that data are developed on a uniform basis by other law schools, and are made available, an individual school will be able to gain a better insight into its own program through comparative analysis. Also the I.C. Equation provides a language and mode of analysis which may facilitate more informed consideration of an individual school's instructional cost when dealing with other parties such as accrediting bodies, university officers, and the like. Moreover, given a predetermined amount of funds for instructional expenditures, the I.C. Equation enables one to develop alternatives and make discriminations in the allocation of such funds. Or, given certain institutional objectives (e.g., reducing the student/faculty ratio, increasing enrollment, or increasing faculty salaries), the I.C. Equation will help determine how the funds necessary to achieve such objectives can be attributed to changes among the three factors.

It should be noted that, for any of these purposes, although changes from year to year may be minimal, definite patterns will emerge over a period of time, and the relative impact of the three factors, Scale, Student/Faculty Ratio and Input Cost, will become readily ascertainable.

Some uses of the I.C. Equation are shown in the examples below. As will be recalled, the I.C. Equation is:

$$\text{Scale factor} \times \text{Student/Faculty Ratio factor}$$
$$\times \text{Input Cost factor} = \text{Instructional Cost factor.}$$

In these examples the following basic data are set forth for each of two years (the earlier year is designated Year 1 and the later year Year 2). All figures are assumed to be constant dollars.

Basic Data

Enrollment
Number of Faculty
Student/Faculty Ratio
Average Faculty Salary
Total Instructional Cost

To give the first example a realistic context, imagine the following memorandum prepared for his files by a new dean; he has discussed with the retiring dean the subject of escalating instructional cost.

> I began the meeting by noting that during the last five academic years instructional cost at our School has increased from $195,000 to $460,000, a 136% increase. I pointed out that this was an enormous increase and quite alarming in view of the severe financial constraints our university has recently experienced. Dean Harris noted that he didn't find this increase particularly surprising in view of the marked growth in student enrollment over the last five years. I responded that while I recognized enrollment had grown by a considerable amount, these increases by no means matched the increase in instructional cost. (I believe we began the period with about 350 students and enroll

about 500 today. I am having the exact figures worked up.) Taking the bull by the horns, I suggested that perhaps large increases in faculty salaries were of particular significance in accounting for increased instructional cost. (We are also computing our average faculty salaries for the two years in question. I will ask my friends in the Economics Department how to convert the earlier salary figure to a constant dollar basis.) Dean Harris pointed out that the past five years have been marked by enormous faculty expansion. In this connection, Harris wondered what had happened to our student/faculty ratio during this period. (We are computing an exact faculty count for the two years.)

Our discussion produced a number of questions but little illumination. After we have worked up the underlying facts, I suggested we get together and try to figure out exactly what happened.

The basic data for *Example 1* are as follows.

	Year 1	Year 2
Enrollment	338	529
Number of Faculty	13	23
Student/Faculty Ratio	26/1	23/1
Average Faculty Salary	$ 15,000	$ 20,000
Total Instructional Cost	$195,000	$460,000

To ascertain the Scale factor:

$$\frac{\text{Year 2 enrollment}}{\text{Year 1 enrollment}} = \text{Scale factor} \qquad \frac{529}{338} = 1.56$$

To ascertain the Student/Faculty Ratio factor:

$$\frac{\text{Year 1 student/faculty ratio}}{\text{Year 2 student/faculty ratio}} = \text{S/F Ratio factor} \qquad \frac{26/1}{23/1} = 1.13$$

To ascertain the Input Cost factor:

$$\frac{\text{Year 2 average faculty salary}}{\text{Year 1 average faculty salary}} = \text{Input Cost factor} \qquad \frac{\$20,000}{\$15,000} = 1.33$$

Thus the I.C. Equation for Example 1 is:

1.56 (Scale) × 1.13 (S/F Ratio) × 1.33 (Input Cost) = 2.36.

Deducting 1.00 from 2.36 and multiplying by 100,[80] we obtain a 136% increase in instructional cost. The increase in percentage terms could also, of course, have been derived by dividing the total instructional cost of Year 1 by the total instructional cost of Year 2, subtracting 1.00 and multiplying by 100, thus:

$$\frac{\$460,000}{\$195,000} = 2.36 \text{ minus } 1.00 = 1.36 = 136\%.$$

However, by deriving the increase in instructional cost via the three factors we can grasp their relative impact. From examining the I.C. Equation alone, it is apparent that Scale has the predominant impact, followed by Input Cost, and

---

80.   See Appendix E.

that the Student/Faculty Ratio factor has the least impact.

Although the relative impact of the three factors has been generally ascertained, because of the compound nature of the I.C. Equation, further steps must be taken to allocate the increase in over-all instructional cost more precisely among the three factors. Thus, the impact of the three factors, operating both singly and in conjunction, is disclosed.[81] For purposes of our analysis the increase in instructional cost is interpreted as consisting of additional expenditures incurred because of faculty growth (the addition of new faculty members) and, also, additional expenditures incurred because of the increased salaries paid to faculty members. Faculty growth in turn is attributed to the addition of some faculty members to parallel enrollment increases, as well as to the addition of others to decrease the student/faculty ratio. Accordingly, to conduct the more detailed examination of increases in instructional cost, three steps are taken. First, an analysis is made of the increase in the size of the faculty. Second, an analysis is made of the increase in instructional cost in terms of faculty growth and increased input cost. Third, these two analyses are combined.

Step One: The Faculty Distribution Equation

The increase in faculty size is attributed to enrollment increases alone, to changes in the student/faculty ratio alone, and to a combination of both factors through the use of an equation designated as the Faculty Distribution Equation. This equation involves the multiplication of the Scale factor by the Student/Faculty Ratio factor. In Example 1, the Faculty Distribution Equation would be as follows.

1.56 (Scale factor) × 1.13 (Student/Faculty Ratio factor)
= 1.77 (Faculty Growth factor).
1.77 minus 1.00 = .77 = 77% (percent increase in faculty).

The product of this equation (1.77) is referred to as the Faculty Growth factor. The Faculty Growth factor minus 1.00, times 100 represents the percent increase in faculty between Year 1 and Year 2. This percentage multiplied by the number of faculty engaged at Year 1, viz., 13, produces the increase in faculty between Year 1 and Year 2 (13 × .77 = 10). According to our hypothesis, these additional ten professors may be allocated among those engaged because of increased enrollment, those engaged because of a reduced student/faculty ratio, and those engaged because of a combination of both factors.

By multiplying the number of Year 1 faculty members (13) by the Scale factor minus 1.00 (.56), we can determine the increase in faculty members attributable to increased enrollment alone, i.e., without any change in the

---

81.   From time to time in the following analysis, reference is made to the "impact" of the factors on instructional cost. Of course, as pointed out above in section 3, these factors, strictly speaking, do not make an "impact" on instructional cost; rather, through the working of the analytical hypothesis, they merely provide one means of interpreting increases in instructional cost. We believe that it is hardly possible to ascertain all the real factors that actually affect instructional cost. However, to foster ready understanding, we frequently talk of "impact" and use other figurative expressions rather than employ more exact but circumlocutory descriptions of all the relevant facts.

school's student/faculty ratio. Thus 13 × .56 = 7.3. By hypothesis, 7.3 faculty members were engaged to provide the additional 191 students with the Year 1 student/faculty ratio of 26/1.[82] By multiplying the number of Year 1 faculty members (13) by the Student/Faculty Ratio factor minus 1.00 (.13), we can determine the increase in faculty attributable to the decreased student/faculty ratio alone, i.e., without any change in the school's enrollment. Thus 13 × .13 = 1.7. By hypothesis, 1.7 faculty members were engaged to provide Year 1 enrollment with the reduced student/faculty ratio of 23/1.[83]

By multiplying the number of Year 1 faculty members (13) first by the Scale factor minus 1.00 (.56) and then multiplying their product by the Student/Faculty Ratio factor minus 1.00 (.13), we can determine the further increase in faculty members attributable to the combined impact of changes in both factors. Thus, 13 × .56 × .13 = 1. By hypothesis, one additional faculty member was engaged to provide the additional 191 students with the reduced student/faculty ratio of 23/1.[84]

In sum, the ten additional professors engaged by the school in Year 2 under our hypothesis are distributed as follows.

Attributable to increased
enrollment alone . . . . .73% or 7.3 professors

Attributable to a reduced
student/faculty ratio alone .17% or 1.7 professors

Attributable to the joint effect
of increased enrollment and
reduced student/faculty ratio . . . . .10% or 1   professor
                                                                                    100% 10   professors

These proportions clearly indicate the relative importance of enrollment growth and student/faculty ratio reduction in interpreting faculty growth.[85]

---

82.   191 ÷ 26 = 7.3.
83.   At a 23/1 student/faculty ratio and an enrollment of 338 students, the school would have engaged 14.7 professors (338 ÷ 23 = 14.7). At a 26/1 student/faculty ratio, it engaged 13 professors (338 ÷ 26 = 13). The difference between 14.7 and 13, or 1.7, represents the impact of the reduced student/faculty ratio on the number of students equal to Year 1's enrollment.
84.   It was shown above that 7.3 professors had to be engaged to provide the additional 191 students with a 26/1 student/faculty ratio. At a 23/1 student/faculty ratio, 8.3 professors had to be engaged. The difference between 8.3 and 7.3, viz., 1, represents the impact of the reduced student/faculty ratio on the additional 191 students.
85.   These same proportions may be derived directly from the Faculty Distribution Equation in the following manner. If the Scale factor minus 1.00 is divided by the Faculty Growth factor minus 1.00, then the result is the percent of faculty growth attributable to increased enrollment alone. Thus, .56 ÷ .77 = .73. If the Student/Faculty Ratio factor minus 1.00 is divided by the Faculty Growth factor minus 1.00, then the result is the percent of faculty growth attributable to a reduced student/faculty ratio alone. Thus, .13 ÷ .77 = .17. If the product of the Scale factor minus 1.00 times the Student/Faculty Ratio factor minus 1.00 is divided by the Faculty Growth factor minus 1.00, then the result is the percent of faculty growth attributable to a combination of increased enrollment and reduced student/faculty ratio. Thus, (.56 × .13) ÷ .77 = .10.

Step 2: The Instructional Dollar Allocation Equation

The increase in instructional cost is attributed to increased faculty alone, to increased input cost alone, and to a combination of both factors through the use of an equation designated as the Instructional Dollar Allocation Equation. In Example 1, the Instructional Dollar Allocation Equation would be as follows.

    1.77 (Faculty Growth factor)

    × 1.33 (Input Cost factor)

    = 2.36 (Instructional Cost factor)

    2.36 minus 1.00 = 1.36 = 136% (percent increase in I.C.)

The product of this equation is equivalent to the product of the I.C. Equation, and, minus 1.00 times 100, represents the percent increase in instructional cost between Year 1 and Year 2 of 136%. This percent when multiplied by Year 1 instructional cost produces the dollar increase in instructional cost between Year 1 and Year 2. Thus, 136% × $195,000 = $265,000. This amount may be allocated in three ways. First, expenditures attributable to increase in faculty size alone, second, expenditures attributable to increase in input cost alone, and, third, expenditures attributable to a combination of increase in faculty size and increase in input cost.

An analysis similar to that made above with respect to faculty distribution may be made and would result in the following dollar allocations.

Attributable to increased

    faculty alone[86] .... 56.5% or $150,000

Attributable to increased

    input cost alone[87] .... 24.5% or $ 65,000

Attributable to the combination

    of increased faculty and

    increased input cost[88] .... 19% or $ 50,000

                                                    100% $265,000

These proportions clearly indicate the relative importance of faculty growth and increased input cost for interpreting the increase in total instructional cost.[89]

Step 3: The Instructional Cost Equation

The two steps presented so far have indicated first, the distribution of faculty growth in terms of enrollment increase and reduction of student/faculty ratio,

---

86.   Year 1 instructional cost × (Faculty Growth factor minus 1.00). $195,000 × (1.77 − 1.00) = $150,000. Ten new faculty members at Year 1 input cost.

87.   Year 1 instructional cost × (Input Cost factor minus 1.00). $195,000 × (1.33 − 1.00) = $65,000. Thirteen original faculty members receiving $5,000 increase in salary each.

88.   Year 1 instructional cost × (Faculty Growth factor minus 1.00) × (Input Cost factor minus 1.00). $195,000 × (1.77 − 1.00) × (1.33 − 1.00) = $50,000. Ten new faculty members, each receiving $5,000 increase in salary.

89.   These proportions can be obtained from the Instructional Dollar Allocation Equation in the same manner that the faculty breakdown was worked out above. See footnote 85.

and, second, the dollar allocation of total increases in instructional cost between faculty growth and increase in input cost. A third step may be taken to break down the increase in total instructional cost, in dollar and percentage terms, among amounts attributable to enrollment (scale) changes alone, student/faculty ratio changes alone, average faculty salary (input cost) changes alone, and amounts attributable to the various combinations of these three factors. This procedure involves the following seven computations.

1. Impact of Scale factor:

> Year 1 instructional cost X (Scale factor minus 1.00).
> $195,000 X .56 = $110,180, or impact of Scale factor alone.

The product ($110,180) represents the increase in instructional cost that would have occurred *if the only change* from Year 1 to Year 2 had been in scale, i.e., that part of salary expenditures paid to the additional 7.3 faculty members (attributable to enrollment increase alone) at the Year 1 salary level of $15,000.

2. Impact of Student/Faculty Ratio factor:

> Year 1 instructional cost X (S/F Ratio factor minus 1.00).
> $195,000 X .13 = $25,440, or impact of Student/Faculty Ratio factor alone.

The product ($25,440) represents the increment in instructional cost that would have occurred *if the only change* from Year 1 to Year 2 had been in the student/faculty ratio, i.e., that part of salary expenditures paid to the 1.7 additional faculty members (attributable to the reduced student/faculty ratio alone) at the Year 1 salary level of $15,000.

3. Impact of Input Cost factor:

> Year 1 instructional cost X (Input Cost factor minus 1.00).
> $195,000 X .33 = $65,000, or impact of Input Cost factor alone.

The product ($65,000) represents the increase in instructional cost that would have occurred *if the only change* from Year 1 to Year 2 had been in input cost, i.e., that part of salary expenditures paid to the 13 original faculty members on hand at Year 1, representing the differential between Year 1 and Year 2 salary level, or $5,000.

4. Combined impact of Scale and Student/Faculty Ratio factors:

> Year 1 instructional cost
> X (Scale factor minus 1.00)
> X (Student/Faculty Ratio factor minus 1.00).
>
> $195,000 X .56 X .13 = $14,370, or the combined impact of Scale and Student/Faculty Ratio factors.

The product ($14,370) represents the increase in instructional cost attributable to a combination of the Scale factor and Student/Faculty Ratio factor, i.e., that part of salary expenditures paid to the one additional faculty member (attributable to the reduced student/faculty ratio as it applies to the increased enrollment alone), at the Year 1 salary level of $15,000.

5. *Combined impact of Scale and Input Cost factors:*

>   Year 1 instructional cost
>   X (Scale factor minus 1.00)
>   X (Input Cost factor minus 1.00).
> $195,000 X .56 X .33 = $36,730, or combined impact
>   of Scale and Input Cost factors.

The product ($36,730) represents the increase in instructional cost attributable to a combination of the Scale factor and the Input Cost factor, i.e., that part of salary expenditures paid to the additional 7.3 faculty members (attributable to increased enrollment alone), representing the differential between Year 1 and Year 2 salary levels.

6. *Combined impact of Student/Faculty Ratio and Input Cost factors:*

>   Year 1 instructional cost
>   X (Student/Faculty Ratio factor minus 1.00)
>   X (Input Cost factor minus 1.00).
> $195,000 X .13 X .33 = $8,480, or combined impact of S/F Ratio and
>   Input Cost factors.

The product ($8,480) represents the increase in instructional cost attributable to a combination of the Student/Faculty Ratio factor and the Input Cost factor, i.e., that part of salary expenditures paid to the additional 1.7 faculty members (attributable to the reduced student/faculty ratio alone), representing the differential between Year 1 and Year 2 salary levels.

7. *Combined impact of Scale and Student/Faculty Ratio and Input Cost factors:*
>   Year 1 instructional cost
>   X (Scale factor minus 1.00)
>   X (Student/Faculty Ratio factor minus 1.00)
>   X (Input Cost factor minus 1.00).
> $195,000 X .56 X .13 X .33 = $4,800,
>   or combined impact of all three factors.

The product ($4,800) represents the increase in instructional cost attributable to a combination of the Scale factor, Student/Faculty Ratio factor, and Input Cost factor, i.e., that part of salary expenditures paid to the additional faculty member (attributable to the reduced student/faculty ratio as it applies to the increased enrollment alone), representing the differential between Year 1 and Year 2 salary levels.

In summary, these seven computations provide the following breakdown of the total increase in instructional cost.

	Impact of	Proportion	Cost Contribution
1.	Scale factor[90]	42%	$110,180
2.	S/F Ratio factor	10%	25,440
3.	Input Cost factor	24%	65,000
4.	Scale & S/F Ratio factors	5%	14,370
5.	Scale & Input Cost factors	14%	36,730
6.	S/F Ratio & Input Cost factors	3%	8,480
7.	Scale & S/F Ratio & Input Cost factors	2%	4,800
		100%	$265,000

If enrollment had not increased (Scale factor would be constant, or 1.00, representing no change), the expenditures represented by items 1, 4, 5, and 7 would not have occurred, and the increase in instructional cost would have been reduced by $166,080, or 63% of the total increase. If the student/faculty ratio had not decreased (Student/Faculty Ratio factor would be constant, or 1.00, representing no change), the expenditures represented by items 2, 4, 6, and 7 would not have occurred, and the increase would have been reduced by $53,090, or 20% of the total increase. If faculty salaries had not increased (Input Cost factor would be constant, or 1.00, representing no change), the expenditures represented by items 3, 5, 6, and 7 would not have occurred, and the increase in instructional cost would have been reduced by $115,010, or 43% of the total increase.

The above example demonstrates how a school might use the I.C. Equation to review the development of its instructional program over a prior period from a fiscal standpoint. Similarly, the I.C. Equation may be used to interpret the results of changes proposed for the future. In such a case Year 1 will presumably be the present year and Year 2 will be some year in the future.[91] A second example involving such a projection follows. In this example, the basic data for Year 1 are:

Enrollment	500
Number of Faculty	20
Student/Faculty Ratio	25/1

90.   Although the factor minus one used in steps 1 through 7 is shown to two decimal places, the breakdown shown here was derived by taking the factor out to six decimal places.
91.   When projecting future expenditures, it should be noted that the I.C. Equation procedure uses constant-dollar figures. After the analysis is completed, therefore, provision can be made for added expenditures due solely to monetary inflation. The simplest procedure is to project the increase in the Consumer Price Index for the period involved, and inflate all figures accordingly.

Average Faculty Salary	$20,000
Total Instructional Cost	$400,000

In planning changes over a five-year period, assume it is desired to increase the faculty by seven additional professors and to let enrollment increase by about 100 students to 600. The net result would be a reduction of the student/faculty ratio to 22/1, which will enable the school to give a larger number of its courses in small classes. In order to maintain its competitive position in the market place, it is decided to plan for an average increase in faculty salary of 5.5% per year. Thus the basic data for Year 2 would be projected as follows.

Enrollment	594
Number of Faculty	27
Student/Faculty Ratio	22/1
Average Faculty Salary	$26,000
Total Instructional Cost	$702,000

Pursuant to these projections, over-all instructional cost would increase by $302,000 (about 75%), from $400,000 in Year 1 to $702,000 in Year 2.

The Instructional Cost Equation in Example 2 is as follows.

Scale factor	Student/Faculty Ratio factor	Input Cost factor	Instructional Cost factor
1.19 X	1.14 X	1.30 =	1.75

The Faculty Distribution Equation in Example 2 provides the following breakdown.

Attributable to increased
enrollment alone . . . . .54% or 3¾ professors

Attributable to reduced
student/faculty ratio alone . . . . .39% or 2¾ professors

Attributable to the combination
of increased enrollment and
reduced student/faculty ratio . . . . 7% or ½ professor

                                                    100%   7 professors

The Instructional Dollar Allocation Equation provides the following breakdown of the increase in instructional cost between faculty growth and input cost.

Attributable to increased
faculty alone . . . . 46% or $140,000

Attributable to increased
  input cost alone .... 40% or $120,000

Attributable to the combination
  of increased faculty and
  increased input cost .... 14% or $ 42,000
                                                 100% $302,000

The detailed contributions of the seven factors and their combinations to the total increase in instructional cost are as follows.

	Impact of	Proportion	Cost Contribution
1.	Scale factor	25%	$ 75,200
2.	S/F Ratio factor	18%	54,400
3.	Input Cost factor	40%	120,000
4.	Scale & S/F Ratio factors	3%	10,300
5.	Scale & Input Cost factors	8%	22,600
6.	S/F Ratio & Input Cost factors	5%	16,400
7.	Scale & S/F Ratio & Input Cost factors	1%	3,100
		100%	$302,000

Per-student Cost

By multiplying the Student/Faculty Ratio factor by the Input Cost factor, we can determine the Per-student Instructional Cost factor. Converting this to a percentage yields the percent increase in per-student cost. For Example 1, the computation would be as follows.

1.13 (Student/Faculty Ratio factor)
X 1.33 (Input Cost factor)
= 1.51 (Per-student Instructional Cost factor).
(1.51 − 1.00) X 100 = 51% (increase in per-student cost).

The per-student cost in Year 1 was $577 ($195,000 ÷ 338 = $577 or $15,000 ÷ 26 = $577). By Year 2, it had increased to $870 ($460,000 ÷ 529 = $870 or $20,000 ÷ 23 = $870), an increase of $293, or 51%. Part of this increase is attributable to the decreased student/faculty ratio, part is attributable to the increased input cost, and part is attributable to a combination of both. An analysis similar to those made above with respect to total instructional cost may be made. It would result in the following breakdown.

Attributable to reduced
   Student/faculty ratio alone[92] .... .26% or $ 75

Attributable to increased
   input cost alone[93] .... .66% or $193

Attributable to the combination
   of reduced student/faculty
   ratio and increased input cost[94] .... 8% or $ 25
                                                    100% $293

These proportions clearly indicate the relative importance of student/faculty ratio reduction and increased input cost for interpreting increases in per-student instructional cost between Year 1 and Year 2.

In Example 2 the Per-student Cost factor is 1.48 (1.14 × 1.30). The Year 1 per-student cost is $800 ($400,000 ÷ 500) and the Year 2 per-student cost is $1,182 ($702,000 ÷ 594), an increase of $382, or 48%. A similar analysis for Example 2 would result in the following breakdown of the increase in per-student cost.

Attributable to reduced
   student/faculty ratio alone .... .28% or $109

Attributable to increased
   input cost alone .... .63% or $240

Attributable to the combination
   of reduced student/faculty
   ratio and increased input cost .... 9% or $ 33
                                                    100% $382

---

92.   Year 1 per-student cost × (S/F Ratio factor minus 1.00). $577 (1.13 − 1.00) = $75.
93.   Year 1 per-student cost × (Input Cost factor minus 1.00). $577 (1.33 − 1.00) = $193.
94.   Year 1 per-student cost × (S/F Ratio factor minus 1.00) × (Input Cost factor minus 1.00). $577 × (1.13 − 1.00) × (1.33 − 1.00) = $25.

Instructional Cost — Content Analysis

Introduction

In chapter 2 we examined increases in instructional cost and showed how these increases could be analyzed in terms of enrollment increases, changes in student/faculty ratios, and increases in the level of average faculty compensation. In this chapter we examine the changes that take place in law school educational programs during a time instructional cost is changing. In brief, in chapter 2 we showed how and why instructional cost has gone up, and in this chapter we show what the law schools get—or can get—for their money as a result of these increased expenditures, and the educational options open to law schools undergoing change. Our examination proceeds by analyzing the changes in the educational programs of law schools. For present purposes, the term "educational program" refers to the number of courses given in a school's curriculum in terms of different subject-matter offerings, the amount of sectionalization of these courses, and the size of these courses and sections in terms of student enrollment.[1]

Ordinarily, educational programs expand as teachers are added to the faculty. More faculty members breed more courses. This phenomenon ties in with Instructional Cost Equation analyses made in chapter 2. As enrollments increase, faculties increase, and we have found that with such increases educational programs expand. Program expansion also occurs when student/faculty ratios decrease, and when enrollments increase and student/faculty ratios decrease concurrently, schools usually enjoy particularly large expansions of their educational programs. Thus, two of the factors that have been used to analyze increases in instructional cost are directly related to the expansion of law school educational programs. A central concern in this chapter will be to show how the scope of law schools' curricula has expanded and how this expansion has produced a mix of classes of different sizes which may be analyzed as costing

---

1. Note that this definition of "educational program" is somewhat narrow; see below for a discussion of the problems concerning quantitative analysis.

different amounts. In addition, we attempt to develop an analytical framework to assist schools in setting priorities and evaluating options.

Before embarking on this examination, a variety of preliminary considerations should be taken into account. In order to analyze changes in a law school's educational program, we make particular use of two measures: teaching hours and student hours. We will first consider teaching hours and, in doing so, will examine the important variable of teaching load. A "teaching hour" is equivalent to a credit hour and is defined as an hour of classroom instruction repeated each week for one semester.[2] Each hour represents a distinct unit of instruction. Most courses entail three teaching hours, although many upperclass curricula contain a large number of two-teaching-hour courses, some four- and five-teaching-hour courses, and, occasionally, courses involving six or more teaching hours. As will be seen below, our analysis of a school's educational program proceeds in part by examining the scope of its curriculum in terms of the number of different subject-matter courses it offers. To do this we break up the curriculum into categories of courses by subject areas called course groupings. We conduct this analysis in terms of the number of teaching hours offered rather than the number of courses offered within each grouping. Thus, we might say that a school has expanded its offering in the corporate grouping from 5 teaching hours in 1955 to 10 teaching hours in 1960. Because law school courses differ in the amount of credit hours they involve, the teaching hour approach is more revealing than comparing the number of courses offered between two years.

An increase in the total number of teaching hours offered does not necessarily mean that a school's educational program has changed in any way other than size. If all or most of the additional teaching hours made possible by the increase in the size of the faculty were used merely to sectionalize existing courses, the change could appropriately be viewed as involving only an increase in the school's dimensions, that is, more students, more faculty, but virtually the same educational program. In effect, a parallel law school would have been created within the existing structure. If, on the other hand, many of the additional teaching hours were used to offer new courses, then one of the results of a school's growth would be expansion of its educational program in the significant sense of going beyond the mere duplication of existing courses. As will be shown, to a considerable extent this is, in fact, what happened at the case-study schools. While expansion of the first-year program involved for the most part the sectionalization of basic courses, sectionalization of courses in the second-and-third-year program was minimal. Most additional teaching hours allocated to the upperclass program, as a result of increases in faculty size, were used to offer new courses.

---

2. Typically, a semester encompasses about 16 weeks and includes 2 weeks for exams. Thus, one teaching hour or credit hour will usually entail about 14 hourly sessions. In many instances, a classroom hour consists of 50 minutes. In a few instances, it is not strictly accurate to equate a teaching hour as it is defined in the text with a credit hour. For example, the number of credit hours awarded for clinical programs is usually not based upon classroom hours. "Teaching hours" is used in this study in a broad enough sense to include credit hours offered for clinical work or other types of instruction which are not related to the classroom hour.

As the number of teaching hours offered by a law school increases, its educational program naturally expands. The total number of teaching hours is the number of faculty members teaching multiplied by their average teaching load per year. (The term, "teaching load," refers to the number of teaching hours a faculty member provides each year.) Thus, for example, a school with 20 faculty members, each of whom teaches on the average of 11 hours a year, will offer 220 teaching hours annually. Although an increase in faculty size usually accompanies an increase in the number of teaching hours offered and a corresponding expansion of a school's educational program, a school might increase the number of teaching hours offered—thus expanding its educational program—by merely increasing its faculty teaching load. In fact, increasing teaching loads and decreasing student/faculty ratios, are, for these purposes, alternative methods of expanding a school's program. Of course, significant differences exist between two schools offering the same number of teaching hours, where one school engages fewer faculty members than the other but has them teach a heavier load.[3]

In considering the variable teaching load, a distinction should be made between a school's stated policy regarding teaching load and the actual average teaching load of its faculty. Most schools have stated guidelines as to the number of teaching hours a faculty member is expected to deliver each year.[4] However, many faculty members teach either more or less than the stated teaching load. In determining teaching load for the case-study schools, we have added the teaching hours of each full-time teacher and divided the sum by the number of full-time teachers, to obtain what we refer to as the "average teaching load."[5] In determining the number of teaching hours a faculty member teaches each year, no distinction is made between teaching separate courses and sections of the same course. If a faculty member teaches 2 three-hour sections of one first-year course, he is credited with a full 6 teaching hours for such efforts. Some methods of calculating teaching hours do not accord full teaching credit for teaching sections, and might, for example, credit the faculty member in the above case with only 4½ teaching hours. As indicated, we do not use this kind of modification for calculating teaching hours.

Information available to us regarding teaching loads has been limited to the case-study schools. The teaching loads of our nine case-study schools for each of the four years examined are set out in Table 1. In the many examples developed below, we use 11 teaching hours per year as the average teaching load. It will be noted that this is higher than the teaching loads in most of the case-study schools in 1970. Teaching loads, of course, vary considerably from school to

3. The relationship between student/faculty ratio and teaching load is discussed below in greater detail.
4. The Consultant to the A.B.A. has informed us that many schools he has visited have 12 hours per year as their stated teaching load.
5. In chapter 2 it was pointed out that the number of equivalent full-time teachers derived from part-time teachers is computed by dividing the sum of all part-time teaching hours by the actual average teaching load. Thus, number of faculty times the average teaching load produces the total number of teaching hours offered by a school.

Table 1

Average Teaching Load per Year at Nine Case-study Schools
1955, 1960, 1965, and 1970
(Semester hours)

Full-time Instructors				Part-time Instructors*			
1955	1960	1965	1970	1955	1960	1965	1970
11.1	11.2	10.6	11.7	2.0	3.5	4.2	2.4
11.9	11.3	10.6	11.6	4.3	3.8	3.0	4.3
14.1	12.2	11.4	11.5	5.1	2.9	4.2	4.0
15.4	13.6	11.4	10.9	4.0	3.9	2.9	3.5
12.6	10.8	10.8	10.7	4.3	3.4	3.9	3.5
14.6	13.8	11.4	10.5	6.3	4.1	2.5	3.4
9.3	8.9	9.8	10.5	2.6	3.2	2.5	3.1
12.0	10.2	11.4	10.3	3.1	3.3	4.1	2.6
9.0	9.6	9.2	8.8	3.3	3.1	2.5	2.5

*Presented for reference only.

school. Indeed the Tunks report, examining the teaching load of faculty members during the academic year 1956-57, concluded that the average teaching load at that time was closer to 15 hours.[6] The significance of a reduction in teaching load is discussed below.[7]

There are a number of hazards involved in using teaching hours as a primary measure of a school's educational program. These problems are discussed in some detail at the end of this chapter. For the present, however, brief consideration should be given to one aspect of the matter. In a sense the logic of our approach to instructional cost assumes faculty time as the sole instructional input and teaching hours as one of the chief instructional outputs.[8] In this connection it will be recalled that instructional cost is defined as consisting solely of salaries paid to faculty members, and that a school's educational program is analyzed in large part in terms of the number of teaching hours

6.   Special Committee on Law School Administration and University Relations of the A.A.L.S., Lehan K. Tunks, Chairman, *Anatomy of Modern Legal Education* (St. Paul, Minn.: West Publishing, 1961), p. 301.
7.   The average faculty teaching load times the number of faculty members teaching produces the number of total teaching hours delivered. It does not, of course, reveal the fact that individual faculty members teach different loads. It is not within the purview of this study's objectives to consider questions relating to the distribution of a school's teaching load. Similar issues arise with regard to different class sizes. These are touched upon below. The inability to gauge or measure classroom performance and the learning experience derived therefrom indicate a principal limit of a wholly quantitative approach to educational matters. Other problems connected with the quantitative approach are discussed below.
8.   The other major instructional output is student hours. Both student hours and teaching hours are based upon the credit-hour system and so much of what is said about teaching hours applies *mutatis mutandis* to student hours.

offered. This scheme, however, obscures the fact that faculty members are expected to devote a substantial part of their time to a number of non-classroom activities, the most important of which is research. Although these activities are directly related to teaching competence and bear fruits as tangible as classroom instruction, they are omitted in the simple correlation of faculty input and teaching hours. In the early stages of our study, we considered dividing instructional cost into two parts by allocating a part of each faculty member's salary to these non-classroom activities. This approach was abandoned, however, because of the extreme difficulties in assigning a quantifiable value to these efforts.[9] For purposes of this study, then, we assume that these other activities are directly related to a faculty member's classroom functions, and, thus, it is proper to include the whole of a faculty member's salary in instructional cost and make the general correlation between instructional cost and teaching hours.

As indicated, we use student hours as another important measure in examining the educational programs of law schools. A student hour is equivalent to a teaching hour, but from a student's standpoint, one "student hour" consists of a student spending one hour in class per week for a semester. Most students take between 13 and 15 credit hours per semester, which means that during the course of a semester, any one student would account for between 13 and 15 student hours of the total amount of student hours taken that semester. In the ensuing analysis we often compute the number of student hours a particular course involves. For instance a 3-credit course enrolling 120 students would cover 360 student hours. Frequently, we work backward from this figure and divide the number of student hours taken in a course or in a group of courses or by an entire class by the corresponding number of teaching hours delivered to these various class groupings, to derive their average class size. Thus, if a first-year class took 3,600 student hours and 30 teaching hours were offered to that class, we would determine that the average-size course for that year was 120 students.

Central to the notion of student hours is the matter of student load, which is the number of credit hours a student must complete each year in order to graduate. Just as total teaching hours may be derived by multiplying the number of faculty by the average teaching load, total student hours may be derived by multiplying the number of students by the average student load. In most cases student load is controlled by a governmental or quasi-governmental agency, the judiciary or an accrediting body. Rules for admission to the bar frequently specify that a law student must have successfully completed a certain number of semester hours of credit at an approved law school. For instance, the New York Court of Appeals requires that 80 semester hours be successfully completed

---

9. In addition to the activities suggested above, faculty members engage in certain pursuits that are not directly related to the teaching function but rather are of an administrative nature, such as serving on admissions committees or disciplinary tribunals. These activities are arguably assignable to the supporting services category, but because of the near impossibility of quantifying their value, they also have not been broken out of instructional cost.

before a student is eligible for the bar.[10] An approved law school is usually a law school that is approved by the A.B.A. At the present time A.B.A. Rules prescribe that a law school require that its students complete at least 1,200 hours of classroom instruction (student hours) in law, and that full-time students have three years of resident study and part-time students, at least four years of resident study.[11]

As indicated above, increases in teaching hours do not necessarily mean that a school has expanded its educational program in the significant sense of adding new subject-matter offerings. When a school has increased the number of teaching hours it offers, the increase could be entirely used for sectionalization of existing courses. This frequently happens when additional teaching hours are added to the first-year program. In most cases the size of each section is reduced. The extent of such reduction is, of course, dependent on changes in student enrollment. If, for example, enrollment has increased substantially, sectionalization of the basic courses might merely reduce the size of sections to the level of the original sections before the enrollment increases occurred.

However, as is usually the case with the second-and-third-year program, when the addition of teaching hours entails the initiation of courses covering new material rather than the sectionalization of existing courses, a quite different situation results from that which occurs when there is mere sectionalization. If most, or all, of the original and the new courses are electives, then it is extremely unlikely that the students will choose equally among them so that each course will be offered to classes of the same size. Rather, what usually happens in such cases is the development of classes of various sizes. As will be demonstrated below, this is exactly what has happened with the second- and third-year programs of most of the case-study schools. Classes of different sizes, of course, may be viewed as costing different amounts.

Specific information regarding the scope of law schools' curricula and the size of law school classes is limited to data we have collected regarding the case-study schools. Consequently, our findings as to the expansion of law school educational programs are limited to these schools. However, since the growth patterns of these schools have virtually the same characteristics (i.e., in terms of student enrollments and changes in student/faculty ratios) as many of the schools included in the larger sample, it is believed that findings made here with respect to the case-study schools have applicability to many schools.

In measuring changes in a law school's educational program we divide it into two components: 1) the first-year program, and 2) the second-and-third-year program or upperclass program. This division has been made for several reasons. For purposes of our analysis, the most important factor, which has been alluded to, involves the different ways in which the two programs expand—the first-year program largely by sectionalizing its basic courses, the upperclass program largely by adding new courses. The reasons for these differences are discussed

10.   22 NYCRR 520.4.
11.   American Bar Association, *Approval of Law Schools: Standards and Rules of Procedure* (A.B.A., 1973).

below. In addition to this, most law schools currently regard their last two years as essentially one program and refer to their "first year" and their "second-and-third-year." The first-year curriculum is usually prescribed and the upperclass curriculum is open to both second-and-third-year students and for this reason no meaningful distinction can be made between the last two years' programs.[12]

In connection with the distinction between the first-year and the upperclass programs, we have found that considerably more student hours are taken in the first year than in either of the last two years. This appears to be the result of two factors. First, there is student attrition between the first year and the second year, and some between the second year and the third year. Second, in the great majority of cases, students are required to take more credit hours in the first year than either of the last two. We have found that the average school has about 37% of its students in the first year class and about 63% in its second-and-third-year classes. This was determined by examining the attrition rates of a sample of 43 law schools, Appendix G sets forth the method used and our findings in detail.

From reviewing slightly over 80 current law school catalogues, we have found that the typical law school requires its students to complete about 84 credit hours and 30 of these are required to be taken in the first year. The basis for these findings are presented in Appendix D. It follows that, on the average, students take 54 credit hours during their second or third year, or average about 27 credit hours a year.[13] A similar analysis was done for the year 1955. The student load requirements were very nearly the same as they are today. In 1955, the typical law school required its students to complete about 83 credit hours and 30 of these were required to be taken in the first year. The results of this examination are also set out in Appendix D.

Section 1 – First-Year Program

In this section we examine the effect of changes in faculty size upon the first-year program. We begin with a simple description of the first-year program. As Packer and Ehrlich recently pointed out, most law schools offer what

---

12. Some courses are open only to third-year students or are open to second-year students only if third-year students have not filled all the course openings. Occasionally, a second-year course or a third-year course will be required. These situations are few and the general proposition stated in the text seems, for our purposes, essentially accurate.

13. A number of further subtleties are pertinent here. During the last two years a number of law schools allow their students to take a small number of courses in other divisions of the university. In this case, these students' hours are not properly attributable to the law school's instructional program for purposes of this analysis. On the other hand, these requirements merely set the minimum number of hours that a student must successfully complete. If a student so desires he may take more than the minimum number. It is our impression, however, that this rarely happens.

amounts to a common first-year curriculum.[14] Course requirements of first-year programs generally involve fully prescribed curricula requiring students to complete 30 credit hours of what are considered to be basic courses. Virtually every school requires torts, contracts, civil procedure, property and criminal law during the first year. Many require a legal method course and a fair number make constitutional law a first-year requirement. Furthermore, most first-year programs require instruction in legal writing, frequently taught by graduate students. A first-year program might prescribe, in addition to a legal writing requirement (for which little, if any, credit might be available), the following courses for the following amount of credit.

Contracts	6
Torts	4
Civil Procedure	6
Property	4
Criminal Law	3
Constitutional Law	4
Legal Method	3
Total credit hours	30

The findings of Alfred Z. Reed published in a 1928 study for the Carnegie Foundation for the Advancement of Teaching suggest that this general pattern has obtained for a long time. The first-year curricula of the Harvard and Michigan Law Schools for the academic year 1925-26 were as follows:[15]

University of Michigan Law School		Harvard University Law School	
Contracts	8	Contracts	6
Torts	5	Torts	6
Property	7	Property	4
Crimes	3	Crimes	4
Pleadings	5	Procedure	4
Equity	2		24
	30		

For purposes of our analysis, by far the most significant aspect of the highly structured nature of the first-year program is that, generally speaking, the first-year program of a school will be about the same whatever its student/faculty ratio is. For example, a small school will offer 30 teaching hours to its first-year class whether it has a low or high student/faculty ratio, and a

14. Herbert L. Packer and Thomas Ehrlich, *New Directions in Legal Education* (New York: McGraw-Hill, 1972), p. 28.
15. Alfred Zantzinger Reed, *Present-day Law Schools in the United States and Canada* (New York: The Carnegie Foundation for the Advancement of Teaching, 1928), p. 233.

large school will offer 60 or 90 teaching hours, depending upon its size,[16] whether it has a low or high student/faculty ratio. The conclusion to be drawn is that changes in a school's student/faculty ratio affect a school's upperclass program far more than its first-year program.

In this connection it will be seen that, as a general rule, when a school remains about the same size and its student/faculty ratio decreases, thereby producing additional teaching hours, the percent of total teaching hours made up by first-year teaching hours tends to decrease. In such cases, most, if not all, of the additional teaching hours are allocated to the second-and-third-year program. It will also be seen that, as student enrollment and faculty size increase together, there is a similar tendency for the percent of total teaching hours made up by first-year teaching hours to decrease. In sum, it will be seen that increases in a school's educational resources tend to benefit the upperclass program far more than the first-year program. Indeed, it is our conclusion that during the period examined nearly all of the significant expansion of the educational programs of law schools took place in the upperclass program. Recently, at some schools, some small sections and elective courses have been added to the first-year program.[17] Some of these innovations are discussed below. But these somewhat specialized classes constitute only a very small proportion of the whole first-year program, and, essentially, the first-year program remains highly structured. Accordingly, our principal interest in this chapter will be with the second-and-third-year program. The first-year program is relevant to our examination primarily as it relates to the upperclass program. In one sense the requirements for the first-year program in terms of teaching hours are fixed, and whatever teaching hours are left over after the first-year assignments have been made are available for the upperclass program. Consequently, much of the analysis in this section is concerned with the relative allocation of teaching hours between the first-year and the upperclass program. It should be remembered as the analysis proceeds, that percentage allocations of teaching hours for these purposes are directly equivalent to percentage allocations of instructional cost.

Expansion of the first-year curriculum at most schools, as a consequence of its fixed nature, occurs solely through the sectionalization of the basic courses, and this happens only when the size of the first-year class becomes so large that it becomes necessary to sectionalize. Thus, as a number of the case-study schools grew in student enrollment, teaching hours allotted to the first-year program tended to increase in blocs of 30; from 30 to 60 teaching hours, from 60 to 90 teaching hours, and so on. During the period studied, at several case-study schools the number of teaching hours delivered to the first-year class was not exactly divisible by 30 nor did curriculum development always entail the addition of exactly 30 teaching hours or some number of teaching hours exactly divisible by 30.[18] Nevertheless, a general pattern along these lines is plainly discernible.

---

16.   Very large schools may offer as many as 120 teaching hours to their first-year class, i.e., four sections.
17.   See Table 4.
18.   Some of the reasons for these differences are explained below.

The above analysis suggests the importance for the whole curriculum of a decision to sectionalize the first-year class. Flexibility in programing for the upperclass years may be appreciably limited by the addition of a section to each first-year course. Before a school sectionalizes its first-year class, it may consider what it gains for the first-year program by offering the core curriculum in smaller classes in return for what it gives up in alternatives for the upperclass program.[19]

Table 2 sets out the number of first-year students at each case-study school

Table 2

**Case-study Schools
Number of First-year Students and Number of
First-year Teaching Hours Delivered**

	1955	1960	1965	1970	Case-study School
En.–1st	51	83	145	165	A
T.H.–1st	30	30	60	60	
En.–1st	62	96	164	190	B
T.H.–1st	32	34	52	58	
En.–1st	72	70	136	167	C
T.H.–1st	31	30	60	60	
En.–1st	117	131	182	208	D
T.H.–1st	32	30	57	101	
En.–1st	145	156	158	171	E
T.H.–1st	30	36	66	94	
En.–1st	183	155	172	176	F
T.H.–1st	53	58	64	68	
En.–1st	277	228	342	410	G
T.H.–1st	60	81	90	103	
En.–1st	324	299	300	307	H
T.H.–1st	62	61	56	77	
En.–1st	516	333	588	517	I
T.H.–1st	110	99	116	123	

19. This point is brought out very well by a problem presented by Professor John Frank of Yale and included in the 1951 Report of the Committee on Teaching and Examination Methods to the A.A.L.S. The report states: "Professor John Frank (Yale) presents this problem: 'A middle-sized school, with 10 or 12 faculty members and a student body of, say,

for each year studied, and underneath that number, the teaching hours delivered to that first-year class. An examination of this Table indicates the curricular progression mentioned. For instance, Schools A, B, and C move from a first-year curriculum of 30 teaching hours in 1955 and 1960 to essentially one of 60 teaching hours in 1965 and 1970. Schools D and E start at about 30 hours in 1955 and 1960, and move to near 60 hours in 1965, and then to 90 hours and more in 1970. School G increases from 60 hours in 1955 to 90 hours in 1965. School I offered over 90 teaching hours to its first-year class in 1955 and 1960, and moved to a first-year curriculum of about 120 hours in 1965 and 1970. Marked increases in first-year enrollment accompanied these increases in teaching hours delivered to the first-year class. It will be observed that two sections of each first-year course, or a total first-year offering of 60 hours, seemed to be the predominant pattern for the first-year curricula of the case-study schools. As well as those instances mentioned above, Schools F and H had essentially 60-hour curricula for each year studied.

It is difficult to generalize about the level of first-year student enrollment that schools reach before they sectionalize or further sectionalize. Wide differences existed among the case-study schools. Obviously, small schools had small first-year classes. For example, in 1955, A, with a total enrollment of 130 students and a first-year enrollment of 51, necessarily had first-year classes no larger than 51 students. One may suppose that those schools in the Small Enrollment Group[20] in 1955 with total enrollments of below 100 students had proportionately smaller first-year classes. As schools increase in size, at some point they sectionalize their first-year class. A, with a first-year enrollment of 145 in 1965, offered two sections of first-year classes, each section enrolling about 70 students. Among the case-study schools, C's 1965 first-year enrollment of 136 represented the lowest level of first-year student enrollment at which sectionalization occurred. In contrast, in 1960, E had a first-year enrollment of 156 students and offered one section. H, in 1955, 1960, and 1965, had first-year enrollments of about 300 students, and offered two sections consisting of about 150 students. In sum, an examination of the case-study schools indicates that where more than one section was offered to the first-year class, the smallest of these sections enrolled about 70 students and the largest enrolled 150 students. Thus, schools offering two sections to their first-year class ranged from schools with first-year enrollments of about 140 students to schools with first-year

---

350, has to make a choice between small sections in the first year or an elective and seminar program for the upper classes. That is to say, if 10 men teach 7 hours a term, 140 class hours is the total offering for the year. If the first-year class is given 15 hours a term, all in one section, 30 of the 140 are thus disposed of. If the number of sections is doubled, 60 are disposed of, leaving 80 for the remainder of the curriculum, and diminishing electives accordingly. What are the educational merits that should effect this choice? With a large entering class next year, Yale is moving to four sections in the first year to keep size down. Our upper class offerings will be somewhat lessened accordingly. Is this sound?' This problem, it could be added, is particularly pressing for the smaller school." *A.A.L.S. Proceedings, 1951.* pp. 225-226.
20.   Small Enrollment Group schools had enrollments between 50 and 150 in 1955. See chapter 2, section 1.

enrollments of 300 students.

To demonstrate the effect of enrollment differences upon the allocation of teaching hours between the first-year and the second-and-third-year programs, we will examine two hypothetical schools: one with a first-year enrollment of 140 students, and one with a first-year enrollment of 300 students. In both cases, two sections are offered to the first-year class.[21] If we assume that the first-year enrollment of both schools' first-year classes constituted 40% of the total enrollment,[22] then the first school had a total enrollment of 350 students and the second school had a total enrollment of 750 students. If we further assume that the two schools had the same student/faculty ratios, it will be seen that there were marked differences between them in terms of the percent of total teaching hours delivered to their first-year classes.

If both schools have a student/faculty ratio of 25/1 and an average teaching load of 11 hours, the smaller school will engage 14 professors who will deliver a total of 154 teaching hours, and the larger school will engage 30 professors who will deliver a total of 330 teaching hours. In both cases only 60 teaching hours will be delivered to the first-year class. Thus, the smaller school will devote about 39% (60/154) of its total teaching hours to its first-year class, and the larger school will deliver about 18% (60/330) of its total teaching hours to its first-year class.

Translating these differences into cost terms, the smaller school will devote 39% of its instructional expenditures to its first-year program, whereas the larger school will devote 18% of its instructional expenditures to its first-year program. At the same time the instructional cost of both schools' first-year programs (assuming no variation in salaries) in absolute terms is identical. To view the same phenomenon from another standpoint, the cost of an average second-and-third-year course at the small school is 21% higher than the cost of one of its first-year sections, whereas the cost of an average second-and-third-year course at the larger school is 246% higher than the cost of one of its first-year sections. This example demonstrates the marked differences that the level of student enrollment makes upon the percentage allocation of total teaching hours to the first-year class and the marked differences in allocation of instructional cost between the first-year and upperclass programs.

Of course, some schools might add a third section before they reach first-year enrollments of 300 students. For instance, a school with a total enrollment of 525 and a first-year enrollment of 210 might have three sections, each consisting of 70 students. However, the same principle applies. The schools with enrollments between 350[23] and 525, having a constant student/faculty ratio and offering only two sections to their first-year class, will follow a pattern such that the higher-enrollment schools will devote a smaller percent of their total teaching hours to their first-year classes than the schools with the lower

21.   Of course, schools might further sectionalize their first-year class before they reach enrollment levels as high as 300. This possibility is discussed below.
22.   See Appendix G.
23.   It will be recalled that a school with a total enrollment of 350 by hypothesis has a first-year enrollment of 140 and first-year sections of 70.

enrollments. Similarly, schools offering three sections to their first-year class might range in size from 525 students to 1,125 students. The latter school would have a first-year enrollment of 450 students with 150 students in each section. In this case also, schools with higher enrollments will devote a smaller percent of their total teaching hours to first-year classes than schools with lower enrollments. Of course, some schools will add a fourth section before they reach first-year enrollments of 450 students.

In sum, as schools increase in size and maintain a constant student/faculty ratio, first-year teaching hours constitute a decreasing proportion of total teaching hours. At some point, however, enrollments reach levels at which an additional section is added to the first-year program and, at this point, the percent of total teaching hours allotted to the first-year class increases sharply. It will decline from this level as enrollment grows until another point is reached where further sectionalization occurs.

Thus far, our analysis has assumed that the schools had identical student/faculty ratios. We shall now examine the effect of student/faculty ratio changes upon the allocation of teaching hours between the first-year and upperclass programs. At any given enrollment level those schools with lower student/faculty ratios will necessarily devote a smaller proportion of their total teaching hours to the first-year program. For instance, assume two schools of 450 students which offer two sections to their identically sized first-year classes of 180 students. The first school has a student/faculty ratio of 25/1 and the second school has a student/faculty ratio of 20/1. With identical teaching loads of 11 hours, the first school will engage 18 professors (450 ÷ 25 = 18) who will deliver a total of 198 teaching hours (18 × 11 = 198), and the second school will engage 22.5 professors (450 ÷ 20 = 22.5) who will deliver a total of 247 teaching hours (22.5 × 11 = 247). Therefore, the school with the larger student/faculty ratio will devote about 30% (60/198) of its total teaching hours to its first-year class, and the school with the smaller student/faculty ratio will devote about 24% (60/247) of its total teaching hours to its first-year class. It is evident that the school with the higher student/faculty ratio offers fewer total teaching hours than the school with the lower student/faculty ratio. Furthermore, the higher student/faculty ratio school devotes a larger percent of its (fewer) total teaching hours to the first-year class than the lower student/faculty ratio school. To regard the same situation from the aspect of the second-and-third-year program, the higher student/faculty ratio school devotes a smaller percent of its (fewer) total teaching hours to its upperclass program than the lower student/faculty ratio school.

Translating these differences into cost terms, the school with the higher student/faculty ratio devotes 30% of its instructional expenditures to its first-year class while the school with the lower student/faculty ratio devotes 24% of its instructional expenditures to its first-year class. At the same time, the cost of both schools' first-year classes is identical. To view the same matter from another standpoint, the cost of an average second-and-third-year course at the school with the higher student/faculty ratio is about 80% higher than one of its first-year sections, whereas the cost of an average second-and-third-year course at the school with the lower student/faculty ratio is 140% higher than one of its first-year sections.

From what has been said so far, it is clear that two major variables—student/faculty ratio and size of student enrollment—affect the relationship involving the allocation of resources between the first-year and upperclass programs. Increases in faculty size attributable to student/faculty ratio decreases or enrollment increases may result in a higher allocation of total teaching hours being made to the second-and-third-year classes and a lower allocation to the first-year class. These two factors may also work in conjunction to produce a proportionately higher allocation of teaching hours to the upperclass program than to the first-year program, or against each other to bring the teaching-hour allocations between the two programs closer together. The first case might involve a situation where enrollment increases are accompanied by decreases in the school's student/faculty ratio. If the extent of the enrollment increases is not such as to cause sectionalization or further sectionalization of the first-year program, the decrease in the proportionate allocation of total teaching hours to the first-year class will be very marked. The second case might involve a situation where enrollment decreases are accompanied by increases in the school's student/faculty ratio. In this case the proportionate allocation of total teaching hours to the first-year class will increase. Finally, it may happen that student/faculty ratio increases are accompanied by enrollment increases such as to cause sectionalization or further sectionalization of the first-year program. In this case the proportionate allocation of total teaching hours to the first-year class will also increase.

We shall now examine our case-study schools in the terms developed above. Table 3 sets out the total enrollment of each case-study school for each year studied, and next to it in parenthesis, the school's student/faculty ratio for that year. The number of first-year students is shown on the second line. The third line shows the number of teaching hours delivered to each first-year class, and next to it in parenthesis, is the percent that this number represents of total teaching hours delivered to all classes at the school. Several of the conclusions reached in the above analysis are illustrated in this Table. School C between the years 1955 and 1960, and Schools F and I between the years 1965 and 1970, are examples of the case where a school's student/faculty ratio decreases and enrollment remains fairly constant, thus producing a larger number of total teaching hours. Because the first-year program remained fixed, virtually all the additional teaching hours were allocated to the upperclass program, and the percent of total teaching hours devoted to the first-year program decreased.[24]

School F between the years 1960 and 1965, and School I between the years 1955 and 1965, are examples of the following development. Student enrollment increased but not to the extent of requiring further sectionalization of the

---

24.   Rarely do the examples exactly parallel the proposition for which they are cited, but the general pattern of the exampled schools' development does provide illustrations of the formulations.

Table 3

Case-study Schools
Total Enrollment, School's Student/Faculty Ratio,
Number of First-year Students, Number of First-year Teaching Hours
Delivered, and Percent of Total Teaching Hours Delivered at School

	1955	1960	1965	1970	Case-study School
En.–Total (S/F Ratio)	130 (15.8/1)	180 (14.5/1)	360 (22.3/1)	440 (20.5/1)	
En.–1st	51	83	145	165	A
T.H.–1st (% of Total)	30 (31%)	30 (24%)	60 (33%)	60 (28%)	
En.–Total (S/F Ratio)	120 (17.5/1)	190 (24.7/1)	350 (29.7/1)	470 (26.8/1)	
En.–1st	62	96	164	190	B
T.H.–1st (% of Total)	32 (32%)	34 (32%)	52 (39%)	58 (32%)	
En.–Total (S/F Ratio)	160 (19.3/1)	150 (14.2/1)	280 (24.1/1)	390 (26.1/1)	
En.–1st	72	70	136	167	C
T.H.–1st (% of Total)	31 (26%)	30 (24%)	60 (45%)	60 (34%)	
En.–Total (S/F Ratio)	230 (23.2/1)	300 (29.6/1)	450 (33/1)	510 (18.6/1)	
En.–1st	117	131	182	208	D
T.H.–1st (% of Total)	32 (27%)	30 (26%)	57 (39%)	101 (32%)	
En.–Total (S/F Ratio)	320 (25.4/1)	370 (20.6/1)	440 (18.2/1)	410 (18/1)	
En.–1st	145	156	158	171	E
T.H.–1st (% of Total)	30 (26%)	36 (22%)	66 (28%)	94 (32%)	
En.–Total (S/F Ratio)	350 (22.5/1)	390 (21.8/1)	480 (21.7/1)	470 (19.6/1)	
En.–1st	183	155	172	176	F
T.H.–1st (% of Total)	53 (30%)	58 (29%)	64 (27%)	68 (23%)	
En.–Total (S/F Ratio)	620 (49.9/1)	500 (30.7/1)	740 (34.6/1)	960 (29.2/1)	
En.–1st	277	228	342	410	G
T.H.–1st (% of Total)	60 (31%)	81 (37%)	90 (37%)	103 (29%)	
En.–Total (S/F Ratio)	740 (28.5/1)	800 (25.3/1)	890 (23.7/1)	1,040 (21.7/1)	
En.–1st	324	299	300	307	H
T.H.–1st (% of Total)	62 (26%)	61 (20%)	56 (16%)	77 (18%)	
En.–Total (S/F Ratio)	900 (41/1)	830 (29.7/1)	1,540 (40.4/1)	1,580 (37.6/1)	
En.–1st	516	333	588	517	I
T.H.–1st (% of Total)	110 (40%)	99 (33%)	116 (28%)	123 (27%)	

first-year class. Growth in faculty size fairly paralleled growth in enrollment, and growth in teaching hours accompanied growth in faculty size. Because of the fixed nature of the first-year program all the additional teaching hours made available by the faculty expansion were allotted to the upperclass program, with the result that the proportion of total teaching hours allotted to the upper classes increased and the proportion allotted to the first-year class decreased.

School A between the years 1955 and 1960, and Schools A, B, and G between 1965 and 1970, are examples where enrollment grew, but not to such an extent as to require sectionalization of first-year courses, and where student/faculty ratio decreased. For the school years in question both changing variables acted together to decrease substantially the percent of total teaching hours devoted to the first-year program and to increase substantially the percent of total teaching hours devoted to the second-and-third-year program.

At some point, however, as a school expands in size, sectionalization of the first-year class will occur. Schools A, C, and D between the years 1960 and 1965 are examples of this development. In these cases the percent of total teaching hours constituted by first-year teaching hours increased. The increase was particularly marked because faculty increases did not keep pace with increases in enrollment. School G between the years 1955 and 1965 is an example of enrollment increase accompanied by a decrease in student/faculty ratio. In this case there was an offset between the two variables, and the percent of total teaching hours made up of first-year teaching hours increased a relatively small amount, notwithstanding the fact that the first-year class sectionalized between these years.

As indicated above, where increases in the percent of teaching hours devoted to the first-year program occur because of sectionalization, it frequently happens that after a period of time the percent decreases to the earlier level. Typically, further enrollment increases occur, but not to the extent of requiring further sectionalization. Furthermore, these increases will be accompanied by parallel increases in faculty, or perhaps even a lowering of the student/faculty ratio, which will produce additional teaching hours that are allocated exclusively to the upperclass program. This results in the lowering of the percent of total teaching hours delivered to the first-year class, which consequently moves down toward its original level. Schools A, B, C, D, and G between the years 1965 and 1970 are examples of this development.

Thus far, the analysis of the first-year program has assumed a standard first-year curriculum. Changes referred to have involved only sectionalization of the basic courses. As indicated above, however, there appears to be a recent trend in legal education involving the institution of small sections in the first-year curriculum. The objective of such a program is to provide the first-year students with some of the benefits of small-class instruction. Among the case-study schools, G in 1960, and E and H in 1970, had such programs. Table 4 sets out the first-year offerings of these three schools. It will be noted that in one case, courses are offered in subject-matter areas usually reserved for the second-and-third-year program.

In connection with the discussion above regarding allocation of teaching hours, it will be observed that two of the three examples cited (E and H) managed to keep the allocation of their first-year teaching hours near 30%. In fact, H offered only 18% of total teaching hours to its first-year class. These schools were able to offer a substantially expanded first-year program, and still manage to keep the percent of total teaching hours devoted to their first-year program proportionately lower than the percent of teaching hours devoted to their upperclass program, because of their low student/faculty ratios. In contrast, G in 1960, with a 31/1 student/faculty ratio, had 37% of its total

Table 4

**First-year Course Offerings and Teaching Hours
at Three Case-study Schools, by Sections**

Course	Number of Students	Number of Teaching Hours Section								
		1	2	3	4	5	6	7	8	9
Torts	171	4	4	4	4	4				
Civil Procedure I		3	3							
Civil Procedure II		2	2							
Contracts I		4	4							
Contracts II		2	2							
Criminal Law		4	4	4						
Legal Process		3	3	3	3					
Property		4	4	4						
Constitutional Law		4	4	4	4					
		30	30	19	11	4				
Torts	228	6	6							
Procedure I		3	3							
Procedure II		3	3							
Contracts I		3	3							
Contracts II		3	3							
Criminal Law		3	3							
Legal Method		3	3	3	3	3	3	3	3	3
Property I		3	3							
Property II		3	3							
		30	30	3	3	3	3	3	3	3
Torts	307	4	4							
Civil Procedure I		4	4							
Civil Procedure II		2	2							
Contracts I		3	3							
Contracts II		3	3							
Criminal Law		3	3							
Legal Method		3	3							
Property		3	3							
Electives		3	3	3	3	3	3	3	3	3
Trade Regulation, Law & Poverty, International Law, Federal Income Taxation, Administrative Law, Labor Law, Constitutional Law										
		28	28	3	3	3	3	3	3	3

teaching hours devoted to its first-year class as a result of its expanded program.[25]

Section 2 — Second-and-Third-Year Program: Static Analysis

We are now in a position to examine the second-and-third-year educational programs of law schools. This examination will have two parts. In this section, through the development of hypothetical or model law schools, an analysis will be made of what schools are likely to be able to do with their upperclass educational programs at different student/faculty ratios and different enrollments. In the next section, a descriptive and historical examination will be made of what, in fact, happened between 1955 and 1970.

To demonstrate more fully the relationship between a school's student/faculty ratio and its second-and-third-year educational program, several hypothetical models will be constructed of schools having differing student/faculty ratios but identical characteristics so far as all other relevant variables are concerned. Initially, four such models will be constructed. In each model the school enrolls 450 students—180, or 40%, in the first-year class, and 270, or 60%, in the second-and-third-year class. First-year students are required to complete 30 credit hours and second-and-third-year students are required to complete, on the average, 26 credit hours each year. In each case it is assumed that first-year courses are given in two sections. Thus, 60 teaching hours are delivered to the first-year class. With a first-year class of 180 students, each first-year section will contain 90 students, which, as indicated above,[26] is not large as first-year sections go. Each school operates with an average teaching load of 11 hours.[27] Each school's second- and third-year students complete a total of 7,020 student hours a year.[28]

It will be noted that the model schools are constructed on the basis of variables that we found to be typical in 1970. It was shown in chapter 2 that the median school enrollment in 1970 was 461 students. In section 1 of this chapter, we indicated that a teaching load of 11 hours per year was typical at many schools in 1970, and that attrition rates usually resulted in the first-year class having about 40% of a school's total enrollment.[29] Furthermore, the four student/faculty ratios used below represent the typical student/faculty ratios

---

25. If School G had offered only 60 hours in 1960 as it offered in 1955 when it had a larger first-year enrollment, only 27% of its total teaching hours would have been devoted to its first-year class.
26. See section 1, Table 3.
27. Between the two years supposed in the examples below, it is assumed teaching load remains constant. On this assumption, the only manner in which a school can increase its teaching hours and thus expand its educational program is by increasing the size of its faculty.
28. 270 students each taking 26 credit hours.
29. As indicated in the Introduction, we have found on the basis of attrition rates that the average proportion of total students in the first-year class is 37% and in the second-and-third-year class, 63%. In constructing the hypothetical models, we use the 40%-60% to simplify the arithmetic. The differences that result in any case are minimal.

that obtained in 1970. Accordingly, while the schools we examine below are only hypothetical models, we believe that they represent, at least in general terms, what is likely to have been the case at a good number of schools in 1970.

The four models are:

School A having a student/faculty ratio of 35/1,
School B having a student/faculty ratio of 30/1,
School C having a student/faculty ratio of 25/1,
School D having a student/faculty ratio of 20/1.[30]

The basic data with regard to these four model schools are set out in Table 5.

Table 5

Basic Data for Four Model Schools

	A	B	C	D
Enrollment, total	450	450	450	450
Student/Faculty ratio	35/1	30/1	25/1	20/1
Faculty size	12.9	15	18	22.5
Average teaching load (hours)	11	11	11	11
Total teaching hours delivered	142	165	198	248
Teaching hours delivered to first-year class	60	60	60	60
Teaching hours delivered to 2nd-&-3rd-year classes	82	105	138	188
Equivalent faculty teaching 2nd-&-3rd-year classes	7.5	9.5	12.5	17.1
Enrollment of 2nd-&-3rd-year classes	270	270	270	270
Effective student/faculty ratio of 2nd-&-3rd-year classes	36/1	28.4/1	21.6/1	15.8/1
Average class size of 2nd-&-3rd-year classes	86	67	51	37

The effective student/faculty ratio for the second-and-third-year class is computed by dividing average teaching load into the number of teaching hours delivered to the second-and-third-year class. This produces the equivalent number of faculty members that would be needed to offer the number of teaching hours actually delivered to the upperclass program. This figure is then divided into the number of second-and-third-year students to determine what we call the "effective student/faculty ratio" for the second-and-third-year class.

It will be noted from Table 5 that the effective student/faculty ratios for the second-and-third-year classes of the four model schools are: School A, 36/1; School B, 28.4/1; School C, 21.6/1; School D, 15.8/1. The effective first-year student/faculty ratio for each model school is 33/1.[31] (In dollar terms, all four

30.   The educational program of a school having a student/faculty ratio of 16/1 is examined below in Table 8.
31.   The effective first-year student/faculty ratio is derived in a similar manner to that explained above regarding the effective second-and-third-year student/faculty ratio. For School A, for example, $60 \div 11 = 5.45$, $180 \div 5.45 = 33$.

schools' first-year programs will have identical instructional costs.) It will be noted that in cases of very high over-all student/faculty ratios, such as School A, the effective first-year student/faculty ratio will be lower than the effective second-and-third-year student/faculty ratio. Consistent with what was said in section 1 regarding the relationship between the first-year program and the second-and-third-year program, the effective second-and-third-year student/faculty ratio decreases at a considerably sharper rate than the over-all student/faculty ratio.

Table 6

Upperclass Total and Per-student Instructional Cost, Assuming Input Cost of $25,000

Model School	Total Upperclass Instructional Cost	Per-student Upperclass Instructional Cost
A	$187,500	$ 694
B	$237,500	$ 880
C	$312,500	$1,157
D	$427,500	$1,583

	First Year Classes	
All Schools	$136,250	$ 757

Table 6 sets out the upperclass total instructional cost and the upperclass per-student instructional cost for each of the schools on the assumption of an average faculty salary of $25,000.[32] The total instructional cost is derived by multiplying the equivalent number of faculty members teaching in the second-and-third-year program at each school by $25,000; the per-student instructional cost by dividing these figures by 270, the enrollment of the second-and-third-year classes. Thus, the instructional cost of the upperclass program of School B will be 27% more expensive than that of School A, the upperclass program of School C will be 32% more expensive than that of School B, and 67% more expensive than that of School A, and the upperclass program of School D will be 37% more expensive than that of School C, 80% more expensive than that of School B, and 128% more expensive than that of School A. Because the schools have identically sized student bodies, the differences among the schools' total instructional costs will be the same as the differences among their per-student costs. Below we shall examine in greater detail the fiscal implications of varying student/faculty ratios.

It will be noted from Table 5 that the schools vary considerably in the number of teaching hours offered to their upperclasses. School A offers 82

---

32. It will be recalled that all four schools have identical first-year instructional costs because all have 180 first-year students and a 33/1 faculty ratio. Each school's first-year-class total instructional cost is $136,250 and per-student instructional cost is $757.

teaching hours to its second-and-third-year classes; School B, 105; School C, 138; and School D, 188. First, we will examine the implications of these differences on the of the four schools' upperclass curricula in terms of subject-matter coverage, and then implications of these differences on the sizes of the second-and-third-year classes of these schools. Unlike the first-year program, where the addition of teaching hours usually involves the sectionalization of basic courses, it will be shown that increments in upperclass teaching hours usually involve not sectionalization but rather the addition of new subject-matter courses. Therefore, it may be assumed that the schools with the lower student/faculty ratios, C and D, have more extensive curricula than the schools with the higher student/faculty ratios, A and B. Table 7 sets forth the number of courses offered to the upperclasses at the four model schools on the assumption that no sectionalization existed in the upperclasses and that the average upperclass course involved 3 teaching hours.

Table 7

Number of Courses Offered to Upperclass

Model School

A	B	C	D
27	35	46	63

School D, for example, offers more than twice as many courses as School A.[33]

Average class size is determined by dividing teaching hours into student hours. Thus, one determines the average class size of Schools A, B, C, and D, by dividing 7,020 by 82, 105, 138, and 188, respectively. This produces an average class size of 86 students for A,[34] 67 students for B, 51 students for C, and 37 students for D.

Average class size does not disclose any detailed information about the mix of a school's classes between large, medium-sized, and small classes. Although it can be inferred that A has mostly large classes and D has mostly small classes, the proportion of each size class to the total number of classes is not revealed. The analysis that follows tests the alternative mixes available for each school.

To do this we have designated in terms of student enrollment three types of classes: Large classes, Medium classes, and Small classes. Large classes are those that enroll over 100 students. Medium classes are those that enroll between 35 and 99 students, and Small classes are those that enroll between 1 and 34

---

33. The nature of the courses added to law school curricula between 1955 and 1970 is discussed in section 3.
34. Thus, the average second-and-third-year class size of School A is nearly the same size as its first-year sections. It might be expected that, because the effective first-year student/faculty ratio is lower than the second-and-third-year effective student/faculty ratio, the first-year sections would be smaller than the average second-and-third-year courses. The variance lies in the different student loads of the first-year and upperclass students.

students. The selection of the enrollment limits for the Large, Medium, and Small classes has been somewhat arbitrary; however, each such class size represents a distinctive type of law school offering. For example, Small classes include seminars, and although this type of offering is frequently limited to 15 or even fewer students, large seminars and colloquia often reach levels of 34. Clinical programs, usually regarded as small class instruction, may also enroll as many as 34 students. The category of Medium classes is, perhaps, the most arbitrary of the three. In our analysis, it involves all those classes that fall between 35 and 99 students. There does, however, appear to be a type of law school course which, in terms of size, is between the seminar, or plainly small class, and the large upperclass offering. Frequently, it will involve a somewhat specialized or advanced course and enroll about 50 students. Large second-and-third-year classes are readily identifiable. The decision to draw the line between Medium and Large classes at 100 is, of course, entirely arbitrary, but second-and-third-year classes of around 120 students or higher are justifiably regarded as Large classes. As the analysis proceeds, it will be recognized that, although the class size distinctions we use are somewhat arbitrary, some such classification had to be made and, for analytical purposes, it does not really matter what the precise limits of each class size are. In any event, our examination of the case-study schools has suggested to us that, at schools of fair-sized and large enrollments, there do exist three types of class sizes. In this connection it should be noted that only schools with fair-sized enrollments have class mixes involving all three types of classes. In section 3 below it will be shown that the schools in the Small Enrollment Group in 1955 had only Small and Medium classes and a few such schools had only Small classes.

In analyzing the case-study schools our method involves grouping all the second-and-third-year classes that fall within the limits of a particular class size and determining the average size of all such classes. In constructing the hypothetical models below we assume that Small classes average 20 students, Medium classes average between 60 and 70 students, and Large classes average 120 students. These levels are fairly representative of what obtained at the case-study schools. To test the alternative mix of class sizes for the model schools, we start by assigning a given percent of each school's total upperclass student hours to Small classes and then observe what alternatives remain for Large and Medium classes. We begin by assuming that a school wishes to offer enough teaching hours so as to enable every upperclass student to enroll in one Small class. If such classes are deemed to consist of 2 credit hours, with a total of 270 students in the second-and-third-years, 540 student hours would be taken in Small classes. If these classes average 20 students, 27 teaching hours would have to be allocated to such Small classes in order to achieve the minimum objective of one Small class offering for each upperclass student.

If School A provided such Small class offerings, 55 teaching hours would be left to cover the remaining classes (82 upperclass teaching hours less 27). As only 540 of the total of 7,020 student hours taken by upperclass students would be taken in these Small classes, the remaining 6,480 student hours (7,020 − 540 =

6,480) would be covered by the remaining 55 teaching hours with the result that all of these remaining student hours would be in classes averaging close to 118 students (6,480 ÷ 55 = 118). In effect, then, all of these remaining student hours would be in Large classes. Schematically this arrangement would look like this.

Student Hours		Class		Teaching Hours	
%	Number	Category	Av. Size	%	Number
92%	6,480	Large	118	67%	55
8%	540	Small	20	33%	27

One-third of upperclass teaching hours would be devoted to instructing 8% of all upperclass student hours and all the remaining upperclass student hours would be Large classes. Thus, nearly all of a student's upperclass experience (and, indeed, virtually all of his law school experience) at School A would be in Large classes. As indicated in section 3 below, the highest percent of student hours taken in Large classes at any of the case-study schools during the period examined was 74%. We believe, therefore, that it is unlikely that a school, such as School A, with a 35/1 student/faculty ratio and a teaching load of 11 hours would choose to offer one class of Small class instruction to each of its second-and-third-year students.[35]

A school with A's characteristics could, however, offer up to 3% of its upperclass student hours in Small classes. If 3% of its student hours are to be in Small classes, then 210.6 student hours (7,020 × .03 = 210.6) will be in such classes, and 10.5 teaching hours (210.6 ÷ 20 = 10.5), or about 13% of the total teaching hours, will be used to instruct these classes. In these circumstances, 60% of the remaining student hours could be in Large classes averaging 120 students and 37% of such student hours could be in Medium classes averaging 71 students. Schematically this arrangement looks like this.

Student Hours		Class		Teaching Hours	
%	Number	Category	Av. Size	%	Number
60%	4,212	Large	120	43%	35.1
37%	2,597.4	Medium	71	44%	36.4
3%	210.6	Small	20	13%	10.5

If less than 60% of student hours were in Large classes, Medium classes would rise above 71 students, and the differences between Large classes and Medium classes would become so attenuated as to be meaningless. Furthermore, if as much as 5% of student hours were taken in Small classes then about 70% of student hours would have to be taken in Large classes as the scheme below demonstrates.

---

35.   Of course, if a school with a 35/1 student/faculty ratio operated with a materially higher teaching load, it would be in a better position to offer a greater number of its upperclass teaching hours in Small classes. The matter of teaching load is discussed below.

Student Hours		Class		Teaching Hours	
%	Number	Category	Av. Size	%	Number
70%	4,914	Large	120	50%	41.0
25%	1,755	Medium	75	28.5%	23.4
5%	351	Small	20	21.5%	17.6

In other words, an increase of 2% in the number of student hours taken in Small classes in these circumstances would produce an increase of 10% in the proportion of student hours taken in Large classes.[36] Furthermore the increase of 2% of student hours taken in Small classes requires an 8.5% increase in teaching hours. This example demonstrates how relatively small changes in the number of student hours taken in Small classes require substantial changes in the rest of the educational program. The leverage effect of Small classes is greatest for schools with high student/faculty ratios, but we will observe below a similar phenomenon in schools with lower student/faculty ratios. These calculations demonstrate that schools with student/faculty ratios of 35/1 and higher are severely limited in their ability to offer a Small class program to their second-and-third-year students. As the percent of student hours in Small classes goes beyond the most minimal level, such schools are forced to give nearly all of their remaining courses in very large classes.

School B, with a 30/1 student/faculty ratio, would be able to offer a program pursuant to which its upperclass students could take about 10% of their student hours in Small classes. Under these circumstances School B would offer only slightly more than one 2-credit-hour course of Small class instruction to each of its upperclass students. (It will be recalled that such a minimum offering would entail 8% of a school's upperclass student hours being taken in Small classes.) Such an arrangement would be as follows.[37]

Student Hours		Class		Teaching Hours	
%	Number	Category	Av. Size	%	Number
50%	3,510	Large	120	28%	29.3
40%	2,808	Medium	69	38.5%	40.6
10%	702	Small	20	33.5%	35.1

36. Note that with these changes the average Medium class has increased to 75 students.
37. Note that if the percentage devoted to Large and Medium classes were reversed the arrangement would be as follows. Here, Medium class size reaches a level that begins to eliminate meaningful distinctions between Large and Medium classes.

Student Hours		Class		Teaching Hours	
%	Number	Category	Av. Size	%	Number
40%	2,808	Large	120	23%	23.4
50%	3,510	Medium	75	44%	46.5
10%	702	Small	20	33%	35.1

An attempt by School B to increase its Small class program to include 15% of student hours would produce a mix which in effect would entail two types—Small classes and Large classes—and the percent of student hours taken in Large classes in these circumstances would constitute a very high amount. Such an arrangement would be as follows.

Student Hours		Class		Teaching Hours	
%	Number	Category	Av. Size	%	Number
75%	5,265	Large	120	42%	43.9
10%	702	Medium	84	8%	8.4
15%	1,053	Small	20	50%	52.7

School C, with a 25/1 student/faculty ratio, can offer 20% of its total student hours in Small classes. Such an arrangement would be as follows.[38]

Student Hours		Class		Teaching Hours	
%	Number	Category	Av. Size	%	Number
35%	2,457	Large	120	15%	20.5
45%	3,159	Medium	67	34%	47.3
20%	1,404	Small	20	51%	70.2

An attempt by School C to raise its Small class program to 25% of total student hours would produce a mix that would begin to move toward a position where the upperclass program would have only two types of classes—Large and Small. Such an arrangement would be as follows.

Student Hours		Class		Teaching Hours	
%	Number	Category	Av. Size	%	Number
60%	4,212	Large	120	25.5%	35.1
15%	1,053	Medium	70	11%	15.1
25%	1,755	Small	20	63.5%	87.8

38. Different combinations of Large and Medium classes could be developed and still result in feasible programs. Two such combinations are as follows.

Student Hours		Class		Teaching Hours	
%	Number	Category	Av. Size	%	Number
40%	2,808	Large	120	17%	23.4
40%	2,808	Medium	63	32%	44.4
20%	1,404	Small	20	51%	70.2
30%	2,106	Large	120	13%	17.6
50%	3,510	Medium	69	36%	50.2
20%	1,404	Small	20	51%	70.2

Note that a 5% increase in the number of student hours taken in Small classes resulted in a 25% increase in the number of student hours taken in Large classes.[39]

School D, with a 20/1 student/faculty ratio, is able to structure its second-and-third-year program in a number of ways that, in comparison with the other schools, allows it to offer a larger number of Small classes. Some of these possibilities are as follows.

Student Hours		Class		Teaching Hours	
%	Number	Category	Av. Size	%	Number
40%	2,808	Large	120	12.5%	23.4
20%	1,404	Medium	58	13%	24.2
40%	2,808	Small	20	74.5%	140.4
30%	2,106	Large	120	9%	17.6
30%	2,106	Medium	70	16%	30.0
40%	2,808	Small	20	75%	140.4
30%	2,106	Large	120	10%	17.6
35%	2,457	Medium	52	25%	47.5
35%	2,457	Small	20	65%	122.9
70%	4,914	Medium	59	44%	82.7
30%	2,106	Small	20	56%	105.3

Obviously, any school with a student/faculty ratio below 20/1 would be able to offer an even larger Small class program than School D. In the Introduction and Summary it was pointed out that the average student/faculty ratio for all divisions of higher education today is about 16/1.[40] Under the circumstances supposed above, the average size of a second-and-third-year class for such a school would be 28. Table 8 sets out the relevant characteristics of a law school similar to those examined above, with a student/faculty ratio of 16/1.

---

39.   If the curriculum was rearranged to reduce the number of student hours being taken in Large classes, the average size of the Medium classes would rise to such a level as, perhaps, to make the change meaningless, as the following shows.

Student Hours		Class		Teaching Hours	
%	Number	Category	Av. Size	%	Number
50%	3,510	Large	120	21%	29.2
25%	1,755	Medium	84	15%	21
25%	1,755	Small	20	64%	87.8

40.   See the Introduction and Summary, Summary.

Table 8

Data for a Model School With
a 16/1 Student/Faculty Ratio

Enrollment, total	450
Student/faculty ratio	16/1
Faculty size	28
Average teaching load (hours)	11
Total teaching hours delivered	308
Teaching hours delivered to first-year class	60
Teaching hours delivered to 2nd-&-3rd-year classes	248
Equivalent faculty teaching 2nd-&-3rd-year classes	22.5
Enrollment of 2nd-&-3rd-year classes	270
Effective student/faculty ratio of 2nd-&-3rd-year classes	12/1
Average class size of 2nd-&-3rd-year classes	28

Such a school would be able to offer a program pursuant to which its upperclass students could take half of their student hours in Small classes and half of their student hours in Medium classes of quite small enrollments. Such an arrangement would be as follows.

Student Hours		Class		Teaching Hours	
%	Number	Category	Av. Size	%	Number
50%	3,510	Medium	48	29%	72.5
50%	3,510	Small	20	71%	175.5

Of course, such a school may choose to offer a number of its upperclass courses in Large classes even though not required to do so in order to cover the requisite number of student hours. For instance, some courses taught by faculty members of particular distinction might be given in Large classes. In addition, some teachers believe that they can better teach certain subject matters in Large classes. Furthermore, teachers might prefer teaching one large section and a separate subject to teaching two small sections of the same course. Assuming a decision was made to offer 10% of its upperclass teaching hours in Large classes, the arrangement of classes at this hypothetical school might be as follows.

Student Hours		Class		Teaching Hours	
%	Number	Category	Av. Size	%	Number
42%	2,976	Large	120	10%	24.8
18%	1,236	Medium	34	15%	36
40%	2,808	Small	15	75%	187.2

It will be noted that, as a result of offering a few of its courses in Large classes, the school would be able to increase the number of its Small class courses and reduce the size of its Medium and Small classes.

It is likely, of course, that a law school with a 16/1 student/faculty ratio would offer a more elaborate first-year program, using more teaching hours than assumed above for Models A, B, C, and D, and such a development would somewhat reduce the number of teaching hours available for the upperclass program. In addition, it is likely that such a school would operate with a lower teaching load than 11 hours per instructor, and this, too, would cause a reduction in the number of teaching hours available for the upperclass program.[41] In any event, it is clear that law schools with fair-sized enrollments and student/faculty ratios of 16/1 would be in a position to provide upperclass programs offering highly enriched curricula, a large number of Small classes, and a considerable amount of individualized instruction.

For schools which possess variables similar to those of the model schools, the various options described above are open. Of course, such pertinent variables differ among law schools. Most importantly, some schools operate with higher teaching loads than 11 hours a year, some with lower teaching loads, and few have their student hours allocated in the same proportion as the hypothetical schools. While these differences alter the exact arithmetic of the analysis, the examination demonstrates the essential relationships between the second-and-third-year instructional programs of schools with differing student/faculty ratios.[42]

We shall now compare the upperclass instructional cost of School C, with a 25/1 student/faculty ratio and a 21.6/1 effective upperclass student/faculty ratio, with the upperclass instructional cost of School D, with a 20/1 student/faculty ratio and a 15.8/1 effective upperclass student/faculty ratio. It will be recalled that we have assumed that both these schools have $25,000 as their average annual faculty salaries. There are a variety of means—different perspectives on the same phenomena—by which to assess differences in instructional cost. First, by comparing the two schools' upperclass student/faculty ratios, it can be determined that the upperclass instructional cost

---

41. See discussion of teaching hours below.
42. Similar to the matter of differences in faculty teaching load, issues relating to the distribution of a school's teaching load among its faculty also come up when differences in class size are considered. For instance, a teacher who has all Small classes covers far fewer student hours than a teacher who has all Large classes, or, for that matter, than a teacher who has a mix of Large, Medium, and Small classes. This aspect of teaching parity is put into sharper focus when it is recognized that faculty members not only differ with respect to the size of classes they teach but also with respect to teaching load. Thus, to make the point most dramatically, one faculty member may teach Small classes at a reduced load of six hours, for example, teaching three seminars each carrying two credits and which enroll about 20 students. Another teacher might lecture to all Large classes at an increased load of 12 hours, for example, teaching four classes each carrying three credits and which enroll about 120 students. In this example, the first teacher will cover 120 student hours and the second 1440 student hours. As indicated above, it is not within the purview of this study's objectives to examine these questions of faculty parity.

at School D is about 37% higher than at School C ($21.6 \div 15.8 = 1.37$). In dollar terms, as School C allotted the equivalent of 12.5 faculty members to its upperclass program, its total upperclass instructional cost would be $312,500 ($12.5 \times \$25,000 = \$312,500$) and its per-student cost would be \$1,157.41 ($\$312,500 \div 270 = \$1,157.41$). School D allotted the equivalent of 17.1 faculty members to its upperclass program and its total upperclass instructional cost amounted to \$427,500 ($17.1 \times \$25,000 = \$427,500$) with a per-student cost of \$1,583.33.

Viewing these differences from another perspective, we determine what the effective upperclass student/faculty ratio and the per-student cost would be if every class were a Small class, if every class were a Medium class, or if every class were a Large class. We have assumed that a Small class enrolls 20 students. If every course that was given in the second and third years averaged 20 students, 351 teaching hours would be given to the upperclass program.[43] With each faculty member averaging 11 hours a year, the equivalent of about 32 faculty members ($351 \div 11 = 31.9$) would be allotted to the upperclass program. At this level of faculty size, a school would have an effective upperclass student/faculty ratio of about 8.5/1 ($270 \div 31.9 = 8.5$). This, of course, would be true for schools of any enrollment with average teaching loads of 11 hours. Thus, such small-class programs may be viewed as operating with a student/faculty ratio of 8.5/1. In dollar terms, the per-student instructional cost at this student/faculty ratio would be \$2,941.18. As each student is expected to complete 26 hours a year, the cost per student hour would be \$113.12.

A similar analysis can be made for Large classes assumed to enroll 120 students and Medium classes assumed to enroll 65 students. Large classes may be viewed as operating at an effective upperclass student/faculty ratio of 50.8/1, at a per-student cost of \$492.13, and a cost per student hour of \$18.93. Medium classes may be viewed as operating at an effective upperclass student/faculty ratio of 27.5/1, at a per-student cost of \$909.09, and a cost per student hour of \$34.96.

Table 9

**Instructional Cost for Upperclass Students
by Size of Class and Student Hours, Assuming Input Cost of $25,000
Model Schools C and D**

	% of Student Hours		Upperclass Per-student Instructional Cost	Instructional Cost per Student Hour
Class Category	School C	School D		
Large class (120)	35%	30%	$ 492.13	$ 18.93
Medium class (65)	45%	30%	$ 909.09	$ 34.96
Small class (20)	20%	40%	$2,941.18	$113.12

43.   270 students enroll in the second and third years, each taking 26 credit hours. Thus, 7,020 student hours are completed a year. If courses enroll 20 students, 351 teaching hours would be needed to cover the minimum student hours necessary for graduation ($7,020 \div 20 = 351$).

Table 9 sets out the mix of class sizes for Schools C and D, developed above in pages 142 and 143, together with the per-student cost and the per-student hour cost of each of these class sizes.[44] Thus, it can be seen that 20% of School C's student hours are in classes which, in terms of the present analysis, cost $2,941 per student or $113 per student hour, whereas 40% of School D's student hours are in classes that cost this amount. Similar observations can be made for Large and Medium classes.

To regard the same situation from the student's perspective, it may be assumed that a typical student in any one year at School C takes 20% of his upperclass student hours, or 5.2 student hours (26 $\times$ .20 = 5.2), in courses that cost $113 per student hour. Thus, the student's Small class instruction costs $588 per year. Similar analyses may be made for Large and Medium classes. The results of such computations for students of Schools C and D are set out in Table 10. It will be noticed that the total is equivalent to the per-student instructional cost for each school. Thus, $588 of the $1,169 per-student instructional cost at School C is attributed to a student's Small class instruction, while $1,176 of the $1,596 per-student instructional cost at School D is attributed to Small class instruction. Similar observations may be made for Large and Medium classes.

Table 10

Number of Upperclass Student Hours Taken in Each Size Class by Each
Student and Instructional Cost to Each Student, Assuming Input Cost of $25,000
Model Schools C and D

Class Category	School C		School D	
	Typical Number of Student Hours in Category	Instructional Cost to Student	Typical Number of Student Hours in Category	Instructional Cost to Student
Large class (120)	9.1 (35%)	$ 172.26	7.8 (30%)	$ 147.65
Medium class (65)	11.7 (45%)	$ 409.03	7.8 (30%)	$ 272.69
Small class (20)	5.2 (20%)	$ 588.22	10.4 (40%)	$1,176.45
Total	26	$1,169.51	26	$1,596.79

In one respect there is a certain artificiality to the analyses made above: they assume that each professor carries an 11-hour teaching load. If this were so, the above calculations would be correct even though some professors taught only Small classes and some taught only Large classes. However, it usually happens that members of a law school faculty do not all teach the same number of hours, even though they average an 11-hour teaching load. If this variation occurred in

44. The per-student instructional cost is affected by our procedure of rounding the student/faculty ratio figure. If the upperclass student/faculty ratio is taken out to three decimal places (for example, a school with all Small classes in its upperclass program would have a student/faculty ratio of 8.462/1), the cost is changed slightly ($25,000 ÷ 8.462 = $2,954.38). The instructional cost per student hour would also change slightly ($2,954.38 ÷ 26 = $113.64). Similar observations may be made for Table 10. In addition, it should be noted that Tables 9 and 10 assume a Medium class size of 65 for Schools C and D whereas the figures given above assume a Medium class size of 67 for School C and 70 for School D. Accordingly, the total per-student cost figures in Table 10 are slightly different than those given above.

the above hypothetical schools, these calculations would not reflect their actual unit costs. For instance, if a number of faculty members taught at a somewhat reduced load, the courses they taught would have slightly higher unit costs than the above calculations indicate. If this were so, then, by hypothesis, other faculty members would have taught at a somewhat increased load, and the courses they taught would have somewhat lower unit costs than the calculations indicate. In addition, the analysis assumes that each professor is paid $25,000. Here, too, it is almost always the case that professors are paid at different salary levels, and this gives rise to similar considerations as those mentioned above regarding the artificiality of assuming identical teaching loads among a faculty. Notwithstanding these difficulties, we believe our analysis is entirely appropriate for indicating general cost differences.

Student enrollments at levels different from those of our hypothetical schools produce significantly different results. Above, we set forth alternative programs and their fiscal implications at various student/faculty ratios for schools of 450 students of whom 270 students were in the second-and-third-year class. Now, we examine what the possibilities are for schools with greater and lesser enrollments while holding the student/faculty ratio constant. In doing this, it is of central importance to consider the position of the first-year program. In the above hypothetical cases it was assumed that the first-year courses would be given in two sections, thus requiring 60 teaching hours. As schools increase in enrollment, at some point, further sectionalization of the first-year classes takes place. When this happens, significant changes occur in the proportion of total teaching hours devoted to the upperclass program. Similar considerations apply as schools become smaller. Much of the discussion that follows iterates many of the points made in section 1 in discussing the first-year program.

Assuming no change in the student/faculty ratio at different enrollment levels, increased enrollment necessarily entails the addition of faculty members and an increase in total teaching hours. In such a case, assuming no additional first-year sections, more can be offered to the second-and-third-year class by way of an extended curriculum and a broader mix of class sizes. By like token, decreased enrollment necessarily entails a reduction in faculty and teaching hours. In such a case, assuming no reduction in first-year sections, less can be offered by way of upperclass curriculum and mix of class sizes. First, we examine schools with enrollments larger than 450, and then, briefly, schools with smaller enrollments.

It is crucial to recognize, as suggested above, that at some point enrollments reach levels sufficiently high to require further sectionalization of the first-year class. As pointed out in section 1 in discussing the first-year program, no clear pattern was found indicating the level at which law schools sectionalize their first-year program. In the hypothetical cases, 180 students were in first-year classes, and their courses were divided into two sections of 90 students each. Some schools with very low student/faculty ratios might have offered their first-year courses in three sections of 60 students each. We expect, however, that most schools will not add a third section to their first-year courses until they reach a first-year enrollment of at least 250 students, i.e., until first-year sections begin to be over 120 students. By hypothesis, such a school enrolls a total of about 600 students. Thus, schools with enrollments of higher than 450 and lower than 600 are in a better position to offer a richer curriculum and a broader mix of classes than the hypothetical cases examined above.

For example, schools with enrollments of 525 and the same variables as the

Table 11

Basic Data for Eight Model Schools

	A	B	C	D
Enrollment, total	450	450	450	450
Student/faculty ratio	35/1	30/1	25/1	20/1
Faculty size	12.9	15	18	22.5
Average teaching load (hours)	11	11	11	11
Total teaching hours delivered	142	165	198	248
Teaching hours delivered to first-year class	60	60	60	60
Teaching hours delivered to 2nd-&-3rd-year classes	82	105	138	188
Equivalent faculty teaching 2nd-&-3rd-year classes	7.5	9.5	12.5	17.1
Enrollment of 2nd-&-3rd-year classes	270	270	270	270
Effective student/faculty ratio of 2nd-&-3rd-year classes	36/1	28.4/1	21.6/1	15.8/1
Average class size of 2nd-&-3rd-year classes	86	67	51	37

	A1	B1	C1	D1
Enrollment, total	525	525	525	525
Student/faculty ratio	35/1	30/1	25/1	20/1
Faculty size	15	17.5	21	26.3
Average teaching load (hours)	11	11	11	11
Total teaching hours delivered	165	192.5	231	289.3
Teaching hours delivered to first-year class	60	60	60	60
Teaching hours delivered to 2nd-&-3rd-year classes	105	132.5	171	229.3
Equivalent faculty teaching 2nd-&-3rd-year classes	9.5	12	15.5	21
Enrollment of 2nd-&-3rd-year classes	315	315	315	315
Effective student/faculty ratio of 2nd-&-3rd-year classes	33.2/1	26.3/1	20.3/1	15.1/1
Average class size of 2nd-&-3rd-year classes	78	62	48	36

model schools have considerably more teaching hours for their second-and-third-year programs than the model schools. Table 11 sets out the basic data of four model schools with enrollments of 450 students, referred to as Schools A, B, C, and D, and four model schools with enrollments of 525 students, referred to as Schools A1, B1, C1, and D1. More upperclass student hours are taken at the larger schools, but the number of upperclass teaching hours offered are proportionately even larger. As a result, the average upperclass sizes at the larger schools are less than at the smaller schools, and the larger schools are able to offer more extensive curricula and a broader mix of class sizes to their second-and-third-year students. The effective second-and-third-year student/faculty ratios at the larger schools are lower than those at the smaller schools, and, consequently, assuming identical input cost at each school, the per-student instructional cost of upperclass students at the larger schools is higher than at the smaller schools. Conversely, the effective first-year student/faculty ratios at the larger schools are higher than those at the smaller schools and, consequently, the first-year per-student instructional cost is lower at the larger schools than at the smaller schools. Of course, the over-all per-student cost of both the larger schools and the smaller schools would be identical as we have assumed identical input cost and constant student/faculty ratios for both sets of schools.

We have assumed above that a school with 600 students and a first-year class of 240 would offer three sections to its first-year class rather than two sections. Table 12 gives the basic data for four such schools which, other than enrollment size, share the same characteristics as the four original model schools. These

Table 12

Data for Model Schools with Larger Enrollments

	A2	B2	C2	D2
Enrollment, total	600	600	600	600
Student/faculty ratio	35/1	30/1	25/1	20/1
Faculty size	17.1	20	24	30
Average teaching load (hours)	11	11	11	11
Total teaching hours delivered	188	220	264	330
Teaching hours delivered to first-year class	90	90	90	90
Teaching hours delivered to 2nd-&-3rd-year classes	98	130	174	240
Equivalent faculty teaching 2nd-&-3rd-year classes	8.9	11.8	15.8	21.8
Enrollment of 2nd-&-3rd-year classes	360	360	360	360
Effective student/faculty ratio of 2nd-&-3rd-year classes	40.5/1	30.5/1	22.8/1	16.5/1
Average class size of 2nd-&-3rd-year classes	96	72	54	39

schools will be referred to as Schools A2, B2, C2, and D2. It is evident from comparing these figures with those above in Table 11 giving data for schools with an enrollment of 525 students, that larger schools are not able to offer as broad a mix of class sizes as the smaller schools. Furthermore, the effective second-and-third-year student/faculty ratios at these 600-student schools are higher and consequently, assuming identical input cost, their upperclass per-student cost is lower than that of the smaller schools examined above.

As schools decrease in enrollment from 450 students, the converse of what has been described occurs. Teaching hours decrease and the ability to offer a wide mix of class sizes lessens. At some point, however, the schools will become so small that only one section will be offered to their first-year students. The mix of classes available to such schools will be the same as that available to schools that have almost but not quite reached a level requiring them to go to three sections. It need hardly be pointed out that, while the mix will be the same because of the tendency against sectionalization of second-and-third-year courses, the curricula of the large schools will be far broader than those of the small schools, although identical percentages of total student hours might be taken in small classes at both sets of schools.

Table 13 sets out the number of teaching hours that would be offered to the second-and-third-year students at hypothetical law schools of varying sizes at four student/faculty ratios, assuming an 11-hour teaching load at all schools. Effective second-and-third-year student/faculty ratios are also given for these schools. It is assumed that schools with total enrollments of 100 to to 250 and first-year enrollments of 40 to 100 will offer only one section of first-year courses. Further it is assumed that schools with total enrollments from 275 to 400 and first-year enrollments of 110 to 160 will offer one or two first-year sections. Teaching hours and student/faculty ratio figures are given on both assumptions. It is assumed that schools with total enrollments from 425 to 775 students and first-year enrollments of 170 to 310 will offer two or three first-year sections, and teaching-hour and student/faculty ratio figures are given under these assumptions. Of course, as first-year enrollments reach levels in the high 200s, schools might offer their first-year program in four sections. We have found, however, that as enrollments increase there is a tendency to let first-year sections grow rather than to attempt to keep first-year class sizes down at levels of 60 to 70 students. It is assumed, therefore, that schools will not divide their first-year class into four sections until they reach an enrollment of 320 or over. Accordingly, it is assumed that schools with total enrollments between 800 and 1,000 students and first-year enrollments between 320 and 400 will offer three or four first-year sections and teaching-hour and student/faculty ratio figures are given under these assumptions.

In considering Table 13, a number of the caveats mentioned earlier should be kept in mind. First, a 30-hour first-year program represents only a rough approximation of what law schools offer to their first-year students. A number of schools have recently developed somewhat specialized components for their first-year program that, in cases where only one section is offered, result in more

Table 13

Second-and-Third-Year Teaching Hours and Effective Student/Faculty Ratios for Schools with the Following Total Student/Faculty Ratios and Enrollments, Assuming One, Two, Three or Four First-Year Sections and an Average Teaching Load of 11 Hours per Year

En-rollment			30/1	25/1	20/1	16/1	30/1	25/1	20/1	16/1
100	Total	T.H.	30	30	30	30	30	30	30	30
40	First Year	T.H.	*	*	*	*	*	*	52.5	55.9
60	2nd-&-3rd-Yr.	S/F r.	*	*	*	*	*	*	18.9/1	14.7/1
125	Total	T.H.	30	30	30	30	30	30	30	30
50	First Year	T.H.	*	*	*	*	*	*	*	*
75	2nd-&-3rd-Yr.	S/F r.	*	*	*	*	*	*	*	*
150	Total	T.H.	30	30	30	30	30	30	30	30
60	First Year	T.H.	*	*	*	*	*	*	*	73.1
90	2nd-&-3rd-Yr.	S/F r.	*	*	*	*	*	*	*	13.5/1
175	Total	T.H.	30	30	30	30	30	30	30	30
70	First Year	T.H.	*	*	*	*	*	*	66.3	91
105	2nd-&-3rd-Yr.	S/F r.	*	*	*	*	*	*	17.4/1	12.7/1

Table 13 (continued)

En-rollment			30/1	25/1	20/1	16/1	30/1	25/1	20/1	16/1
200	Total	T.H.	30	30	30	30				
80	First Year	T.H.	*	58	80	107.5				
120	2nd-&-3rd-Yr.	S/F r.	*	22.8/1	16.5/1	12.3/1				
225	Total	T.H.	30	30	30	30				
90	First Year	T.H.	52.5	69	93.8	124.7				
135	2nd-&-3rd-Yr.	S/F r.	28.3/1	21.5/1	15.9/1	11.9/1				
250	Total	T.H.	30	30	30	30				
100	First Year	T.H.	61.6	80	107.5	141.9				
150	2nd-&-3rd-Yr.	S/F r.	26.8/1	20.6/1	15.4/1	11.6/1				
275	Total	T.H.	30	30	30	30	60	60	60	60
110	First Year	T.H.	70.9	91	121.3	159.1	*	61	91.3	129.1
165	2nd-&-3rd-Yr.	S/F r.	25.6/1	20.0/1	15.0/1	11.4/1	*	29.7/1	19.9/1	14.1/1
300	Total	T.H.	30	30	30	30	60	60	60	60
120	First Year	T.H.	80	102	135	176.3	50	72	105	146.3
180	2nd-&-3rd-Yr.	S/F r.	24.8/1	19.4/1	14.7/1	11.2/1	39.6/1	27.5/1	18.9/1	13.5/1
325	Total	T.H.	30	30	30	30	60	60	60	60
130	First Year	T.H.	88.8	113	148.8	193.4	58.8	83	118.8	163.4
195	2nd-&-3rd-Yr.	S/F r.	24.4/1	19.0/1	14.4/1	11.1/1	36.5/1	25.8/1	18.1/1	13.1/1

Table 13 (continued)

Enrollment			30/1	25/1	20/1	16/1	30/1	25/1	20/1	16/1
350	Total	T.H.	30	30	30	30	60	60	60	60
140	First Year	T.H.	98.4	124	162.5	210.6	68.4	94	132.5	180.6
210	2nd-&-3rd-Yr.	S/F r.	23.5/1	18.6/1	14.2/1	11/1	33.8/1	24.6/1	17.4/1	12.8/1
375	Total	T.H.	30	30	30	30	60	60	60	60
150	First Year	T.H.	107.5	135	176.3	227.8	77.5	105	146.3	197.8
225	2nd-&-3rd-Yr.	S/F r.	23.0/1	18.3/1	14.0/1	10.9/1	31.9/1	23.6/1	16.9/1	12.5/1
400	Total	T.H.	30	30	30	30	60	60	60	60
160	First Year	T.H.	116.6	146	190	245	86.6	116	160	215
240	2nd-&-3rd-Yr.	S/F r.	22.6/1	18.1/1	13.9/1	10.8/1	30.5/1	22.8/1	16.5/1	12.3/1
425	Total	T.H.	60	60	60	60	90	90	90	90
170	First Year	T.H.	95.9	127	173.8	232.2	65.9	97	143.8	202.2
255	2nd-&-3rd-Yr.	S/F r.	29.2/1	22.1/1	16.1/1	12.1/1	42.6/1	28.9/1	19.5/1	13.9/1
450	Total	T.H.	60	60	60	60	90	90	90	90
180	First Year	T.H.	105	138	187.5	249.4	75	108	157.5	219.4
270	2nd-&-3rd-Yr.	S/F r.	28.3/1	21.5/1	15.8/1	11.9/1	39.6/1	27.5/1	18.9/1	13.5/1
475	Total	T.H.	60	60	60	60	90	90	90	90
190	First Year	T.H.	114.1	149	201.3	266.6	84.1	119	171.3	236.6
285	2nd-&-3rd-Yr.	S/F r.	27.5/1	21.0/1	15.6/1	11.8/1	37.3/1	26.3/1	18.3/1	13.3/1

Table 13 (continued)

Enroll-ment			30/1	25/1	20/1	16/1	30/1	25/1	20/1	16/1
500	Total	T.H.	60	60	60	60	90	90	90	90
200	First Year	T.H.	123.4	160	215	283.8	93.4	130	185	253.8
300	2nd-&-3rd-Yr.	S/F r.	26.7/1	20.6/1	15.4/1	11.6/1	35.3/1	25.4/1	17.8/1	13/1
525	Total	T.H.	60	60	60	60	90	90	90	90
210	First Year	T.H.	132.5	171	228.8	300.9	102.5	141	198.8	270.9
315	2nd-&-3rd-Yr.	S/F r.	26.1/1	20.3/1	15.1/1	11.5/1	33.8/1	24.6/1	17.4/1	12.8/1
550	Total	T.H.	60	60	60	60	90	90	90	90
220	First Year	T.H.	141.6	182	242.5	318.1	111.6	152	212.5	288.1
330	2nd-&-3rd-Yr.	S/F r.	25.6/1	19.9/1	15.0/1	11.4/1	32.5/1	23.9/1	17.1/1	12.6/1
575	Total	T.H.	60	60	60	60	90	90	90	90
230	First Year	T.H.	150.9	193	256.3	335.3	120.9	163	226.3	305.3
345	2nd-&-3rd-Yr.	S/F r.	25.2/1	19.7/1	14.8/1	11.3/1	31.4/1	23.3/1	16.8/1	12.4/1
600	Total	T.H.	60	60	60	60	90	90	90	90
240	First Year	T.H.	160	204	270	352.5	130	174	240	322.5
360	2nd-&-3rd-Yr.	S/F r.	24.7/1	19.4/1	14.7/1	11.2/1	30.5/1	22.8/1	16.5/1	12.3/1
625	Total	T.H.	60	60	60	60	90	90	90	90
250	First Year	T.H.	169.1	215	283.8	369.7	139.1	185	253.8	339.7
375	2nd-&-3rd-Yr.	S/F r.	24.4/1	19.2/1	14.5/1	22.1/1	29.6/1	22.3/1	16.3/1	12.1/1

Table 13 (continued)

En-rollment			30/1	25/1	20/1	16/1	30/1	25/1	20/1	16/1
650	Total	T.H.	60	60	60	60	90	90	90	90
260	First Year	T.H.	178.4	226	297.5	386.9	148.4	196	267.5	356.9
390	2nd-&-3rd-Yr.	S/F r.	24.0/1	19.0/1	14.4/1	11.1/1	28.9/1	21.9/1	16.0/1	12/1
675	Total	T.H.	60	60	60	60	90	90	90	90
270	First Year	T.H.	187.5	237	311.3	404.1	157.5	207	281.3	374.1
405	2nd-&-3rd-Yr.	S/F r.	23.8/1	18.8/1	14.3/1	11/1	28.3/1	21.5/1	15.8/1	11.9/1
700	Total	T.H.	60	60	60	60	90	90	90	90
280	First Year	T.H.	196.6	248	325	421.3	166.6	218	295	391.3
420	2nd-&-3rd-Yr.	S/F r.	23.5/1	18.6/1	14.2/1	11/1	27.7/1	21.2/1	15.7/1	11.8/1
725	Total	T.H.	60	60	60	60	90	90	90	90
290	First Year	T.H.	205.9	259	338.8	438.4	175.9	229	308.8	408.4
435	2nd-&-3rd-Yr.	S/F r.	23.2/1	18.5/1	14.1/1	10.9/1	27.2/1	20.9/1	15.5/1	11.7/1
750	Total	T.H.	60	60	60	60	90	90	90	90
300	First Year	T.H.	215	270	352.5	455.6	185	240	322.5	425.6
450	2nd-&-3rd-Yr.	S/F r.	23.0/1	18.3/1	14.0/1	10.9/1	26.8/1	20.6/1	15.4/1	11.6/1
775	Total	T.H.	60	60	60	60	90	90	90	90
310	First Year	T.H.	224.1	281	366.3	472.8	194.1	251	336.3	442.8
465	2nd-&-3rd-Yr.	S/F r.	22.8/1	18.2/1	14.0/1	10.8/1	26.4/1	20.4/1	15.2/1	11.5/1

Table 13 (continued)

En-roll-ment			30/1	25/1	20/1	16/1	30/1	25/1	20/1	16/1
800	Total	T.H.	90	90	90	90	120	120	120	120
320	First Year	T.H.	203.4	262	350	460	173.4	232	320	430
480	2nd-&-3rd-Yr.	S/F r.	26.0/1	20.2/1	15.1/1	11.6/1	20.5/1	22.8/1	16.5/1	12.3/1
825	Total	T.H.	90	90	90	90	120	120	120	120
330	First Year	T.H.	212.5	273	363.8	477.2	182.5	243	333.8	447.2
495	2nd-&-3rd-Yr.	S/F r.	25.6/1	19.9/1	15.0/1	11.4/1	29.8/1	22.4/1	16.3/1	12.2/1
850	Total	T.H.	90	90	90	90	120	120	120	120
340	First Year	T.H.	221.6	284	377.5	494.4	191.6	254	347.5	464.4
510	2nd-&-3rd-Yr.	S/F r.	25.3/1	19.8/1	14.9/1	11.3/1	29.3/1	22.1/1	16.1/1	12.1/1
875	Total	T.H.	90	90	90	90	120	120	120	120
350	First Year	T.H.	230.9	295	391.3	511.6	200.9	265	361.3	481.6
525	2nd-&-3rd-Yr.	S/F r.	25.1/1	19.7/1	14.8/1	11.3/1	28.8/1	21.8/1	16.0/1	12/1
900	Total	T.H.	90	90	90	90	120	120	120	120
360	First Year	T.H.	240	306	405	528.8	210	276	375	498.8
540	2nd-&-3rd-Yr.	S/F r.	24.8/1	19.4/1	14.7/1	11.2/1	28.3/1	21.5/1	15.8/1	11.9/1
925	Total	T.H.	90	90	90	90	120	120	120	120
370	First Year	T.H.	249.1	317	418.8	545.9	219.1	287	388.8	515.9
555	2nd-&-3rd-Yr.	S/F r.	24.5/1	19.3/1	14.6/1	11.2/1	27.9/1	21.3/1	15.7/1	11.8/1

Table 13 (continued)

Enrollment			30/1	25/1	20/1	16/1	30/1	25/1	20/1	16/1
950	Total	T.H.	90	90	90	90	120	120	120	120
380	First Year	T.H.	258.4	328	432.5	563.1	228.4	298	402.5	533.1
570	2nd-&-3rd-Yr.	S/F r.	24.3/1	19.1/1	14.5/1	11.1/1	27.5/1	21.0/1	15.6/1	11.8/1
975	Total	T.H.	90	90	90	90	120	120	120	120
390	First Year	T.H.	267.5	339	446.3	580.3	237.5	309	416.3	550.3
585	2nd-&-3rd-Yr.	S/F r.	24.0/1	19.0/1	14.4/1	11.1/1	27.1/1	20.8/1	15.5/1	11.7/1
1,000	Total	T.H.	90	90	90	90	120	120	120	120
400	First Year	T.H.	276.6	350	460	597.5	246.6	320	430	567.5
600	2nd-&-3rd-Yr.	S/F r.	23.9/1	18.9/1	14.4/1	11/1	26.8/1	20.6/1	15.4/1	11.6/1

Note: The asterisk indicates that the second-and-third-year teaching hours total less than 50. This means that the school could not provide the minimum number of credit hours required for admission to most bars.

than 30 teaching hours being offered to their first-year classes.[45] Second, as first-year enrollments increase, schools may sectionalize some first-year courses, but not every one. Thus, teaching hours delivered to the first-year program do not always increase in blocs of 30 as the table assumes. Third, teaching loads differ among schools. In this connection, it will be recalled that teaching loads tend to lower as student/faculty ratios decrease. Finally, the assumed enrollment breakdown of 40% total enrollment in the first-year class and 60% total enrollment in the second-and-third-year class is, of course, only an approximation of what obtains at any one school. These differences do not, however, affect the general patterns illustrated by the Table. Furthermore, as indicated, the Table has been based on assumed variables which, we believe, closely approximate (with the exception of the 16/1 student/faculty ratio) those of many law schools today.

We began our analysis in this section by assuming constant enrollments and varying student/faculty ratios. We then assumed constant student/faculty ratios and varying student enrollments. As has been shown in chapter 2, as law schools develop over a period of time, it is usually the case that neither of these variables remain constant. During the period of 1955-1970, enrollments increased at virtually every school, and student/faculty ratios changed in a number of different ways. Table 13 provides the number of teaching hours that would be provided at various enrollment levels at four different student/faculty ratios. Thus, in determining the effect of an enrollment change on the number of deliverable teaching hours, Table 13 allows one to assess the change on the assumption that a school's student/faculty ratio will not remain constant.

The explanation accounting for differences between any actual law school and the one closest to it in Table 13 will be readily ascertainable, and such an analysis should provide the investigator of any particular school with useful insights into the school he is examining. For example, we will suppose that an investigator wishes to compare a school against the one in the Table that most closely approximates it. Throughout this example we will refer to the school being examined by the investigator as the "actual" school. Assume the actual school enrolls 478 students and has a student/faculty ratio of 20/1. The investigator finds that the actual school offers 144 teaching hours in its second-and-third-year program. This would present him with a startling difference between the number of teaching hours delivered by the actual school and those delivered by the school in the Table closest to the actual school. According to the Table, a school with an enrollment of 475 students and a student/faculty ratio of 20/1 delivers 201 teaching hours to its second-and-third-year class if 2 first-year sections are offered, and 171 teaching hours if 3 first-year sections are offered. In this example, however, the actual school offers only 144 hours to its second-and-third-year class.

The investigator might first note that the actual school's first-year program offers a number of Small classes in addition to two sections of the remaining

---

45.   See section 1.

courses. Because of this special first-year component, 74 teaching hours are delivered to the first-year class, rather than 60 or 90 as assumed in the Table. As the Table shows that a school of 475 students offering 90 teaching hours to its first-year class offers 171 teaching hours in its upperclass program, the investigator would have to look further to determine why the teaching hours delivered in the second-and-third-year program at his school are so low.

First, he might find that the actual school engages only 20.8 professors when properly counted. The 20/1 student/faculty ratio counted the Dean, Librarian, and a professor on sabbatical leave as full-timers. The Dean and Librarian taught only one course and should have been counted as part-timers. The professor on sabbatical leave should not have been counted at all.[46] In fact, the actual school's student/faculty ratio is 22.9/1.

Second, the actual school's calculated teaching load is 10.5 hours rather than 11; so, with 20.8 faculty members teaching, this school delivered a total of 218 teaching hours. With 74 of these teaching hours allotted to the first-year program, as indicated, 144 teaching hours were left for the second-and-third-year program.

We have noted above that differences in teaching load produce quite different results. We have also observed that as student/faculty ratios decrease, teaching loads frequently decrease. Thus, among our case-study schools with low student/faculty ratios, it was not unusual for a school to operate with a teaching

Table 14
Model School D with Different Teaching Loads

	Teaching Load	
	11 Hours	9 Hours
Enrollment, total	450	450
Student/faculty ratio	20/1	20/1
Faculty size	22.5	22.5
Average teaching load (hours)	11	9
Total teaching hours delivered	248	203
Teaching hours delivered to first-year class	60	60
Teaching hours delivered to 2nd-&-3rd-year classes	188	143
Equivalent faculty teaching 2nd-&-3rd-year classes	17	15.9
Enrollment of 2nd-&-3rd-year classes	270	270
Effective student/faculty ratio of 2nd-&-3rd-year classes	15.8/1	17/1
Average class size of 2nd-&-3rd-year classes	37	49

46.   In addition, one of the professors counted as a full-timer should have been counted as a part-timer.

load as low as 9 hours. If School D with a student/faculty ratio of 20/1, had a teaching load of 9 hours instead of the supposed 11 hours, its ability to offer a Small class program to the second-and-third-years would be considerably limited. Table 14 sets out the basic data for School D assuming, as above, an 11-hour teaching load and assuming a teaching load reduced to 9 hours.

Preliminarily, it will be observed that the second-and-third-year effective student/faculty ratio increases as a result of the lowering of School D's teaching load. This results because of the fixed nature of the first-year program.[47] Assuming identical input cost, the upperclass per-student instructional cost in the case where School D has an average teaching load of 11 hours will be 7% higher than the case where School D operates with a teaching load of 9 hours. Conversely, per-student first-year cost at School D with an 11-hour teaching load is 18% less than with a 9-hour teaching load. Considerably fewer teaching hours, of course, are offered to the upperclasses as a result of the reduced teaching load. With an average teaching load of 9 hours, School D would be able to have no more than 25% of its upperclass student hours in Small classes. Such an arrangement, in schematic form, would be as follows.

Student Hours		Class		Teaching Hours	
%	Number	Category	Av. Size	%	Number
50%	3,510	Large	120	20%	29.3
25%	1,755	Medium	69	18%	25.5
25%	1,755	Small	20	62%	87.7

Comparing this arrangement with the possibilities set out above[48] for School D with an 11-hour average teaching load, demonstrates the manner in which School D's ability to conduct a Small class program is limited as a result of a reduced teaching load.

It has already been pointed out that student/faculty ratio and teaching load, from the standpoint of teaching hours alone, are interchangeable. In the above two examples of School D its student/faculty ratio is 20/1, both where it operates with an 11-hour teaching load and where it operates with a 9-hour teaching load. For School D to operate with a 9-hour teaching load and deliver the same number of teaching hours it delivers with an 11-hour load, it would have to increase its faculty from 22.5 to 27.5 and thus decrease its student/faculty ratio from 20/1 to 16.4/1. Assuming identical input cost, its per-student cost would increase about 22%.

Conversely, if School D operates with an 11-hour teaching load and delivers as many teaching hours as it does when it operates with a 9-hour teaching load at a 20/1 student/faculty ratio, it would be able to decrease its faculty from 22.5 professors to 18.4 and thus increase its student/faculty ratio from 20/1 to

---

47.   See section 1.
48.   See above.

24.5/1. Again, assuming identical input cost, its per-student cost would decrease 18%.

In section 5 of chapter 2 it was shown how the Instructional Cost Equation might be used to facilitate a better understanding of a school's fiscal development. The analysis developed in this chapter can be combined with the analyses using the Instructional Cost Equation to demonstrate what program changes may accompany fiscal changes. To show how this may be done we will return to the second example given in section 5. It will be recalled that this example involved a school that planned to increase its enrollment and reduce its student/faculty ratio. The basic data for such a school are set out in Table 15. It is assumed that the school will operate with a teaching load of 11 hours both years. It will be noted that the Table assumes that all the additional teaching hours resulting from the increase in faculty size are allocated to the upperclass program which, as a result, has an increase in teaching hours of almost one-half.

Table 15

Data for a Model School with
Increasing Enrollment and Decreasing Student/Faculty Ratio

	Year 1	Year 2
Enrollment, total	500	594
Student/faculty ratio	25/1	22/1
Faculty size	20	27
Average teaching load (hours)	11	11
Total teaching hours delivered	220	297
Teaching hours delivered to first-year class	60	60
Teaching hours delivered to 2nd-&-3rd-year classes	160	237
Equivalent faculty teaching 2nd-&-3rd-year classes	14.5	21.5
Enrollment of 2nd-&-3rd-year classes	300	356
Effective student/faculty ratio of 2nd-&-3rd-year classes	20.6/1	16.5/1
Average class size of 2nd-&-3rd-year classes	49	39

Under these conditions the upperclass curriculum would expand substantially. Assuming that an upperclass course averages three hours and that little sectionalization of existing upperclass courses occurs, about twenty-six new courses would be added to the upperclass curriculum. In addition, as the difference in average class size suggests, the school would be able to offer a much enlarged Small class program. Before the changes, the school could have had a Small class program covering about 25% of its upperclass student hours, with about 50% of its upperclass student hours in Large classes and about 25% in

Medium classes. After the change, the school could have a Small class program covering about 35% of its upperclass student hours, with only 40% of its upperclass student hours in Large classes and 25% in Medium classes.

The variables given in Table 15 for the projected Year 2 represent, of course, only one of an almost infinite number of alternatives. This alternative should be viewed as a starting point from which the analysis might proceed. Having established one alternative, it is easy to ascertain the effects on the program of lowering teaching loads, adding more teaching hours to the first-year program and the like.

A possible danger exists in a study such as this where, for analytical purposes, so much emphasis is placed on data which are easily quantifiable. For example, teaching hours are the primary measure we use in comparing the educational program of law schools. A logical response to this type of analysis might be to call for an increase in teaching hours by simply increasing the faculty's teaching load. This would be the cheapest and most expedient way of increasing teaching hours. In this context, the danger of an approach that deals with only quantifiable material becomes apparent at once. A great deal of value that is inherently incommensurable may be lost when a faculty member's teaching load is increased. Professors with heavy teaching loads are likely to have little time for meetings with students on an individual basis. A number of the schools we have studied with low teaching loads conduct quite extensive upperclass writing programs during which several students engage in individual research under the supervision of a professor. Usually the joint effort involves written submissions and faculty evaluations and criticism, but does not count as course credit for the student nor as teaching credit for the professor. Such programs may have to be reduced if teaching loads are forced upward. Other considerations exist. For example, schools with low teaching loads can offer more informal meetings between teachers and students involving individual after-class discussion, and there is greater opportunity for professor and student to review performance at a number of junctures during the term. Finally, and most importantly, the imposition of high teaching loads restricts the opportunities for faculty to engage in sustained research and writing. Since law professors do a great deal more than teach and research, a school must carefully weigh what it would be giving up when it increases its teaching load.

There are, of course, a number of other problems in using teaching hours or credit hours as a chief means for measuring output. To begin with, it is evident as an almost a priori matter that learning cannot be measured in exact quantitative terms, as seems to be an important (implied) objective of the use of the credit system. Credits consist of units of time rather than units of knowledge or competence. Even assuming that time is an adequate measure of educational accomplishment, credit hours do not take into account time spent outside the classroom by both students and professors, which may be different in courses that entail identical credit hours. Some courses, most notably clinical courses, assign credit hours for reasons that are wholly unrelated to classroom attendance. As suggested above, basing faculty workload on a standard of productivity that uses credit hours conveys a distorted notion of a faculty member's actual activities and output. From the student's standpoint, a substantial portion of his learning may come through various "un-credited" educational experiences, such as work on a law review or moot court. Although these problems with the credit-hour system must be kept in mind, we believe an analysis geared to teaching hours gives an accurate enough measure of the educational program in quantitative terms to justify the use made of it in this study.

Section 3 – The Development of the Second-and-Third-Year Program between 1955 and 1970

In this section we explore, in terms of the analysis developed in section 2, the manner by which the upperclass educational programs of the case-study schools actually evolved between 1955 and 1970. The analysis first covers case-study schools that were in the Small and Middle Enrollment Groups and then discusses those in the Large Enrollment Group. We believe that, in terms of general patterns, the changes that occurred at the case-study schools are similar to those which occurred at other schools in the same Enrollment Group. A group of schools whose enrollments, student/faculty ratios, and teaching loads changed in a similar manner will necessarily have similar teaching-hour changes and, accordingly, similar changes in educational program, at least with respect to the quantitative characteristics developed in this chapter.

As in section 2, our principal focus in this section is an examination of how schools' curricula expanded and how the enrollment mix of their classes changed as a result of faculty growth. With respect to curriculum expansion, to understand more clearly the changes that have taken place, we have divided the law school curriculum into the following fourteen course groupings: corporations, commercial, procedure, property, taxation, jurisprudence,[49] criminal law, urban affairs,[50] labor law, law and the person,[51] international law, administrative law, constitutional law, and a grouping designated as general that includes all those courses not included in the above groupings. Appendix H lists under each course grouping the titles of every course included therein offered by the case-study schools for each year that data were collected. For purposes of this study, the fourteen course groupings have been divided into two categories. The first five course groupings (corporations, commercial, procedure, property, and taxation) constitute the First Category, and the remaining nine course groupings (jurisprudence, criminal law, urban affairs, labor

49.   Jurisprudence is conceived broadly and includes legal history, legal ethics, and sociology and the law offerings.
50.   Urban affairs is something of a misnomer and really designates a number of current-interest courses that are not necessarily suggested by the term "urban affairs." These include environmental protection and Indian rights courses. See Appendix H for a complete listing of the course titles included under the urban affairs grouping.
51.   Law and the person includes such courses as family law and psychoanalysis and law.

law, law and the person, international law, administrative law, constitutional law, and general) constitute the Second Category. These two Categories of course groupings have been determined on the basis of the number of student hours taken in each grouping at the case-study schools. Generally, each course grouping in the First Category had over 10% of total student hours taken, and each course grouping in the Second Category had under 10%. At the start of the period examined, over 70% of all student hours were taken in the First Category at virtually every case-study school. Consequently, in terms of averages, about 14% of total student hours were taken in each First Category course grouping, and about 3% of total student hours were taken in each Second Category course grouping. As will be shown below, by 1970 at most schools, the proportion of total student hours taken in the First Category and the Second Category were about equal. However, because the First Category contains fewer groupings than the Second Category, in most instances fewer student hours were still taken in the individual course groupings of the Second Category than in the individual course groupings of the First Category.

In chapter 2 it was shown that schools in the Small Enrollment Group (50 to 150 students in 1955) were characterized by student/faculty ratios which would be considered low by today's standards. These schools had low student/faculty ratios because they had to engage a minimum of 6 professors in order to provide the minimum credit-hour requirements without placing too heavy a teaching load upon their faculty. Because of their small enrollments, faculties of this size were large enough to produce low student/faculty ratios. In this connection, it will be recalled that most Small Enrollment Group schools in 1955 engaged between 6 and 10 professors. Schools with low enrollments and minimum faculties necessarily had low student/faculty ratios. Notwithstanding their low student/faculty ratios, however, schools with small faculties had relatively limited upperclass curricula.[52]

---

52. The general thesis developed in the text was expressed very well by Harry W. Jones in an address delivered at the Southeastern Regional Law Teachers Conference during the summer of 1957. In discussing the differences between local and national law schools, Jones said:

Under the second major heading, adequacy of faculty resources, each "national" law school will report a large faculty and, what is incomparably more significant, a favorable relationship between faculty manpower and the minimum lawyer-training job that has to be done. Right here is where the literature of legal education needs some clarifying, and I am rash enough to have a try at it. We will all agree that the gross, numerical size of a law faculty is not the significant figure in a check-list of school resources. A faculty of twenty full-time members would be perfect for the University of North Carolina but quite skimpy for Harvard. The length of the faculty list must be measured against the educational job at hand. But the law schools, and particularly the smaller "local" law schools, have been victimized by that pet cliche of the educational statisticians, the faculty-student ratio. According to this plausible theory, the adequacy of a faculty is determined by a simple process of dividing the number of students enrolled by the number of full-time faculty members and comparing the mathematical quotient with that prevailing at other, high-prestige, schools. University presidents love the faculty-student ratio, for its precision and simplicity, and rumor has it that a good many law school deans walk into the booby-trap and discuss their faculty needs in these terms.

Two of the case-study schools were in the Small Enrollment Group in 1955. They had very low enrollments, small faculties, low student/faculty ratios, and limited upperclass curricula. Their basic data are set out in Table 16. For the sake of reference the schools are designated School A and School B.[53]

School A offered only 17 teaching hours more than the average required minimum of 82[54] hours, and School B offered only 15 hours more than the minimum. In other words, they offered about five courses more than the required minimum. As might be expected, neither School A nor School B offered any upperclass course in more than one section. Both schools offered virtually the same number of courses in the First Category. School A offered 50 teaching hours in the First Category, and School B offered 51. In terms of the number of teaching hours offered in each grouping, the two schools had nearly identical programs. This similarity is depicted in Table 17.

Why is it that the faculty-student ratio furnishes a false and misleading comparison between the "national" and the "local" law schools? Let me illustrate with two hypothetical law schools, one "local" and one "national," at both of which I have been a hypothetical teacher. School *L* is a "local" law school, with a full-time faculty of eight members and a total student body of one hundred and twenty-five. School *N* is a "national" law school, with a full-time faculty of thirty-five and a total student body of approximately seven hundred. Apply the faculty-student ratio, and you will see how fortunate School *L* is: one faculty member to fifteen students, as compared to the "national" law school's ratio of one faculty member to twenty students. Educational statisticians will assure you that this means that the teachers at School *L* will have far more time for research and public service activities than their more heavily-burdened brothers at School *N*.

Now just why does this lead us down the garden path? Compare School *L* with School *N* not in terms of student enrollment, but in terms of the number of courses that have to be offered to provide adequate training for today's profession, and you get a very different picture. School *L*, in my time, offered a few more than the irreducible minimum, forty one-semester courses. School *N* offers fifty-five. In terms of what I am going to call the faculty-course ratio, this works out as five courses per faculty member at the "local" school and somewhat less than two courses per man at the "national" school. Seminars and the sectionalization of large classes at the "national" school will reduce the disparity somewhat, but the essential fact is clear as a bell: the teacher at the typical "local" law school has to keep up with—and teach—at least twice as many fields of law as his brother at Harvard, Yale, or Columbia. When one of my younger colleagues at Columbia is troubled in soul by the burden of preparing as many as two new courses for a coming year, I think of twenty years ago at School *L*, when I had as light a teaching load as any member of our faculty and got off with a program limited to Sales, Wills, Bankruptcy, Conflicts, Legislation, and the post of faculty advisor to the law review. Here—far more, I think, than the matter of geographical distribution—is a difference to be kept in mind in comparing the functions and opportunities of the "national" and the "local" law schools.

Jones, *Local Law Schools vs. National Law Schools: A Comparison of Concepts, Functions and Opportunities*, 10 J. Legal Ed. 281, 286-287 (1958).

53.   Case-study school designations in this section do not correspond to case-study school designations in section 1, i.e., School A above is not the same as School A in section 1.

54.   Several jurisdictions required the completion of more than 82 credit hours (teaching hours) for admission to the bar; so these figures are conservative. See Appendix D for a survey of minimum hours required for graduation in 1955 and in 1970.

Table 16

1955 Data for Case-study Schools A and B

	School A	School B
Enrollment, total	117	128
Student/faculty ratio	17.5/1	15.8/1
Faculty size	6.7	8.1
Average teaching load (hours)	14.6	12.0
Total teaching hours delivered	99	97
Teaching hours delivered to first-year class	32	30
Teaching hours delivered to 2nd-&-3rd-year classes	67	67
Equivalent faculty teaching 2nd-&-3rd-year classes	4.6	5.6
Enrollment of 2nd-&-3rd-year classes	55	77
Effective student/faculty ratio of 2nd-&-3rd-year classes	12/1	13.8/1
Average class size of 2nd-&-3rd-year classes	20	31

Table 17

First Category Teaching Hours Offered by School A and School B in 1955

First Category Course Grouping	Upperclass Teaching Hours	
	School A	School B
Corporate	6	6
Commercial	9	5
Procedure	19	19
Property	8	13
Taxation	8	8
Total	50	51

As shown in Table 18, School A offered 17 teaching hours, and School B, 16 teaching hours in the Second Category. It will be noted that both schools in 1955 offered by far the larger number of teaching hours in the First Category (75% for School A and 76% for School B).

These two schools provide an example of the interchangeable impact of teaching load and student/faculty ratio discussed above in section 2. School A, with a higher student/faculty ratio, was able to offer about the same number of total teaching hours as School B with a lower student/faculty ratio, although A

Table 18

Second Category Teaching Hours Offered by School A and School B in 1955

Second Category Course Grouping	Upperclass Teaching Hours	
	School A	School B
Jurisprudence	3	2
Criminal	2	0
Urban Affairs	0	0
Labor	0	3
Law & The Person	0	2
International	3	0
Administrative	3	3
Constitutional	4	0
General	2	6
Total	17	16

engaged only 6.7 professors as compared with B's 8.1 professors. School A was able to do this because its faculty teaching load (14.6 hours) was considerably higher than the faculty teaching load of School B (12.0 hours). If School A had operated with an average teaching load of 12.0 hours instead of 14.6 teaching hours, and had offered the same standard first-year curriculum, it would not have been able to offer the minimum number of credit hours required for its upperclass program.

In chapter 2 it was pointed out that in 1955 many Middle Enrollment Group schools had faculties about the same size as, or only slightly larger than, schools in the Small Enrollment Group.[55] Because, by definition, their enrollments were larger than those of the Small Enrollment Group, their student/faculty ratios were necessarily higher. Two of the case-study schools were Middle Enrollment schools in 1955. We shall examine one in detail; this school is designated School C. The basic data for School C are presented in Table 19.

School C offered about 20 more teaching hours in its upperclass curriculum than Schools A and B. Compared with School B which engaged 8.1 faculty members in 1955, School C engaged 10.1 faculty members in 1955. Both schools offered about the same number of teaching hours to their first-year classes, although School C engaged two more faculty members than School B. All the extra teaching hours that School C offered because of its larger faculty were allotted to the second-and-third-year program.[56]

Table 20 presents the number of teaching hours offered in each course

55. We assumed that once a minimum number of faculty members was reached, permitting a school to offer the minimum curriculum, enrollment growth was not inevitably accompanied by faculty growth.

56. This is an example of what was shown in section 2 regarding the impact of increased enrollment on the upperclass program where the increase is not so great as to cause sectionalization of the first-year class. Note that this is so even though the student/faculty ratio of School C is considerably higher than the student/faculty ratios of Schools A and B.

grouping by School C in 1955. None of these teaching hours consisted of sections. It will be noted that in 1955 School C offered about 70% of its upperclass teaching hours in the First Category and about 30% in the Second Category.[57]

Table 19

1955 Data for Case-study School C

Enrollment, total	234
Student/faculty ratio	23.2/1
Faculty size	10.1
Average teaching load (hours)	11.9
Total teaching hours delivered	120
Teaching hours delivered to first-year class	32
Teaching hours delivered to 2nd-&-3rd-year classes	88
Equivalent faculty teaching 2nd-&-3rd-year classes	7.4
Enrollment of 2nd-&-3rd-year classes	117
Effective student/faculty ratio of 2nd-&-3rd-year classes	15.8/1
Average class size of 2nd-&-3rd-year classes	37

All the schools that have been considered so far had very small upperclass enrollments by today's standards, so it is not surprising that they had low average size classes. School A had an average upperclass size of 20 students, School B, 31 students, and School C, 37 students. None of the three schools had Large classes as we have defined that term. School A had all of its upperclass courses in what we have defined as Small classes. School B had 35% of its upperclass student hours in Small classes and 65% in what we have defined as Medium classes. School C had 23% of its upperclass student hours in Small classes and 77% in Medium classes.[58]

---

57.   The second case-study school that was a Middle Enrollment Group school in 1955 (which will be designated School D) enrolled 161 students, considerably fewer than School C. In 1955, it engaged 8.4 faculty members and had a student/faculty ratio of 19.2/1. That year School D's faculty members carried a teaching load of 14 hours, a high teaching load. Because of this fact, while School D's faculty was much closer in size to School B than C, the number of teaching hours it offered to its second-and-third-year classes was nearly identical to School C. However, School D had a smaller enrollment than School C and accordingly, School D had an average upperclass size of 26 students as compared with School C's 37 students. In 1955, School D had 52% of its upperclass student hours in Small classes and 48% in Medium classes. School D offered about 66% of its upperclass teaching hours in the First Category and 34% in the Second Category.

58.   A Large class enrolls 100 or more students per course. A Medium class enrolls between 35 and 99 students per course. A Small class enrolls between 1 and 34 students per course. See section 2.

Table 20

School C's Teaching Hours in the
Course Groupings in 1955

Course Grouping	Upperclass Teaching Hours 1955
First Category	
Corporate	11
Commercial	10
Procedure	22
Property	9
Taxation	10
Subtotal	62
Second Category	
Jurisprudence	3
Criminal	0
Urban Affairs	0
Labor	4
Law & The Person	3
International	2
Administrative	0
Constitutional	2
General	12
Subtotal	26
Total	88

It is notable that although School C had a substantially higher student/faculty ratio than Schools A and B and, consequently, larger class sizes, both indices of lower per-student costs, it, nevertheless, had a considerably broader curriculum in terms of subject-matter coverage than the other two schools. Students at School C did not have the small second-and-third-year classes of Schools A and B, especially School A, but they had available to them a wider range of electives. This pattern was common during the early part of the period examined. Schools in the Middle Enrollment Group had somewhat larger faculties and considerably higher student/faculty ratios (because of their larger enrollments) than schools in the Small Enrollment Group. The larger schools' upperclass sizes tended to be greater than those of smaller schools, but they offered more upperclass teaching hours and their curricula were more extensive. It should be noted that, compared with the average size law school today, all three of these schools had very small upperclasses and relatively limited curricula.

Of the 83 schools that were in the Small and Middle Enrollment Groups in 1955, 56 had enrollments of fewer than 170 students. Most of the Small Enrollment schools had between six and ten professors, and many of the Middle Enrollment schools had faculties of this same size. It may be assumed that such schools shared many characteristics described above with respect to the smaller case-study schools. In addition, these schools were similar, in some of the quantitative characteristics detailed above, to a number of law schools as they existed prior to 1955.

In 1928, The Carnegie Foundation for the Advancement of Teaching published Alfred Z. Reed's *Present-day Law Schools in the United States and Canada*, which examined 75 of the 92 approved American law schools for the academic year 1925-26. The schools ranged in enrollment from 20 to 1,443 students with the median school enrolling 130 students. Most (40 of the 75) had enrollments between 50 and 170 and most engaged five or six professors.[59]

Reed made a full examination of the number of credit hours required to obtain a degree and the total amount of instruction offered by these schools. They required between 68 and 91 credit hours for their degrees, with most schools requiring between 72 and 84 credit hours.[60] Credit hours in excess of the amount required were referred to as "excess instruction." Thirty-three of these schools offered no electives[61] or only a limited number of electives, defined as less than 12 "excess credit" hours.[62] Thirty offered a moderate number of electives, defined as between 12 and 32 "excess credit" hours,[63] and twelve offered a large number of electives, defined as over 40 "excess credit" hours.[64] Many of the schools that Reed studied shared common characteristics with 1955 schools in the Small Enrollment Group and a number of schools in the Middle Enrollment Group. Both groups of schools had small faculties, relatively low student/faculty ratios, and limited curricula.

In contrast, by 1970, only a handful of law schools had small enrollments; the great majority of the Small and Middle Enrollment schools of 1955 had grown to schools of substantial size. It was the enormous growth in faculty and enrollment that took place at these schools between 1955 and 1970, as detailed in chapter 2, which produced significant changes in the educational programs of so many American law schools. The extent and nature of these changes are described below. As about 65% of the institutions included in the larger sample of schools were in the Small and Middle Enrollment Groups in 1955, it is apparent that the period of 1955 to 1970 was a time of substantial change—at least in quantitative terms—for American legal education.

As the enrollments of Small and Middle Enrollment Group schools increased during the period of 1955 to 1970, three general patterns developed. The first pattern involved 38 schools whose faculties increased very little and at a much lower rate than their student enrollments. As a result, their student/faculty ratios increased very substantially. Indeed, as was pointed out in section 4 of chapter 2, their enormous increases in student enrollment and relatively small increases in faculty size resulted in actual decreases in per-student cost during this period at a large number of these schools even though input cost uniformly

59.   Reed, pp. 540-541.
60.   Ibid., pp. 240-245.
61.   Ibid., pp. 239-241.
62.   Ibid., pp. 241-242.
63.   Ibid., pp. 242-244.
64.   Ibid., pp. 244-246.

increased. These schools tended to be in subgroups L and M of the Small Enrollment Group and in subgroup L of the Middle Enrollment Group. The second pattern involved 28 schools whose faculties increased at a lower rate than their student enrollments, but whose student/faculty ratios did not increase as much as those schools included in the first pattern. These schools tended to be in subgroup H of the Small Enrollment Group and in subgroups L and M of the Middle Enrollment Group. The third pattern involved 17 schools whose faculties increased at a higher rate than their student enrollments.[65] These schools had their student/faculty ratios decrease and tended to be in subgroups M and H of the Middle Enrollment Group.

School C, between 1955 and 1965, represents a school in the first pattern. The basic data for School C for the years 1955, 1960, and 1965 are set out in Table 21. During this ten-year period, School C's enrollment increased from 234 to 452 students, close to a 100% increase, and its faculty increased from 10.1 to 13.7 members, a 36% increase. As a result, its student/faculty ratio increased from 23/1 in 1955 to 33/1 in 1965. If input cost had remained constant between 1955 and 1965, per-student cost would have declined 30% as a result of these changes.[66]

As indicated, School C's faculty was slightly larger in 1965 than in 1955 and

Table 21

Data for Case-study School C
for 1955, 1960 and 1965

	1955	1960	1965
Enrollment, total	234	305	452
Student/faculty ratio	23.2/1	29.6/1	32.8/1
Faculty size	10.1	10.3	13.7
Average teaching load (hours)	11.9	11.3	10.6
Total teaching hours delivered	120	117	145
Teaching hours delivered to first-year class	32	30	57
Teaching hours delivered to 2nd-&-3rd-year classes	88	87	88
Equivalent faculty teaching 2nd-&-3rd-year classes	7.4	7.7	8.3
Enrollment of 2nd-&-3rd-year classes	117	174	270
Effective student/faculty ratio of 2nd-&-3rd-year classes	15.8/1	22.6/1	32.5/1
Average class size of 2nd-&-3rd-year classes	37	56	73

65.   Theoretically, some schools' enrollments and faculties could have increased at exactly the same rate. It is understandable that, over a period as long as fifteen years, this did not occur in any case examined.

66.   In fact, because of increases in input cost, per-student cost decreased only 11%.

it was therefore able to deliver a total of 25 more teaching hours. However, as it added a second section to most of its first-year classes, it actually offered the same number of teaching hours to its second- and third-year students in 1965 as it did ten years earlier. In fact, School C offered virtually the same number of teaching hours and nearly identical curricula to its second- and third-year students in 1955, 1960 and 1965. In effect, the same number of faculty members were allocated to the second-and-third-year programs in each of these years.

During the same time, however, its second-and-third-year enrollment increased as follows: 1955, 117 students; 1960, 174 students; 1965, 270 students. Its upperclass curriculum remained the same, but the average size of its second-and-third-year classes increased substantially: 1955, 37 students; 1960, 56 students; 1965, 73 students.[67] In 1955, 23% of its upperclass student hours were in Small classes and 77% were in Medium classes. In 1960, the proportion of its upperclass student hours in Small classes had decreased to 14% and the proportion in Medium classes had increased to 86%. By 1965, upperclass student hours in Small classes had further decreased to 6% of total student hours taken by second- and third-year students, 41% of such student hours were in Medium classes, and for the first time, a number of such student hours (53% of the total) were taken in Large classes.[68]

School B is an example of a small school that fell in the second pattern mentioned, schools whose student/faculty ratios increased, but at a lower rate than those of schools in the first pattern. The basic data of School B for the years 1955 and 1970 are set out in Table 22. Between 1955 and 1970, enrollment increased 240% (128 students to 435) and the faculty also increased, but at the lower rate of 162%. As a result of these changes, its student/faculty ratio increased from about 16/1 to 21/1. Thus, if input cost had remained at the same level between 1955 and 1970, per-student cost would have decreased 25%.[69]

Even though School B's student/faculty ratio increased between 1955 and 1970, because its faculty increased substantially (although not at the rate of its enrollment increase), the number of teaching hours it delivered also increased substantially. In 1955, it offered 97 total teaching hours, 30 to its first-year class and 67 to its second-and-third-year classes; in 1970, it offered 215 teaching hours, 56 to its first-year class and 159 to its second-and-third-year classes.[70] Of the 159 teaching hours delivered to the second-and-third-year classes in 1970, 14

67. School C's effective second-and-third-year student/faculty ratio increased roughly from 16/1 in 1955 to 23/1 in 1960 to 33/1 in 1965.

68. As indicated, by 1965, School C's enrollment had grown to 452 students. Thus, in terms of the enrollment classifications, School C had become a Large Enrollment Group school. Between 1965 and 1970, its enrollment increased about 12% and its faculty 98%. As a result, its student/faculty ratio was reduced from 33/1 in 1965 to 19/1 in 1970. Accordingly, School C's pattern of development between 1965 and 1970 was similar to those of many of the schools that were in the Large Enrollment Group in 1955. The evolution of the Large Enrollment Group is discussed below.

69. In fact, because of increases in input cost, per-student cost increased 8%.

70. It may be noted that teaching hours increased 126% as compared with a faculty increase of 162%. The difference is explained by the fact that School B's teaching load decreased from 12 hours in 1955 to 10.3 hours in 1970.

consisted of sections.[71] Thus, in terms of new subject-matter offerings, School B's upperclass curriculum more than doubled between 1955 and 1970.

Table 22

Data for Case-study School B
for 1955 and 1970

	1955	1970
Enrollment, total	128	435
Student/faculty ratio	15.8/1	20.5/1
Faculty size	8.1	21.2
Average teaching load (hours)	12	10.3
Total teaching hours delivered	97	219
Teaching hours delivered to first-year class	30	60
Teaching hours delivered to 2nd-&-3rd-year classes	67	159
Equivalent faculty teaching 2nd-&-3rd-year classes	5.6	15.4
Enrollment of 2nd-&-3rd-year classes	77	270
Effective student/faculty ratio of 2nd-&-3rd-year classes	13.8/1	17.5/1
Average class size of 2nd-&-3rd-year classes	31	48

Table 23 sets out the number of teaching hours offered in each course grouping in 1955 and 1970. The figures in parenthesis next to the 1970 figures represent the number of teaching hours within that grouping that consisted of sections. It will be noted that enormous expansion took place in the Second Category, especially in the jurisprudence, urban affairs, international law, and general groupings. In the First Category, growth took place in the number of teaching hours delivered in the corporation and taxation groupings, but as a percent of total upperclass teaching hours delivered, they remained at about the same level as they were in 1955. Most other groupings in the First Category decreased substantially in terms of the percent of total teaching hours delivered in those groupings.

Table 24 sets out the percent of total teaching hours offered and the percent of total student hours taken in the First and Second Categories in 1955 and 1970. By 1970, almost the same percent of teaching hours was delivered to the First Category as was delivered to the Second Category, in contrast to the 76% to 24% breakdown in 1955. The percent of student hours taken in the First Category also decreased between 1955 and 1970, but not to the extent of teaching hours. In 1955, the average size of classes in the First and Second Category was about the same. As a result of the changes noted above, in 1970,

---

71.   None of the 67 upperclass teaching hours in 1955 consisted of sections.

Table 23

School B's Teaching Hours in the Course Groupings in 1955 and 1970

Course Grouping	Upperclass Teaching Hours	
	1955	1970
First Category		
Corporate	6	17
Commercial	5	10 (2)
Procedure	19	22
Property	13	12
Taxation	8	21 (6)
Subtotal	51	82
Second Category		
Jurisprudence	2	10 (4)
Criminal	0	4
Urban Affairs	0	17
Labor	3	7
Law & The Person	2	6
International	0	9
Administrative	3	3
Constitutional	0	3
General	6	18 (2)
Subtotal	16	77
Total	67	159

Table 24

School B's Percent of Total Teaching Hours and Percent of Total Student Hours in the First Category and Second Category, 1955 and 1970

	1955		1970	
	Student Hours	Teaching Hours	Student Hours	Teaching Hours
First Category	79%	76%	71%	52%
Second Category	21%	24%	29%	48%

the average size of classes in the First Category was considerably larger than the average size of classes in the Second Category.

Consistent with the increase in student/faculty ratio between 1955 and 1970, the average size of the second-and-third-year classes increased from 31 in 1955 to 48 in 1970. Table 25 shows the breakdown of student hours between Large, Medium, and Small classes. In 1955, School B had just two types of classes, Medium and Small, and they were actually relatively close together in size: Small classes averaging 22 students and Medium classes averaging 41 students. By 1970, the proportion of its student hours in Small classes had dropped from 35% to 23%, and its remaining student hours were divided fairly evenly between Medium and Large classes. Although in 1970 the average size of Small classes remained about 20 students, the average size of Medium classes had increased to 60 students and the average size of Large classes was 127 students.

The nature and extent of School B's curriculum development between 1955 and 1970 may be assumed to be generally similar to the development of many other schools which were small schools in 1955 and whose faculty and student body increased between that year and 1970 in such a manner that enrollment increases outpaced faculty increases, resulting in student/faculty ratio increases. Originally, such schools were very small and, in view of the small size of their faculty, offered few more than the necessary minimum of teaching hours to their second- and third-year students. As a result, most of their upper classes necessarily had about the same number of students in each course. In this respect they were similar to first-year courses. As these schools increased in size and their faculties expanded, it may be assumed that, in a similar manner to School B, their second-and-third-year educational programs changed in two essential ways: their curricula broadened, and their classes began to differ in size.[72]

There follows a description of how the upperclass curricula of schools that were small in 1955 developed as the schools grew in size, concentrating

---

72.   Between 1955 and 1970, School A's enrollment increased from 117 to 467, a 300% increase. During the same time, its faculty increased from 6.7 to 17.6, a 163% increase, and its student/faculty ratio increased from 17.5/1 to 26.7/1. Its upperclass teaching hours increased from 67 to 126. Of the total increase of 59 upperclass teaching hours, 16 were in the First Category (from 50 to 66, a 32% increase) and 43 were in the Second Category (from 17 to 60, a 253% increase). In 1955, School A offered 65 separate subject-matter teaching hours to its upperclasses. By 1970, this amount had increased by 51 teaching hours to 116 (10 teaching hours were in sections), a 78% increase in separate subject-matter offerings. Average class size of second-and-third-year classes increased from 20 in 1955, when all of such classes were Small classes, to 56 in 1970, when 15% of total upperclass student hours were in Small classes, 43% in Medium classes, and 42% in Large classes. (Over 90% of student hours in Large classes were in the First Category.)

Between 1955 and 1970, School D's enrollment increased from 161 to 393 students, a 144% increase, while its faculty increased from 8.4 to 15, a 79% increase. As a result of these changes, its student/faculty ratio increased from 19.2/1 to 26.2/1. Its upperclass teaching hours increased from 87 to 106.5. Virtually all of the increase in new separate subject-matter teaching hours delivered to the upperclass constituted Second Category courses. Average class size of second-and-third-year classes increased from 26 in 1955, when 52% of total upperclass student hours were in Small classes and 48% were in Medium classes, to 41 in 1970, when 21% of such student hours were in Small classes, 67% were in Medium classes, and 12% were in Large classes. (All of the upperclass student hours in Large classes were in the First Category.)

particularly on the manner in which the upperclass curricula evolved into a mix of different size classes. Of particular importance to this explanation is our finding, mentioned above, that, unlike the expansion that took place in the first-year programs, the addition of teaching hours to the second-and-third-year programs of case-study schools in the Small and Middle Enrollment Groups did not usually involve the sectionalization of basic courses. Rather, new courses

Table 25

**School B's Student Hours and Size of Classes
in 1955 and 1970**

1955		1970	
Percent of Student Hours	Size of Classes	Percent of Student Hours	Size of Classes
0%	Large	40%	Large
65%	Medium	37%	Medium
35%	Small	23%	Small

were offered involving new fields of study or new materials on existing subjects. As the upperclass curricula expanded, students did not distribute evenly among all the courses offered, and a pattern of class sizes emerged involving a mix of Large, Medium, and Small classes. This phenomenon will now be explained in more detail.

Until quite recently, a number of upperclass courses were required at most law schools. Nearly all these required courses consisted of what we have called First Category courses, such as corporations, commercial transactions, evidence, property, trusts and estates, and federal income taxation. Because these schools rarely sectionalized their upperclass courses, as their enrollments increased, these courses became Large class offerings. However, as the credit hours received from completing these required courses in most cases constituted a relatively small proportion of the minimum hours required during the last two years, the students chose among the available electives to complete their upperclass credit-hour requirements. As indicated, at the start of the period examined, schools in the Small and Middle Enrollment Groups had few electives, and all their upperclass courses were about the same size. With the passage of time, however, the number of teaching hours delivered to the upper classes increased, and with this increase, the number of elective courses offered also increased. (Many of these elective courses fell within what we have called the Second Category of course groupings.) Students, however, did not distribute themselves evenly among these elective courses. Some courses were more fully subscribed than others. At the same time, a number of these upperclass electives consisted of seminars whose enrollments were limited. Thus, there resulted a mix of classes by enrollment size. In recent years many schools have abandoned the system of upperclass requirements, but a similar pattern of class mix prevails. For example, at School A of the case-study schools, a large number of the First Category courses that were required in earlier years, such as evidence, corporations, trusts and estates, and the basic tax course, continue to draw relatively large numbers of students, while the enrollment in the remaining courses differs considerably from class to class.

When schools were small, there were only two sizes of class—Medium and Small. Courses in the First Category tended to be given in Medium classes, and courses in the Second Category tended to be given in Small classes. As enrollments increased, Large classes evolved and became part of the upperclass mix. At the end of the period studied, most Large classes involved courses in the First Category. Medium and Small classes were fairly evenly distributed between the First and Second Categories, although frequently a larger proportion of the Small classes fell within the Second Category.

So far we have discussed only schools in the Small and Middle Enrollment Groups whose student/faculty ratios increased between 1955 and 1970, that is, schools that followed the first and second patterns of development mentioned above. Of the 83 schools in these two Groups, only 17 (or about 20%) followed the third pattern, i.e., schools that had their student/faculty ratios decrease during this period.[73] Virtually all these third-pattern schools had student/faculty ratios of 20/1 or higher in 1955. Because these schools had relatively high enrollments and student/faculty ratios, their evolution was more typical of the Large Enrollment schools which are discussed below. No case-study school that was a Small or Middle Enrollment school in 1955, had its student/faculty ratio decrease between 1955 and 1970. For these reasons schools following the third pattern will not be discussed.

Virtually no school within the Small or Middle Enrollment Group which had an extremely low student/faculty ratio (16/1 and lower) in 1955 maintained or decreased its student/faculty ratio between 1955 and 1970 while its enrollment increased. At the start of this section, it was pointed out that these schools had extremely low student/faculty ratios because of small enrollments together with faculties of a minimum size. It has also been suggested that, in view of the fact that law schools with large enrollments have had a tradition of high student/faculty ratios and large classes, it is understandable that, as enrollments of small schools increased, their student/faculty ratios should also increase.[74] In this connection there is examined above in section 2 a hypothetical model of a school of 450 students and a student/faculty ratio of 16/1 which might have been a Small or Middle Enrollment school in 1955 and kept its student/faculty ratio constant between that year and 1970.

We now turn to an examination of the development of the upperclass educational programs of schools in the Large Enrollment Group (schools with enrollments in 1955 of 250 and higher). In one sense these schools began the period examined in a position similar to that attained by many of the Small and Middle Enrollment schools at the end of the period. Thus, they offered fairly

---

73.   Of these schools, five were in subgroup H of the Middle Enrollment Group, four were in subgroup M of the Middle Enrollment Group, and one was in subgroup M of the Small Enrollment Group.
74.   See chapter 2, section 4.

extensive curricula to their second-and-third-year classes, and in addition, their upperclass curricula, in terms of class size, usually consisted of a mix of Small, Medium, and Large classes. Chapter 2 has demonstrated that Large Enrollment schools developed quite differently from most of the schools in the Small and Middle Enrollment Groups. As shown there, during the fifteen-year period examined, while virtually every school had its enrollment increase, most of the student/faculty ratios of the smaller schools increased, and most student/faculty ratios of the larger schools remained constant or decreased. As might be expected, the Large Enrollment Group's upperclass curricula developed very substantially, and in cases where their student/faculty ratios lowered, average class sizes were reduced. It will be recalled from chapter 2 that these latter schools were those in which rising input cost combined with decreasing student/faculty ratios to produce extremely large increases in cost per student.

As Large Enrollment schools' enrollment increased between 1955 and 1970, two general patterns developed. First, a number of schools began the period with relatively low student/faculty ratios, and, as their enrollments increased, their faculties increased at a somewhat faster rate. As a result, their student/faculty ratios decreased, but not by a great extent. A sizeable number of schools in subgroup L and a few schools in subgroup M of the Large Enrollment Group followed this pattern. Second, a number of schools began the period with moderate to high student/faculty ratios, and, as their enrollments increased, their faculties increased at a considerably faster rate. As a result, their student/faculty ratios decreased quite substantially.[75] A large number of schools in subgroups M and H of the Large Enrollment Group followed this pattern.

None of the case-study schools fell within the first pattern mentioned above. However, the effective second-and-third-year student/faculty ratios of two of these schools decreased a relatively small amount between 1955 and 1970 because they had a considerably smaller percentage of total students in their second and third years in 1955 than in 1970. These schools' upperclass development thus approximates the first pattern. They will be designated as Schools X and Y. We will begin by examining School X's development.

Table 26 presents the basic data with respect to School X for the academic years 1955-56 and 1970-71. The table reveals a 59% increase in students and a 124% increase in faculty. Consistent with these changes, School X's student/faculty ratio decreased from 25/1 to 18/1. As a result of its faculty increase, total teaching hours increased 178 hours, from 118 hours in 1955 to 296 hours in 1970, or 151%.[76] Upperclass teaching hours increased 114 hours, from 88 teaching hours in 1955 to 202 in 1970, a 130% increase.[77] As fewer teaching hours consisted of sections in 1970 than in 1955, the increase of new subject-matter teaching hours was even greater, viz., 186%. Table 27 exhibits School X's distribution of upperclass teaching hours among the course groupings

---

75.   Among the schools in the Large Enrollment Group, a small number (13 out of 43) had student/faculty ratios that increased during the period examined.

76.   Because School X's teaching load increased somewhat (from 9.3 hours in 1955 to 10.5 hours in 1970), total teaching hours grew at a faster rate than faculty size.

77.   Upperclass teaching hours in percentage terms increased a smaller amount than total teaching hours because first-year teaching hours increased an even greater amount.

Table 26

Data for Case-study School X
for 1955 and 1970

	1955	1970
Enrollment, total	321	510
Student/faculty ratio	25.3/1	18/1
Faculty size	12.7	28.4
Average teaching load (hours)	9.3	10.5
Total teaching hours delivered	118	296
Teaching hours delivered to first-year class	30	94
Teaching hours delivered to 2nd-&-3rd-year classes	88	202
Equivalent faculty teaching 2nd-&-3rd-year classes	9.5	19.2
Enrollment of 2nd-&-3rd-year classes	176	339
Effective student/faculty ratio of 2nd-&-3rd-year classes	18.5/1	17.7/1
Average class size of 2nd-&-3rd-year classes	51	46

in 1955 and 1970.[78] It will be noted that, of the 119-hour increase in upperclass teaching hours, 33 such hours, or 30%, were in the First Category, and 80 such hours, or 70%, were in the Second Category. In the First Category significant increases occurred only in the corporation and tax groupings, although as a percent of total teaching hours in 1970, they only slightly exceeded the percent of total teaching hours they constituted in 1955. The other groupings in the First Category remained at about the same level in terms of actual teaching hours and, consequently, decreased substantially as a percent of total teaching hours. In the Second Category, enormous expansion took place in the criminal law and urban affairs groupings, and substantial expansion took place in the jurisprudence, law and the person, and international law groupings.

Table 28 gives the percent of total teaching hours offered and the percent of total student hours taken in the First and Second Categories in 1955 and 1970. Between these two years, both the percent of teaching hours and the percent of student hours decreased in the First Category and increased in the Second Category, reflecting the fact that 70% of the teaching hours added to the upperclass curriculum during that time were in the Second Category. Whereas the average class size of First Category classes was larger than that of Second Category classes both in 1955 and 1970, by 1970 the average class size of First Category classes had increased and that of Second Category classes had decreased. The effective upperclass student/faculty ratio at School X dropped

---

78.   The figures in parenthesis represent the number of teaching hours that consisted of sections.

Table 27

School X's Teaching Hours in the Course Groupings in 1955 and 1970

Course Grouping	Upperclass Teaching Hours	
	1955	1970
First Category		
Corporate	9.4 (1.4)	25 (4)
Commercial	6.7 (2.0)	6
Procedure	12.7 (4.0)	12
Property	12.1 (2.1)	19 (3)
Taxation	8.7 (4.7)	21 (4)
Subtotal	49.6 (14.2)	83 (11)
Second Category		
Jurisprudence	4.7	15.5 (2)
Criminal	0	20 (5)
Urban Affairs	2.7 (1.4)	25
Labor	5.4 (1.4)	6
Law & The Person	0	8
International	5.3 (2.6)	24
Administrative	2.7	3
Constitutional	6 (2.0)	6
General	11.3 (2.0)	11
Subtotal	38.1 (9.4)	118.5 (7)
Total	87.7 (23.6)	201.5 (18)

Table 28

School X's Percent of Total Teaching Hours and Percent of Total Student Hours in the First Category and Second Category, 1955 and 1970

	1955		1970	
	Student Hours	Teaching Hours	Student Hours	Teaching Hours
First Category	72%	57%	61%	41%
Second Category	28%	43%	39%	59%

from about 18.5/1 in 1955 to 17.7/1 in 1970. Consistent with this change, the average size of the second-and-third-year classes decreased from 51 students in 1955 to 46 students in 1970, and the percent of upperclass student hours in Small classes almost doubled.

The second Large Enrollment case-study school we will examine will be referred to as School Y. As in the case of School X, School Y began the period with a relatively low effective second-and-third-year student/faculty ratio, which, over the next fifteen years, decreased a moderate amount. The basic data for School Y for the years 1955 and 1970 are given in Table 29.

Table 29

Data for Case-study School Y
for 1955 and 1970

	1955	1970
Enrollment, total	743	1,035
Student/faculty ratio	28.5/1	21.8/1
Faculty size	26.1	47.5
Average teaching load (hours)	9	8.8
Total teaching hours delivered	236	418
Teaching hours delivered to first-year class	62	77
Teaching hours delivered to 2nd-&-3rd-year classes	174	341
Equivalent faculty teaching 2nd-&-3rd-year classes	19.3	38.8
Enrollment of 2nd-&-3rd-year classes	419	728
Effective student/faculty ratio of 2nd-&-3rd-year classes	21.7/1	18.8/1
Average class size of 2nd-&-3rd-year classes	64	57

Between 1955 and 1970, enrollment at School Y increased 39% and the faculty increased 82%. As a result, the school's student/faculty ratio decreased from 29/1 to 22/1. Total teaching hours increased 77%, this increase being somewhat less than the faculty increase because of the slightly reduced teaching load in 1970. Upperclass teaching hours increased 167 hours, from 174 to 341, a 96% increase. Upperclass teaching hours increased at a greater rate than total teaching hours because 92% of the increase in total teaching hours was allocated to the second-and-third-year program. In 1955, 25 of the 174 teaching hours delivered to the second-and-third-year classes consisted of sections.[79] In 1970, 79 of the 341 teaching hours delivered to the upperclass consisted of sections.[80] Thus, the number of separate subject-matter offerings grew from 149 in 1955 to

---

79.   Of these 25 teaching hours, 11, or 44%, were in the First Category, and 14, or 66%, were in the Second Category.
80.   Of these 79 hours, 46, or 58%, were in the First Category, and 33, or 42%, were in the Second Category.

262 in 1970, a 76% increase. Table 30 shows School Y's distribution of upperclass teaching hours among the course groupings in 1955 and 1970.[81] It will be observed that of the 167 additional teaching hours offered in 1970, 57, or 34% of the total, were in the First Category, and 110, or 66% of the total, were in the Second Category. In 1955, 67 separate subject-matter teaching hours were offered in the First Category, and in 1970, 89 such teaching hours were offered in the First Category, an increase of 22 hours, or 33%. In 1955, 82 separate subject-matter teaching hours were offered in the Second Category, and in 1970, 173 such teaching hours were offered, an increase of 111%. In the First Category, only the corporation group expanded, increasing from 15 teaching hours in 1955 to 50 hours in 1970, or from 9% of total teaching hours to 15% of total teaching hours. Teaching hours offered in the procedure grouping also expanded but not as a percent of total teaching hours. The number

Table 30

**School Y's Teaching Hours in the
Course Groupings in 1955 and 1970**

Course Grouping	Upperclass Teaching Hours	
	1955	1970
First Category		
Corporate	15	50 (16)
Commercial	10 (2)	9 (3)
Procedure	18 (2)	39 (18)
Property	15	18 (3)
Taxation	20 (7)	19 (6)
Subtotal	78 (11)	135 (46)
Second Category		
Jurisprudence	6	30
Criminal	2	24 (8)
Urban Affairs	2	21 (2)
Labor	7	10
Law & The Person	3	3
International	27 (4)	55 (5)
Administrative	6	6
Constitutional	18 (3)	30 (12)
General	25 (7)	27 (6)
Subtotal	96 (14)	206 (33)
Total	174 (25)	341 (79)

81.   The figures in parenthesis represent the number of teaching hours within that grouping which consisted of sections.

of teaching hours offered in the other groupings of the First Category remained constant or reduced, and, naturally, as a percent of total teaching hours, reduced substantially. In the Second Category, substantial expansion occurred in the jurisprudence, criminal law, urban affairs, and international law groupings.

School Y's effective upperclass student/faculty ratio was about 22/1 in 1955. By 1965, it had decreased to 19/1. Between 1965 and 1970, its upperclass student/faculty ratio remained at 19/1. The average class size of second-and-third-year classes at School Y dropped from 64 to 57 students between 1955 and 1970 and the percent of upperclass student hours in Small classes increased somewhat.

The third Large Enrollment case-study school we shall examine had an extremely high student/faculty ratio in 1955 which over the next fifteen years lowered substantially. This school falls within the second pattern of Large Enrollment schools mentioned above. It will be referred to as School Z. The basic data of School Z are given in Table 31.

Table 31

Data for Case-study School Z
for 1955 and 1970

	1955	1970
Enrollment, total	618	958
Student/faculty ratio	49.8/1	29.2/1
Faculty size	12.4	32.8
Average teaching load (hours)	15.4	10.9
Total teaching hours delivered	191	356
Teaching hours delivered to first-year class	60	103
Teaching hours delivered to 2nd-&-3rd-year classes	131	253
Equivalent faculty teaching 2nd-&-3rd-year classes	8.5	23.2
Enrollment of 2nd-&-3rd-year classes	341	548
Effective student/faculty ratio of 2nd-&-3rd-year classes	40.1/1	23.6/1
Average class size of 2nd-&-3rd-year classes	70	64

It will be noted that in 1955 School Z was a large school with a high student/faculty ratio, engaging only a few more faculty members than many of the smaller schools. Its faculty carried an extremely heavy teaching load. If they had taught an 11-hour load, in order to have offered the same number of total teaching hours as were actually delivered (191 hours), the school would have had to increase the size of its faculty by close to one-third (from 12.4 to 17.4). If this had been the case, its student/faculty ratio would have been 35/1, still high but considerably lower than the 50/1 student/faculty ratio under which it actually operated.

In 1955, School Z offered 131 teaching hours to its upper classes and the average size of these classes was 70; students took only 6% of upperclass student hours in Small classes. The student enrollment at School Z increased from 618 students in 1955 to 958 in 1970, a 55% increase, and its faculty increased from 12.4 professors to 32.8, a 165% increase. As a result of these changes, School Z's student/faculty ratio decreased from 50/1 in 1955 to 29/1 in 1970. If input cost had remained constant during these years, per-student cost would have increased 70%. As it was, input cost increased 110%, and this increase combined with the decrease in the student/faculty ratio to produce a per-student cost increase between 1955 and 1970 of 259%.

School Z's upperclass curriculum expanded enormously as a result of the increased size of its faculty. In 1955, it offered 131 teaching hours to its second-and-third-year students, 35 of which were sections; in 1970, it offered 253 teaching hours, of which 45 were sections. In other words, School Z's upperclass curriculum in terms of separate subjects increased by 112 teaching hours, or 117%. Eighty-seven, or 78%, of these additional teaching hours were in the Second Category and 25, or 22%, were in the First Category.

Table 32 sets forth School Z's distribution of upperclass teaching hours among the course groupings in 1955 and 1970. The figures in parenthesis represent the number of teaching hours within that grouping which consisted of sections.

In the First Category, substantial increases took place in the corporation grouping. The remaining First Category groupings either decreased or remained at about the same level in terms of number of teaching hours offered, and decreased substantially as a percent of total teaching hours. In the Second Category, substantial increases occurred in the criminal law, urban affairs, law and the person, and international law groupings, both in terms of the number of teaching hours offered and as a percent of total teaching hours.

Table 33 gives the percent of total teaching hours offered and the percent of total student hours taken in the First and Second Categories in 1955 and 1970. The changes between these two years indicate a definite shift of both teaching hours and student hours toward courses in the Second Category. This is not surprising, as most of School Z's curriculum growth was in the Second Category.[82]

School Z's effective upperclass student/faculty ratio decreased from 40/1 in 1955 to 24/1 in 1970. Consistent with these changes, the average size of second-and-third-year classes at School Z dropped from 70 students in 1955 to 64 students in 1970, and the number of upperclass student hours in Small classes doubled from 6% in 1955 to 12% in 1970.

In sum, tremendous expansion in the curricula of all three schools occurred between 1955 and 1970 as enrollments increased and student/faculty ratios fell. Their curriculum expansion in terms of new subject matter more than doubled. Most of this expansion took place in the Second Category, particularly in the

82. Although the average class size of First Category courses was larger than that of Second Category courses both in 1955 and 1970, by 1970, the average class size of the First Category courses had increased and that of Second Category courses had decreased.

Table 32

**School Z's Teaching Hours in the
Course Groupings in 1955 and 1970**

Course Grouping	Upperclass Teaching Hours	
	1955	1970
First Category		
Corporate	12 (3)	41 (10)
Commercial	14 (6)	20 (7)
Procedure	31 (8)	34 (9)
Property	30 (12)	25 (9)
Taxation	12	14 (4)
Subtotal	99 (29)	134 (39)
Second Category		
Jurisprudence	7 (2)	9
Criminal	0	16 (3)
Urban Affairs	0	22
Labor	3	9
Law & The Person	2	18 (3)
International	5	18
Administrative	3	6
Constitutional	8 (4)	6
General	4	15
Subtotal	32 (6)	119 (6)
Total	131 (35)	253 (45)

Table 33

**School Z's Percent of Total Teaching Hours
and Percent of Total Student Hours in the First
Category and Second Category, 1955 and 1970**

	1955		1970	
	Student Hours	Teaching Hours	Student Hours	Teaching Hours
First Category	80%	76%	70%	53%
Second Category	20%	24%	30%	47%

urban affairs, international law, criminal law, and law and the person groupings, although in the First Category considerable expansion took place in the corporation grouping. For Schools X and Y, whose effective upperclass student/faculty ratios decreased the least, this expansion may be attributed as much to increased enrollment as to decrease in student/faculty ratio, whereas, for School Z, whose student/faculty ratio decreased substantially, a large part of this expansion may be attributed to favorable student/faculty ratio development. Both Schools X and Y began the period with low upperclass student/faculty ratios and, accordingly, had a fairly high percent of student hours in Small classes from the start. As their upperclass student/faculty ratios decreased somewhat between 1955 and 1970, the number of student hours taken in Small classes increased further, but the mix of classes did not alter essentially. School Z, on the other hand, had its upperclass student/faculty ratio decrease substantially and, consequently, the number of student hours taken in Small classes increased to a considerable extent.

Section 4 — The Costs of Clinical Legal Education

Before leaving the subject of instructional cost, a brief examination will be made of the cost of clinical legal education programs.[83] The institution of such programs during the past five years or so has been a major new development in legal education and their costs have become a central concern for law schools.

In analyzing the costs of these programs it is appropriate to distinguish instructional cost from noninstructional cost. Following the somewhat narrow definition of instructional cost used in the rest of this chapter, the instructional cost of clinical programs involves only the salaries paid to faculty members who teach and supervise these programs. On the other hand, noninstructional cost includes all of those expenditures made to defray what might be characterized as the law office expenses of a clinical program.[84] For example, court costs, duplicating costs in connection with litigation, travel, costs incurred in telephoning clients, and the like fall within the compass of noninstructional cost. In addition to these nonpersonnel items, compensation paid to secretaries, to office managers, and, in some cases, to attorneys whose primary responsibility is to help manage a clinic's caseload (rather than supervise students) are included within noninstructional cost.[85]

To begin with, we will examine the instructional cost of clinical programs.

---

83. This section has been based in large part upon the close familiarity of one of the co-authors with clinical education derived from his four years as a program officer with the Council on Legal Education for Professional Responsibility.

84. The noninstructional cost of clinical education might, as a matter of sheer consistency, be more properly examined in the chapter on Supporting Services. However, as most people include both instructional and noninstructional cost in their concept of the costs of clinical education, both costs are covered in this section.

85. Strictly analyzed, considerable overlap may occur between instructional and noninstructional cost. Supervising faculty members will necessarily be involved in helping prosecute a clinic's caseload and, conversely, attorneys whose major responsibility is to manage the clinic's caseload will from time to time supervise students.

Instructional cost is determined in large part by the number of students a clinical faculty member can supervise in the course of a semester. Little consensus exists among clinical educators regarding the maximum number of students a clinical instructor can manage at any one time. Salient to this issue is a consideration of the type of cases being handled by the clinic, and the experience of the faculty member or supervising attorney, and the nature of his teaching load, i.e., whether he devotes his full time to the clinical program or whether he has other teaching assignments in the school's nonclinical curriculum. Some have argued that for an individual instructor to provide thoroughly adequate supervision, no more than seven students should be assigned to him. In practice, it appears that one instructor for every 20 students is more nearly the typical arrangement, although there are a number of programs where as many as 35 students will be supervised by one clinical instructor. In analyzing the instructional cost of these programs, consideration must also be given to the teaching loads of the clinical instructors. In many cases, clinicians devote their full time to teaching their clinical programs. Indeed, it is because of this fact that they are able to provide adequate supervision to as many as 20 students.

Most clinical programs today award 3 hours of credit a semester and, in this respect, are similar to the great preponderance of upperclass courses.[86] In these circumstances, a clinical instructor will carry a 6-hour teaching load each year. In terms of the analysis developed in section 2, an upperclass program involving one instructor teaching 20 students for 6 credit hours implies a student/faculty ratio of about 4.5/1, i.e., if every upperclass course were limited to 20 students and each faculty member teaching in the upperclass curriculum taught only 6 hours a year, the school would operate with an upperclass student/faculty ratio of 4.5/1.[87] In section 2 it was demonstrated that Small class instruction, on this analysis, implies a student/faculty ratio of about 8.5/1.[88] The difference between the student/faculty ratio determined for such Small classes and that determined for our typical clinical program inheres in the fact that the Small class student/faculty ratio computation in section 2 assumed an average teaching load of 11 hours whereas the student/faculty ratio for the clinical program assumed a 6-hour teaching load. It appears, therefore, that the instructional cost of Small class clinical education of the kind supposed is relatively high. In many cases, however, the clinical instructor will teach courses in the nonclinical curriculum and so will approximate a full teaching load. In these instances, on the analysis developed above, the instructional cost of clinical programs is no greater than that of other Small class programs.

---

86.   As suggested at the end of section 2, clinical enterprises are examples of educational programs where the credit system, based as it is on classroom attendance, begins to break down. Most of the time that students and faculty members devote to clinical work is in the field or in preparing cases in the clinic. Usually an organized seminar will also attach to the program, but time spent in the seminar constitutes a small portion of total time devoted to the program.

87.   Assume 100 upperclass students, each taking 26 credit hours a year. They will produce 2,600 student hours. If classes are limited to 20 students, 130 teaching hours will be required to cover these student hours. Further, if each faculty member teaches only 6 hours, about 21.5 faculty members will be required to furnish these teaching hours. This works out to a student/faculty ratio of about 4.5/1. ($100 \div 21.5 = 4.65$).

88.   See above.

As suggested in section 3, the relation between credit hours and teaching hours makes little sense when applied to clinical programs. By their intrinsic nature, these are not classroom programs. Although typically they involve a classroom component, the bulk of a participating student's work usually is with the "clinical" component of the program. The classroom component usually involves weekly sessions that last for about two hours. Frequently, reading assignments are given in connection with these meetings; so, in many respects these classroom meetings are like the traditional seminars for which two hours of credit is usually awarded.[89] As pointed out, most clinical programs award three hours of credit. However, because so much more of a student's total work is on clinical matters than on classroom preparation and attendance, it cannot reasonably be said that credit is allocated on the basis of two hours for the classroom component and one hour for the clinical work. Indeed, from the standpoint of learning, the classroom component is usually regarded as a supplement to the student's principal educational experience, which is derived from working on cases. It is difficult to ascertain, then, the precise basis on which these three units of credit are assigned. The most likely basis would appear to be that clinical programs are regarded as full law school courses, and the typical law school course is a three-point offering. It may well be that, in terms of credit awarded, many clinical programs are undervalued. In any event, a determination of the proper amount of credit to be accorded to a clinical program must necessarily be on grounds other than classroom attendance. It is intriguing to speculate on what these grounds might be, and such speculation effectively raises many of the most fundamental issues of legal education. It is not, however, in the scope of this study to examine such questions. Nevertheless, it should be noted that, to the extent that clinical programs are undercredited, their per-student-hour cost may be overestimated.

Thus far, nothing has been said about the salaries of faculty members teaching clinical programs—the other major factor involved in instructional cost. Insofar as regular faculty members are concerned, no distinction has been found in the salary levels of faculty members who teach clinically and those who teach in the traditional curriculum. However, a number of clinical programs use recent graduates as teaching fellows, and these instructors are paid at levels appreciably below those of regular faculty members. In these cases the instructional cost of clinical programs will be somewhat lower than might otherwise be the case.

The cost of a clinical program may be substantially affected by the type of program involved. While differences in type of clinical program are significant in determining the noninstructional cost of these programs, there is one type-distinction that has particularly important impact on instructional cost. This is the difference between "farm-out" programs and "in-house" programs. Farm-out programs place students in non-law school agencies, such as local prosecutors' or public defenders' offices. In some instances nearly all the clinical supervision that students need is produced by attorneys employed by the agency. From a law school's standpoint, these programs may involve only part of

---

89.   In the traditional seminar there is, of course, a direct relation between time spent in the classroom and the amount of credit awarded.

the time of an administrative dean, who arranges for the students' placements, and the cost of such programs may be minimal.[90] In-house programs are run and solely controlled by the law school. Supervision of the students' clinical work is performed by faculty members and attorneys on the law school payroll. Usually all the costs for such programs are defrayed by the law school, and, over-all, they are far more expensive than farm-out programs. Hybrid programs combining the features of both types of program exist. Some farm-out programs involve faculty members working with and supervising students in the outside agencies, and the instructional cost of these programs may be as high as those of in-house programs. Conversely, a few law schools run programs that assume responsibilities for local legal service agencies, and attorneys from these agencies (and on their payrolls) are assigned to them. In these cases the supervisory cost of the in-house program will be reduced.

To complete this examination of the costs of clinical education programs, brief consideration will be given to their noninstructional cost. As indicated, these costs differ widely among the various types of clinical programs. Clinical programs involving law school "clinics" with large caseload responsibilities entail considerable noninstructional cost. Frequently they are located in spaces outside the law school building and, accordingly, incur rent, utility, and office-maintenance expenses. For such clinics with large caseloads, staff attorneys may be hired primarily to handle the caseload. In addition, these clinics may require their own secretarial pools and libraries.[91] Few, if any, of these expenses are incurred by smaller clinical programs operating in the law school building with restricted caseloads. These smaller programs, however, incur noninstructional costs of appreciable dimensions. Typically, secretarial services are supplied to clinical programs at a much higher level than to nonclinical instructional programs. Secretaries attached to clinical programs, because of the complexities of their work, are frequently among the highest paid secretaries at the law school. In addition, all clinical programs incur markedly higher expenses for office supplies, duplicating, telephone, and postage than the regular law school program. Many clinical programs carry liability insurance on their students. Travel expenses vary widely with the type of program. For example, an inmate-assistance program, pursuant to which students travel to penitentiaries far distant from the law school, may incur substantial travel expenses. On the other hand, an in-house clinic located in a law school, accessible to its clients and near the court houses, may incur minimal travel expenses. Finally, most clinical programs entail special litigation expenses, such as filing fees, compensation for court reporters, witness fees, and the like.[92]

90. In addition to being inexpensive, these programs may also appeal to law schools because they do not involve law schools assuming caseload responsibilities. Of course, lack of law school control is an important factor in many legal educators' doubts about such programs. These doubts may be particularly strong if the school awards academic credit for participation in such programs.
91. For a comprehensive examination of the library component of clinical education, see: Grossman, *Clinical Legal Education and the Law Library*, 67LLJ60 (1974).
92. For a detailed analysis of the costs of clinical education, see Swords, *Including Clinical Education in the Law School Budget*, in "Clinical Education for the Law Student," pp. 314-324 (New York: CLEPR, 1973).

Chapter 4

Library Costs

Introduction

As a purely a priori matter, library costs may be expected to increase even if instructional cost and expenditures for supporting services of legal education remain constant or decline. Growth is an inherent characteristic of law school libraries. Libraries will continue to expand regardless of the increase or decrease in student enrollment and faculty size. This is so for a number of reasons. Law school libraries are research libraries, and as new books and materials are published, they must be acquired if the libraries are to remain serviceable. Furthermore, the kinds of books law libraries predominantly acquire, viz., serials,[1] tend also to produce inherent growth in library acquisitions. Increases in the number of volumes added and total volumes held make it necessary to engage additional library personnel to maintain and run the library.

This chapter analyzes two major components of library costs: books, dealt with in section 1, and personnel, dealt with in section 2. Our examination is based upon two general sources of information. Some information regarding a large number of law school libraries has been derived from statistical data published by the American Association of Law Libraries in a publication entitled

---

1. See below.

Directory of Law Libraries.[2] This is a biennial publication, and in using the data from this source, we have chosen to commence our investigation with the year 1954 rather than the year 1956. Thus, certain of our data span a sixteen-year period (1954 to 1970) rather than the fifteen-year period used elsewhere in this study. In addition, we have used information regarding a large number of law school libraries published in the "Annual Statistical Survey of Law School Libraries and Librarians" authored by Alfred J. Lewis and appearing each year in the May issue of the *Law Library Journal.* These surveys have only recently been instituted. The first survey reported figures for the fiscal year July 1968 to June 1969, and at the time of this writing a total of four such surveys have been completed and published. They are based on information collected from virtually every accredited law school.[3] These surveys, containing an enormous amount of significant information, will be extremely useful for future examinations of law libraries.

For analytic purposes we have broken the large number of law school libraries for which information is available into four groups on the basis of volumes held in 1970. Group 1: Large libraries, consists of those libraries with over 200,000 volumes. Group 2: Medium-large libraries, consists of those libraries with between 100,001 and 200,000 volumes. Group 3: Medium libraries, consists of those libraries with between 50,001 and 100,000 volumes. Group 4: Small libraries, consists of those libraries with fewer than 50,001 volumes. This breakdown is used by Professor Lewis in his surveys. For comparative purposes we have used only those 112 libraries for which both 1954 and 1970 data were reported. These 112 libraries were ranked according to the number of volumes held in 1970 and then divided into the four groups. On this basis there are 15 Large libraries, 28 Medium-large libraries, 42 Medium libraries, and 27 Small libraries. The other general source of information is data collected from our case-study schools. In addition, some information was derived from interviews with law librarians and others.

Section 1 – Books

Annual expenditures for law library books are, of course, a function of two variables: the number of books purchased and their price. First, we will examine library acquisitions without regard to price. Between the years 1955 and 1970 many law libraries tended to acquire each year more books than in the previous year, i.e., the number of volumes added increased from one year to the next.[4]

---

2.   *Directory of Law Libraries,* The Committee on Directories, American Association of Law Libraries, ed.: (New York; Commerce Clearing House, Inc.), June 1970; June 1964; June 1960; June 1954. Prior to the 1964 edition this was entitled *Law Libraries in the United States and Canada.*
3.   In 1969, 145 law school libraries were surveyed and 137 responded, 63 LLJ 267 (1970); in 1970, 147 were surveyed and 141 responded, 64 LLJ 218 (1971); in 1971, 148 were surveyed and 148 responded, 65 LLJ 221 (1972); in 1972, 149 were surveyed and 148 responded, 66 LLJ 189 (1973).
4.   It will be noted in Table 1 below that during the latter part of the period examined this phenomenon did not prevail among the Large libraries. Indeed, at over one-half of the

Table 1 sets out for each school in each of the four groups the volumes held in 1954 and 1970 and the compound average annual rate of increase for five periods of time: 1954-1960, 1960-1964, 1964-1970, 1954-1970, and 1969-1972. The data for the first four periods were obtained from the *Directory of Law Libraries* and for the last time interval (1969-1972) from the Annual Survey.[5] Table 2 presents the distribution of these average annual growth rates within each of the four groups. It will be noted that the growth rate at the Large and Medium-large libraries was less during the latest time period (1969-1972) than during the preceding time period examined (1964-1970). At the Medium libraries the growth rate remained about the same and it increased at the Small libraries.

Table 1

Annual Growth Rates of Library Volumes Held by 112 Law School Libraries for Five Periods of Time, by Groups 1954-1972

1954 Volumes Held	1970 Volumes Held	6-Year Annual Growth Rate 1954-1960	4-Year Annual Growth Rate 1960-1964	6-Year Annual Growth Rate 1964-1970	16-Year Annual Growth Rate 1954-1970	3-Year Annual Growth Rate 1969-1972 *
		Group 1	—	Large Libraries		
785,000	1,175,000	2.9%	2.7%	2.1%	2.6%	1.5%
330,000	500,000	2.7	2.4	2.7	2.6	1.7
351,000	490,000	1.9	1.0	3.0	2.1	2.1
241,000	402,000	2.3	4.1	3.6	3.2	2.5
130,000	325,000	4.1	4.9	8.4	5.9	4.6
199,000	321,000	3.5	2.9	2.6	3.0	2.5
158,000	280,000	2.4	3.5	5.1	3.7	3.5
120,000	276,000	4.3	7.0	5.4	5.4	3.9
133,000	272,000	.1	7.8	7.0	4.6	4.2
106,000	260,000	4.0	7.2	6.5	5.7	6.5
130,000	215,000	1.9	3.6	4.3	3.2	4.5
100,000	212,000	1.6	5.3	7.8	4.8	8.5
101,000	206,000	4.3	5.0	4.5	4.5	4.8

schools included in this group, the rate of increase between 1964 and 1970 was lower than the rate of increase between 1960 and 1964.

5.   A somewhat smaller group of schools (107) is included in the last time interval than is included in the first four, because of lack of data for five schools. Because of some difference in the figures reported, this last time interval should be regarded as a separate series. (See note to Table 1.)

Table 1   (continued)

1954 Volumes Held	1970 Volumes Held	6-Year Annual Growth Rate 1954-1960	4-Year Annual Growth Rate 1960-1964	6-Year Annual Growth Rate 1964-1970	16-Year Annual Growth Rate 1954-1970	3-Year Annual Growth Rate 1969-1972 *
105,000	205,000	2.4	6.2	4.9	4.3	4.5
80,000	205,000	6.8	5.3	5.8	6.1	4.0

Group 1 — Averages

204,600	356,200	2.8%	3.7%	4.1%	3.5%	3.2%

Group 2 — Medium-large Libraries

127,000	198,000	1.1%	3.5%	4.1%	2.8%	3.9%
81,000	179,000	4.3	2.4	7.7	5.1	4.6
32,000	175,000	3.7	3.5	24.0	11.2	5.4
95,000	163,000	2.4	3.3	4.6	3.4	2.7
88,000	160,000	2.7	3.3	5.1	3.8	3.9
106,000	155,000	2.5	1.4	3.0	2.4	4.9
40,000	150,000	8.4	7.9	9.3	8.6	6.4
70,000	150,000	4.3	4.9	5.4	4.9	2.6
47,000	146,000	6.4	14.8	3.8	7.4	4.3
45,000	145,000	10.5	11.1	2.5	7.6	2.2
22,000	137,000	23.9	7.7	4.0	12.0	4.7
55,000	130,000	5.7	8.8	3.1	5.5	0
73,000	128,000	3.4	3.6	3.7	3.5	5.5
65,000	127,000	4.5	1.8	5.6	4.2	3.4
26,000	124,000	9.2	14.5	8.2	10.1	6.0
59,000	123,000	9.1	.8	3.1	4.7	3.1
84,000	123,000	2.3	2.3	2.7	2.5	4.0
23,000	123,000	3.1	9.3	21.3	11.2	8.1
27,000	122,000	2.8	7.1	19.4	9.9	8.6
75,000	113,000	2.6	2.9	2.4	2.6	2.6
57,000	111,000	3.4	3.2	3.1	3.3	1.7
32,000	111,000	2.6	7.5	14.2	8.0	7.6
31,000	106,000	9.7	4.9	8.4	8.0	5.9
28,000	106,000	11.3	6.3	9.2	9.2	7.7
50,000	105,000	5.8	3.3	4.7	4.7	6.5
44,000	105,000	3.9	6.6	6.7	5.6	5.2
45,000	104,000	5.2	5.3	5.6	5.4	4.1
42,000	102,000	4.7	2.0	9.2	5.7	2.0

Group 2 — Averages

56,300	132,900	4.9%	5.0%	6.4%	5.5%	4.4%

Table 1   (continued)

1954 Volumes Held	1970 Volumes Held	6-Year Annual Growth Rate 1954-1960	4-Year Annual Growth Rate 1960-1964	6-Year Annual Growth Rate 1964-1970	16-Year Annual Growth Rate 1954-1970	3-Year Annual Growth Rate 1969-1972 *
Group 3 — Medium Libraries						
30,000	100,000	10.3%	7.2%	6.1%	7.9%	4.8%
31,000	100,000	4.6	0	16.5	7.6	8.5
38,000	99,000	8.3	3.3	5.9	6.1	6.4
44,000	98,000	3.4	6.9	5.7	5.1	3.4
41,000	92,000	3.8	7.7	4.9	5.2	10.4
53,000	92,000	2.4	1.7	5.9	3.5	4.3
33,000	90,000	7.2	8.8	4.3	6.5	7.2
20,000	90,000	9.0	5.2	14.0	9.9	9.6
34,000	90,000	7.0	5.2	6.3	6.3	5.2
30,000	86,000	2.6	6.5	11.3	6.8	13.5
13,000	85,000	15.0	9.9	11.7	12.5	5.5
33,000	85,000	6.3	3.0	7.9	6.1	7.3
40,000	84,000	2.0	3.7	8.3	4.7	3.7
54,000	83,000	1.6	3.1	3.5	2.7	3.3
19,000	80,000	9.4	3.8	13.4	9.5	6.5
45,000	80,000	4.9	2.0	3.5	3.6	2.7
33,000	79,000	6.7	3.5	6.1	5.7	8.1
50,000	77,000	.5	4.7	3.7	2.7	6.8
21,000	76,000	3.5	8.7	13.3	8.4	7.0
38,000	75,000	4.9	7.6	1.9	4.4	3.2
28,000	72,000	2.6	10.0	7.0	6.1	6.2
28,000	72,000	3.3	4.8	9.8	6.1	9.6
30,000	71,000	10.3	3.4	2.5	5.6	4.8
40,000	70,000	1.3	4.8	5.0	3.6	6.8
25,000	69,000	8.3	4.5	5.9	6.5	5.0
17,000	68,000	15.6	7.4	3.9	9.0	3.5
27,000	67,000	2.9	13.4	4.2	5.9	n.a.
42,000	64,000	1.2	2.2	4.6	2.7	7.7
30,000	63,000	2.8	2.7	8.1	4.7	8.7
32,000	61,000	5.4	3.0	3.7	4.2	3.6
22,000	61,000	8.9	4.6	5.9	6.7	5.4
20,000	61,000	4.7	17.8	3.4	7.3	2.1
30,000	61,000	3.3	3.8	5.9	4.4	5.5
14,000	60,000	10.1	11.0	8.0	9.6	6.0
23,000	60,000	8.5	2.2	6.3	6.1	2.7
30,000	58,000	6.3	2.8	2.9	4.1	4.6
22,000	57,000	2.9	2.2	12.3	6.1	5.7
25,000	56,000	4.7	3.9	6.5	5.2	13.2
26,000	55,000	6.3	3.0	4.5	4.8	n.a.

Table 1   (continued)

1954 Volumes Held	1970 Volumes Held	6-Year Annual Growth Rate 1954-1960	4-Year Annual Growth Rate 1960-1964	6-Year Annual Growth Rate 1964-1970	16-Year Annual Growth Rate 1954-1970	3-Year Annual Growth Rate 1969-1972 *
23,000	54,000	6.0	8.0	3.5	5.5	8.4
24,000	53,000	1.1	1.8	12.0	5.2	4.0
20,000	52,000	4.6	4.1	9.2	6.2	8.5

Group 3 – Averages

30,400	73,900	5.2%	5.2%	6.6%	5.7%	6.3%

Group 4 – Small Libraries

1954 Volumes Held	1970 Volumes Held	6-Year Annual Growth Rate 1954-1960	4-Year Annual Growth Rate 1960-1964	6-Year Annual Growth Rate 1964-1970	16-Year Annual Growth Rate 1954-1970	3-Year Annual Growth Rate 1969-1972
21,000	50,000	3.7	7.3	6.4	5.6	11.8
9,000	50,000	9.9	13.0	12.6	11.7	25,0
19,000	50,000	2.7	7.7	8.9	6.2	7.7
20,000	50,000	5.2	4.0	7.7	5.8	11.9
19,000	50,000	2.5	17.5	2.9	6.2	6.2
30,000	50,000	6.2	1.4	1.6	3.2	3.6
27,000	49,000	5.4	2.5	3.0	3.8	10.3
12,000	49,000	10.2	5.5	10.1	9.0	6.7
22,000	48,000	3.2	4.8	7.4	5.1	9.1
10,000	48,000	16.5	8.0	5.7	10.2	3.6
17,000	46,000	8.8	6.3	4.7	6.6	12.6
19,000	45,000	7.6	3.7	4.7	5.5	8.0
22,000	45,000	5.5	2.0	5.8	4.7	14.3
15,000	45,000	5.4	4.2	10.4	7.0	9.3
7,000	43,000	0	9.9	27,0	12.0	n.a.
23,000	42,000	5.3	3.5	2.6	3.8	10.1
20,000	41,000	2.9	4.7	6.2	4.6	5.0
16,000	41,000	5.7	4.1	7.2	5.9	4.5
24,000	41,000	1.5	4.1	4.8	3.4	3.2
25,000	39,000	0	3.9	5.1	2.9	4.4
25,000	38,000	2.2	1.7	4.0	2.8	7.8
21,000	36,000	4.4	4.2	2.1	3.5	5.2
10,000	36,000	7.0	7.5	10.3	8.3	11.5
20,000	35,000	.8	5.3	4.9	3.4	1.8
19,000	30,000	4.1	3.9	1.1	2.9	13.8
9,000	30,000	8.6	2.6	11.4	8.1	n.a.
7,000	23,000	8.7	4.7	10.5	8.3	n.a.

Group 4 – Averages

18,000	43,000	5.0%	5.1%	6.3%	5.5%	8.6%

Table 1   (continued)

1954 Volumes Held	1970 Volumes Held	6-Year Annual Growth Rate 1954-1960	4-Year Annual Growth Rate 1960-1964	6-Year Annual Growth Rate 1964-1970	16-Year Annual Growth Rate 1954-1970	3-Year Annual Growth Rate 1969-1972 *
		Total: 112 Libraries — Averages				
57,200	118,900	4.0%	4.5%	5.5%	4.7%	4.8%

n.a. = Not available.

* These data are from Lewis' Annual Statistical Survey which began in 1969. Although a larger number of libraries appeared in the survey, only those schools which appear in the 1954-1970 sample are included here; in 5 cases, either the 1969 or the 1972 data were not available. There were some discrepancies in the comparative data (for instance, in 37 of the libraries, some 1969 figures reported were the same as the 1970 figures in the 1954-1970 series, some were much smaller, some were much larger) and these figures should therefore be regarded as a different series.

Sources: *Directory of Law Libraries*, op. cit. and Lewis, op. cit.

These Tables clearly demonstrate the exponential nature of increases in volumes acquired by law school libraries.[6] Even though a wide variation occurred in such increases among the schools examined, the average annual increase for all schools for the sixteen-year period of 1954-1970 was at the compound rate of 4.7% with a median increase of 5.5%. The volume increases have been enormous. The libraries in the three smaller groups have increased at a faster rate than those in the largest group. This is not surprising since large libraries started the period with a much larger base than the smaller libraries. On the basis of this information the average Small library (group 4) held 43,000 volumes in 1970 as compared to 18,000 volumes in 1954, a 138% increase. The average Medium library (group 3) held 73,900 volumes in 1970 as compared to 30,400 in 1954, a 143% increase. The average Medium-large library (group 2) held 132,900 volumes in 1970 as compared to 56,300 in 1954, a 136% increase, and the average Large library (group 1) held 356,200 volumes in 1970 as compared to 204,600 in 1954, a 74% increase. The Large library group includes one library that held 1,175,000 volumes in 1970, over twice as many as the next largest library. If this figure is omitted, the average Large library held 298,000 volumes in 1970 and 163,000 in 1954, an increase of 82%. For all 112 libraries examined, the increase averaged 108%, from 57,200 volumes in 1954 to 118,900 volumes in 1970. This growth is demonstrated in Figure 1 which shows the distribution of the 112 libraries by size in 1954 and 1970.

6.   It should be noted that Tables 1 and 2 are based on volumes added each year and not on volumes acquired. The rate of volumes acquired may be higher than that of volumes added, the difference being the number of volumes withdrawn from the collection.

Table 2

Distribution of Growth Rates for Five Periods of Time
for 112 Law School Libraries, by Groups

Compound Average Annual Increase	Group 1 Large Libraries (over 200,000 volumes) Number of Libraries					Group 2 Medium-Large Libraries (100,001 to 200,000 volumes) Number of Libraries					Group 3 Medium Libraries (50,001 to 100,000 volumes) Number of Libraries					Group 4 Small Libraries (under 50,000 volumes) Number of Libraries					Total Number of Libraries				
	1954 to 1960	1960 to 1964	1964 to 1970	1954 to 1970	1969 to 1972	1954 to 1960	1960 to 1964	1964 to 1970	1954 to 1970	1969 to 1972	1954 to 1960	1960 to 1964	1964 to 1970	1954 to 1970	1969 to 1972	1954 to 1960	1960 to 1964	1964 to 1970	1954 to 1970	1969 to 1972	1954 to 1960	1960 to 1964	1964 to 1970	1954 to 1970	1969 to 1972
12.0%+						1	2	4	1		2	2	6	1	2	1	2	2	1	4	4	6	12	3	6
11.5%–11.9%							1					1							1	3	1			1	3
11.0%–11.4%						1			2		1		2		2				1		2	1		2	
10.5%–10.9%						1	1	3	1		1	1	1	3		1	1		1		3	3	3	4	3
10.0%–10.4%						1	1	1	1		1	1	1	1	2	1		3	1	2	3	4	4	4	2
9.5%–9.9%					1	2	2	2	1		2	2	2	2	1		1			2	4	1	6	5	4
9.0%–9.4%			1			2	1	1	2		2	1	3	1		1	1	1	3		5	4	4	5	5
8.5%–8.9%			1				3	2	1	1	4	2	1	8	3	3		3	1		3	6	1	9	3
8.0%–8.4%			1				1	2	1	3	1	5	1	4	3		1	2	1	1	3	3	6	3	6
7.5%–7.9%			1			3	3	2	2	1	1	1	1	4	3	1	1	4			5	5	3	7	5
7.0%–7.4%	1	2	1	1		1	1	2	2		1	5	4	3	3	3	3	2	4		6	13	6	10	6
6.5%–6.9%		1	1			1	1	2	2	3	6	6	6	3	3	1	4	1	6	2	8	8	11	5	6
6.0%–6.4%		3	1	4	4	2	2	2	2	2	2	2	3		3	5	2	1	8	2	6	12	6	9	11
5.5%–5.9%		1	1	2	2	2	3	4	3	1	3	4	6	4	3	4	1	1	6		8	5	9	6	8
5.0%–5.4%	3	1	1	2		2	2	2	2	3	5	2	1	4	2	1	3	2	7	1	6	9	7	9	6
4.5%–4.9%	1	1	1	1	2	2	2	2	2	3	2	4	2	3	3	1	5	1	8	2	7	8	8	7	4
4.0%–4.4%	1	2	2	1		2	2	4	4		5	2	6	4	3	3	4	1	5	1	9	8	9	11	4
3.5%–3.9%	2		1	1		5	5	2	2	2	2	1	2		2	1	2		3		8	9	3	2	4
3.0%–3.4%	3	1	1	1	2	2	2	3	3	3	1				2	1	1	1	1	1	7	2	2	1	1
2.5%–2.9%			1	1	2	3	1	1	1						1		1	1	3		2	1	1		
2.0%–2.4%						2	1			1							1	1	1		2				
1.5%–1.9%						1	1														1				
1.0%–1.4%	1										1	1									3				1
.5%–.9%																									
0%–.4%																									
Average	2.8%	3.7%	4.1%	3.5%	3.2%	4.9%	5.0%	6.4%	5.5%	4.4%	5.2%	5.2%	6.6%	5.7%	6.3%	5.0%	5.1%	6.3%	5.5%	8.6%	4.0%	4.5%	5.5%	4.7%	4.8%
Median	2.7%	4.9%	4.1%	3.5%	4.0%	4.3%	4.3%	5.3%	5.5%	4.5%	4.7%	4.3%	5.9%	5.4%	6.1%	5.3%	4.2%	5.8%	5.6%	9.2%	4.5%	4.3%	5.6%	5.5%	5.2%

Number of Law School Libraries

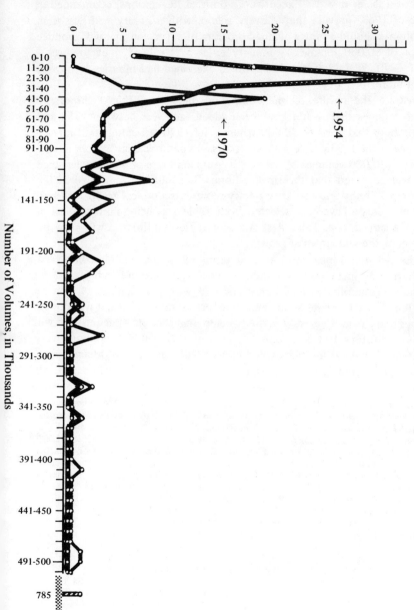

Distribution of 112 Law School Libraries
by Number of Volumes
1954 and 1970

Figure 1

It may be that the revision of the American Association of Law Schools standards in the late 1960's caused a number of small libraries to build their collection at a faster rate. Its Executive Committee Regulations, as amended in December of 1968, provide that: "Every school with a library with less than 60,000 volumes should adopt a planned program of expansion that will produce a collection of 60,000 volumes by January 1, 1975."[7] Table 1, above, indicates that as of 1970, 78 out of the 112 schools examined had libraries of 60,000 volumes or more.

To illustrate the nature of the compound increases, Table 3 shows the number of volumes that would have been added each year between 1954 and 1970 at a school that grew to 80,000 volumes by 1970 at a compound rate of 5.3% per year since 1954. Table 3 also presents a hypothetical law school library that grew to 270,000 volumes by 1970 at a compound rate of 4% per year since 1954. It will be noted that the smaller library is about the same size as the median group 3 library and the larger library represents a typical group 1 library. The rates of increase have been selected from Table 1 as being fairly typical of libraries of a similar size. Table 4 shows how these two libraries will grow by 1980, assuming the same rates of growth.[8]

As indicated, the Tables show that in terms of all the schools considered, libraries have been increasing the number of books they acquire each year at the average annual compound rate of increase of 4.7% with a median rate of increase of 5.5%. If a library increases at an annual compound rate of 5.0%, it will double its holdings every fifteen years. We assume below that the rate of acquisition will decrease in the future. If it slows to 4.4%, a library will double its holdings every 16 years, and if it slows to 4%, it will double its holdings every eighteen years.[9]

Returning to Figure 1, it is evident that the great bulk of law school libraries

---

7.   Regulations Sec. 8.1(d) *A.A.L.S. Proceedings, 1968* (Part Two), 234. Prior to this change the maximum number of volumes required was 20,000. This standard was adopted in 1952 (*A.A.L.S. Proceedings, 1952*, 224) after having stood at 10,000 volumes since 1930. Bade, *Library Standards*, 4 J. Legal Ed. 427 (1952). Between the end of 1962 and 1968, however, the A.A.L.S. Standards provided for no minimum number of volumes but rather set out a list of required publications. This list, in a slightly expanded form, was continued in the 1968 amendments. A related amendment passed in 1968 required that libraries of member schools expend a minimum of $40,000 for new acquisitions designed to extend their collections. Regulations Sec. 8. 4(c) *A.A.L.S. Proceedings, 1968* (Part Two), 236. In 1971, the minimum was raised to $50,000. *A.A.L.S. Proceedings, 1971* (Part One), 233.

8.   It is unlikely, however, that a large library that held 270,000 volumes in 1970 would increase its holdings over the next 10 years in the exponential manner shown in Table 4. As indicated above, the rate of acquisition at most of the libraries included in the Large library group decreased from the period 1960-1964 to the period 1964-1970. Similarly, a comparison of the rates of increase at these libraries between the period 1969-1972 and the period 1964-1970 indicates a further decrease. (As indicated these two periods are not comparable. See note to Table 1.) An examination of volumes added by these Large libraries between 1969 and 1972 indicates that, as a general matter, each of these libraries has recently been acquiring the same number of books as it did the year before. Thus, their rate of acquisition has been decreasing. If a library of 270,000 volumes adds 10,000 volumes a year over a ten-year period, it will increase its holdings at a compound rate of 3.2% rather than 4% as assumed in the Table. The Table, however, uses the 4% figure to demonstrate what would happen if Large libraries continue to increase their holdings in an exponential manner.

9.   On the other hand, if the rate of acquisition increases to a compound rate of 6% per year, a library will double its holdings every 12 years; if it increases to 6.5%, every 11 years.

Table 3

Illustration of Volume Increase at an Average Medium and an Average Large Size Law School Library, 1954 to 1970, at Different Growth Rates

	Medium Library Compound Average Annual Rate of Increase = 5.3%		Large Library Compound Average Annual Rate of Increase = 4.0%	
	Total Volumes	Added Volumes	Total Volumes	Added Volumes
1970	80,000		270,000	
1969	75,974	4,026	259,617	10,383
1968	72,150	3,824	249,631	9,986
1967	68,519	3,631	240,030	9,601
1966	65,070	3,449	230,798	9,232
1965	61,795	3,275	221,921	8,877
1964	58,685	3,110	313,386	8,535
1963	55,731	2,954	205,179	8,207
1962	52,926	2,805	197,287	7,892
1961	50,262	2,664	189,699	7,588
1960	47,732	2,530	182,403	7,296
1959	45,330	2,402	175,388	7,015
1958	43,048	2,282	168,642	6,746
1957	40,881	2,167	162,156	6,486
1956	38,824	2,057	155,919	6,237
1955	36,870	1,954	149,922	5,997
1954	35,014	1,856	144,156	5,766

in 1970 had holdings between 30,000 and 130,000 volumes, with a concentration of these schools in the 50,000 volume range. Twenty-three percent of all schools examined had libraries in 1970 that contained over 130,000 volumes, and these schools were distributed fairly evenly between that number and 500,000, with one school having slightly over 1,000,000 volumes. Figure 2 shows the distribution of libraries by size in 1970 (thus repeating part of Figure 1) and the projected distribution of libraries in 1980 on the assumption that each library will increase its holdings between 1970 and 1980 at the average annual compound rate of increase of 3.2% for Large libraries (group 1) and 5.3% for all other libraries (groups 2, 3 and 4).

Not surprisingly, the libraries of the case-study schools had similar growth patterns to those of the schools examined above. The time period for which data were compiled at the case-study schools is slightly different from that of the 112 schools: a fifteen-year period extending from 1955-56 to 1970-71. Table 5 presents the percent increases in volume holdings of the nine case-study school libraries between 1955 and 1970 and their annual compound rates of increase.

Table 4

Projected Volume Increase at an Average Medium
and an Average Large Size Law School Library, 1970 to 1980,
at Different Growth Rates

	Medium Library Compound Average Annual Rate of Increase = 5.3%		Large Library Compound Average Annual Rate of Increase = 4.0%	
	Total Volumes	Added Volumes	Total Volumes	Added Volumes
1980	134,083		399,666	
1979	127,334	6,749	384,294	15,372
1978	120,925	6,409	369,514	14,780
1977	114,839	6,086	355,302	14,212
1976	109,059	5,780	341,636	13,666
1975	103,569	5,490	328,496	13,140
1974	98,356	5,213	315,862	12,634
1973	93,406	4,950	303,713	12,149
1972	88,705	4,701	292,032	11,681
1971	84,240	4,465	280,800	11,232
1970	80,000	4,240	270,000	10,800

The median and average percentage increases in total volumes of the nine schools between 1955 and 1970 were 119% and 95%, respectively. This works out to average annual compound growth rates of 5.4% and 4.6%, respectively. Two of the libraries are in group 1 and the remaining seven are in group 2. The group 1 libraries averaged a 3.5% growth rate and the group 2 libraries averaged a 5.5% growth rate over the fifteen-year period.

To provide an indication of the amount of books that law school libraries have been acquiring recently, Table 6 sets forth for each of the four groups the average volumes added per year during the three academic years 1969-70, 1970-71, and 1971-72. This Table has been constructed from information contained in the Annual Surveys.

The exponential nature of the growth of law libraries noted above appears to be a characteristic of all research libraries. Freemont Rider argued almost three decades ago that American research libraries have been increasing in size at an exponential rate since at least 1831 and perhaps as early as the seventeenth century. In his view research libraries doubled in size every sixteen years.[10] More recently, a study conducted at Purdue University arrived at similar conclusions for the members of the Association of Research Libraries.[11]

10.   Freemont Rider, *The Scholar and the Future of the Research Library* (New York: Hadham Press, 1944).
11.   O.C. Dunn, W.F. Seibert and Janice A. Scheuneman, *The Past and Likely Future of 58 Research Libraries: 1951-1980* (Lafayette, Ind.: University Libraries and Audio Visual Center, Purdue, 1967).

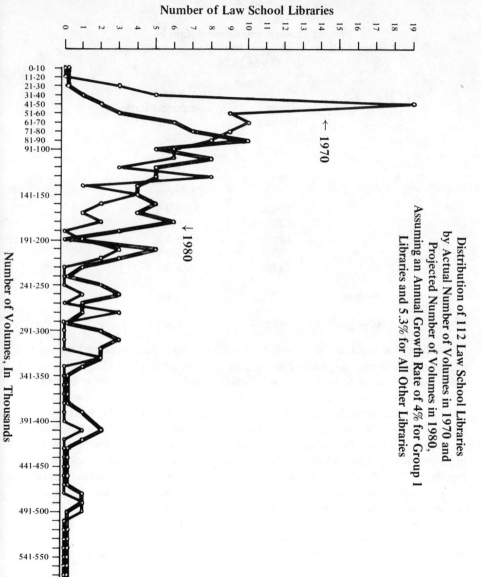

Figure 2

Distribution of 112 Law School Libraries
by Actual Number of Volumes in 1970 and
Projected Number of Volumes in 1980,
Assuming an Annual Growth Rate of 4% for Group 1
Libraries and 5.3% for All Other Libraries

Table 5

Percent Increase and Growth Rate in
Library Volume Holdings of Nine Case-study Schools
1955 to 1970

	Percent Increase	Annual Compound Rate of Increase
	49%	2.7%
	57%	3.0%
	91%	4.4%
	114%	5.2%
	119%	5.4%
	126%	5.8%
	158%	6.5%
	205%	7.7%
	217%	8.0%
Median	119%	5.4%
Average	95%	4.6%

Much of the exponential growth of law library holdings is explained by the nature of the books acquired. The bulk of any law library's holdings is serial volumes. A serial is defined as "a publication issued in successive parts bearing numerical or chronological designations and intended to be continued indefinitely. Serials include periodicals, newspapers, annuals (reports, yearbooks, etc.), the journals, memoirs, proceedings, transactions, etc., of societies, and numbered monographic series."[12] Examples of typical serials acquired by law libraries include case reports, codes and session laws, rules and regulations, digests and citators, law reviews, and loose-leaf services. The other major category of books acquired by law libraries is monographs. A monograph is defined as "a work, collection, or other writing that is not a serial."[13] Monographs for law libraries include treatises, texts, and the like.[14]

---

12.   *Anglo-American Cataloging Rules* (Chicago: American Library Association, 1967), p. 346.

13.   Ibid., p. 345.

14.   Frequently, library holdings are divided into three groups: Monographs, Periodicals, and Serial Services. Periodicals are a special kind of serial and the term is defined as "a serial appearing or intended to appear indefinitely at regular or stated intervals, generally more frequently than annually, each issue of which normally contains separate articles, stories or other writings. Newspapers disseminating general news, and the proceedings, papers, or the publications of corporate bodies primarily related to their meetings are not included in this term." Ibid. Law reviews, for example, are considered to be periodicals. A serial service is a publication issued by an agency supplying information, especially current data, in easily available form, but not readily available otherwise. The information may be issued in printed, multigraphed, loose-leaf, or other form, and may be supplied regularly and/or on request. See Thompson, Elizabeth H., *A.L.A. Glossary of Library Terms* (Chicago:

For purposes of explaining the exponential growth of law libraries, the particularly significant aspect of serials is that once a particular serial has been acquired, continuations[15] of that serial will necessarily be acquired each year until it terminates. In a sense, acquisitions begin each year with continuations of serials subscribed to in the past, and then, in addition, new serials are acquired each year. It is estimated below that over 70% of law school libraries' acquisition budgets have been spent on serials. Although serials are more expensive than monographs, this finding clearly supports the assertion that serials constitute the largest proportion (numerically) of law library holdings.[16] It is shown below

Table 6

Number of Library Volumes Added
During Fiscal Years 1969, 1970, and 1971
by the Four Groups of Law School Libraries

	Group 1	Group 2	Group 3	Group 4
Total Number of Volumes Added	532,020	512,430	579,040	302,230
Average Number Added Per Year Per Library	11,800	6,100	4,600	3,700

that between 1955 and 1970 at the case-study schools serials came to constitute a larger proportion and monographs a smaller proportion of the total amount of book expenditures. This change emphasizes the impact of serials on law library acquisitions.[17]

Although the acquisition of serials increased at the case-study schools at a greater rate than that of monographs, in absolute terms the number of monographs acquired also increased. At many of the case-study schools, international law and, to a lesser extent, foreign law collections were built up during this period and a number of the books acquired in developing these collections were monographs.[18] In chapter 3 we have shown that law schools'

American Library Association, 1943), p. 125.

15.   The term continuation is defined as "1. A work issued as a supplement to one previously issued. 2. A part issued in continuance of a book, a serial, or a series." Op. cit., *Anglo-American Cataloging Rules*, p. 334.

16.   This is in contrast to general college and university libraries, which spend 73% of their acquisition budget on books and 20% on serials (and 7% on binding). 1968 data from *The Bowker Annual - 1970* (New York: R.R. Bowker Company), p. 21.

17.   Every expanding library necessarily faces the problem of increased annual expenditures for continuations. With the purchase of each new serial, the budget percentage allocated for continuations will tend to grow.

18.   It is also true that these collections, particularly in their initial development, were heavily serial in nature.

curricula have expanded, particularly in the international law, urban affairs (which includes environmental law), law and the person, and criminal law groupings. Many of the books required by courses in these groupings also tend to be monographs. In this connection it has been observed that as the function of law and the lawyer in society has broadened, librarians of law schools have felt increasingly obliged to acquire nonlegal materials chiefly in the social sciences; for example, education, sociology, political science, labor economics, psychology, housing and urban planning, ecology, and statistics.[19] Besides acquiring current serials and monographs, libraries had to enter the out-of-print books market in order to purchase items their directors felt should have been acquired when originally issued. Several head librarians at the case-study schools have indicated this as one reason for increased acquisitions. Another reason is so-called "knowledge explosion" resulting in a growth of books being published throughout the world which has induced higher acquisitions by university libraries and, no doubt, by law libraries affiliated with them.[20]

The figures for the last time period examined in Tables 1 and 2 indicate that the rate of book acquisition is slowing. Between 1964 and 1970, Large libraries grew at a median compound rate of 4.9% and an average annual compound rate of 4.1% as compared to 4.0% and 3.2%, respectively, for the period 1969 to 1972. A similar reduction prevailed for the Medium-large libraries. While the two smaller groups had higher rates of increase during the most recent time period, the figures for all libraries also show median and average rate reductions—from 5.6% and 5.5%, respectively, for the period 1964 to 1970 to 5.2% and 4.8%, respectively, for the period 1969 to 1972. In the future it may well be that the general rate of acquisition will decrease. The data suggest that as libraries grow larger their rates of acquisition tend to decrease. On the basis of past rates of increase, particularly among the smaller libraries, it may be anticipated that more libraries will reach substantial size and then level off. In addition, the period of financial stringency that appears to have settled upon higher education for the foreseeable future will also operate to hold acquisitions down. Strong pressures will be exerted to keep library budgets from increasing by more than a marginal amount, and with inevitable increases in the cost of books and amounts paid to library personnel, it will be difficult to merely maintain a constant level of book acquisition.

Mounting annual acquisitions are only part of the law book story. We shall now turn to an examination of increases in the price of law books. Statistics show that libraries have been buying more and more books at sharply increased unit costs. A review of rising book prices is presented by *Bowker Annual's*[21] calculations of average prices. It divides prices into three categories: hardbound books,[22] serial services, and periodicals. Taking inflation into account, in the

---

19. Willard, *What Is Happening in Your Law Library?* 23 J. Legal Ed. 457 (1971). Dee, *Library Purchasing in an Interdisciplinary Age,* 63 LLJ 19 (1970).
20. William S. Dix, "Cause and Effect on University Libraries," *American Libraries*, vol. 3 (1972), pp. 725-726.
21. See note to Table 7.
22. Based on tabulation of wholesale prices of all newly published books recorded in the

sixteen-year period from 1954 to 1970, hardbound law books rose 166%, law periodicals rose 114%, and law serial services rose 195%. If converted to constant 1970 dollars, hardbound law books rose 78%; law periodicals, 43%; and law serial services, 98%. The average price per volume and the price indices are as follows.

Table 7

Average Price and Price Index for Hardbound Books, Periodicals, and Serial Services, 1954 to 1970

	Average Price 1954		Average Price 1970	Price Index 1954 = 100		16-Year Growth Rate
	Current Dollars	Constant 1970 Dollars		Current Dollars	Constant 1970 Dollars	Constant Dollars
Law Hardbound Books	$ 6.17	$ 9.20	$16.41	266.0	178.4	3.7%
All Hardbound Books	4.28	6.38	11.66	272.4	182.8	3.8%
Law Periodicals	4.60	6.86	9.84	213.9	143.3	2.3%
All Periodicals	4.34	6.47	10.41	239.9	160.9	3.0%
Law Serial Services	24.69	36.80	72.78	294.8	197.8	4.3%
All Serial Services	40.04	59.67	85.44	213.4	143.2	2.3%

Note: Data are converted from the 1947-49 and 1957-59 base period reported in order to make a continuous series. Estimates for missing data are made from either the price or the index reported. The category "All" includes only technical materials (business, law, medicine, social sciences, etc.) and not general readership items such as novels.
Sources: Schick and Kurth, *The Cost of Library Materials* (U.S. Office of Education, Library Services Branch, 1961). *The Bowker Annual* (New York: R.R. Bowker Company), 1964, pp. 82-84; 1965, pp. 102-104; 1966, pp. 102-105; 1970, pp. 37-38; 1971, pp. 87-90. *Library Journal* (Oct. 1, 1962), v. 87, pp. 3396-98.

Figure 3 shows that hardbound law books and law periodicals had not risen as steeply in price by 1970 as hardbound books and periodicals in other fields of study, whereas law serial services showed a larger increase than the composite of all serial services. Since definitive data are unavailable, we can only estimate from the above figures that, between 1954 and 1970, in constant-dollar terms, the price of law monographs increased approximately 78% and the price of law serials increased approximately 84%.[23]

As indicated, the price of serial services has increased more than any other type of law acquisition. As "loose-leaf" or serial services make up the largest component of serial acquisitions, and since serial acquisitions make up the largest component of total acquisitions, it is not surprising to find that, in the

Weekly Record Section of *Publishers Weekly*. The hardbound books do not include paperbacks, textbooks, government documents, or encyclopedias.
23. Assuming serial services constitute three-quarters of serial expenditures and periodicals constitute one-quarter of serial expenditures. (97.8 × .75) + (43.3 × .25) = 84.

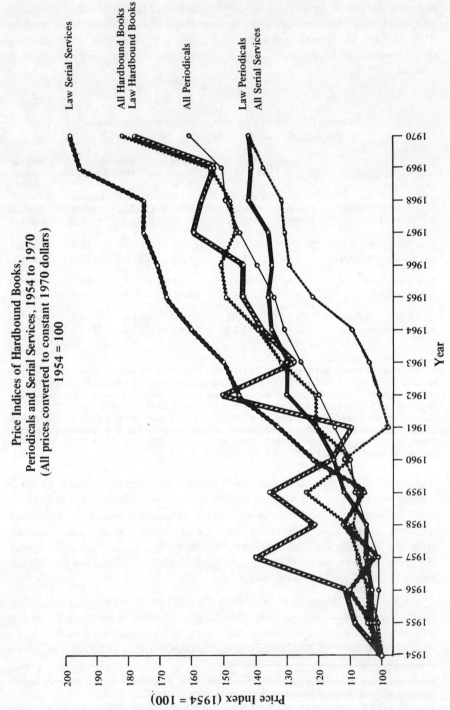

Figure 3

Price Indices of Hardbound Books,
Periodicals and Serial Services, 1954 to 1970
(All prices converted to constant 1970 dollars)
1954 = 100

recent past, serials account for over 70% of total acquisition expenditures. Table 8 sets out, for each of the four groups of libraries, the four-year (1969-1972) average of the percent of total dollars spent on books, spent on serials and monographs.

Table 8

Percent of Library Book Expenditures Spent on Serials and Monographs, for Four Groups of Law School Libraries Average for 1969-1972

Group	Serials	Monographs
Group 1	64.1% (72.1%)	24.8% (27.9%)
Group 2	68.7% (74.4%)	23.6% (25.6%)
Group 3	65.4% (72.6%)	24.6% (27.4%)
Group 4	67.2% (72.4%)	25.5% (27.6%)

Note: The two percentage figures for serials and monographs do not total 100 because the total amount spent on book expenditures (which constitutes the denominators of the fractions on which these percents are based) includes amounts spent on binding and on a category called "other." In parenthesis next to these figures are set out the percentages spent on serials and monographs where the denominators have included only the total amounts spent on these two items.

Table 9 sets out for eight case-study schools the percent of total dollars spent on books constituted by serials and monographs for 1955 and 1970. It will be noted that between 1955 and 1970 serials came to constitute a larger proportion and monographs a smaller proportion of book expenditures.

If we assume that, as a rough average, over the period examined serials constituted about 70% of the acquisition budget and mongraphs about 30%,[24] and that during this period the cost of serials increased about 84% and the cost of monographs about 78%, then the over-all cost of law books increased about 82% in constant 1970 dollars.[25]

What has been the budgetary impact on law school libraries of purchasing larger quantities of books at higher unit costs? We have shown above that, as a rough approximation, law libraries increased their annual acquisitions by about 108% from 1954 to 1970. During the same period the cost of law books, in constant dollars, has been estimated to have increased about 82%. Combining these two figures, we estimate that law library acquisition costs computed in constant dollars increased, on the average, 279% between 1954 and 1970. This is

24.   For this computation a distinction is made between the "acquisition budget" and the "amount spent on book expenditures." The latter includes the acquisition budget plus amounts spent on binding and other items.
25.   It should be noted that these figures are necessarily rough estimates. $(84 \times .70) + (78 \times .30) = 82$.

Table 9

**Percent of Library Book Expenditures Spent on Serials and
Monographs by Eight Case-study Schools
1955 and 1970**

	1955	1970
Group 1 Libraries (2 schools)		
Serials	67.4% (73.7%)	70.8% (79.0%)
Monographs	24.1% (26.3%)	18.5% (21.0%)
Group 2 Libraries (6 schools)		
Serials	64.9% (70.6%)	71.5% (77.6%)
Monographs	27.0% (29.4%)	20.6% (22.4%)

Note: See note to Table 8 for explanation of figures.

equivalent to an average annual compound growth rate of 8.7%. The figures with which these computations have been made omit amounts spent on book binding[26] and certain other expenditures charged to the book budget. However, these expenditures are relatively small as a percent of total book expenditures, and it may be conjectured that expenditures for these items increased at about the same rate as book acquisitions.[27]

Table 10 shows that eight case-study schools, on the average, almost quadrupled their acquisition budgets from 1955 to 1970, which means that their average annual rate of growth of acquisition expenditures was 8.8%. Figure 4 shows the 1955 and 1970 acquisition budgets, for each of these case-study-school libraries, separated into group 1 and group 2 size libraries, with the amount spent on serials, monographs, and other in constant 1970 dollars.

To provide an indication of the amount of money that libraries have recently spent on book acquisitions, Table 11, based on information contained in the Annual Survey, sets out the four-year average (1969-1972) of dollars expended on book acquisitions for each of the four groups of libraries. Dollar figures have not been corrected for inflation in this instance.

Certain costs related to larger acquisitions and holdings will be briefly mentioned before we turn to the area of personnel, although sufficient data is unavailable for analysis. The first of these involves binding of new acquisitions

26. Binding costs at the case-study schools increased about 200% on the average (constant dollars) between 1955 and 1970.
27. A recent appraisal of increases in law library acquisition cost is provided in the 1973 report of the Committee on Libraries of the A.A.L.S. Part of this report contained a report of Subcommittee C, "A.A.L.S. Executive Committee Regulations Review," addressing itself to the question of whether the $50,000 minimum for new acquisitions should be increased.

Table 10

Increase in Library Acquisition Expenditures
from 1955 to 1970 for Eight Case-study Schools

	15-Year Increase (Constant dollars)	15-Year Growth Rate
	135%	5.9%
	178%	7.1%
	217%	8.0%
	274%	9.2%
	283%	9.4%
	293%	9.6%
	454%	12.1%
	528%	13.0%
Median	278%	9.3%
Average	257%	8.8%

and rebinding of old volumes, both of which, of course, contribute to increased library costs. The second involves the quantity of shelving required. As library holdings expand exponentially, more shelf space is needed either in the library stacks proper, or in storage, and eventually in an entirely new library. (Other components of total library costs, such as expenditures for typewriters, office supplies, telephone, duplicating, security, certain special maintenance

---

See footnote 7. It sets out the conclusions of Professor Richard G. Hutchins of the University of Iowa (Chairman of Subcommittee A, "Statistical Survey of Law School Libraries") that from 1970 to 1972:

"(1)   The average cost of monographic titles in law increased 4.5%;

(2)   The number of monographic titles in law published increased 18.5%;

(3)   The cost of purchasing a given percentage of monographic law titles published increased 23.9%;

(4)   The average cost of monographic titles in the social sciences increased 28%;

(5)   The number of monographic titles published in the social sciences increased 9.5%;

(6)   The cost of acquiring a given percentage of titles published in the social sciences increased 40.1%; and

(7)   The average cost of periodical titles in law increased 13.3%.

The Bowker Annuals do not report the number of periodical titles published. Consequently the cost of purchasing a given percentage of the titles cannot be determined. However, it is possible to make an estimate. If it is assumed that the number of periodical law titles published increased 5% per year, then the cost of purchasing a given percentage of those titles increased 24.9%. Even if it is assumed that the number of titles increased by 4% or even 3%, the cost of acquiring a given percentage increased by 22.6%, or 20.2% respectively. The number of periodical titles received at the University of Iowa Law Library increased 9.75% per year from 1970 to 1972.

To recapitulate, the amount needed to maintain a given level of adequacy in acquisitions in law libraries has increased during the past two years by the following amounts:

(1) monographs in law   23.9%

(2) monographs in the social sciences   40.1%

(3) periodicals in law   20.2%"

A.A.L.S. Proceedings, 1973 (Part One), 35.

Figure 4

Library Book Budgets of Eight Case-study Schools by Size of Library, 1955 and 1970 (Constant 1970 dollars)

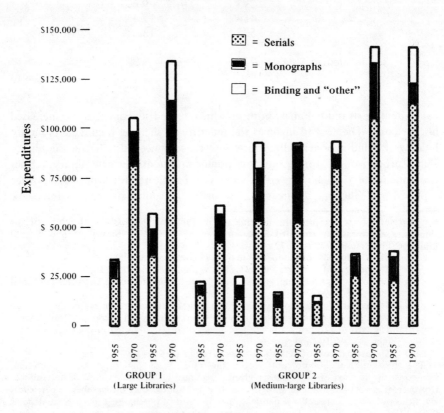

Table 11

**Average Annual Expenditures for Library Book Acquisitions
for Four-year Period, 1969 to 1972, for Four Groups of
Law School Libraries**

Group	Annual Average (Current dollars)
Group 1	$147,000
Group 2	$ 91,800
Group 3	$ 66,000
Group 4	$ 46,000

expenditures, and the like, are not dealt with because of lack of adequate data for comparative purposes.) Finally, two fairly recent developments, not necessarily related to acquisitions but bound to add to the upward pressure on library costs, will be mentioned. First, increasing demand for individualized seating in library reading areas[28] will, in many libraries, require new equipment and possible expansion of library space. This change in seating style will inevitably result in reduced seating capacity since carrels or single seats require more space than the large reading room tables used in the past. Second, many law libraries have been taking various steps to improve physical conditions, such as, installing air conditioning systems, fire detection and prevention systems, and tighter anti-theft security systems. Where installed, such systems invariably involve substantial capital expense and sometimes additional operating costs.[29]

Section 2 — Personnel

We shall now examine library personnel, the second major component of library costs. Information relating to library personnel was gathered from the case-study schools and from the *Law Library Journal*'s Annual Surveys. First, an analysis will be made of the increase in the number of personnel serving law libraries and then an analysis will be made of the increase in the salary levels of library personnel.

Between 1955 and 1970, the case-study schools had a significant increase in the numbers of both professional librarians and nonprofessional supporting staff. The average professional staff rose from 3.75 to 7.2 full-time members. At the same time, full-time and full-time-equivalent nonprofessionals rose from 3.5 to 15.8. As for percent increases in staff size, we find considerable fluctuation. The

28. See Report of the Committee on Libraries, *A.A.L.S. Proceedings, 1971* (Part One), 56.
29. A related expense is insurance coverage for books and materials which many libraries are considering in the aftermath of the disastrous Temple University Law Library fire in 1972. See Trelles, *Protection of Libraries*, 66 LLJ 241 (1973).

two case-study schools which had Large libraries (group 1) increased their professional staff 41%; the six case-study schools[30] which had Medium-large libraries (group 2) increased their professional staff 156%. The two group 1 schools increased their nonprofessional staff 214%, and the six group 2 schools increased their nonprofessional staff 499%. Total increase of all staff was 217%. On the whole, the case-study schools showed a growth rate for all library staff of about 8% per year compounded.[31]

Among the case-study schools there was little uniformity in staff composition and in the functions of each professional librarian and supporting staff member. However, comparing the personnel data of these schools in 1955 with the data in 1970 reveals some interesting patterns. Generally included in the ranks of professionals in 1955 were a head librarian, an assistant librarian, and a cataloger. This was true of four law school libraries in our survey. In addition, a slightly larger number of clerks, library assistants, and students performed various nonprofessional tasks. By 1970, while the professional staff still included the three positions mentioned above, additional members had come into existence. For example, there were librarians in charge of acquisitions, circulation, foreign and international law, government documents, and reference. A parallel trend toward staff specialization is even discernible among nonprofessionals, with library clerks and assistants in 1970 having more defined functions. Many more student assistants were used in 1970.[32] In sum, during the fifteen-year period, appreciable development occured in the expansion of the law library's work force and the division of its labor.

The rising number of professional and nonprofessional library employees is not difficult to explain. The exponential growth of library holdings required more professional librarians to select books for acquisition and more to catalog them once they were received. The development of international and foreign law holdings resulted in the hiring of librarians in these areas by three law schools. Two law school libraries became partial government depositories and required the services of documents librarians. Meanwhile, increased student enrollment and library use led to the hiring of reference and circulation librarians, and at least two of the case-study school libraries had to increase the length of their operating day in order to accommodate the increased student use. In general, growing library holdings and use have been prime contributors to the need for more professional librarians and nonprofessional employees of all kinds to assist them. Therefore, instead of a single librarian or clerk performing in a variety of capacities, larger libraries require professionals and nonprofessionals in greater numbers to render more specialized services. The revision in 1968 of the A.A.L.S. Library Standards regarding professional staffing may have been a significant factor in staff growth toward the end of the period examined. The amendments required, for libraries with over 60,000 volumes, three professional librarians in addition to the head librarian, and many libraries may have enlarged

---

30.   Data were unavailable for one case-study school.
31.   On this basis the staff would double approximately every 9 years. However, as will be explained below, it is unlikely that library staffs will continue to grow at this rate in the future.
32.   Presumably, a number of such students were engaged under work-study programs.

their staffs to meet these requirements.[33]

Information regarding the staff size of law school libraries is contained in the *Law Library Journal* Annual Surveys of 1969-70-71-72. The Survey divides the library staff into three components: 1) professionals, 2) full-time

Table 12

Size and Growth of Library Staff
for Four Groups of Law School Libraries
1969 to 1972

		Group 1 (Large)	Group 2 (Med-large)	Group 3 (Medium)	Group 4 (Small)
Average number of professionals					
	1969	6.4	2.1	.9	.5
	1972	9.0	5.1	2.7	2.1
Average change		41%	143%	200%	320%
Average number of full-time non-professionals					
	1969	17.8	5.4	2.6	1.0
	1972	14.7	5.6	3.1	1.9
Average change		−17%	4%	19%	90%
Average number of part-time non-professionals					
	1969	6.3	5.6	4.3	3.5
	1972	6.1	6.8	5.2	4.0
Average change		−4%	21%	21%	14%

Source: Lewis, *Statistical Survey of Law School Libraries and Librarians.*

33.   The 1968 amendments to the Executive Committee Regulations provided, in part, that: "In the case of a library of 60,000 volumes or more, the librarian, where practicable, should be provided with at least the following staff: three professional assistants, qualified through training or experience, with responsibility in the following functions, acquisitions, cataloging, reference and administration, and other necessary professional and clerical assistance." Regulations Sec. 8.3(b) *A.A.L.S. Proceedings, 1968* (Part Two), 235. Prior to this time the standards merely required that the librarian be furnished with such professional and clerical assistance as was necessary to properly conduct the library. It will be recalled that 78 out of the 112 libraries examined had over 60,000 volumes in 1970, and that another 1968 amendment requires that all member schools have libraries of this size by 1975.

nonprofessionals, and 3) part-time nonprofessionals (data converted to full-time equivalents). For each of the four groups of libraries we have determined the average growth in these three categories of library personnel between the years 1969 and 1972. This is presented in Table 12.

The Annual Survey's questionnaire uses a very restrictive definition of a professional law librarian, defining the term as "a person who has both a graduate degree in library science and a law degree and at least 2 years of professional library experience, or who has a law degree and at least 4 years of professional library experience, or who has a graduate degree in library science and at least 6 years of professional library experience, or who has long-term professional library experience."[34] The Table indicates that the greatest growth took place in the full-time professional ranks. This may have been the result of the 1968 amendments regarding professional staffing referred to above.[35] Whatever the reasons may be, the increases in both the professional and nonprofessional categories appear somewhat distorted; the increases in the professional category being unusually large and those in the nonprofessional category being unusually small. To eliminate such distortion, Table 13 simply presents the growth of all full-time library personnel (excluding part-time nonprofessional staff).

Table 13

Size and Growth of Full-time Library Staff for Four Groups of Law School Libraries, 1969 to 1972

		Group 1	Group 2	Group 3	Group 4
Average number of full-time professionals and non-professionals					
	1969	24.2	7.4	3.5	1.4
	1972	23.7	10.7	5.8	4.0
Average change		−2%	44%	65%	185%
Average annual compound rate of growth		0	12.8%	18.2%	41.7%

It is evident that, in percentage terms, the greatest growth in personnel during this period occurred in the schools with smaller libraries. Indeed, those schools with large libraries experienced a slight decrease in total personnel between 1969 and 1972.[36] It is unlikely that law school library staffs will continue to grow at

---

34.   63 LLJ 267 (1970).
35.   See footnote 33. In addition, what may have happened during this four-year period is that a number of the full-time nonprofessionals in 1969 completed their years-of-service requirements and thus were classified as full-time professionals by 1972.
36.   Reporting on the averages of 111 member schools from which information was

the rates they grew over the period examined. Much of this period was a time of general expansion in higher education. In addition, the growth that has been shown, particularly in the smaller libraries, may have been related in part, at least, to the more demanding accreditation standards.[37] In a period of financial stringency in all aspects of legal education it is unlikely that growth will continue at the same rate. Moreover, with the unavoidable pressures which may be anticipated from book expenditures, it will be difficult to finance personnel costs, even at existing levels.

Information regarding salary levels of law library personnel is scant. Beteeen 1955 and 1970 increases in the salaries (ex-fringe) of head librarians at the case-study schools for which information is available[38] ranged from a low of 65% to a high of 120% in constant dollars, with an average increase of about 95%. The average salary for all professional law librarians in eight case-study schools was about $6,400 in 1955. The average salary in 1970 was about $10,200, an increase of 60%. However, the range of increases among the schools was so wide (from 13% to 159%) that little weight can be accorded to this average figure. The Annual Survey states that in 1970, the median salary for head law librarians was $17,340 and for 376 full-time professional law librarians (excluding head librarians) was $9,650, for an over-all average professional salary of $11,750. Combining the case-study and Annual Survey data, the average professional salary increased approximately 85% over fifteen years (from $6,400 to $11,750) at an annual compound rate of 4.2%. In the 1972 Annual Survey, a brief review of salary statistics concludes, "In the last 3 years (1970-71-72), the median salaries for *head law librarians* have risen about 10 percent while those for *other than head law librarians* have risen only about 1 percent."[39] A 10% rise in salaries over three years works out to an annual compound rate of increase of 4.9%. Inadequate data for the year 1955 and the changing composition of library staffs thereafter precludes a determination of trends in the salary levels of nonprofessional library personnel. The information that is available suggests that increases in these individuals' salary levels were considerably smaller than the increases registered by professionals during the same period. The Annual Survey contains no information regarding changes in the salary levels of nonprofessional library personnel.

In sum, although the available information does not permit conclusive findings as to salary increases of professional law school librarians, it does appear that over the course of the period examined they have enjoyed slightly higher increases than law school instructors. It will be recalled that the average increase in faculty salaries on a compound basis during this period was about 3.4%,[40]

received, the 1970 Libraries Report of the Committee of Libraries of the A.A.L.S. stated: "In 1970, there was an average of 4.2 professional librarians, 5.4 full-time clericals and 5.9 part-time clericals on the staff of A.A.L.S. libraries. The total staff averaged 15.5 persons. Professionals, full and part-time clericals constituted 27.1%, 37.8% and 38.1% of the staff respectively." *A.A.L.S. Proceedings, 1971* (Part One), 55.
37.   See footnote 33.
38.   Data on the salaries of head librarians were available for only six of the nine case-study schools.
39.   Lewis, *1972 Statistical Survey of Law School Libraries and Librarians*, 66 LLJ 189 (1973).
40.   See chapter 2.

compared with a compound annual increase of roughly 4.2% for professional librarians. This phenomenon of higher increases in the compensation of law librarians is not easily explained, although we can suggest several contributing factors which may be involved. Considerable progress has been made toward improvement in the educational levels of professional law librarians. A comparison of data from studies published in 1961 and 1970 clearly shows a trend in the direction of greater educational qualifications; there has been an increase in the percentage of law school librarians holding both library and law degrees.[41] This has been the case for many case-study school librarians. Undoubtedly, one of the reasons why professional librarians' salaries increased between 1955-56 and 1970-71 was to bring them in line with the salaries of comparably educated people in other fields. From an examination of case-study school data, it appears that the average salary for professional librarians in 1955 was about $6,400. It will be recalled from chapter 2 that the average faculty salary for schools in the Small, Middle, and Large Enrollment Groups in 1955 was $10,100, $11,300, and $14,300, respectively (in constant 1970 dollars). The factors contributing to higher salaries for nonprofessionals include the unionization of supporting staff, job reclassification, and affirmative action programs.

The above figures indicate that between 1955 and 1970 personnel costs at libraries increased at a greater rate than acquisition costs. As a result, personnel costs came to constitute a greater portion, and acquisition costs a lesser portion, of total library costs. At the case-study schools personnal costs constituted an average of 52.6% of total library costs in 1955, and in 1970, they constituted 55.2%.

Section 3 – Prospective Developments

Research libraries in general, and law libraries in particular, appear to be at a watershed in their development. Three interrelated factors have developed which may produce a period of change for law libraries. They are fiscal stringencies, technological developments, and cooperative arrangements between libraries. Indeed, technological innovations and cooperative ventures may be used to maintain or expand library services in the context of restricted funding. The heavy fiscal pressures felt by law libraries have been indicated above. Each year they are compelled to acquire a large number of books at ever-increasing prices. On the one hand, those libraries whose collections have grown to substantial size

---

41.   The earlier report shows that 38.9% of law school librarians surveyed in 1961 had only a law degree, 45.4% only a library degree, and 15.7% both degrees. This means that 54.6% had at least a law degree, 61.1% at least a library degree, and the same 15.7% both degrees. Special Committee on Law School Administration and University Relations of the A.A.L.S., Lehan K. Tunks, Chairman, *Anatomy of Modern Legal Education* (St. Paul, Minn.: West Publishing, 1961), p. 443. A more recent report indicates that 52% of law school librarians surveyed in 1970 had at least a law degree, 73% at least a library degree, and 34% both degrees. These categories are not mutually exclusive and show an advancing level of law librarian education. *Law Library Salaries*, 63 LLJ 473 (1970).

and whose rates of book acquisition no longer increase exponentially nevertheless acquire an extremely large number of books each year. On the other hand, smaller libraries are still increasing their holdings exponentially. While the rate of staff expansion may decrease, salary and wage increases for existing staff are unavoidable.[42] Thus, libraries will continue to experience expanding budgets merely to keep them where they are and this will occur in the context of university-wide fiscal constraint. Libraries are considering developments in new technology with increasing seriousness, at least in part in response to fiscal considerations. Expanded use is being made of microforms although they constitute a relatively small part of library operations. Hard copy material that is deteriorating, or seldom used and occupying valuable shelf space, is being converted to various types of microforms. Some new materials are available only on microforms. While microform materials do not lend themselves readily to legal research, new types of readers are making such material more usable.[43] In the future, facsimile transmission between libraries, or between the library and the professor's office, may become one of the functions of library services. A second major technological development which is bound to change law school libraries in the future involves automation and the computer. There are two aspects of the application of computers to libraries. First, they may be used to help with a number of purely administrative tasks involving repetitive clerical functions, such as catalog-card production and circulation control. Second, they may be used as a research tool for information-retrieval purposes. At the start, at least, many of these technological innovations will undoubtedly add to library costs. Large initial outlays for equipment will have to be made without immediate savings to offset these developmental costs. In addition, it will be necessary to provide new reader spaces, storage spaces, supplies, and the like. Eventually, however, it is likely that a number of technological innovations will become cost-effective and thus help in meeting budgetary pressures. Increased cooperation among libraries may be a third major development producing significant changes in libraries. Cooperative ventures have not been particularly successful in the past, but here, too, in response to fiscal pressures, libraries may move into forming effective consortium arrangements or other cooperative schemes.

---

42.   In connection with personnel changes, unionization of library staff should be noted. Few library staffs are organized today, and those that are involve for the most part only the nonprofessional staff. But as will be indicated below in chapter 5, increasing unionization of university personnel appears certain. And so we can expect more of this activity in our libraries. For an excellent description of the impact of unionization on law libraries, see Morris L. Cohen's remarks made on a panel of American Association of Law Libraries in *Law Library Salaries*, 63 LLJ 496-502 (1970).

43.   There are now available "reader-printers" which print out micromaterials in normal size in a manner similar to a Xerox machine reproducing normal-size pages.

Chapter 5

Supporting Services

Introduction

Our examination of operating costs has been broadly divided between costs
relating to three functions: instructional, library, and supporting services.[1] As
explained above, our analyses of instructional and library costs[2] were based on
direct costs that were involved in those areas. With respect to supporting
services, however, our analysis divides costs into two main categories designated
"direct costs" and "indirect costs." The first category, "direct costs," consists of
those costs which are defrayed by dollar allocations made explicitly available to
law schools for supporting-service functions. The second category, "indirect
costs," consists of those costs which are also incurred for supporting-service
functions of the law school but which are defrayed by dollar allocations made
available to various central university services (e.g., plant operations) for the
benefit of several departments and activities. Expenditures incurred for similar
supporting-service functions may, of course, constitute direct costs at some law
schools and indirect costs at other law schools. For example, for some law
schools, tuition and fees are collected by the law school, and thus expenditures
incurred for this function constitute direct costs. In most instances, however,
this function is performed by a central university service (bursar), and

---

1. See Introduction and Summary.
2. See chapter 2, "Instructional Cost – Factor Analysis"; and chapter 4, "Library Costs."
It should be noted that library costs in this study consist of law library acquisitions and
personnel costs, both of which are designated as direct costs of the law school. In many
cases such items will not appear on the law school budget as such, but will be part of a
central university library budget. See section 2, "Indirect Costs," for a more refined
explanation of the distinction between "direct" and "indirect" costs.

expenditures for it constitute indirect costs. On the other hand, some supporting-service functions of a law school may be accounted for as both direct and indirect costs. For example, the registration function may be shared by both the law school and a central university office. Thus, the expenditures incurred for the registration of law students constitute both direct and indirect costs. In sum, structural variations in the performance of specific functions, between universities and their law schools, serve as the basis for distinctions between direct and indirect costs among law schools.

If, despite variations in the structure of supporting services between universities and their law schools, more precise fiscal data regarding supporting services is elicited, the relative proportion of allocations among instructional, library, and supporting-service costs can be ascertained. To the extent that proportionate dollar allocations for law school instructional, library, and supporting-service purposes are ascertained, law school funds may be more easily managed, and the shifting of funds to serve changing law school needs may take place with greater facility. However, since indirect-cost expenditures are not by their nature easily ascertainable, since such expenditures are not the responsibility of the law school, and since such expenditures may involve a number of fixed-cost items, the dollars expended for indirect costs are not as susceptible to law school influence.

Section 1 — Direct Costs

We first examine supporting services accounted for by direct costs. These costs are deemed to be those which are met by direct dollar allocations for purposes other than instructional salaries and library functions, and thus constitute a "catch-all" category. In soliciting information from the case-study schools, supporting-service direct costs were divided into the following categories: instructional support, student activities, and administration. Instructional support was deemed to include those funds which were provided for such items as secretarial assistance, supplies, duplicating, telephone and postage, and traveling. Other items were included, such as research assistance specified for the use of the instructional staff and not supported by restricted project funds.[3] Student activities were deemed to include those funds which were provided for a variety of student-operated functions, such as the student government, moot court, and publications (e.g., the *Law Review*).[4] The administration category was deemed to include those funds which were provided for such activities as admissions, placement, student counseling, alumni and development programs, and general administrative operations. Costs were elicited for each area on the basis of the following classifications: salaries, supplies and equipment, duplicating, telephone and postage, travel, and other items. In turn, salary classifications were divided into three grades: senior

---

3. See Appendix A, Part III of the Questionnaire.
4. See Appendix A, Part VI of the Questionnaire.

officers, junior officers, and supporting staff, such as clerical and secretarial personnel.[5]

Relationship among Supporting-Services,
Instructional, and Library Direct Costs

We shall first examine the over-all relationship among instructional, library, and supporting-service direct costs as drawn from the data submitted by the case-study schools.[6] Table 1 sets forth the percentage distribution of direct costs

Table 1

Relationship in Percents among Supporting-service, Instructional, and Library Direct Costs at Case-study Schools

Case-study School	Year	Supporting-Service Cost	Instructional Cost	Library Cost
A	1970-71	45%	35%	20%
	1955-56	45	40	15
B	1970-71	36	48	16
	1955-56	23	58	19
C	1970-71	33	53	14
	1955-56	45	45	10
D	1970-71	27	50	23
	1955-56	24	51	25
E	1970-71	25	60	15
	1955-56	22	60	18
F	1970-71	24	47	29
	1955-56	37	53	10
G	1970-71	24	53	23
	1955-56	27	47	26
H	1970-71	19	61	20
	1955-56	23	60	17
I	1970-71	17	62	21
	1955-56	15	64	21

5.   See Appendix A, Part IV of the Questionnaire. In view of the inevitable difficulties in determining and allocating such cost data, close communication was maintained with the case-study schools in order to ensure as much uniformity as possible in the treatment of the data.
6.   For one school, in addition to the information supplied by the school, data for 1955-56 were derived from an inspection report prepared by the then Adviser to the Section of Legal Education and Admission to the Bar of the A.B.A.

for each of the three categories at the case-study schools for the years 1955-56 and 1970-71. It should be noted that since supporting services may involve a greater proportion of indirect costs, the supporting-service categories may be artificially low.

A review of the average and median percentages in Table 2 for each of the three categories for the years shown, appears to indicate a slight increase in the percentage of funds available for library functions.

Table 2

Comparison between 1955-56 and 1970-71 of the
Relationship among Supporting-service, Instructional,
and Library Direct Costs at Case-study Schools

	Supporting-Service Cost		Instructional Cost		Library Cost	
	1955-56	1970-71	1955-56	1970-71	1955-56	1970-71
Average	29.0%	27.8%	53.1%	52.1%	17.9%	20.1%
Median	24	25	53	53	18	20
Range	15-45	17-45	40-64	35-62	10-26	14-29

Additional data regarding these relationships are available from a review of the reports prepared for the schools that were jointly inspected by the A.B.A. and A.A.L.S. in 1972-73.[7] The data are set forth in Table 3.

Table 4 sets forth the average and median percentages for the inspected schools.

Although the average and median percentages approximate those for the case-study schools, the figures in Table 1 and Table 3 show the variations that exist in the allocation of dollars made available for the direct costs of the law school program and, therefore, underscore the difficulty in making generalizations regarding the relation among supporting-service, instructional, and library direct costs. Nevertheless, from the foregoing data a broad model of a contemporary law school program might be constructed which would apportion direct costs at somewhat less than 30 percent for supporting services, about 50 percent for the instructional program, and somewhat more than 20 percent for the library. In view of the limited number of schools upon which the model is based and the broad variation among such schools, we are not suggesting that the proportions set forth are necessarily reflective of average relationships or should be construed as a standard. The usefulness of such broadly interpreted allocations is limited to examining possible trends and developing comparative insights among law schools and with other disciplines. Since presumably, although not necessarily, increases in costs of supporting

---

7. Data for 10 of the 31 inspected schools were provided in a form to make the analysis shown in Table 3. The information in Table 3 was based on budgeted costs for the year 1972-73, rather than actual costs.

Table 3

Relationship in Percents among Supporting-service, Instructional, and Library Direct Costs at Inspected Schools

Inspected School	Year	Supporting-Service Cost	Instructional Cost	Library Cost
J	1972-73	47%	36%	17%
	1970-71	38	38	24
K	1972-73	45	38	17
	1970-71	41	40	19
L	1972-73	37	35	28
	1970-71	50	32	18
M	1972-73	33	46	21
	1970-71	22	56	22
N	1972-73	30	41	29
	1970-71	28	44	28
O	1972-73	26	52	22
	1970-71	36	43	21
P	1972-73	22	61	17
	1970-71	13	63	24
Q	1972-73	21	50	29
	1970-71	18	52	30
R	1972-73	18	62	20
	1970-71	19	57	24

Table 4

Relationship among Supporting-service, Instructional, and Library Direct Costs at Inspected Schools

	Supporting-Service Cost		Instructional Cost		Library Cost	
	1970-71	1972-73	1970-71	1972-73	1970-71	1972-73
Average	29.4%	31.0%	47.2%	46.8%	23.3%	22.2%
Median	28	30	44	46	24	21
Range	13-50	18-47	32-63	35-62	18-30	17-29

services will divert dollars otherwise available for instructional and library purposes, procedures for developing more complete information regarding the "mix" would be useful.[8]

Table 5 sets forth for the case-study schools, in 1970, the lowest, highest and median costs on a unit basis of the direct-cost components and shows their range.

Table 5

1970-71 Per-student Allocation of Direct-cost Components at Case-study Schools

	Low	High	Median
Instructional	$643	$1,300	$935
Library	$200	$ 716	$420
Supporting Services	$198	$1,661	$487

Note: The range of figures indicates the variations that exist, and the median figures should be interpreted with this factor and the small number of schools in mind.

A more refined view of the nature of supporting-service costs may be developed by examining the variance in the costs of supporting services against other factors involving the size and nature of an individual law school program. The data from the case-study schools indicate that a closer relationship between supporting-service expenditures and size of faculty and median instructional salaries may exist than between such expenditures and student enrollment.

Components of Supporting Services

As previously indicated, supporting services consist of all law school costs not attributed to the instructional and library programs. The main direct-cost supporting-service components are categorized as administration, instructional support, and student activities. Subcategories exist for each of the three components. For example, admissions and placement would be subcategories of administration. Personnel costs, plus other operating expenses, such as duplicating, telephone, and supplies, were obtained for the various subcategories.[9]

The supporting-services area, particularly with respect to personnel costs, is subject to wide variations among law schools. This is so, since identical functions may be performed at different schools by persons occupying widely different levels of rank and enjoying different degrees of seniority. Thus, the cost of a person in charge of placement may be substantially more at a law school where such a person is of high rank and high seniority, than at a law school where the

8.   See section 4, regarding a matrix system for gathering more precise data.
9.   See Appendix A.

same position is occupied by a person of low rank and low seniority. In addition to these variations, one individual may be performing two or more functions (e.g., placement and alumni programs).

Although the study did elicit detailed fiscal data for supporting services from each of the case-study schools, and some general relationships can be shown, conclusions of general applicability are difficult to draw from widely differing local situations. Keeping in mind these differences, Table 6 sets forth the percentage distribution of costs for major supporting-service categories at the case-study schools during 1970-71.

Table 6

1970-71 Allocation in Percents of Supporting-service Direct Costs at Case-study Schools

Supporting-Service Category	Average	Median	Case-study School								
			A	B	C	D	E	F	G	H	I
Administration:											
General	27%	28%	27%	33%	31%	15%	28%	34%	18%	26%	30%
Admissions	9	8	13	8	8	13	1	11	7	4	14
Placement	4	5	7	6	2	1	1	7	5	5	1
Student Counseling	5	4	4	5	4	–	1	–	9	6	4
Alumni and Development	7	5	6	18	15	2	2	–	2	7	5
Instructional Support:	40%	34%	23%	26%	28%	66%	66%	33%	43%	34%	39%
Student Activities:	10%	12%	20%	4%	12%	3%	1%	15%	16%	18%	7%

– indicates separate figures are unavailable.

Although variations are apparent, a prototype, based on the foregoing percentages, might suggest that for the direct costs of supporting services somewhat more than one-third would be for instructional support, somewhat less than one-third for general administration, and the balance divided roughly as follows: admissions and student activities about one-tenth each; and placement, counseling, and alumni programs about one-twentieth each. A review of the data supplied by the case-study schools over the fifteen-year period indicates that instructional-support, admissions, and alumni activities experienced a somewhat greater rate of increase in cost than placement, student activities, counseling, and general administration. Allocations for alumni and development activities were generally greater at private schools, and also reflected the extent to which these activities were decentralized.

No single item within the supporting-services area is apt to be of more personal concern to the individual instructor than secretarial or clerical assistance. The cost of additional secretarial services is of course low compared to the cost of using the instructor to perform similar services. An instructor's productivity is inevitably reduced by the need to file papers, undertake small errands, write longhand, and engage in similar activities which could be handled by clerical personnel with less distraction of the instructor from teaching and research. Nevertheless, in a period of fiscal restraint, schools may be tempted to decrease such clerical assistance, because it is an area of least resistance, and savings in faculty time that would otherwise be devoted to clerical functions is not likely to be regarded as translatable into increased teaching hours. In the instructional-support area, a review of case-study school data suggests that salaries constitute about 60 percent of an instructional-support budget, and the proportion between salaries and other operating expenses remained relatively static over the period 1955 to 1970. Although technological devices, e.g., elaborate duplicating equipment, may have influenced faculty productivity, expending funds for such devices does not seem to have reduced personnel costs. Moreover, technological devices may lead to increases in instructional-support costs, merely through the ease with which new matter can be reproduced.

During the period examined, with increasing stress in admissions,[10] it was inevitable that this function placed a greater demand on resources. Two factors have tended to offset these pressures. With the recent introduction of a national center for transcript processing[11] expenditures in the admissions area (e.g., measuring undergraduate grade point averages, etc.) have been either modified or reallocated to meet the costs of other functions related to the selection process; and admissions as a support area has often generated fees to offset costs. Application fees may be credited toward the law school admissions process itself, or for general law school purposes; or they may be credited to the university for general purposes. In the latter case, of course, such fees do not accrue directly to the law school. It should be noted that, in many instances, although application fees may offset admission costs, the income received is less than the total cost involved in the admission process.

Annual gift campaigns, alumni postgraduate conferences, and other types of alumni hand-holding have become a significant form of support activity at a number of institutions since 1955. As mentioned, the figures in Table 6 reflect the greater emphasis on alumni activities at some private schools. The average salaries of chief development officers may exceed those of other administrative officers. In part this could result from the fact that costs for development programs are frequently offset against contributions, and to that extent are not treated as a drain on general income.[12]

---

10.   See chapter 6, section 6.

11.   Under a program developed by the Law School Admission Council, the applicant for admission to law schools is directed to have all academic records submitted to the Law School Data Assembly Service (LSDAS) in Princeton, New Jersey; thus the admissions offices at participating schools are relieved of the necessity to assign personnel to the function of assembling and calculating grade-point averages.

12.   *The Chronicle of Higher Education*, June 24, 1974. Additional data would be required to determine the relationship between the costs of developmental activities and growth in annual giving.

Section 2 — Indirect Costs

We next examine supporting services accounted for by indirect costs. In the previous section, our focus was on the direct costs associated with law school supporting services. As previously mentioned, certain supporting-service functions accounted for as direct costs at some institutions may at other institutions be accounted for as indirect costs, to the extent that a central university office performs such functions in whole or part. In addition, there exists a large variety of other indirect costs produced by central university activities and plant operations. This section deals with these several forms of indirect costs.[13]

Within the instructional-cost category, indirect costs involve such items as law students taking courses in other divisions of the university; and in the library cost area, they involve such items as use by law faculty or law students of the business school library.[14] These costs, however, are often relatively small compared with indirect costs associated with supporting services. Indeed, from the standpoint of many law schools, the topic of indirect costs, for the most part, is centered on supporting services. Generally, such indirect costs consist of those which arise in the performance of a variety of central institutional support functions and plant operation services. The elements of supporting-service indirect costs are described more particularly below.[15]

The concept of indirect costs developed above involves the objective of genuinely accounting for all the costs of legal education, i.e., the full costs of legal education, by attempting to ascertain direct and indirect costs as they

---

13.   As in the case of many enterprises, the "full costs" of legal education consist of the combination of two broad categories of expenditures. The first category, designated "direct costs," generally includes all those expenditures for goods and services which can easily, and often definitively, be traced to particular law school functions, since specific budget allocations were made to support these functions. For example, such costs might be those involving law school instructional salaries, acquisitions for the law library, and dean's office supplies. The second category, designated "indirect costs," includes all those expenditures which, though not precisely or readily traceable to particular functions, are incurred to support the operation of law schools. "Direct Costs," are defined by the Office of Management and Budget as "those costs which can be identified specifically with a particular ... instructional ... or any other institutional activity or which can be directly assigned to such activities relatively easily with a high degree of accuracy"; "Indirect Costs" are defined as "those that have been incurred by common or joint objectives and therefore cannot be identified with a particular ... institutional activity" (Attachment A Circular A-21, Revised, issued by the Executive Office of the President, September 2, 1970, p. 6). See also "Direct Cost" and "Indirect Cost" as terms defined in standards promulgated by the Cost Accounting Standards Board, Federal Register, vol. 37, no. 40, p. 4171. A workable concept of indirect costs precludes defining it in a precise and entirely consistent manner. For example, the notion that, in order to classify a particular expenditure as a direct or indirect cost, one must ascertain whether it is directly traceable to a particular law school function, strictly speaking, would appear to place some buildings-and-grounds or plant-operation costs, traditionally classified as indirect costs, in the direct-cost category. Amounts spent to provide electricity to the law school building, if metered, or the salary of a janitor assigned exclusively to the law school constitute expenditures directly traceable to a law school function, and might accordingly be defined as direct costs. Convention, however, usually designates these expenditures as indirect costs.

14.   Data regarding such use were not available.

15.   Sections 4 and 5 below.

actually relate to law school operations.[16] There is another approach to "indirect costs" which in many instances is the more usual one. This approach begins with the total amount of resources actually generated by the law school, and then subtracts the funds made available to the law school. Although direct costs may be precisely defined under this approach, the amount of indirect costs is arbitrary and may have little relation to genuine indirect costs.[17] This alternative approach is discussed in greater detail below.[18]

The significance of indirect costs derives from the inherent logic that, since full costs comprise both direct and indirect costs, any study of the *full* costs of legal education will necessarily be limited to the extent that access to indirect-cost data is limited. In addition, the significance of indirect costs is also revealed when it is recognized that the level of dollars available for direct-cost items may be a function of the level of dollars expended for indirect-cost items. This can be seen by examining the relationship between "primary" and "support" programs. In this context, all instructional programs would be considered "primary," and are largely accounted for as direct costs, while a variety of central university activities and plant operations would be considered "support" programs, and are accounted for as indirect costs. Many expenditures incurred by central support programs are fixed-cost items. (For example, students must be registered and billed, and light and heat must be provided.) As these fixed costs are met, the funds available for primary programs contract. In this connection, if the dollars available for a law school's instructional program were not affected by expenditures for indirect costs, this fact in itself would be critically significant.

Despite their significance, actual data regarding indirect costs are either unavailable or severely limited. This is due in large part to their intrinsic character, since indirect costs by definition are not easily traceable to the activities of divisions and departments, and since, even when adequately traced, their measurement is difficult. Even where indirect-cost information is available, it often does not lend itself to comparative analyses, owing to a substantial lack of uniformity in categorization and treatment by diverse institutions. Thus the value of such information, for the present, is more apt to be confined to intra-university rather than inter-university comparisons.

Another aspect of indirect costs which renders imprecise data is the fact that indirect-cost categories are not likely to be parallel among different universities. Obviously, variations will continue to exist. Therefore, parallel classification systems for eliciting cost data, irrespective of whether the costs are "direct" or

---

16. With respect to indirect costs that are law school "related," interpretative distinctions will arise. For example, opinion will vary about whether the support of other university instructional divisions properly constitutes an "indirect cost" of the School of Law.

17. Assume, for example, that the resources generated by a law school consisted of $1,000,000 in tuition income, $80,000 in gifts, and $50,000 in endowment income. Total resources would, therefore, be $1,130,000. Suppose that funds allocated for the law school were $500,000 for instructional salaries, $220,000 for library acquisitions and personnel, and $280,000 for supporting services. If the funds were expended, direct costs would amount to $1,000,000, and so-called "indirect costs" might be regarded as $130,000. See section 3.

18. Section 3.

"indirect," have to be developed while recognizing that corresponding structural approaches to the same functional activity are not likely to evolve. The essential objective is to insure that direct cost *and* indirect cost information related to the same function will be available regardless of the internal organizational structure of individual universities. A system for comparing cost information among law schools can be created regardless of whether, in the case of an individual law school, a particular function is performed by the law school, by both the law school and a central institutional support program, or by the latter alone; and regardless of whether expenditures related to a particular function are classified internally as direct-cost items or indirect-cost items.[19]

In general, direct and indirect costs must be combined in any area where a similar function is shared by both the law school and a central institutional support program. Naturally, many functions which benefit the law school are not sustained by a combination of both direct and central support dollar allocations, but lie exclusively within a central institutional support-program area. In that event the appropriate pro-rata share of such central institutional support costs would be designated as indirect-cost items by the law school. By developing a basic classification system for supporting services generally performed by and for all law schools, the full costs of such services can be measured regardless of organizational distinctions and regardless of variations in the treatment of direct- and indirect-cost items. If such a system is developed, the fiscal dimensions of different law schools' activities can be more precisely gauged and evaluated. Accordingly, the means for ascertaining and handling comparative law school cost data are dependent on a broad system of classification regarding functions shared by all (or most). Meanwhile, existing figures relating to the full operating costs of law schools, comparisons of over-all direct-cost data, surveys eliciting "indirect cost" and "overhead" data and the like have only limited use. Classification systems and formulae to measure indirect costs are discussed below.[20]

Section 3 — Another Approach to Indirect Costs

The foregoing approach to indirect costs presumes that a reasonable basis for classifying and allocating such costs can and should be developed so as to enable law schools to come as close as feasible to an understanding of the full costs of legal education. Naturally, apart from the concerns of law schools, universities may be prompted to allocate their central institutional support expenditures along departmental or divisional lines in order to meet their own concerns or the concerns of other disciplines and constituencies. There is, as previously

---

19.   For instance, to the extent that a law school is allocated funds for its admissions process, such funds would fall within the admissions subcategory of supporting services and constitute direct costs. At the same time, some part of the law school admissions process may be supported by the operations of a central university admissions office and thus constitute indirect costs. In that event, from the law school perspective, both direct costs and indirect costs are incurred by the law school admission process. Accordingly, in this case, to develop a complete understanding of the cost of the law school admission process, direct costs and indirect costs would have to be combined.

20.   Section 4.

mentioned, an alternative approach to indirect costs which, from a narrow law school point of view, is occasionally, and sometimes with naivete, thought to be completely sufficient to satisfy the concerns, if any, of individual law schools regarding indirect costs. (Indeed, the first approach outlined above may be deemed undesirable by a law school in any situation where there is no apparent fiscal discomfort regarding the extent, if any, to which its actual or potential resources are being utilized for indirect costs.) Such an alternative approach stems from a law school perspective directed exclusively to the amount of law school resources, if any, which are devoted to all non-direct-cost items.[21] This amount can be ascertained by simply calculating the total amount of resources generated by a law school from tuition, endowment, and gift income, etc., and deducting the sum of law school direct-cost items from the total.[22] From this view the difference is perceived to be the "overhead" or "indirect costs" of the law school. In fact, although the difference represents the total amount which is made available from law school resources toward the "indirect costs" of the law school, the extent of its relationship to the actual or reasonable indirect costs sustained by the law school is not known.[23] Moreover, although the alternative approach may produce a figure bearing little relationship to actual indirect costs, it may, as explained above,[24] influence the amount available for meeting the direct costs of the law school program. Of course, if the difference is negative, then both the indirect costs incurred and part of the direct costs are met through resources which are not directly generated by the law school.

A brief examination of the private case-study schools illustrates three conditions. In 1955, at three schools, the direct costs exceeded total resources; at one school, direct costs equaled total resources; and at two schools, direct costs were less than total resources. In 1970, in all such schools, total resources exceeded direct costs. In this examination, total resources are deemed to consist of tuition income, endowment and gift income, and receipts. After subtracting grants for financial aid and direct-cost items for instructional, library, and supporting-service purposes, if a positive difference existed, it presumably was available for non-direct-cost items. Since more definitive data are unavailable, it is not possible to ascertain the extent to which such additional law school resources met, fell below, or exceeded the reasonable indirect costs of the law school. What can be ascertained is the proportion of the positive difference to total resources (tuition, plus endowment income, plus gifts, plus receipts), or net resources (tuition, plus endowment income, plus gifts, plus receipts, less financial-aid grants). If, for this purpose, the positive difference is labeled "overhead," then the percent of total or net resources presumably applied

21. Such a calculation might overlook or underestimate the extent to which the law school should benefit from unrestricted university endowment or the extent to which it should participate in overhead factors imposed on government or foundation grants.

22. See footnote 17 for an example of this process. In the public law school sector, tuition-subvention factors would have to be introduced into the equation in order to reach a basis for calculating resources.

23. The term "reasonable" indirect costs refers to an amount which is systematically derived according to classification techniques and measurement formulae such as those discussed in section 4.

24. See section 2.

toward "overhead" can be determined. Table 7 sets forth the relationship between the "overhead" differential and resources for the private case-study schools in 1955 and 1970.[25]

Table 7

"Overhead Differential" in 1955-56 and 1970-71 at the Private Case-study Schools

School		A	B	C	D	E	F
% of Total Resources	1955-56	40%	(30%)	27%	(75%)	(50%)	——
	1970-71	29%	18%	13%	6%	5%	3%
% of Net Resources*	1955-56	41%	(40%)	28%	(84%)	(66%)	(18%)
	1970-71	31%	20%	15%	8%	6%	9%

Note: Figures in parenthesis indicate extent to which direct costs exceeded total or net resources, respectively.

* Total resources less scholarship grants

—— indicates Direct Costs equaled Total Resources

These "overhead" differentials among the case-study schools illustrate how the use of the alternative approach may produce distinctions in attitudes regarding "indirect costs." Regardless of what reasonably allocated indirect costs might actually be, schools which find themselves in a position similar to the historic pattern of a D school, will look upon "overhead" differently from schools whose positions resemble an A school.

The Tunks Committee report, based on 1956-57 data, also reflects the attitudes that fiscal phenomena of this type produce. The report, having examined 108 law schools for which data were reported, in a Table headed *"University Law Schools' Income from Tuition and Fees Related to Direct Operating Expenses,"* shows 90 schools with "income producing no excess"; 7 schools with "excess going to law school reserve"; 6 schools with "excess to state"; and 5 schools with "excess to university coffers." The Committee concludes "it would appear that there need be very little current concern about the possibility of a university drain on law student generated income for the benefit of other university operations."[26] Available figures for 1948-49 from the *Survey of the Legal Profession*[27] indicate that, of 83 law schools for which it was possible to calculate a surplus or deficit based on tuition and fees, 73

25. See footnote 22.
26. Special Committee on Law School Administration and University Relations of the A.A.L.S., Lehan K. Tunks, Chairman, *Anatomy of Modern Legal Education* (St. Paul, Minn.: West Publishing, 1961), p. 85.
27. Lowell S. Nicholson, *The Law Schools of the United States* (Baltimore, Md.: The Lord Baltimore Press, 1958), p. 84 f.

university-connected schools "show a small average deficit." Thus, the 1948-49 data and the 1956-57 data suggest that for most law schools there was minimal concern regarding indirect costs. Actual indirect costs were apparently absorbed by resources not directly attributed to law schools.

A different attitude may emerge when examining recent law school data from the perspective of the alternative approach. The fiscal reports of the private and university-affiliated schools which were inspected by the A.B.A. and A.A.L.S. during 1972-73 indicate that, for this group, law school related resources exceeded direct costs plus financial-aid grants (if any) in a predominant number of schools. Thirty-one reports were examined, two were of unaffiliated schools, and nine of public law schools. The breakdown of the remaining twenty university-affiliated private law schools is as follows:

Total resources exceeded direct costs plus
    financial-aid grants (if any):   13

Total resources were used exclusively for
    direct costs and financial-aid grants: 2

Total resources were less than direct costs
    plus financial-aid grants: 2

Insufficient data: 3

The percent of total resources which was not allocated for direct costs and financial-aid grants, if any, is shown in Table 8 for ten[28] of the thirteen schools whose total resources exceeded allocations for direct costs and financial-aid grants, if any.

Table 8

**Percent of Total Resources Not Allocated for Direct Costs
and Financial-aid Grants at Inspected Schools**

School	1970-71	1971-72	1972-73
J	49%	44%	47%
K	24	39	39
L	46	50	37
M	22	30	28
N	40	33	19
O	11	23	18
P	38	41	15
Q	12	08	15
R	21	29	13
S	22	21	13

Note: Fiscal data for 1972-73 were reported during the spring of 1973, and actual figures, although available for 1970-71 and 1971-72, were not available for 1972-73. Accordingly, 1972-73 data are based on budget figures. The figure for School R was due to increase to 29% in 1973-74.

28.   Data for three of the thirteen schools were not sufficient for calculating respective percentages.

It should be noted that in six of the ten schools an overhead figure was listed.[29] However, in five of those schools, a difference still existed between total resources and the sum of direct costs, financial aid, and overhead. In 1970-71, eight of the ten schools devoted in excess of 20 percent of total resources to non-direct-cost items. In 1971-72, there were nine such schools. Budget figures for 1972-73 indicate this number was reduced to four such schools, but one school reported a contemplated increase to 29 percent for 1973-74.[30] Similar relationships existed with respect to the percent of net resources (total resources less financial-aid grants) which were unallocated for direct costs. Table 9 sets forth the percent of net resources which were not allocated for direct costs at the respective schools.

Table 9

Percent of Net Resources Not Allocated for Direct Costs at Inspected Schools

School	1970-71	1971-72	1972-73
K	25%	40%	40%
L	49	53	39
M	24	32	29
O	13	26	19
P	40	43	17
R	——	32	14

Note: —— indicates figure was not available. Financial-aid data were not available for 4 of the inspected schools.

Currently, there are available only limited surveys and general impressions upon which to conjecture about the extent to which law school resources are being used for non-direct-cost items. Reliance on these means will continue until more uniform methods of collecting data from law schools are developed, and until such data are systematically analyzed. Whatever the degree of reasonableness or unreasonableness of the difference that exists between resources and direct costs, the data of the case-study and inspected schools indicate that the relationship has apparently changed significantly for many law schools since 1956-57, at which time a substantial number of schools reported income producing no excess over operating expenses.[31] Case-study- and inspected-school data suggest that many law schools will seek a more definitive and reasonable basis for the allocation of resources within a university system. The standards and policies of the American Bar Association and the Association of American Law Schools also support the trend toward more refined methods

29.   In a number of the inspection reports concern was expressed over the failure to furnish any overhead figures or to provide an adequate cost-accounting basis on which to pro-rate overhead charges properly.
30.   See note to Table 8.
31.   At that time, for many schools, the funds expended for university supporting services may have more closely approximated a fair share of university unrestricted funds.

of collecting and interpreting data. The American Bar Association's Standards for the Approval of Law Schools provides that "If the law school is affiliated with or part of a University, that relationship shall serve to enhance the program of the law school."[32] The Association of American Law Schools stipulates as approved Association policy that "A member school ... should have wide discretion, compatibly with its university's over-all interests, to ... Determine the financial support needed to operate its program."[33] Presumably, programs for providing law schools with more sufficient data are needed in order to meet these standards and concerns.

Section 4 — Classification and Allocation Systems

Before considering classification systems and diverse bases for allocating indirect costs, it should be understood that variations in the treatment of indirect costs are likely to be a function of the objectives which are sought to be achieved through the realization of indirect-cost information. These objectives may be influenced by a university's or law school's desire to gain access to particular kinds of resources. For example, some indirect-cost information may be developed as a basis for insuring full recovery of the total "actual" expenditures involved in the performance of a research contract, or some indirect-cost information may be developed for creating in alumni ranks a more complete understanding of the full costs involved in particular programs of a law school. Unlike direct-cost information which is based on hard dollars, indirect-cost information may be derived from "estimates" which are construed to be reasonable, and which are meant to serve as a fair pro-rata share for the particular service which has been provided. Since formulae for such estimates may be conceived on a somewhat arbitrary basis, they are susceptible to development and adjustment depending on the purposes sought to be served by the use of the indirect-cost information which is produced.

In the "alternative approach"[34] to indirect costs, the focus is on the difference in amount between resources and direct costs of instructional, library, and supporting-services functions. The actual relationship between this amount and the amount reasonably allocated as indirect costs for the support of a law school program will remain elusive until program-classification systems have been developed and put into use. Such systems and associated cost-finding techniques are exemplified in the activities and proposals of the National Center for Higher Education Management Systems (NCHEMS) and are developing in response to varying needs. In public education a primary need is to assure the reasonable allocation of tax dollars among a number of institutions. For these purposes a variety of institutional functions are defined and allocation systems

---

32. American Bar Association, *Approval of Law Schools: Standards and Rules of Procedure* (A.B.A., 1973), p. 4.
33. Association of American Law Schools, *Association Information*, (Washington, D.C., February, 1972), By-Laws of the Association, pp. 10-11.
34. See section 3.

created which may be applied across differing institutions in meeting legislative objectives. On the other hand, the needs of private universities are often served by developing cost-classification and allocation systems based on individual school programs without undue concern for insuring that such individual systems can be accommodated to produce comparative data from similarly situated universities. In such situations the comparative focus, if any, will be directed toward intra-university departmental relationships among the many divisions of the single university rather than toward inter-university departmental relationships involving the same discipline or activity at several universities. Regardless of distinctions between classification and allocation systems among diverse institutions, whether public or private, it presumably would be useful for law schools as a whole to create an elementary classification system that would be able to generate, without undue stress, the basic data for making comparisons among law schools. Thus, from the law school perspective, a desirable classification system is one that would embrace those particular categories which are related to law school functions; provide for a system of categorization which is neither so broad nor narrow as to make inter law school comparisons obscure or complex; enable the law school to provide and interpret data with facility; and provide compatibility with pre-existing or developing systems.

NCHEMS

Law schools may wish to look to the National Center for Higher Education Management Systems (NCHEMS) Program Classification Structure for guidelines in the development of a classification system that satisfies the foregoing criteria. NCHEMS at the Western Interstate Commission for Higher Education was established in 1969. Its primary mission is "to assist colleges and universities with the development of improved resource allocation and management systems"[35] and to develop procedures that facilitate the exchange of comparable data among institutions. Numerous task forces and advisory panels, in addition to the professional staff, are engaged in the development of NCHEMS programs.[36] For fiscal 1974 the federal government has provided 97% of NCHEMS budget of almost $1.9 million.[37] The work of NCHEMS is apt to exert considerable influence among many educational institutions in the creation and refinement of their respective classification structures. In turn, it will affect the internal fiscal and data-reporting schemes of law schools associated with universities that make reference to NCHEMS programs and techniques.

In the development of a Program Classification Structure (PCS), NCHEMS has recognized that modifications may be necessary to conform with changes in higher education. In addition, NCHEMS has emphasized that the PCS should not be construed "as a specification of a new organization system to be imposed on

35. NCHEMS at WICHE, *Program Classification Structure*, Technical Report No. 27 (Boulder, Colo.: NCHEMS, 1972) first edition, p. 5.
36. A co-author of the study (Walwer) serves on the Advisory Review Panel of the Cost Finding Principles Project.
37. *The Chronicle of Higher Education*, April 1, 1974.

higher education" but rather as a design "to supplement the institution's own unique data system."[38] A brief description follows. The Program Classification Structure categorizes Instruction, Research, and Public Service as "Primary Programs," and Academic Support, Student Service, and Institutional Support as "Support Programs."[39] In order to permit institutions to assign costs with various degrees of refinement, within each of the Primary and Support Programs, five subordinate levels[40] are provided. The first level is designated "Sub-Program." Examples of Sub-Programs within Support Programs are: "Computing Support" as a Sub-Program of Academic Support and "Fiscal Operations" as a Sub-Program of Institutional Support. The next level, designated "Program Categories," is based on discipline area or major function.[41] Two levels follow: "Program Subcategories" and "Program Sectors." Program Sectors identify the level of the course (e.g., courses at the professional level). The ultimate component is the "Program Element" level. This level is designed to enable each institution to identify and define its own additional cost categories. The expectation is that associated coding structures developed by individual institutions will facilitate the transfer of data to the Program Classification Structure (PCS). To perform the transfer of institutional fiscal data to the PCS system, a "cross-over procedure" is being developed.[42] Thus the PCS coding structure enables each institution to maintain its own accounting structure while relating it to the NCHEMS Program Classification Structure.

Allocation of Indirect Costs

In the NCHEMS system, ideally, all support-program costs would be allocated to a primary program, such as the law school instructional program.[43] For example, if it were deemed appropriate to allocate part of the office costs of a central registrar to the law school, two methods might be employed. The first method, described as the "direct allocation technique," is one which assumes that all support-program activities contribute directly to primary programs. In using this method, the costs associated with support programs are not, as an

---

38.   NCHEMS at WICHE, op. cit., p. 1.
39.   Support programs are described as "those activities within the institution that provide campuswide support to the other programs." See NCHEMS at WICHE, op. cit., pp. 15-19.
40.   Ibid., pp. 21-24.
41.   Program categories for the Instructional Program correspond to the standard taxonomy of fields of study used in the Higher Education General Information Survey (HEGIS). Numerical designations are assigned for each program classification and level. See Robert A. Huff and Marjorie O. Chandler, "A Taxonomy of Instructional Programs in Higher Education" (Washington, D.C.: U.S. Government Printing Office, 1970).
42.   In the preliminary stages only data from the first four levels are utilized. Thus, for example, the Support Program: Institutional Support (6.0), has a Subprogram: "Physical Plant Operation" (6.5) which has a Program Category: "Maintenance Operations" (6.5.8300) which in turn has a Program Subcategory: "Building Maintenance" (6.5.8320).
43.   The Law General Discipline category within the General Academic Instruction Sub-Program carries the code designation 1.1.1401, which will presumably become part of the vocabulary of many of those who wrestle with law school fiscal data.

intermediate step, allocated to other support programs as is the case in the second method described below. Thus, for a central registrar office, statistical data would be gathered relating to each instructional subprogram (e.g., the number of students registered for each division). A corresponding percent ratio is then computed and cost allocations can be made on a pro-rata basis directly from the central registrar's office[44] to the law school and other divisions.

It should be noted, however, that some support programs interrelate with and support other support programs. Consequently, a second method for allocating indirect costs has been developed which, assumedly, reflects more accurately the internal workings of universities. This method, described as the "recursive allocation technique,"[45] unlike the direct allocation technique, makes allowances for the contribution of support-cost centers to other support-cost centers. Through this technique the support-cost centers which are allocated first are those assumed to provide the broadest support to all other cost centers; those that provide the next broadest support are allocated second; and so on. For example, suppose that fringe benefits are applicable to most employees of the central registrar's office. Before the appropriate pro-rata share of the central registrar's office is allocated to the law school, the appropriate pro-rata share of fringe benefits must be allocated to the registrar's office.[46] Implicit in the recursive allocation technique is the ordering of support programs in such a way that all direct costs of a support program can be allocated to either primary programs or to other support programs which are deemed to function at a later stage in the process. In the use of the recursive allocation technique, once all allocations are made from a support-cost center, no further allocations are made back to it. Thus, some arbitrary decisions must be made in ordering support-cost centers according to a system which, as indicated, begins with the support center theoretically providing the broadest support and proceeds downward. Assume, for example, that all costs of "Executive Management," have been allocated first, on the theory that Executive Management, by definition,[47] is concerned with the management and long-range planning of the entire institution. Allocations will therefore have been made not only to all primary cost centers but also to all support-cost centers such as Physical Plant Operations. Obviously, in addition to Executive Management providing services for Physical Plant Operations, Physical Plant Operations provides services for Executive Management. As mentioned, the recursive method assumes that a contribution is made only one way, and thus slippage will exist. This problem may, or may not, be minimal, relative to more fundamental concerns in the initial development of indirect-cost allocations. Once elementary indirect-cost-allocation procedures are

44.   In this case the Registrar's Office would carry the classification: 6.3.8200, where 6 represents the Support Program designated Institutional Support Program, 3 represents the General Administrative Services Sub-Program, and 8220 represents a "functional operation program category" viz., student admissions and records.
45.   See James R. Topping, *Cost Analysis Manual* (Boulder, Colo.: NCHEMS, 1974), chap. 6.
46.   Fringe benefits that involve cash outlays, e.g., Social Security taxes, can, of course, be more readily allocated than such fringe benefits as the use of university recreational facilities by employees.
47.   NCHEMS at WICHE, op. cit., p. 59.

introduced, it may be possible to create a computational system that takes into account a variety of reciprocal relationships among support centers.[48]

In addition to proposing a program classification system and a method for the allocation of indirect costs, NCHEMS is endeavoring to determine what "allocation parameters" or statistical data are apt to most closely reflect the actual utilization of support-center services. Ideally, allocations of support-center costs would be made on the basis of actual usage. Normally records of such usage are not maintained, since the costs of maintaining precise statistical records usually outweighs any perceived advantage which might result from the availability of such data. If, however, such records were maintained, they might include the actual number and category of student users of a particular facility, e.g., the main library, or the actual number of hours a particular type of equipment is used by a department.[49] Generally, instead of maintaining elaborate use records, the more feasible approach is to develop

Table 10

Indirect Costs: Alternative Allocation Parameters

Cost Center	Alternative Allocation Parameters		
Executive Direction	Total Operating Expense	or Total Budget	or Head Count of Employees
Financial Operations	Total Operating Expense	or Total Budget	or Number of Accounts or Transactions
Employee Personnel and Records	Head Count of Employees	or Full-time Equivalent Employees	or Total Salaries
Purchasing and Materials	Number of Transactions	or Total Operating Expense	or Costs of Supplies and Services
Custodial Services	Assignable Square Feet	or Full-time Equivalent Employees	
Student Health Service	Target Population		
Academic Administration	Full-time Equivalent Faculty by Discipline	or Full-time Equivalent Employees by Discipline	or Faculty Salaries by Discipline

48. See John H. Powel, Jr., and Robert D. Lamson, *Elements Related to the Determination of Costs and Benefits of Graduate Education* (Washington, D.C.: The Council of Graduate Schools, 1970), p. 170.
49. With respect to computer time such use data may be maintained. Also see John C. Gardner, "Plant Maintenance," *American School and University* (September 1971), p. 6 regarding distinctions in allocating plant maintenance costs based on usage rather than simple square footage.

substitute measures known as "proxies" or "allocation parameters." Examples of alternative "allocation parameters" are found in Table 10.[50]

Obviously, a variety of statistical data could be applied in developing allocation parameters. Moreover, for a single support center, allocation parameters could be created which involve more than one measure with different assigned weights.[51] In sum, the allocation parameters of individual institutions will be created on the basis of measuring use, either in terms of actual usage if feasible, or more likely, in terms of parameters which seem the most relevant and expedient.

A Law School Matrix

As has been seen, the allocation of support or indirect costs to primary cost centers is dependent upon the development of classification systems and parameters for assigning such costs. While universities struggle with the creation

Table 11

Law School Program Areas

Instructional

Organized Research

Library

Supporting Services:
    General Administration
    Admissions
    Career Guidance and Placement
    Development and Alumni
    Student Services:
        Counseling
        Publications
        Activities
    Instructional Support
    Unassigned

Public Service

Unassigned

---

50.   See James R. Topping, op. cit. Thus, the pro-rata distributions of the costs of Financial Operations, for example, could be made by taking the total costs of that support program and allocating such costs in alternative ways. The actual total operating expenses for each university department could be determined. Based on the respective amounts for each department a proportionate percent of all university operating expenses would be derived. These percentages would then be applied to the total costs of Financial Operations and those costs would be allocated accordingly among the departments. A similar procedure could be followed using departmental budgets as the basis. Another alternative would be for the Financial Operations division to keep track of the proportionate amount of transactions for each department and allocate costs on that basis.
51.   For a discussion of alternative parameters see Raymond J. Woodrow, "Budgeting and Accounting," *College and University Business*, vol. 54, no. 4 (April 1973), pp. 6-10.

of over-all classification systems and the determination of appropriate parameters, law schools (in addition to other departments) may wish to develop broad classification systems which will provide the basic data for inter law school comparative purposes. A broad classification system based on contemporary law school functions might embrace the law school program areas set forth in Table 11.

Depending on organizational differences that exist between individual law schools and their universities, the foregoing program areas may be supported by a variety of other university activities and departments. Using the NCHEMS Program Classification System as a guide, such activities might embrace the program areas set forth in Table 12 below.

Table 12

University Program Areas

Instructional

Organized Research

Academic Support
>   Libraries
>   Computing Centers
>   Academic Administration and Personnel
>   Unassigned

Student Services
>   Career Guidance/Placement
>   Unassigned

Institutional Support
>   Executive Management
>   Fiscal Operations
>   General Administrative Services
>>   Student Admissions and Records
>>   Unassigned
>   Logistical Services
>   Physical Plant Operations
>   Faculty and Staff Services
>   Community Relations
>>   Alumni Relations
>>   Development
>>   Unassigned
>   Unassigned

Based on the two foregoing classification structures, Law School Program Areas which have their origins in contemporary law school functions, and University Program Areas, a matrix could be developed which would provide considerable insight into the full costs of a law school program. Such a matrix would be as shown on the following page.

LAW SCHOOL PROGRAMS→

- Salaries
- Other
- Total Direct Costs

UNIVERSITY PROGRAMS ↓

Instructional:

Organized Research:

Academic Support:

- Libraries
- Computing Centers
- Admin & Personnel
- Unassigned

Student Services:

- Career Guidance/Placement
- Unassigned

Institutional Support:

- Executive Mgt.
- Fiscal Operations
- Gen Administrat Serv
- Admissions and Records
- Unassigned
- Logistical Services
- Physical Plant Operations
- Faculty and Staff Services

Community Relations

- Alumni Relations
- Development
- Unassigned
- Unassigned

Total Indirect Costs

Total Full Cost

	Total	INSTRUCT.	ORG. RES.	LIBRARY	SUPPORTING SERVICES									PUBL. SERV.	UNA.
					Total Support Services	Gen. Adm.	Admissions	Career Guidance Placement	Develop and Alumni	Counseling	Public. Activ.	Instruct. Support	Unassigned		
										Student Service					

The Law School Program Areas need little explanation. Two general categories exist for each program area, salaries and other. A total column is provided for all Supporting Services, so as to make it unnecessary to make subordinate refinements in individual situations if such are cumbersome. General Administration is a "catch-all" category to include administrative costs that cannot be included in one of the other defined areas. Instructional Support includes such items as salaries for secretaries of the faculty, duplicating expenses, etc. An "Unassigned" category provides for the allocation of all the costs that cannot be included in some specified area. The foregoing matrix system is not, of course, definitive. It serves simply to introduce for consideration one method for broadly classifying law school costs so as to interrelate conventional law school functions with conventional university program areas. Similarly the University Program Areas are classified according to a system which, in itself, is highly experimental and subject to modifications.[52]

With respect to the University Program Areas, the Instructional category provides a place for those costs related to Instructional services offered by other divisions to the law school. Within the Academic Support category, Libraries recognizes the use by the law school of non-law school library materials and services. Career Guidance, Admissions and Records are specifically set forth in order to ascertain the relationships, if any, between the law school and the central university placement, admissions, and registrar offices. The Institutional Support category sets forth the major operational areas where support is most likely being rendered for the law school.

The matrix could be used as follows. All direct costs would be allocated to various categories of the Law School Program. If feasible, distinctions would be made between salaries and other expenditures within each category. To the extent possible, indirect costs would be allocated according to the University Program categories, recognizing that many subcategories would yield "rough" figures. Although some University Program costs might be distributed among several Law School Program areas, total figures would suffice in the many instances where such a procedure would be unrealistic or not feasible. Thus, if the total costs of a University Program category were not distributed among the various Law School Program categories in the Supporting Services area, the total University Program costs would simply appear in the Total Supporting Services column. If the total costs of a University Program were distributed among specific Law School Program areas, it would then be possible to ascertain the full costs of the particular Law School Program area. For example, if the admissions process of the law school involved both direct and indirect costs, these costs would appear in the admissions category on the respective Law School and University Programs, and the sum of both costs would constitute the full costs of law school admissions. The sum total of all Law School Program direct costs plus University Program indirect costs would, of course, represent the full costs

52.   During 1973, six highly diverse institutions were directly involved in the NCHEMS Cost Finding Principles pilot test. One institution has a law school. It is anticipated that a collection of the special statistics and analyses used in the test, *Cost Finding Principles: Summary of the Analyses of the Pilot Test Data*, will be published in the fall of 1974.

of the law school, as then ascertainable. Accordingly, if a law school matrix system was introduced and if law schools were able to provide the data called for (even in a summary and "rough" fashion), then a clearer idea of the full costs of legal education at individual law schools could be developed, and comparative studies among law schools made.

Section 5 — Increasing Costs of University Supporting Services

The lack of appropriate classification and measurement devices severely hampers any comparative analysis of increases in the indirect costs of supporting services. Nevertheless, recognition can be given to some underlying developments which, during the period of the study, contributed to substantial cost increases in this area. Basically, two types of phenomena have produced the increases; the growing number of support activities, and the increases in the cost of goods and services related to these activities. By examining a variety of relatively new and expanding universitywide support services, we can consider the impact of these phenomena on the fiscal state of the university and thus on the fiscal state of legal education. To the extent that university costs have increased by enlarging or taking on a variety of new support activities, the indirect costs of its divisional components have similarly increased. Moreover, even when the resources generated by particular university divisions are sufficient to sustain their own full costs, if the resources of other divisions are insufficient to meet their full costs, those divisions with sufficient resources will be affected by increasing costs of university supporting services. Since 1955, developments contributing to the growing number and the increased costs of university support activities have included federalization, automation, unionization, specialization, and the need for greater protection of university plant personnel.

Before examining some of the ways in which these developments have influenced the indirect costs of the law school, we broadly outline those university support activities which may serve as supporting services for the law school and, thereby, contribute to the indirect costs of the law school.

One class of university support activities forming the basis for indirect costs includes:

- Executive Management consisting of high-level universitywide direction, long-range development and planning, legal affairs, university external relations and other high-level administrative functions.
- Fiscal Operations consisting of the receipt, control, disbursement, and investment of funds.
- Physical Plant Operations consisting of buildings and grounds maintenance, alterations, janitorial services, utilities, security, and safety.
- Student Record Operations consisting of the preparation and maintenance of student records, certifications of records, issuance of transcripts, preparation of student charges, preparation and issuance of identification cards, and other activities conventionally assigned to a registrar. (Such operations are performed, at least to some degree, on a central service basis at many institutions.)

-   Personnel Affairs consisting of the maintenance of permanent records, recruitment, hiring practices, counseling, job classification and training.
-   Computer Operations. (At many institutions computer operations provide support not only for academic exercises and research, but also for a variety of administrative functions).

The foregoing categories are not comprehensive; they merely illustrate support activities that are contributing to increases in indirect costs at virtually every university.

Another class of university support activities includes Community programs, University Development and Alumni programs, Student Services (recreation, intra-mural athletics, foreign student centers, minority group programs), Audio-visual Services, and other operations forming a potpourri of supporting services, the costs of which might properly be allocated to law schools. This second class of university support activities is distinguished from the first class insofar as some operations within this class may not be conducted by individual universities.

Another class of university support activities includes a range of auxiliary services such as food, housing, health services, and a variety of retail operations, which are distinguished from other operations in that they generate income. These operations will, of course, contribute to indirect costs if expenditures exceed the income produced by such activities.

Finally, a number of universities sustain a class of support activities which, either in kind or degree of expenditures involved, are exceptional and virtually unique to the particular institution. For example, the upkeep of historic monuments, or elaborate gardens, and the like, serve to generate expenditures which, in a manner similar to more basic support activities, are part of the indirect costs of the respective divisions.[53]

We shall next consider some of the developments that contributed to the growing number of university support activities. We begin by examining the influence of increased federalization and the effect of new forms of governmental regulation and operations on the university. A number of examples exist. In the personnel area, universities as government contractors were obligated to comply with requirements of affirmative-action programs growing out of the civil rights legislation of the mid-sixties. Before universities faced the substantive aspects of affirmative-action programs such as the development of plans to remove under-representation of minority workers, they

---

53.   To illustrate an aspect of this situation, assume that maintenance services are provided for law school classrooms, and a historic campus monument. The law school is thus receiving maintenance support for its own classrooms; and it also benefits, theoretically, from the existence of the monument which also receives maintenance services. At the same time, income from endowed funds may exist for the care of the monument but not for the maintenance services being provided for the law school classrooms. These assumedly are being met through tuition income. Accordingly, janitorial expenditures incurred for both functions are components of the indirect costs of the law school, although they are being met through a combination of endowment and tuition income. This relationship may, of course, exist in other classes of supporting services.

first had to demonstrate whether or not such under-representation existed. This process involved an analysis of the composition of the work force of the university, and a comparison of such data with the local availability of minorities according to job classification. Thus, in addition to the costs of meeting program objectives, such as the development of training programs, substantial costs were also incurred in the enormous data gathering and reporting processes. A second example of federalization involves the recovery of indirect costs under government contracts which required the development of appropriate formulae and often a negotiation process involving considerable expense.[54] The Occupational Health and Safety Act of 1970[55] provides an example of the impact of federalization on indirect costs in the area of physical plant operations. Some of its essential provisions require the maintenance of occupational injury records at the place where employees usually report to work, the maintenance of logs and supplementary records of each injury, and the reporting of certain accidents to the Secretary of Labor. In addition, medical examinations are prescribed, and universities are required to correct many potential hazards through the installation of railings, the provision of showers for those working in chemical laboratories, the purchase of goggles, and the like. Another example involves the processing requirements of the extensive federal loan programs which have added considerably to the personnel and paperwork costs of the student records area. Finally, in a period of political tensions, the very existence of federal contracts, such as those involving research affecting national security and Reserve Officer Training Programs, have acted as a trigger for disruptions and caused increased expenditures for repairs and additional security measures.

The foregoing examples are illustrative of the relationships among federalization, burgeoning support functions, and increases in indirect costs. The advent and expansion of federalization inevitably fostered the obligation to meet certain standards. In turn, compliance with such standards created new demands on the support functions of the university, and these demands often involved data collection, processing, and interpretation for which the managements of universities were unprepared. Government reporting requirements engulfed the often unsophisticated and informal university bureaucracies. Coincidental with the ensuing demands placed on the data processing divisions of the university was the development of automation in order to meet the demands.

The apparent need for automation, as a method to solve record-keeping and reporting problems, led university management into the use of highly sophisticated and expensive computer technology. The first computers had their origins on university campuses. In the beginning they were used primarily for research purposes; and then they developed into significant instruments, not only for the primary functions of instruction and research, but also as essential

54. See Attachment A, Circular A-21, Revised, issued by the Executive Office of the President (September 2, 1970).
55. Department of Labor, Occupational Safety and Health Administration, "Occupational Safety and Health Standards," *Federal Register*, vol. 37, no. 202 (October 18, 1972).

tools for support functions. In 1962-63, less than $40 million was spent for computer services in higher education by 200 institutions that were leaders in the field. By the end of the decade, 1,250 institutions, constituting about half of the accredited colleges and universities in the United States, were spending more than $350 million.[56] Thus, during the period covered by the study, significant costs were incurred for both installation purposes and for meeting the problems associated with the utilization of new equipment.

As mentioned, in the 1950's and 1960's, university computer hardware was largely shared by both those concerned with academic utilization (research and instruction) and those involved with administrative data processing. The diversity of the university created inescapable tensions among competing-interest and managerial staffs regarding access to computer time, and bureaucratic arrangements had to be developed merely to respond to pressures for computer services. In addition to the managerial stress which was created by both primary and support functions contending for computer time, other administrative problems arose within the support areas when the managers of such functions as student records, fiscal operations, etc., found themselves dependent on the computer to meet ongoing processing requirements. Thus, for example, although the registrar had the ultimate responsibility for registration of students, he may have had to rely on the computer center for actually doing much of the job. In some instances, dual systems, with their attendant costs, were created in order to avoid such reliance. To compound these difficulties, high-level university management had to resolve these problems within the alien framework of computer technology. Other cost factors accompanying the introduction of the computer were those associated with recruiting and training readers and programers, adapting existing personnel to computer techniques, acquiring additional data-processing paraphernalia, and responding to nearly immediate obsolescence.

Unionization also has indirect-cost implications for individual university divisions such as law schools. Although collective bargaining arrangements in higher education are expanding, generalizations are difficult to make without more experience regarding the impact of collective bargaining by academicians,[57] or by white collar workers, on the indirect costs of the respective divisions of the university. In any event, collective bargaining is likely to become an increasing force in apportioning university resources. While the unionization of academics may be affected, in part, by the attitude and maneuvers of national academic societies and by peer influences extending beyond regional areas, the unionization of white collar supporting staff is more likely to be related to local labor conditions.

Collective bargaining arrangements in various segments of the university may change the nature of support functions as well as the dimensions of indirect

---

56. Charles Mosmann and Einar Stefferud, "Campus Computing Management," *Datamation*, vol. 17, no. 5 (March 1, 1971), p. 20.
57. In a 1973 survey, 212 institutions of higher learning with collective bargaining agencies were identified. *The Chronicle of Higher Education*, Nov. 26, 1973.

costs. In a static resource situation, if deficits are to be avoided, increased costs for primary functions will most likely be offset by decreased costs for support functions. For example, collective bargaining of academics in other divisions[58] may tend to increase allocations for instructional services (a primary function) and, thus, allocations for support functions may tend to be reduced.[59] If, at the same time, collective bargaining arrangements with units within support-function areas are creating pressures for increased salaries and wages, then, in a static resource situation, funds for different types of support functions may be further reduced. Whenever support functions are reduced, the reductions might include such items as curtailment of cleaning services, needed repairs, etc. Since greater institutional stress is created by assuming negative postures toward salary increases than by assuming negative postures toward maintenance and repairs, allocations for salary increases are apt to be favored over allocations for maintenance and repairs. When the relation between instructional take-home pay and support-function expenditures becomes more apparent to the constituents involved, there may be less incentive to create more elaborate support functions. Conventional bureaucratic delays due to reduced personnel or more modest equipment may then become more tolerable to instructors, given the alternative; and the tendency to increase indirect costs by greater dollar outlays for more efficient or elaborate support functions may be diminished. If collective bargaining arrangements tend to increase expenditures for support functions, students may similarly be willing to accept greater bureaucratic inefficiencies as an alternative to higher tuition. In summary, indirect costs may not necessarily increase as a result of collective bargaining arrangements since universities may be influenced by other considerations to hold expenditures for support functions at a constant, or near constant, level, or to reduce expenditures for some support functions in order to make more funds available for primary functions. Thus, although individual wage scales and salaries may tend to increase, the total funds expended may remain relatively constant through staff reductions.

The effect of specialization on indirect costs depends on the extent to which more highly skilled, and therefore, more costly, personnel are engaged to operate the support services of the university. While automation over a period of time tends to reduce some personnel needs, the proportionate share of specialists will increase. As a variety of support services become more sophisticated, universities will start engaging greater numbers of supporting staff technicians who bring to their jobs a greater degree and quality of experience. More highly skilled personnel will presumably seek greater opportunities for advancement and the rate of job turnover may thus increase. As the rate of job turnover increases, the proportion of supporting staff with long standing relationships to the university will decrease. This factor may have a bearing on employee morale and esprit, and a greater number of personnel working within the academic

58. We are not here discussing law faculties.
59. Of course, individual instructional salary increments can also be met, in a static situation, by reducing the instructional work force.

environment will perceive themselves in a more conventional employment relationship, sharing more conventional employee objectives, such as higher salaries, medical benefits, etc. Thus, the compensations for the job will not (as it may have been, heretofore, for large numbers of "old timers") be satisfied by the mere values of being associated with an academic institution and enjoying such fringe benefits as the possibility of participating in the academic program. As compensation for the job is increasingly viewed in terms of hard cash, or dollar equivalents, the employee price tag will go up and indirect costs will be pushed higher.

The costs of plant preservation have exerted and will probably continue to exert a substantial impact on indirect costs. Plant preservation is meant to embrace a number of the activities associated with physical plant operations, such as janitorial services, buildings and grounds maintenance, security, insurance, and the general supervision entailed in such operations. In a period of fiscal stringency, these university operations will be subject to short term "skimp and save" measures. Certain basic services must be provided, but floors can be waxed less often and walls painted with less frequency. Therefore, in an inflationary period, cutbacks can be made easily which are tactically palatable but may be fiscally shortsighted. In the years since 1955, we have witnessed a combination of significant physical plant expansion and inflationary pressures, without, in many cases, adequate provision of funds for the maintenance of the increasing number of buildings. Furthermore, the fancier species of new buildings require fancier grooming, all contributing to greater indirect costs.

Campus security, itself, has also added to indirect costs. From the simple watchman operations of the mid-fifties, which were mainly concerned with fire and weather hazards, security forces have evolved, trained in police techniques and equipped with the latest vehicular and electronic paraphernalia. Although greater security must be provided for individual buildings, laboratory and library components, the diversity and ethos of the university require that campuswide meandering remain free. Therefore, university plants require particularly difficult and costly security techniques.

Chapter 6

Resources

Section 1 — Endowment Income and Gifts

As stated in the overview, the resources for the operating costs of legal education consist of tuition income, endowment income, gifts, grants,[1] receipts,[2] and public support.[3] Tuition income is the predominant resource of private schools; and tuition income together with public support are the predominant resources of public schools.[4] Before considering these major sources of support, we shall briefly examine the relative proportion of total resources that are provided by endowment and gift income.[5] Although

---

1. A grant for a specific purpose may be used as a resource for operating costs or to support an activity considered to be outside law school operating costs. Research funds might be considered in either category. Grants from public agencies are included under public support.
2. Receipts include such items as income from vending-machine operations, duplicating services, and the like.
3. With the exception of funds provided by work-study programs and student loans and their interest subsidization, the case-study data suggest that public support toward the operating costs of private law schools is generally minimal, although individual law school research or clerical projects have received some public support. At public law schools, the amount of public support could be measured by a specific subvention factor as prescribed by legislative and executive formulae. In fact, the actual amount of public funds which are used to support the operating costs of public law schools would be the full operating costs of the law school less the resources made available toward such costs from tuition, endowment, gifts, grants, and receipts.
4. See Manning "Financial Anemia in Legal Education: Everybody's Business," A.B.A. Journal (December 1969), pp. 1123-1128.
5. For these purposes, grants made toward operating costs are included in the gift category. Receipts for operating costs are similarly treated.

Table 1

Percent of Total Resources represented by Endowment and Gift Income at the Case-study Schools, 1955-56 and 1970-71

School	Endowment Income		Gift Income	
	1955-56	1970-71	1955-56	1970-71
A	15%	20%	11%	12%
B	5	20	3	9
C	–	9	–	13
D	1	1	0	8
E	0	–	0	7
F	4	6	0	5
G	0	3	1	22
H	–	1	–	3
I	0	0	0	0

Note: In some instances income from grants and receipts was included under gift income. See footnote 5.

– indicates less than 1%.

information for the larger sample of schools[6] is unavailable, an examination of data from the case-study schools and from the reports of schools which participated in a joint A.B.A.-A.A.L.S. inspection in 1972-73 offers some insight into the relative extent of the support provided by endowment and gift income.[7] Table 1 sets forth the percent of total resources represented by endowment and gift income at the case-study schools in 1955-56 and 1970-71.[8]

6.　See chapter 2, section 1.

7.　As indicated, resources, in the form of either endowment or gift income, which were designated for capital improvements, e.g., a new building, are not part of this examination. Also, beyond the purview of the study is an examination of investment policies. Of course, the amount of income which endowments will generate is dependent not only on the amount of the gift which produced the endowment but on variations in investment policies . For a discussion of the management of and legal problems of endowment funds see William L. Cary and Craig B. Bright, *The Law and The Lore of Endowment Funds* (New York: Ford Foundation, 1969).

8.　For public schools, total resources are considered to be the sum of funds allocated to the law school by the university (rather than tuition income) plus endowment and gift income generated by the law school. For private schools, total resources are considered to be the sum of gross tuition income (number of students × the tuition rate) plus endowment and gift income (including grants and public support) generated by the law school. Thus, in the case of public schools, total resources will equal the direct costs of the law school. However, in the case of private schools total resources may exceed, equal, or be less than direct costs. With respect to both public and private schools, the actual percent that endowment and gift income comprise in relation to the total actual funds available for law school operating costs, both direct and indirect, is not known since the specific amount and source of funds necessary to sustain indirect costs is not known.

Table 2 sets forth the percent in 1970-71 of total resources represented by endowment and gift income at schools that participated in a joint A.B.A.-A.A.L.S. inspection in 1972-73.[9] Of seventeen schools for which data were available, six had neither endowment nor gift income for operating costs. Data for the remaining eleven schools are shown.

Table 2

Percent of Total Resources Represented by Endowment and Gift Income at the Inspected Schools in 1970-71

School	Endowment Income	Gift Income
A	0%	20%
B	0	11
C	0	11
D	1	8
E	–	7
F	0	5
G	–	3
H	–	2
I	0	2
J	2	1
K	–	–

In some instances income from grants and receipts was included under Gift Income. See footnote 5.

– indicates less than 1%.

A review of the foregoing Tables suggests that endowment and gift income constitute a relatively insubstantial source for meeting the operating costs of most law schools.[10] Tuition income is the predominant form of financing for private schools. In the case of state schools, public subvention, together with tuition income, is the predominant form of financing. An examination of tuition levels in both private and public schools for the period 1955 to 1970 indicates the growth that has taken place in tuition income. Such an examination is made in the next section.

Section 2 — Law School Tuition: 1955-1970

This section examines tuition increases at 122 law schools between 1955 and

9. See footnote 8.
10. It will be noted that Tables 1 and 2 indicate that in some cases such income is consequential.

1970.[11] The law schools examined are divided into two groups: 76 privately supported schools and 46 publicly supported (or state) schools. Because of the tax-supported subvention that public schools receive, tuition at these schools tends to be considerably lower than tuition at private schools,[12] and, for this reason, the two groups of schools are treated separately and no direct comparisons are made between their tuition increases. This section also examines how tuition at private schools increased in comparison with per-student instructional cost. A similar analysis is not made for public schools because subvention contributions make up a relatively significant proportion of their operating budgets.

Tuition Increases at Private Law Schools

Like many statistics we have examined in this study, tuition increases between 1955 and 1970 at private schools varied widely, and, therefore, average and median figures have only limited significance. For general comparative purposes, however, the average tuition in constant dollars[13] at the 76 private schools examined was $728 (median $669) in 1955, and $1,629 (median $1,705) in 1970.[14] Thus, their average tuition increase between 1955 and 1970 was 124% (median about 120%). By Enrollment Groups,[15] the average tuition increase of the 28 private schools in the Small Enrollment Group was 139% (median 126%), the average increase of the 23 private schools in the Middle Enrollment Group was 123% (median 111%), and the average increase of the 25 private schools in the Large Enrollment Group was 113% (median 119%).

Table 3 gives the 1955 and 1970 tuitions of the 76 private schools. Tuition increases at these schools will now be considered in more detail. To begin, we will examine the increases in the Small and Middle Enrollment Groups. Tuition levels of schools in the Small and Middle Enrollment Groups were very similar in 1955. For both Groups, tuition ranged from about $300 to about $900, with a majority of the schools charging between $500 and $750.[16] By 1970, tuition at

---

11.   These are the same schools that were examined by Enrollment Group in section 1 of chapter 2 except that four such schools are not included because they changed their status from private to public between 1955 and 1970. See footnote 41. The tuition figures examined are only those reported for full-time students. No analysis has been made of tuition charges made to part-time students.

12.   Public school tuition is usually divided between resident and nonresident tuition, and nonresident tuition is usually appreciably higher than resident tuition. Nevertheless, we have found that nonresident tuition charged at public schools, in most cases, is lower than tuition charged at private schools. See below.

13.   As in other parts of the study, unless stated to the contrary, all figures are in constant 1970 dollars, that is, 1955 dollars have been converted to 1970 dollars to eliminate increases due solely to inflation.

14.   All tuition data used in this section has been derived from the 1955 and 1970 editions of the *Review of Legal Education*.

15.   For the definition of the three Enrollment Groups, see chapter 2, section 1.

16.   Of the 51 schools in these two Groups, 27 had tuition within this range, 10 above and 14 below. The average tuition of schools in the Small Enrollment Group in 1955 was $622 (median $604); of the Middle Enrollment Group $667 (median $669).

Table 3

Annual Tuition at 76 Private Law Schools
1955-56 and 1970-71
(1955 figures converted to 1970 dollars)

Small Enrollment Group			Middle Enrollment Group			Large Enrollment Group		
1955-56	1970-71	Percent Increase	1955-56	1970-71	Percent Increase	1955-56	1970-71	Percent Increase
$446	$1,042	34%	$ 669	$ 844	26%	$ 602	$ 915	52%
594	900	52	520	735	41	1,263	2,275	80
455	756	66	594	1,000	68	1,337	2,450	83
535	909	70	1,114	1,875	68	966	1,800	86
588	1,005	71	981	1,750	78	782	1,460	87
817	1,400	71	802	1,520	90	669	1,260	88
594	1,125	89	594	1,155	94	1,189	2,235	88
316	618	96	669	1,310	96	1,189	2,250	89
817	1,645	101	669	1,337	100	1,189	2,350	98
669	1,350	102	446	900	102	1,204	2,424	101
891	1,848	107	409	854	109	1,003	2,100	109
743	1,550	109	669	1,410	111	1,114	2,400	115
892	1,950	119	743	1,600	115	892	1,950	119
613	1,350	120	817	1,858	127	669	1,500	124
698	1,620	132	773	1,774	129	1,097	2,475	126
728	1,740	139	624	1,500	140	817	1,863	128
498	1,190	139	669	1,650	147	802	1,850	131
624	1,500	140	825	2,175	164	817	1,900	133
743	1,780	140	565	1,500	165	639	1,500	135
632	1,754	178	728	1,960	169	743	1,800	142
669	1,900	184	669	1,880	181	817	2,030	149
713	2,030	185	446	2,000	348	428	1,080	152
594	1,700	186	349	1,587	355	749	1,895	153
499	1,585	218				743	1,950	162
520	1,750	237				832	2,240	169
594	2,040	243						
446	1,710	283						
490	1,920	292						
Average			**Average**			**Average**		
$622	$1,488	139%	$667	$1,486	123%	$902	$1,918	113%

Total 76 Schools

$728	$1,629	124%

these schools ranged from about $600 to $2,200. In most cases tuition ranged from $1,300 to $1,900, with some slight concentration between $1,500 and $1,750.[17] Percentage increases over the fifteen years differed widely among these schools, ranging from about 25% to 355%. There was no particular concentration between these limits, although 31 of these 51 schools fell between

---

17.   The average tuition of schools in the Small Enrollment Group in 1970 was $1,488 (median $1,603) and of the Middle Enrollment Group, $1,486 (median $1,520).

a 60% and a 140% increase.[18] Unlike the Large Enrollment Group, which is discussed below, little correlation existed between the relative tuition levels in 1955 and 1970; that is, many schools that were at the bottom, middle, and top of the tuition scale in 1955 were not similarly situated in 1970.[19]

Schools in the Large Enrollment Group had considerably higher tuition than schools in the Small and Middle Enrollment Groups both in 1955 and 1970. In 1955, the 25 schools in the Large Enrollment Group were distributed fairly evenly between tuition levels of about $600 and $1,250.[20] By 1970, most of these schools were distributed between tuition levels of about $1,800 and $2,475.[21] For the fifteen-year period, percentage increases among these schools ranged from 80% to 169%.[22] As indicated above, unlike the smaller schools, these schools showed a very high correlation between their relative tuition levels in 1955 and 1970.[23]

Tuition Increases Compared with Increases in Per-student Instructional Cost at Private Law Schools

Of particular interest is a comparison of private school tuition figures and the instructional-cost-per-student figures developed in chapter 2. Table 4 sets forth by Enrollment Group the 1955 and 1970 tuitions and the per-student

18.   Schools in the Small Enrollment Group had somewhat higher average and median percent increases than schools in the Middle Enrollment Group because a few of them reached considerable tuition levels in 1970.
19.   It will also be shown below that no correlation occurred among these schools between increases in their per-student instructional cost and tuition increases.
20.   Two schools which had very low and very high tuitions ($428 and $1,337) are not included. The average tuition at schools in the Large Enrollment Group in 1955 was $902 (median $817). The 25 private schools in the Large Enrollment Group are divisible into two subgroups: 12 schools which are in the Fourth (top) Quartile of the Resource Index and are generally regarded as leading national law schools, and 13 schools which are in lower quartiles and may be regarded as more representative schools. The tuition range of the top Quartile schools in 1955 was $743 to $1,263, and their average tuition was $1,057 (median $1,151). The tuition range of the other group of schools was $602 to $1,097 (except for the two schools mentioned above with very low and very high tuitions), and their average tuition was $759 (median $792). The preponderance of schools in the more representative subgroup ranged from $640 to $830. It will be noted that the tuition range of the second group of schools is similar to the tuition range of most of the schools in the Small and Middle Enrollment Groups that year, viz., $500 to $750.
21.   Their average tuition was $1,918 (median $1,950). The tuition range of the schools included in the Fourth (top) Quartile of the Resource Index in 1970 was $1,895 to $2,450, and their average tuition was $2,192 (median $2,242). The tuition range of the second group of schools was $915 to $2,475, with most schools falling between $1,460 and $1,900, and their average tuition was $1,703 (median $1,800). Here also the tuition range of the second group of schools in 1970 is very similar to that of most of the schools in the Small and Middle Enrollment Group that year, viz., $1,300 to $1,900.
22.   One school had a percentage increase in tuition between 1950 and 1970 of 52%, the rest fell within the limits mentioned.
23.   The above figures demonstrate that tuition levels among the preponderance of schools in each group (i.e., taking the Small and Middle Enrollment Groups as one group and dividing the Large Enrollment Group into two subgroups, as described in footnote 20) were much closer together in 1955 than they were in 1970. This was particularly true for schools in the Small and Middle Enrollment Groups and for schools in the second, more

instructional cost of 66 private schools.[24] Table 5 shows the average tuition and per-student instructional cost of schools in each Enrollment Group in 1955 and 1970 and, for each group, the percent by which average tuition exceeded average per-student instructional cost in each year.

Table 4

Tuition and Per-student Instructional Cost
at 66 Private Law Schools, 1955-56 and 1970-71
(1955 figures converted to 1970 dollars)

	Annual Tuition			Per-student Instructional Cost	
1955-56	1970-71	Percent Increase	1955-56	1970-71	Percent Change
		Small Enrollment Group			
$446	$1,042	34%	$ 801	$ 407	−49%
455	756	66	465	688	48
535	909	70	595	678	14
588	1,005	71	1,237	669	−46
817	1,400	71	680	772	14
594	1,125	89	805	779	− 3
316	618	96	911	1,489	63
817	1,645	101	470	536	14
669	1,350	102	789	950	20
891	1,848	107	803	671	−16
743	1,550	109	748	569	−24
892	1,950	119	910	1,000	10
613	1,350	120	538	444	−17
698	1,620	132	889	854	− 4
728	1,740	139	569	512	−10
624	1,500	140	715	1,057	48
743	1,780	140	703	1,052	50
632	1,754	178	620	624	1
669	1,900	184	1,644	1,197	−27
713	2,030	185	1,493	1,169	−22
594	1,700	186	853	513	−40
499	1,585	218	693	889	28

representative, subgroup of the Large Enrollment Group. In 1955, the spread for both of these groups was about $200, and by 1970, it widened to about $500. The spread among the top Quartile group of the Large Enrollment schools also widened, from $520 in 1955 to $550 in 1970, but not to the extent of the other groups.

24.   Table 4 includes 66 of the 76 private schools shown in Table 3. Instructional-cost data were not available for 10 of the 76 schools. Of these 66 schools, 21 were in the Large Enrollment Group, 21 were in the Middle Enrollment Group, and 24 were in the Small Enrollment Group.

Table 4 (continued)

	Annual Tuition			Per-student Instructional Cost	
1955-56	1970-71	Percent Increase	1955-56	1970-71	Percent Change
594	2,040	243	1,011	889	−12
490	1,920	292	631	869	38

		Average			
$640	$1,505	135%	$816	$770	− 6%

Middle Enrollment Group

1955-56	1970-71	Percent Increase	1955-56	1970-71	Percent Change
$ 669	$ 844	26%	$ 375	$1,022	173%
520	735	41	320	436	36
594	1,000	68	524	706	35
1,114	1,875	68	1,027	923	−10
981	1,750	78	535	1,051	96
802	1,520	90	547	543	− 3
594	1,155	94	381	442	16
669	1,310	96	512	306	−40
669	1,337	100	280	608	117
446	900	102	581	663	14
669	1,410	111	629	440	−30
743	1,600	115	433	740	71
817	1,858	127	653	906	39
773	1,774	129	744	906	22
624	1,500	140	466	712	53
669	1,650	147	316	529	67
825	2,175	164	362	894	147
565	1,500	165	538	417	−22
728	1,960	169	443	718	62
669	1,880	181	565	619	10
446	2,000	348	893	1,277	43

		Average			
$695	$1,511	117%	$530	$708	34%

Large Enrollment Group

1955-56	1970-71	Percent Increase	1955-56	1970-71	Percent Change
$1,263	$2,275	52%	$ 790	$1,607	103%
1,337	2,450	83	1,462	2,224	52
966	1,800	86	557	577	4
782	1,460	87	265	502	89
669	1,260	88	345	336	− 3
1,189	2,235	88	782	1,437	84

Table 4 (continued)

	Annual Tuition			Per-student Instructional Cost	
1955-56	1970-71	Percent Increase	1955-56	1970-71	Percent Change
1,189	2,250	89	1,207	1,278	6
1,189	2,350	98	912	1,889	107
1,204	2,424	101	955	1,177	23
1,003	2,100	109	843	1,382	64
1,114	2,400	115	1,102	1,486	35
892	1,950	119	629	1,193	90
669	1,500	124	396	527	33
817	1,863	128	246	918	273
817	1,900	133	293	593	102
639	1,500	135	268	435	62
743	1,800	142	643	938	46
817	2,030	149	662	1,081	63
749	1,895	153	359	1,004	180
743	1,950	162	359	883	146
832	2,240	169	365	862	136

Average

$934	$1,982	112%	$640	$1,063	66%

Total 66 Schools

$751	$1,659	121%	$669	$843	26%

It will be observed that in 1955 the average tuition at schools in the Middle and Large Enrollment Groups was higher than their average per-student instructional cost. Average tuition of schools in the Large Enrollment Group exceeded average per-student instructional cost by about 46%.[25] Average tuition of schools in the Middle Enrollment Group exceeded average per-student instructional cost by

25.   Of course there were differences in the relation of tuition to per-student instructional cost among the 21 schools. On an individual basis, the relation of tuition to per-student instructional cost ranged from one school whose tuition exceeded per-student instructional cost by 232% to one school whose tuition was 9% less than per-student instructional cost. Schools were fairly evenly distributed between these extremes. If the Large Enrollment Group is divided into the two subgroups described in footnote 20, the average 1955 tuition of the first subgroup of 12 top Quartile schools was $1,057 (median $1,151) as compared to an average per-student instructional cost of $839 (median $817). Average tuition thus exceeded average per-student instructional cost by 26%. The average tuition of the second, more representative, subgroup of Large Enrollment schools was $759 (median $782), as compared to an average per-student instructional cost of $375 (median $345). Average tuition thus exceeded average per-student instructional cost by 102%. This second subgroup of schools contains only nine schools in this part of the analysis because data regarding per-student instructional cost are not available for four schools.

Table 5

**Average Tuition and Per-student Instructional Cost at 66
Private Law Schools, by Enrollment Groups, 1955-56 and 1970-71
(1955 figures converted to 1970 dollars)**

Group	Average Annual Tuition	Average Per-student Instructional Cost	Percent by Which Average Tuition Is Less Than or Exceeds Average Per-student Instructional Cost
1955-56			
Small Enrollment Group	$640	$816	−22%
Middle Enrollment Group	$695	$530	31%
Large Enrollment Group	$934	$640	46%
1970-71			
Small Enrollment Group	$1,505	$770	95%
Middle Enrollment Group	$1,511	$708	113%
Large Enrollment Group	$1,982	$1,063	86%

about 31%.[26] In sharp contrast, average tuition of schools in the Small Enrollment Group in 1955 was considerably lower than average per-student instructional cost. Average per-student instructional cost of schools in this Group exceeded average tuition by about 28%. In keeping with the above analysis, average tuition was about 22% lower than average per-student

---

26.   On an individual basis, the relation of tuition to per-student instructional cost ranged from one school whose tuition exceeded per-student instructional cost by 139% to one school whose tuition was 50% less than per-student instructional cost. Schools were fairly evenly distributed between these extremes.

instructional cost.[27] The difference in the relationship of tuition to per-student cost in 1955 between the Small Enrollment Group and the two larger Groups is understandable when it is recalled that Small Enrollment Group schools, for the most part, had very low student/faculty ratios in 1955 and, accordingly, high per-student instructional costs.[28] Table 6 shows the relationship of tuition to per-student instructional cost at each of the 66 private schools for which data are available.

Table 6

Relationship of Tuition to Per-student Instructional Cost at 66 Private Law Schools

Percent by which tuition is less than (−) or exceeds (+) per-student instructional cost

1955-56		1970-71	
Small Enrollment Group			
−65%	−13%	−58%	+ 90%
−59	−10	+10	95
−52	− 2	34	121
−52	− 2	42	129
−44	− 1	42	156
−41	+ 2	44	172
−30	6	50	175
−28	11	59	181
−26	14	69	204
−22	20	74	207
−21	28	78	231
−15	74	81	240
Middle Enrollment Group			
−50%	+34%	−17%	+116%
−23	47	+36	120
+ 4	56	42	143
5	63	57	161
6	64	67	173
8	72	69	180
13	78	96	204
18	83	103	212
25	112	105	220

27. On an individual basis, the relation of tuition to per-student instructional cost at these schools ranged from one school whose tuition exceeded per-student cost by 74% to one school whose tuition was 65% less than per-student instructional cost.
28. See chapter 2, section 4.

Table 6 (continued)

1955-56		1970-71	
31	128	111	260
	139		328

Large Enrollment Group

− 9%	+60%	+10%	+ 92%
− 1	69	24	103
+ 1	73	42	106
16	94	52	121
19	107	56	160
23	109	62	185
26	128	63	191
30	138	76	212
42	179	88	220
52	195	89	245
	232		275

Between 1955 and 1970, tuition increased at a greater rate than per-student instructional cost. At the Large Enrollment schools, average tuition increased 112%, and average per-student instructional cost, 66%.[29] At the Middle Enrollment schools, average tuition increased 117%, and average per-student instructional cost, 34%; and at the Small Enrollment schools, average tuition increased 135%, and average per-student instructional cost decreased 6%. As a result of these changes, for the Large and Middle Enrollment Groups, tuition came to exceed per-student instructional cost in 1970 by even greater amounts than in 1955. Furthermore, whereas per-student instructional cost exceeded tuition at over 70% of the schools in the Small Enrollment Group in 1955; by 1970, tuition at these schools exceeded per-student instructional cost in all but one case.

As shown in Table 5, in 1970, the average tuition of schools in the Large Enrollment Group was $1,982, and the average per-student instructional cost about $1,063. The amount by which average tuition exceeded average per-student instructional cost increased from 46% in 1955 to 86% in 1970.[30]

29.   At the first subgroup of the Large Enrollment Group schools, on the average, tuition increased 107% and per-student instructional cost 65%; at the second subgroup, tuition increased 121% and per-student instructional cost 69%. (See footnote 20 for description of the division of the Large Enrollment Group into two subgroups.)
30.   On an individual basis, the relation of tuition to per-student instructional cost at these schools ranged from one school whose tuition exceeded per-student instructional cost by 10% to one school whose tuition exceeded per-student instructional cost by 275%, with schools being distributed fairly evenly between these extremes. If the Large Enrollment Group is divided into the two subgroups described in footnote 20, the average 1970 tuition of the first subgroup of 12 top Quartile schools was $2,192 (median $2,242) as compared to an average per-student instructional cost of $1,387 (median $1,330). Thus, the amount by

The average tuition in 1970 of the schools in the Middle Enrollment Group was $1,511, and the average per-student cost about $708. The amount by which average tuition exceeded average per-student instructional cost increased from 31% in 1955 to 113% in 1970.[31] The average tuition in 1970 of schools in the Small Enrollment Group was $1,505, and the average per-student instructional cost about $770. The spread between average tuition and average per-student instructional cost in Small Enrollment schools changed from average per-student instructional cost exceeding average tuition by about 28% in 1955 to average tuition exceeding average per-student instructional cost by 95% in 1970.[32] For all three Enrollment Groups, those schools with the highest increases in per-student instructional cost did not necessarily have the highest increases in tuition.

To summarize, in 1955, tuition at nearly every school in the Large and Middle Enrollment Groups exceeded per-student instructional cost. This was not the case, however, for schools in the Small Enrollment Group; at most of these schools (17 of 24, or over 70%), per-student instructional cost exceeded tuition. Thus, at schools in the Small Enrollment Group gross tuition income[33] was insufficient to cover instructional cost and, therefore, direct costs.[34] It may be, of course, that the direct costs of these schools were supported by endowment and gift income. We have found, however, that most law schools receive only small amounts of endowment and gift income, and that they received less of this income in 1955 than in 1970.[35] It appears, therefore, that a number of these small schools received support from their universities in meeting their direct

which tuition exceeded per-student instructional cost at this subgroup increased from 26% in 1955 to 58% in 1970. The average tuition of the second, more representative, subgroup of schools was $1,073 (median $1,800) in 1970 as compared to an average per-student instructional cost of $632 (median $577). Thus, the amount by which tuition exceeded per-student instructional cost at this subgroup decreased from 105% in 1955 to 69% in 1970.

31.   On an individual basis, the relation of tuition to per-student instructional cost at these schools ranged from one school whose tuition exceeded per-student instructional cost by 328% to one school whose tuition was 17% less than per-student instructional cost, with schools being distributed fairly evenly between these extremes.

32.   On an individual basis, the relation of tuition to per-student instructional cost at these schools in 1970 ranged from one school whose tuition exceeded per-student instructional cost by 240% to one school whose tuition was 58% less than per-student instructional cost.

33.   The phrase "gross tuition income" assumes no reduction of tuition income on account of scholarships. See section 3.

34.   Direct costs, it will be recalled, consist of instructional cost, library cost, and the cost of supporting services. See Introduction and Summary. It has been estimated that instructional cost typically constitutes somewhat over 50% of total direct costs. See chapter 5, section 1. In 1955, the supporting-services category may have constituted a smaller percent of direct costs than in 1970, because a number of supporting-service functions, conducted at a law school and included in its direct-cost budget in 1970, may have been conducted by central university offices in 1955, and, therefore, included in the indirect costs of the law school. In these cases instructional cost would have constituted a larger percent of direct costs in 1955 than in 1970.

35.   See section 1.

costs.[36] As indicated above, in 1955, tuition exceeded per-student instructional cost at schools in the Large and Middle Enrollment Groups, but, in many cases, the excess was less than 50%.[37] Indeed, at schools in the Large Enrollment Group average tuition exceeded average per-student instructional cost by only 46%, and at schools in the Middle Enrollment Group by only 31%.[38] It appears, therefore, that in 1955 a number of these larger schools also received support from their universities in meeting their full costs.[39] Between 1955 and 1970, the situation changed markedly; and by 1970, for all three Enrollment Groups, tuition exceeded per-student instructional cost by far greater amounts than it had in 1955. See Tables 5 and 6. In 1970, therefore, tuition income was covering a much greater proportion of full costs at these law schools than it covered in 1955.[40] Table 6 suggests that in a number of cases tuition income may have exceeded full costs.

Tuition Increases at Public Schools

We shall now briefly consider increases in tuition at public schools between 1955 and 1970. In most instances two separate tuition charges are made at public schools—one charge for resident students and one for nonresident students, resident tuition usually being appreciably lower than nonresident tuition. In 1955, considerable uniformity existed in the tuition charged by public schools.[41] Their average resident tuition was $229 and their average nonresident tuition was $537. As an average matter in 1955, nonresident tuition

---

36.   As these schools were unable to meet all of their direct costs out of the income they generated, it follows that no such money was available for the schools' indirect costs. In brief, in these cases, the universities must have met all the indirect costs of their law schools as well as some of their direct costs. Since these schools were very small, with small enrollments, small faculties, and presumably small operating budgets, the amount, in absolute terms, of non-law school tuition or university support needed to supplement law school tuition may have been quite small.
37.   See Table 6. Of the 21 schools in the Middle Enrollment Group, 12 had tuition that exceeded their per-student instructional cost by less than 50%. Of the 21 schools in the Large Enrollment Group, 10 had tuition that exceeded their per-student instructional cost by less than 50%. (This includes one school whose tuition exceeded its per-student instructional cost by 52%.) All these schools were in the first subgroup of the Large Enrollment Group. (See footnote 20.)
38.   See Table 5.
39.   The term "full cost" is defined to be the sum of direct costs and indirect costs. See Introduction and Summary.
40.   The extent to which tuition exceeded per-student instructional cost in 1970 may have been influenced by the appreciable increases in scholarship awards that occurred at some schools between 1955 and 1970. See section 3. In cases where a substantial portion of gross tuition income derives from scholarship grants, and where, in addition, a fair proportion of the funds for such grants derives from full tuition payments, for purposes of the above analysis, the tuition figure should be lowered. Furthermore, it should be noted that indirect costs, a component of full costs, increased appreciably during this period.
41.   We have examined 46 public schools. In 1970, 57 such schools were included in the Totality, but 4 of these schools were private schools in 1955 (a significant fact in itself), and 7 schools enrolled fewer than 50 students in 1955, so that only 46 public schools are examined in this section.

exceeded resident tuition by 135%.[42] By 1970, average resident tuition increased to about $523, a 129% increase since 1955,[43] and average nonresident tuition increased to about $1,235, a 130% increase since 1955. As an average matter in 1970, nonresident tuition exceeded resident tuition by 136%.[44] Comparing tuitions at private schools and public schools, on the whole, in both 1955 and 1970, tuition for private schools was about three times as high as tuition for resident students at public schools and about one-third higher than tuition for nonresident students at public schools.

Section 3 — Tuition and Financial Aid

An examination was made above of the relationship between tuition and per-student instructional cost. We now examine the relationship between tuition and financial aid.

From the institutional point of view, tuition is a resource and financial aid is a cost.[45] From the student's point of view, the reverse is true. This section examines developments in tuition and financial aid from the points of view of both parties. From the institutional standpoint, the ultimate concern is likely to be the net amount of resources that remain after financial aid (in the form of scholarships) is offset against gross tuition income. From the student standpoint, the ultimate concern is likely to be the net amount of costs that must be met after financial aid (in the form of scholarships and loans[46]) is offset against tuition and living expenses. Although "financial aid" within this section is considered to be those explicit grants and loan funds which go toward meeting the tuition and living expenses of the student, another form of financial aid exists when the tuition income of the institution is not sufficient to meet the full costs[47] of a law school. In these circumstances every student is receiving a

---

42.   The bulk of the schools' resident tuitions ranged between no tuition and $400 (excluding four schools with tuitions higher than $400), and their nonresident tuitions ranged between $200 and $800, with most schools having nonresident tuitions between the range of $400 and $800.

43.   In 1970, resident tuition spread between $300 and $750, with four schools charging more and three less. Resident tuition at schools in the Large Enrollment Group was slightly higher than at schools in the other two Groups. Average resident tuition of the Large Enrollment Group schools was $549 in 1970 as compared to $499 and $518 for the Middle and Small Enrollment Schools, respectively.

44.   Nonresident tuition spread between about $900 and $1,900, with three schools charging more and eight schools charging less. Nonresident tuition at schools in the Large Enrollment Group was slightly higher than at schools in the other two Groups. Average nonresident tuition of Large Enrollment Group schools was $1,451 in 1970 as compared to $1,115 and $1,141 for the Middle and Small Enrollment Group schools, respectively.

45.   In fact, financial aid, in most cases, acts to reduce resources rather than to increase costs. Costs would be increased in those cases where the scholarship grant exceeds the tuition charge and students receive funds toward living expenses.

46.   Of course, for the long term, the student will be additionally concerned about the indebtedness which he is accumulating in loans. See section 5.

47.   See footnote 39.

form of financial aid, since each student is receiving more than he or she is paying for and, to that extent, is being subsidized.

Although data for the larger sample of schools is unavailable, figures from the case-study schools provide an insight into the expansion of scholarship awards during the period 1955-1970. Scholarships may be awarded in such a way as to meet either all or part of students' tuition and living expenses. However, for comparative purposes, Table 7 sets forth the percentage of students who could have been provided with full tuition grants on the basis of total scholarship awards in 1955-56 and in 1970-71 at the case-study schools.[48]

Table 7

**Percent of Students who could have been provided
with full tuition Scholarships for 1955-56
and 1970-71 at the Case-study Schools**

School	1955-56	1970-71
A	7%	23%
B	7	22
C	6	20
D	19	19
E	6	16
F	11	13
G	1	11
H	2	8
I	0	4

Note: See footnote 48.

Table 7 reveals, in most instances, considerable increases in scholarship grants over the period of the study. During this period there were also considerable increases in enrollment and tuition charges.[49] The case-study school data in Table 7 also indicate that, as tuition charges have increased,[50] substantial changes have taken place in the proportion of credits that have been made against tuition charges.[51] In order to illustrate the dimensions of the increases set forth in Table 7, there follows a hypothetical example of a school whose

48.   In view of separate tuition charges, for comparative purposes in the case of public law schools, the funds were hypothetically equally divided between resident and nonresident students.
49.   See chapter 2 regarding enrollment patterns and section 2 regarding tuition patterns.
50.   See section 2 regarding increases in tuition charges.
51.   A credit against a tuition charge is the amount of a scholarship grant that is equal to, or less than, the tuition charge. In such cases, the scholarship grant is applied as a "credit" against tuition, and the student would make up the balance due in tuition, if any, through loan proceeds or available cash. In some cases, of course, scholarship grants may exceed the tuition charge. In these instances students then receive funds toward their living expenses. Scholarship grants in either case, if not supported by endowment or gift income, must be realized through a higher tuition rate than would otherwise be applicable. See section 4.

enrollment and tuition increased considerably and whose grant pattern is similar to those of some of the schools in Table 7. The example assumes that, in 1955-56, a school with an enrollment of 600 and a tuition charge of $500 was able to provide scholarships in an amount equivalent to its full tuition charge to 7 percent of its students. In the example, the gross sum of scholarships would be $21,000 ($500 × 42 students). Assume that in 1970-71, enrollment was 1,000, the tuition charge was $2,000, and the school endeavored to provide scholarships in an amount equivalent to its tuition charge for 20 percent of its students. Under these circumstances, $400,000 ($2,000 × 200 students) would be required. In current dollars, total scholarships would have increased from $21,000 to $400,000. In constant dollars, total scholarships would have increased from $31,164 to $400,000.[52] If the school had no endowment or gift income to support its scholarship program, its net tuition income would have been as shown in Table 8.[53]

Table 8

	1955-56	1970-71
Number of students	600	1,000
Number of students who could have received full tuition scholarships	42	200
Percent of students who could have received full tuition scholarships	7	20

	1955-56 current dollars	1955-56 constant dollars	1970-71 dollars
Tuition	$500	$742	$2,000
Gross tuition income	$300,000	$445,200	$2,000,000
Credits against tuition (total scholarships)	$21,000	$31,164	$400,000
Net tuition income	$279,000	$414,036	$1,600,000

52.   In this study 1955 dollars have been inflated to 1970 levels. See Introduction and Summary.
53.   Net tuition income is gross tuition income (number of students × tuition charge) less the total amount of scholarship awards applied against tuition. See section 4 for a further discussion.

In percentage terms, enrollment increased by 67%, the number of students who could have received full tuition scholarships increased by 376%, and based on constant dollars the following changes would have occurred:

Increase in tuition	170%
Increase in gross tuition income	349%
Increase in scholarships	1,184%
Increase in net tuition	286%

These figures illustrate the tremendous expansion that occurs in the total amount of scholarships offered when the theoretical[54] percent of students offered such aid changes from 7% to 20% as shown in the hypothetical school.

A static view of the extent to which tuition charges are not being met by student payments[55] can be gained by examining the proportion of gross tuition charges represented by scholarships at law schools which participated in the joint A.B.A.-A.A.L.S. inspections of 1972-73. Because of the limited data, the figures in Table 9 are meant to be illustrative only.[56]

Table 9

Percent of Tuition Income represented by Scholarships during 1972-73 at 8 private schools jointly inspected by the A.B.A.-A.A.L.S.

School	Percent
A	11%
B	11
C	9
D	9
E	8
F	7
G	7
H	4

The resources to support a scholarship program may be endowment or gift income or grants from various agencies. Frequently, however, a student's scholarship may not be supported by such income.[57] In both instances, a scholarship is generally first applied as a credit toward the tuition charge for

54.   The term "theoretical" is used since in actuality a number of students receive less than a full tuition scholarship. To that extent the percent of students receiving scholarships would be greater.

55.   To the extent that credits against tuition charges are supported by endowment and gift income for scholarship purposes, the dollars available for institutional operations are not proportionately reduced. To the extent that credits against tuition charges are not so supported, the dollars available for institutional operations are proportionately reduced.

56.   It should be noted that the percents reflected in Tables 7 and 9 are comparable for private schools since the equivalent percent of students receiving full tuition scholarships is the same as the percent of gross tuition income represented by scholarships. For Table 9 sufficient information was unavailable for 9 other private schools.

57.   In this context, tuition income is not considered as a resource for the support of the scholarship program. Of course, the total amount of scholarship grants often exceeds the

RESOURCES 269

each student.[58] In the latter case, a credit is made toward the tuition charge, even though endowment or gift income to support such credit does not exist. In

Table 10

Percent of Scholarships supported and unsupported by Endowment and Gift Income for the Case-study Schools 1955-56 and 1970-71

School		Unsupported by Endowments or Gifts	Supported by Endowments	or Gifts
A	1955-56	100%	0%	0%
	1970-71	100	0	0
B	1955-56	81	0	19
	1970-71	28	16	56
C	1955-56	42	58	0
	1970-71	55	4	41
D	1955-56	—	—	—
	1970-71	23	38	39
E	1955-56	0	14	86
	1970-71	21	47	32
F	1955-56	/	/	/
	1970-71	14	79	7
G	1955-56	0	100	0
	1970-71	0	64	36
H	1955-56	0	28	72
	1970-71	0	25	75
I	1955-56	0	0	100
	1970-71	0	77	23

Note: In this table schools F, H, and I are public schools. / indicates no scholarships were awarded. — indicates breakdown unavailable.

total amount of endowment or gift income used as support for the scholarship program. In these cases, the law school is able to charge some students lesser amounts toward full tuition charges through its scholarship program, since some students are paying greater amounts toward full tuition charges.
58. If the scholarship award exceeds the tuition charge, the student would then receive the balance in the form of a cash stipend.

effect, the actual cash tuition income of the institution is the net amount that is available after credits for scholarships which are not supported by endowment or gift income have been deducted.[59] Thus, the proportionate share of gross tuition income represented by scholarships not supported by endowment and gift income determines the actual cash from tuition income that is available to the institution.

Table 10 sets forth the variations among the case-study schools in the relative proportion of scholarships supported and not supported by endowment and gift income and which presumably exist generally. In reviewing the data in Table 10, it should be stressed that relatively small sums were involved in 1955-56 as compared with 1970-71[60] Therefore, even if in a particular category there was a percentage drop from 1955-56 to 1970-71, the gross funds involved in 1970-71 may have been considerably greater than in 1955-56.

As explained above, to the extent that financial aid is in the form of scholarships not supported by endowment and gift income, the total amount of such scholarships reduces the funds that would be generated by tuition charges if such awards were not made. Table 11 shows for the case-study schools the

Table 11

Percent of Gross Tuition Income at the Case-study Schools represented by Scholarships unsupported by Endowment or Gift Income

	1955-56	1970-71
A	11%	13%
B	1	12
C	1	4
D	0	4
E	–	4
F		1
G	0	0
H	0	0
I	0	0

Note: – indicates breakdown unavailable. 1 is one percent or less. In 1955-56 no scholarships were awarded at school F.

59.   As a hypothetical example, assume a law school with an enrollment of 500, and an annual tuition charge of $2,000. Thus, gross tuition income would be $1,000,000. Assume further that $200,000 is awarded in "tuition scholarships" of which income from endowments supports $40,000 and an annual alumni program has made $90,000 available. Assume no additional outside income for scholarships exists. In these circumstances, the actual funds available for operating costs would be $930,000, since $70,000 of the $200,000 awarded for scholarships is not supported by endowment or gift income.
60.   See Table 7.

percent of gross tuition income (number of students X tuition charge) represented by scholarship awards not supported by endowment and gift income.

Table 11 figures are illustrative only, and, in view of the limited data, are set forth to suggest that since 1955 more schools may be relying to a greater degree on sustaining financial-aid programs through unsupported scholarships. Generalizations regarding the dimensions of these changes would require more precise information from a larger number of schools.

In examining the proportion of scholarships that are supported and unsupported by endowment and gift income, as in Table 10, one may compare the extent to which students are being supported by benefactors with the extent to which some students are being supported by other students. If scholarships are supported by endowments or gifts, the income from such sources is available for operating costs.[61] If such income is made available through the scholarship program, the tuition rate would presumably be lower than otherwise. Under these circumstances, students who are not receiving scholarships benefit from the existence of a financial-aid program supported by endowments and gifts as well as those students who are receiving scholarships.[62] This is so, since the students who are not receiving scholarships would otherwise have to pay a higher tuition. In sum, whenever income from endowments or gifts is unavailable for scholarships, and the law school wishes to maintain a scholarship program, tuition must be increased. Students who are not receiving scholarships would provide a larger share of the resources through a higher tuition rate.

From the institutional perspective, a distinction must also be made between supported and unsupported financial-aid programs. As indicated above, presumably a higher tuition is charged to generate resources than would be the case if scholarship grants were supported by endowment and gift income. At the same time, it should be noted that, by increasing tuition and decreasing the amount of supported scholarships, endowment and gift income, to the extent that it is unrestricted, can be used for expanding the law school program at a faster rate than if endowment and gift income is used to support the scholarship program.

Section 4 — Setting Tuition Levels

We next consider the function of setting tuition levels by examining some of the factors that influence such a determination. We also suggest a method through which tuition can be set which takes account of these factors.

---

61.   Thus the scholarship program is one mechanism through which endowment and gift income is provided for institutional operations except insofar as scholarship awards supported by endowment or gift income exceed the tuition charges.

62.   Of course, many students receive partial tuition scholarships and are thus paying tuition in part and to that extent are assisting, in part, all who are receiving unsupported scholarship grants. Also, see discussion regarding the tuition increment formula in section 4.

We assume that the objective in increasing the tuition level is to produce more funds for the full costs[63] of law school operations and to provide for a financial-aid program to enable a given number of students to enroll without having to pay the full tuition charge.[64] Therefore, in determining tuition charges, the following factors must be taken into account: the total number of students enrolled, the number of students receiving scholarships, the amount of living expenses to be recognized, and the amount in net tuition revenues desired. It should be noted that, when tuition charges are increased, additional funds are made available through net tuition revenue for the full costs of law school operations, except under the extraordinary circumstances when the additional resources created by the tuition increase are totally used for financial-aid purposes. This might occur, for example, in a situation in which the cost of living spirals, a substantial proportion of students receives scholarship grants, the school endeavors to increase the grant allocations to students to meet cost-of-living increases, and the tuition increase for all students is not sufficient to do any more than meet that need.[65] A tuition-increment formula provides a means for determining the amount by which each student's tuition must be increased in order to achieve two objectives: first, to produce additional net tuition revenues in order to make more funds available for full costs so as to meet inflationary pressures and possibly expand the law school program; second, to maintain those who are receiving financial aid on a parity basis with the previous year, by taking into account increases in both tuition and the cost of living. The Tuition Increment Formula is as follows:[66]

$$TI = \frac{(CL \times F_2) + [(F_2 - F_1) \times AA] + AR}{N_2}$$

---

63.   See footnote 39. See Introduction and Summary.

64.   In some cases students may receive scholarships which, in addition to providing credits toward tuition, contribute cash funds to defray living expenses. See footnote 51. It is assumed throughout that any increases in endowment and gift income are not sufficient to meet increases in full costs.

65.   Living expenses will, of course, vary according to the status of the student: single or married, resident or commuter, and the need to support children or other dependents. Such expenses can be regarded as falling into two areas, basic and special. Basic expenses consist of rent, food, clothing, laundry, recreation, drugs, and other miscellaneous items that apply to all students. Special expenses include long-distance transportation, medical-dental care, and other items that vary according to the needs of the individual student.

66.   The formula takes into account three factors: first, the difference in dollars required to adjust for increases (or decreases) in the cost of living for all students who will receive scholarships during the following year; second, the difference in dollars which would result from increases (or decreases) in the number of students who will receive scholarships; and third, the difference in dollars which would result from the need for more (or less) funds for institutional operations. The sum of the differences is then divided by the number of students who will not receive financial aid, in order to determine the increase or decrease in tuition for the following year.

where

TI = The tuition increment per student from Year 1 to Year 2,

CL = the cost-of-living expense increment per student from Year 1 to Year 2,

F_1 = the number of students receiving scholarships during Year 1,

F_2 = the number of students receiving scholarships during Year 2,

N_2 = the number of students not receiving scholarships during Year 2,

AA = the average scholarship awarded in Year 1,

AR = additional resources desired for Year 2 for purposes other than scholarship grants.

As a hypothetical example assume the following in Year 1:

- a total student body of 500
- a tuition of $2,000
- a nine-month cost-of-living expense budget of $2,500
- 20% of the students receiving scholarship grants, i.e., 100; thus 80% of the students are not receiving scholarship grants, i.e., 400
- an average scholarship grant of $1,000[67]

Thus, in Year 1, the gross tuition income is $1,000,000, the amount of scholarship grants, $100,000; and, therefore, net tuition income (or cash resources) left available to contribute toward the full costs of the law school program is $900,000.

Assume the following for Year 2:

- the cost-of-living expense budget is expected to rise 5%, or $125.
- the total student body will remain the same size, i.e., 500.
- it is desired to increase the percent of students receiving scholarship grants to 25% of the student body, i.e., from 100 to 125 students. Thus, 75%, or 375 students, will not be receiving scholarship grants.
- it is desired to produce $75,000 in additional net tuition income in order to meet inflationary pressures and expand the law school program.

The Tuition Increment Formula provides a way to determine the tuition increment that would be necessary to provide for both the additional scholarships and the additional resources. In this example, CL is 125, F_1 is 100, F_2 is 125, N_2 is 375, AA is 1,000, and AR is 75,000. Thus, by applying the Tuition Increment Formula:

$$TI = \frac{(125 \times 125) + [(125 - 100) \times 1,000] + 75,000}{375}$$

$$\text{or} \quad \frac{15,625 + 25,000 + 75,000}{375}$$

$$\text{or} \quad \frac{115,625}{375} \quad \text{or} \quad 308.33$$

67. This hypothetical example assumes there are no funds from endowment or gift income for scholarship purposes. When such income exists, the average scholarship grant in

Therefore, the tuition increment from year 1 to Year 2 is $308.33; and in Year 2, tuition per student would be $2,308.33, or, as would be likely, rounded off to $2,310. From the institutional perspective the following would result in Year 2:

- gross tuition income would be $1,155,000, or $2,310 (Year 2 tuition) multiplied by 500 (Year 2 enrollment);
- total scholarship grants would be $179,375, or $1,000 (the Year 1 average scholarship award) plus $310 (the tuition increment) plus $125 (the cost-of-living increment), i.e., $1,435, multiplied by 125 (the number of students receiving scholarship awards);
- net tuition income would be $975,625,[68] or $1,155,000 (gross tuition income) less $179,375 (total scholarship grants)
- additional resources would be $75,625.[69]

Accordingly, the desire to produce $75,000 in additional income after satisfying financial-aid objectives, would be met. From the perspective of a student receiving a hypothetical average scholarship grant, the following would result in Year 2:

- "out of pocket" costs would be $3,500, and, thus, the same as in Year 1.

In Year 1, the 100 students who were scholarship recipients received an average credit of $1,000 toward the tuition charge of $2,000. Thus, in Year 1, each grantee was "out of pocket" an average of $1,000 for tuition and $2,500 for living expenses, or a total of $3,500. By Year 2, tuition had increased to $2,310, but since each grantee received an average credit of $1,435 toward the tuition charge, each was "out of pocket" an average of $875 for tuition. For continuing students, this amount would be $125 less than in Year 1. For these students, the $125 could then be applied toward living expenses which in Year 2 amounted to $2,625. Thus, each grantee was "out of pocket" an average of $875 for tuition and $2,625 for living expenses, or a total of $3,500. It should be noted that, although in theory such a continuing grantee has maintained a parity position, in fact his position has improved, since his "out of pocket" dollars are of course cheaper (i.e., easier to obtain) owing to inflation.

If the additional 25 students receiving scholarship grants averaging $1,435 were upperclassmen, they would be considerably better off than they were the previous year since each, on the average, is paying $875 in tuition after the $1,435 grant is deducted. The $1,435 grant represents $125 toward the cost-of-living increase and $1,310 in cash savings in the form of average tuition credits. The $1,310 in cash savings would modify the need for these students to beg, borrow, draw on savings, or work. It is more likely, however, that most, if not all, of the 25 additional students receiving awards would be entering students rather than upperclassmen.[70] In this case, the tuition increment would,

---

Year 1 would be the total amount of scholarship funds unsupported by endowment or gift income divided by the total number of students receiving scholarship grants.
68.   This is $625 more due to the adjustment in tuition to $2,310 for convenience.
69.   See footnote 68.
70.   It should also be recognized that the formula assumes that the theoretical average Year 1 award for first-year students entering in Year 2 is the same as the actual Year 1 average award for continuing students.

in effect, be used to improve the quality of the student body.

Obviously, the Tuition Increment Formula can be applied to many variations depending on particular institutional objectives.[71] For example, the Tuition Increment Formula may also be used when it is determined, perhaps unrealistically, that the number of students receiving scholarships will be reduced. In this case, in making projections for a subsequent year, the school might take its current enrollment, endeavor to maintain a parity[72] award for ongoing students, and then determine the average award and proportion of incoming students, if any, who would receive scholarship grants. Another example also involves alternatives available to a school with respect to its incoming students. The Tuition Increment Formula assumes that the average award for the incoming class will be the same as for ongoing students. However, since greater flexibility exists in setting the average award for incoming students, a school can, if it wishes, expand the number of students in the first-year class who would receive financial aid by reducing their average awards.

Although the Tuition Increment Formula produces the amount by which tuition must be increased in order to theoretically maintain each scholarship recipient in an absolute parity position between Year 1 and Year 2, substantial adjustments may, of course, be made on the basis of changes in law school financial-aid policies or changes in the circumstances of the individual student. As mentioned, more students in the incoming class could be given grants if the average first-year awards were reduced. Such an approach would be taken if it were determined, for example, that a greater proportion of aid for incoming students should be in the form of loans rather than grants. Or, for instance, it may be deemed unessential to maintain ongoing students in a parity position. Thus, if ongoing students were receiving financial aid in the form of a combination of grants and loans, it would be possible here, also, to readjust from class to class. In this case, the proportion of loans could be made higher during each subsequent year. To implement this policy, a law school might inform incoming students that cost-of-living and tuition increases, if any, would be met through loans and not through scholarships.

Although the Tuition Increment Formula can be used to ascertain the tuition increment that would be necessary to produce a certain gross amount of scholarship grants, the amount of a student's individual grant may depend on the resolution of certain basic issues involving the applicant's particular circumstances. For example, with respect to ongoing students who are renewing financial-aid applications, such issues might include the extent to which adjustments, if any, would be made on the basis of: an increase in the resources available to the student, e.g., through a well-paying job; a decrease in resources available to the student, e.g., through participation in summer activities that do not generate sufficient income, such as a position on a journal, or studying abroad. Other issues arise when a spouse converts from student status to

71. The formula may be applied, of course, when there are decreases in any one, or all, of the several factors.
72. "Parity" is used as previously explained. Some, however, believe that ongoing students should receive less in scholarship awards as they advance closer to their degrees.

employee, or vice-versa, or when total indebtedness increases beyond a predetermined level. With respect to the last-mentioned factor, presumably consideration would be given to the reasons why the indebtedness had reached the higher limits. If high indebtedness resulted from borrowing in excess of what would seem reasonable to meet educational expenses, presumably the student should not benefit through a financial-aid package containing a larger proportion of grants than loans, on the mere grounds that his indebtedness has reached a certain level.

Section 5 – Loans

During the period of the study, loans, like scholarships, became a significant resource in financing law students' education. Although specific information from four of the case-study schools was not available, the data from three schools showed percent increases between 1955 and 1970 of 2,592%, 7,100%, and 10,133% in current dollars, and 1,712%, 4,746%, and 6,788%, respectively, in constant dollars. The enormous percent increases in the amount of loans is a function of the fact that in 1955 the amount of loans in absolute terms was extremely limited.[73] (Two case-study schools had no loan funds available in 1955.) Measuring the dimensions of a loan program in terms of the percent of students whose tuition could be underwritten by loan proceeds may not, of course, be an accurate reflection of the actual use of all such loan funds, since the proceeds students receive from loans may be applied toward both tuition and living expenses. Nevertheless, for comparative purposes, by drawing on the information in Table 7 (where the percent of students whose full tuition could have been supported by scholarship grants was measured) the proportionate relationship between scholarship grants and loans can be shown. Table 12 shows

Table 12

Percent of Students whose full tuition could have been supported by Grant and Loan Funds in 1970-71 at the Private Case-study Schools

School	A	B	C	D	E	F
Grants	23%	22%	19%	16%	13%	8%
Loans	24	24	28	4	13	7
Total	47%	46%	47%	20%	26%	15%

---

73. Thus, if in 1955 a school had $3,000 in loan funds (which would be $4,457 in 1970 constant dollars) and in 1970 the school had $300,000 in loan funds, such funds would have increased by 9,900% in current dollars and 6,630% in constant dollars.

the percent of students whose tuition could have been supported by grant and loan funds in 1970-71 at the private case-study schools.[74]

The figures indicate that loan funds as such, or in conjunction with scholarship grants, form a significant basis for enabling students to obtain a legal education. As mentioned, loan funds may often be applied to living expenses rather than tuition. When an individual scholarship recipient is receiving both a scholarship and a loan, and the scholarship is equivalent to or exceeds the tuition charge, the loan proceeds will, of course, be fully applied toward the living expenses of the student. In these instances, therefore, the loan proceeds, from an institutional standpoint, do not provide dollar resources for the law school. To the extent that the loan recipient is not receiving a scholarship, or the scholarship is less than the full tuition charge, the loan proceeds, even if not internally credited toward tuition, will provide the means for the student to pay all or part of the tuition charge. Undoubtedly, the expansion in loan sources for students over the period of the study was a major factor in the expansion of law school resources and, consequently law school programs.[75] Under some loan plans a deposit by a school of $10,000 will create $100,000 in loan capacity. Thus, by converting some scholarship funds to a deposit for such purposes, considerable additional resources become available for more students.[76] If loan funds continue to expand, and more students are willing to borrow or to borrow more, then law school programs may continue to expand. If loan funds contract, law school programs may similarly contract.[77]

From the student standpoint, the type of loan plan, the amount of personal indebtedness that would be incurred, and the terms of repayment may influence a basic career choice or the selection of a law school. Loan plans can be divided into three major categories. The first consists of institutional loan funds, which comprise those loans provided by the university through its own capital. These loans originate with the institution and are made directly to the student. The funds for institutional loans derive from endowment, gift or tuition income, or

74. The loan data obtained from the case-study schools included loans provided by all sources, i.e., the university, state-guaranteed loan programs, the National Defense Education Act, etc.
75. In 1964, there was created within the A.B.A. Fund for Public Education, the American Bar Association Fund for Legal Education. The Legal Education Fund was created in order to start a revolving "Student Guaranty Loan Fund" for law students and to attract the interest of promising students to the profession. In 1972, United Student Aid Funds created a new loan program designed specifically for students attending law, medical, business, and dental schools. For every $1,000 deposited by a law school with USA Funds it will endorse $10,000 in loans to the school's students. When these loans are repaid, the same $1,000 underwrites $10,000 more in loans for each new generation of students. The minimum deposit is $10,000, creating $100,000 in loan capacity. See "A New Student Loan Program for Graduate and Professional School Students" (New York: United Student Aid Funds, Inc., 1973).
76. See the United Student Aid Funds program described in footnote 75.
77. In section 4 it was shown that both scholarship funds and funds available for the law school program could be increased by obtaining a higher net tuition from students with greater individual resources. Thus, expansion of the law school program could occur without an expansion of loan funds, but the quality of the student body might be affected. In a similar manner, contraction of the law school program might be avoided through the expansion of scholarship rather than loan funds.

public support. If endowed, the loans may be provided under the terms of a fiduciary agreement that stipulates an extremely low rate of interest. Gifts for the purpose of providing loans may also stipulate low interest. Although such low-interest loans are particularly attractive for students, from the institutional standpoint, the administration of such funds is often cumbersome, owing to their variety and differing terms.

A second category of loan plans consists of those which are provided directly to the student by banks and other financial institutions and which are governmentally guaranteed. Under these programs the federal government, or the federal government in conjunction with a state agency, insures the principal and interest. In addition, these programs provide the lender with a supplemental interest payment from the federal government. If the student meets certain guidelines,[78] the federal government will pay the interest on the loan while the student is enrolled and for a brief period of time thereafter.[79] Under these plans the capital is provided by private lenders, and, accordingly, the student is dependent on the extent to which funds are made available by private lenders, which, in turn, is related to general market conditions.

A third category of loan plans is, in part, a combination of the first two categories. In this category, the institution provides the capital as in the first category, and occupies the status of the private lender as in the second category, thereby benefiting from the governmental guarantees that exist in the second category. Under these arrangements the loan originates with the university and, as in the second category, the university is eligible for the interest supplement paid by the federal government. Since the loans are guaranteed, the university, with the loan paper as collateral, may be able to create new lines of credit or sell the loan paper to a secondary market.[80] As mentioned, under the first category of loan plans, the origin and servicing of the loans rests with the institution; and under the second category, with the private lenders. The third category of loan plans enables the institution to be responsible for the origin of the loan, but, if the paper is sold, the servicing may be taken over by private lenders. In addition to these advantages, the capital risks are assumed by the government and not by the university.

As loans become a more significant resource for providing funds to students and thus to the institution, the total indebtedness of law students will of course increase. In order to meet the concerns of students regarding repayment of high indebtedness, various contingent repayment plans have been developed.[81]

---

78. See U.S. Office of Education, Office of Guaranteed Student Loans, Fact Sheet, June 2, 1974.
79. Nine months, unless a student has taken a leave of absence, in which case the period of the leave is deducted.
80. The Student Loan Marketing Association ("Sallie Mae"), a U.S. Government sponsored private corporation, was created by the 1972 amendments to the Higher Education Act of 1965, to provide liquidity, primarily through instituting secondary market and warehousing facilities for insured student loans. See materials provided by Sallie Mae, 1750 K Street N.W., Washington, D.C. 20006.
81. See D. Bruce Johnstone with Stephen P. Dresch, *New Patterns for College Lending: Income Contingent Loans*, A Ford Foundation Report (New York: Columbia University Press, 1972), pp. 3-7.

"Pay-as-you-earn"[82] is the basic concept underlying these plans, which, unlike conventional loans, permit the borrower to repay at some percent of future income. In addition, limits are imposed on the repayment period and the total repayment liability. Under conventional loan plans, the lender assumes the risk that the borrower will fail to meet the repayment obligations. Income-contingency plans carry the additional risk that the income of the borrower will not increase as anticipated. Since government-insured plans do not presently cover income-contingent loans and private lenders are reluctant to assume the risks except at very high rates of interest, such loans must be capitalized by the institutions themselves. It has therefore been suggested that "the only way . . . income contingent-fixed schedule plans can become generally available is either through direct governmental capitalization . . . or through state and/or federal assumption of the capital risk . . . "[83]

Regardless of the exact terms of individual income-contingent plans, such plans involve a group of borrowers, or "cohort," who contract for a repayment rate at a specified percent of income, a maximum repayment period beyond which the borrower need no longer pay, and an upper limit of accumulated payments. Under these conditions "surplus" payments from higher earners within the cohort will compensate for lower payments from the lower earners.[84] Since law school graduates constitute a group whose income potential may be higher than other groups, a question exists as to whether law students would wish to be tied into a universitywide cohort. A study of law, medical, and business students at a single university found that the "pay-as-you-earn" concept was "unable to generate a sufficient base of support to warrant its introduction."[85] Students with high average income expectations were "well satisfied with a fixed obligation loan whose term of repayment reflects the size of the initial debt." Not surprisingly, students "with low income expectations" formed the bulk of support for the "pay-as-you-earn" plan.[86]

It may be that, to accommodate varying concerns, loan plans will develop which are not tied into a cohort, but which provide for graduated payments related to income. For example, a repayment schedule might be arranged with the borrower obliged to repay either the specified amount or a fixed percentage of future annual income. The unpaid amount would be refinanced by the university; and if the indebtedness of a low earner was ultimately forgiven, the university, in effect, would have given a grant. Thus, some grants would be made not on a need basis reflecting the relatively low current income of the parents of the student, but on the basis of the actual low future earnings of the student. In sum, a variety of loan plans are emerging designed to meet the demand for

---

82.   These plans are sometimes referred to as "PAYE" plans.
83.   D. Bruce Johnstone, *Pay-As-You-Earn: Summary Report and Recommendations* (New York: Ford Foundation, 1972), p. 11.
84.   See footnote 81.
85.   George S. Day, Associate Professor, Graduate School of Business, Stanford University, "Loan Plans for Professional Schools: An Appraisal of Student Responses," A Report to the Ford Foundation (not published).
86.   See footnote 85.

increased institutional and student resources through loans. The tremendous expansion in loan funds which took place from 1955 to 1970 suggests that these years may have been the brink of a period when loan funds become the prevailing factor in meeting the costs of legal education. At the present time, it is too early to tell what the impact of various loan plans will be. The plans described above suggest some alternative loan plans and their implications.

Section 6 — Demand for Legal Education and Financial Aid

We next consider enrollment as a function of the demand for legal education, and such demand in relation to the amount of financial aid available. During the period of the study, the demand for legal education increased considerably. Table 13 provides a broad overview of changes during the period of the study between the number of Law School Admission Test (LSAT) candidates and the number of first-year enrolled law students.[87]

Table 13

Number LSAT Candidates		Number of Enrolled First-year Students in the following year	
11,755	(1955-56)	16,771	(1956-57)
23,800	(1960-61)	17,698	(1961-62)
45,268	(1965-66)	26,720	(1966-67)
107,147	(1970-71)	37,724	(1971-72)

See footnote 87.

During the period covered, the number of LSAT candidates increased 812% and enrolled first-year law students 125%. The percentages do not precisely reflect demand patterns.[88] They clearly indicate, however, that during this period the demand for legal education progressively outgrew the places available. These conditions are related to developments in financial aid, insofar as financial aid might have been construed by law schools as a recruitment device. At the

87.   See *Annual Meeting*, Law School Admission Council (ETS, Princeton, N.J., 1973), p. 92.
88.   One should not conclude that over 100,000 students were seriously seeking admission to law school during 1970-71. Included in the number of LSAT candidates are students who took the LSAT more than once. Therefore, repeaters must be discounted. Furthermore, in 1955, only 36 of 129 A.B.A. approved schools required the LSAT, whereas, by 1970-71, 142 of 147 A.B.A. approved schools required the LSAT. Furthermore, a number of students may be taking the test in an effort to determine whether legal education is an appropriate course of study. More likely, closer to 80,000 were in fact seeking admission. See Winograd "Law School Admissions: A Different View" A.B.A. Journal (August 1973).

threshold of the period, the Tunks Report[89] described financial aid in large measure as a recruitment mechanism. However, as the number of candidates seeking enrollment expanded,[90] the objective of attracting more and better students began to be met in considerable measure apart from the use of financial aid as a recruitment device.[91] Since the total number of students seeking admission expanded so greatly, the number of more highly qualified applicants, on the basis of academic accomplishments and aptitudes, similarly increased. As a result, financial aid has come to be used more as a means to lessen the financial strain of needy students and less as a recruitment device. Assuming that among the applicant population the group who are well qualified consists of students both with adequate resources and with minimal resources, a financial-aid program could be developed that would seek to maintain or enhance the over-all academic quality of the student body by drawing funds from those well-qualified students who are capable of meeting higher tuition charges in order to defray the expenses of students who have greater need.[92] Thus, with the increase in the number of well-qualified applicants and an increase in the number of well-qualified students with greater resources, financial-aid opportunities for students with less adequate resources were expanded. More students of limited means were in a position to seek a legal education despite rising expenses.

Section 7 — Tuition, Living Expenses, and Student Resources

We now turn to an analysis of the relationship between tuition and living expenses and more fully consider financial aid from the students' perspective. As indicated above, for the student, financial aid is a resource which governs the net amount he or she must obtain elsewhere in order to meet educational and living expenses. The student's expectations regarding the limits on these available resources will influence the tuition charge.[93] Since 1955 the proportionate share of student resources that have been allocated to tuition versus living expenses

---

89.   Special Committee on Law School Administration and University Relations of the A.A.L.S., Lehan K. Tunks, Chairman, *Anatomy of Modern Legal Education* (St. Paul, Minn.: West Publishing, 1961), ch. 4.
90.   Vaughn Ball, Professor, University of Southern California Law School, attributes the increasing number of LSAT candidates to population factors. For a discussion of his views and other considerations underlying increased pressures for admission see Report of the Task Force on Professional Utilization, A.B.A. 1972, Part II.
91.   During the period of the study, law as a career among adult Americans 18 and over increased in preference from 6% to 14% of those recently surveyed. A.B.A. Journal (March 1974), p. 315.
92.   The Tuition Increment Formula provides a method for making the necessary projections. See section 4.
93.   Another factor related to student expectations is the value of the student's educational investment relative to its subsequent return. This factor involves complex economic considerations regarding the costs of obtaining an education, loss of earnings during the period of schooling, and the prospective earnings of law graduates. A study of these factors has been proposed. See Boyer and Cramton, *American Legal Education: An Agenda for Research and Reform*, 59 Cornell L. Rev. 221 (1974).

has changed substantially. As indicated in section 2, the average tuition expense in 1955 was about $650 (in 1970 dollars) at private schools in the Small and Middle Enrollment Groups, and about $900 at private schools in the Large Enrollment Group. By 1970, these amounts had risen to about $1,500 in the Small and Middle Enrollment Groups and to about $1,900 in the Large Enrollment Group. If, for comparative purposes, we assume that the average living expenses of students were roughly $1,800 during 1970-71, we can use this amount as a constant-dollar measure for 1955.[94] On this assumption, in 1955, tuition expense at the average Small and Middle Enrollment Group schools consisted of about one-quarter of a student's total expenses, and in 1970, about one-half of total expenses. At the average Large Enrollment Group school, tuition expense consisted of about one-third of total expenses in 1955, and somewhat more than one-half in 1970. Since basic living expenses of about the same level must be incurred under any circumstances, the investment for educational purposes (tuition) became a substantially greater proportion of total expenses.[95] The figures show that, in 1955, many students could obtain a legal education by spending from one-third to one-half more than they spent on living expenses, whereas by 1970, for many students, the tuition expense of a legal education was almost equal to, and in some cases even exceeded, living expenses. As has been seen, although, in individual cases, scholarship programs acted as an offset against these tuition increases, substantial numbers of students, nevertheless, met total expenses by going into debt. Like other extraordinary expenditures which approach or exceed basic living expenses, for example, purchasing an automobile or buying and furnishing a home, such educational expenditures were amortized over a period of time through a variety of loan programs. Thus, significant increases in student indebtedness have taken place.

We next consider some factors that affect the capacity of students to meet increases in tuition and living expenses. Of three kinds of law school resources, tuition, endowment, and gift income, tuition income can be set by educational decision makers, whereas the extent of prospective endowment and gift income is dependent upon the future and, thus, uncertain attitudes and actions of benefactors. Therefore, as part of the decision process, it is essential, in the development of law school resources, to ascertain the capacity of students to meet increases in tuition and living expenses. In this process, the institution will ascertain the extent to which those students who have a greater capacity to meet law school costs can, through the financial-aid policies of the school, provide resources which those of lesser capacity are unable to provide.[96]

Three kinds of resources, other than financial aid, are potentially available to the law student: those provided by the student himself or herself, those provided

94. Obviously, particular components of a student's living expenses will vary at different universities and under different local conditions.

95. Depending on local conditions, a student's campus housing expenses may often be less than the prevailing cost of off-campus housing. Loss of potential earnings during the period of schooling is sometimes characterized as an "expense" of obtaining an education. This factor is not herein considered.

96. See Tuition Increment Formula, section 4.

by the spouse, and those provided by parents.[97] In ascertaining the funds that might be available from each, both policy and factual determinations must be made. Policy issues involve such matters as whether imputations will be made regarding the student's summer earnings, the earnings of a spouse, or the ability of parents to contribute.[98] Factual determinations will be made regarding the financial status of each party and the dollars that are available from each to underwrite tuition and living expenses.[99] Some insight into the capacities of law students and their families to finance tuition and living expenses may be gained from the data that were collected from financial-aid applicants through the Law School Financial Aid Service (LSFAS). In an effort to ascertain the extent of resources available to law school financial-aid applicants, their spouses and parents, LSFAS made an analysis of the financial data submitted as part of its program in 1971-72.[100]

Table 14

Comparison of the Income (before taxes) of
U.S. Families with Children in College and LSFAS Parents

Parents' Income	U.S. Families[a]	LSFAS[b]
$15,000 - over	34.0%	35.6%
10,000 - 14,999	27.2	22.6
5,000 - 9,999	23.4	23.3
0 - 4,999	8.3	10.3
Not Reported	7.1	8.2
Totals	100.0	100.0

[a]Source: U.S. Bureau of the Census, *Current Population Reports*, Series P-20, no. 241, "Social and Economic Characteristics of Students: October 1971," (Washington, D.C.: U.S. Government Printing Office, 1972) p. 28.

[b]Sample size is 917. Estimates of income were made in 1971-72 for 1972-73. See footnote 100 for source of Table.

97. Gifts which are made to the student by others: relatives, friends, organizations, are construed in this context as the resources of the student.
98. With respect to parental contributions, it is sometimes asserted that a contribution from parents is unwarranted or unrealistic. Thus, in developing criteria for ascertaining a student's need, policy guidelines must be created for determining under what conditions, if any, emancipation will be recognized. In some cases, in developing guidelines for the purpose of awarding scholarship grants, emancipation is not recognized. However, loan funds might be provided to compensate for estimated parental contributions which, for whatever reason, are not forthcoming. See section 4 regarding other issues of a policy nature.
99. The Graduate and Professional School Financial Aid Service (GAPSFAS) was created in 1971 in order to provide professional school financial aid officers with a determination of the resources an applicant has for educational expenses. See a GAPSFAS "Manual For Financial Aid Officers" (Princeton, N.J.: Educational Testing Service, November 1973).
100. In 1969, the Law School Admission Council decided to establish the Law School Financial Aid Service (LSFAS) to assist law schools in the systematic evaluation of the

With respect to the financial status of parents of law school financial-aid applicants, Table 14 sets forth a comparison of the gross incomes of U.S. families with children in college and parents of LSFAS applicants.

It should be noted that the percents set forth for the LSFAS parents represent only those families applying for financial aid, whereas the percents set forth for U.S. families represent all families with students in college regardless of whether they are financial-aid applicants or not.[101]

Although income was the primary factor in determining the financial strength of parents, the LSFAS rationale recognized that assets enhance a family's ability to contribute to education.[102] Therefore information regarding parental assets was also examined. This information is set forth in Table 15.

Table 15

Percentage Distributions and Summary Statistics for Assets Held by Parents of LSFAS Applicants for 1972-73

Amount in Dollars	Residence Equity	Other Real Estate Equity	Bank Accts.	Other Invmts.	Bus./ Farm	Total Assets
over $35,000	3.4%	1.0%	1.2%	2.8%	0.9%	17.7%
30,001 - 35,000	2.8	0.3	0.2	0.8	0.3	5.7
25,001 - 30,000	4.8	0.3	0.4	1.0	0.1	7.5
20,001 - 25,000	9.3	0.5	1.3	1.5	0.8	10.5
15,001 - 20,000	15.8	1.0	2.0	2.1	0.3	11.9
10,001 - 15,000	16.7	1.9	3.9	2.9	1.0	14.2
5,001 - 10,000	16.2	1.5	8.8	7.0	1.5	11.5
1 - 5,000	7.6	5.8	66.7	16.5	6.7	15.6
zero	23.3	87.7	15.4	65.4	88.3	5.6
Mean	$12,500	$1,741	$3,642	$4,637	$1,407	$25,056

Note: sample size was 917. See footnote 100 for source of Table.

Considering all assets together, LSFAS parents had median assets of $16,353. In arriving at an amount that parents might reasonably be expected to contribute,

financial need of applicants. As part of the LSFAS application process, fiscal and personal data were elicited from such applicants, their parents and spouses. At the close of the 1971-72 processing year, since the data were not on tape, a sample consisting of 917 (of about 11,000) filers was systematically drawn in order to develop some information regarding the over-all financial characteristics of the applicant group. It should be noted that students who applied for financial aid through LSFAS were not necessarily representative of law school applicants generally, since only 53 schools used the service and not all law students apply for financial aid. The study *Law School Financial Aid Service: A Description of Students and Parents Who Completed the 1972-73 LSFAS Application* (Dwight H. Horch Educational Testing Service, 1973); was undertaken under the direction of a special committee of the Law School Admission Council: Richard D. Lee (Davis), Russell A. Simpson (Harvard), Frank K. Walwer (Columbia).

101.   In view of the limited size of the sample and the fact that not all applicants for financial aid completed the LSFAS application, more comprehensive data would be required to more definitively ascertain the financial postiion of the parents of law school applicants. The GAPSFAS program contemplates studies of this nature.

102.   See also GAPSFAS, op. cit., sec. 5.

LSFAS made two determinations: one, on the basis of family income after allowances, known as "effective income"; the other, on the basis of "effective income" plus the family's net assets, known as "adjusted effective income." The amount that parents would theoretically be expected to contribute and the amount that parents are willing to contribute differ. Table 16 sets forth a comparison of these differences.

Table 16

Comparison of Percentage Distributions, LSFAS–Expected Parental Contributions with Amounts Offered by Parents for 1972-73

Amount in Dollars	Contribution from Effective Income	Contribution from Adjusted Effective Income	Parents' Offer from Income	from Assets
over $5,000	4.4%	8.5%	0.1%	0.0%
4,501 - 5,000	1.6	1.4	0.0	0.1
4,001 - 4,500	1.2	2.2	0.0	0.0
3,501 - 4,000	2.0	2.6	0.1	0.0
3,001 - 3,500	4.4	4.6	0.1	0.0
2,501 - 3,000	3.4	4.1	0.4	0.0
2,001 - 2,500	6.2	6.7	1.3	0.1
1,501 - 2,000	8.1	8.3	3.1	0.3
1,001 - 1,500	12.2	11.9	4.0	0.4
501 - 1,000	20.2	17.2	14.1	2.6
1 - 500	22.6	20.5	16.5	5.3
0 - 0	13.8	12.0	60.3	91.2

Note: sample size was 917. See footnote 100 for source of Table.

Table 16 reveals that 39.7 percent planned to make a contribution from income but only 8.8 percent planned to use any of their assets to help meet law school expenses.[103] On the basis of both income and assets, in theory, 30.1 percent could have contributed over $2,000; 37.4 percent could have contributed between $500 and $2,000; 20.5 percent could have contributed some funds up to $500; and 12.0 percent would have been unable to contribute. The median contribution from income would have been $836 and from income and assets, $1,011.

With respect to the financial status of the students themselves, in the year preceding entry into law school, about 94 percent of the students reported earnings from employment. Presumably, a number had been working full time, since the median earnings reported were $2,314. However, reflecting the inclination to devote full time to law studies, 65 percent indicated they would not be working during the law school academic year. Sixty-nine percent indicated they would have cash funds available at the beginning of the law

103.   Twenty-four percent of the students expected aid from their parents in comparison with about 40 percent of the parents who indicated they would contribute some funds from income.

school year. The median amount of such funds was $743. Of the 40 percent who reported indebtedness in the form of undergraduate loans, the median amount was $1,736.

With respect to the applicants' spouses, 29 percent of the applicants indicated they would be married when entering law school. However, about 36 percent of the spouses were also planning to be students. Of the spouses who contemplated employment while the students were in law school, the median earnings for the academic year were expected to be $3,396.

In sum, of this small sample, based on median statistics for the unemployed and unmarried student who anticipated some cash on hand at the start of the school year, the parental contribution would have been about $1,010 and the cash on hand would have been about $740, or a total of $1,750. For the married student, the median figure provided by a working spouse would be about $3,400, for a total of $5,150. The net resources available to a law student for educational expenses is the difference between total resources and living expenses for the academic year. Assume for the 1972-73 academic year that a single student applying for financial aid had $1,750 available for living and educational expenses, and a married student had $5,150. Based on Bureau of Labor statistics for the age level 20 to 35, updated to February 1973 price levels, and readjusted to a 9-month basis, the single student would have required about $1,650 on a "low" budget standard and $2,450 on a "moderate" budget standard for living expenses. Comparable figures for the married couple without children were about $2,200 and $3,300. In 1972-73, based on figures derived from the *Review of Legal Education*, the median tuition at private law schools was $2,100. In this instance, therefore, total tuition and living expenses at the moderate level for the single student might have been $4,550. Similar expenses for the married student would have been $5,400. Thus for the single student, total expenses would have exceeded total resources by $2,800 ($4,550 less $1,750). For the married student with a working spouse, the total resources of $5,150 would have closely approximated the total expense of $5,400.

On these assumptions, if on the basis of median figures, undergraduate indebtedness was $1,736, and the amount by which expenses exceeded resources of the single student had to be borrowed for each successive year in law school (plus somewhat more to meet cost-of-living and tuition increases), accrued total indebtedness by June 1975 would exceed $10,000. It should be further noted that, if grants are made on a need basis, and the student is not, in fact, receiving the theoretical parental contribution, this amount may have to be compensated for by additional loans, thus pushing indebtedness higher. As mentioned, this analysis is based on a small sample involving a single year. As more data are collected both nationally and by individual law schools, a sharper understanding of the students' resources and expenses can be acquired.

Appendices

Appendix A

Questionnaire

PART I   **Enrollment - Tuition - Fees**

	'55-'56	'60-'61	'65-'66	'70-'71
Tuition				
Fees				
Enrollment as of October 1				

A) Full-time Day
- 1st Year
- 2nd Year
- 3rd Year
- Graduate
- Other

Part-time Evening
- 1st Year
- 2nd Year
- 3rd Year
- Graduate
- Other

PART I (continued)

	'55-'56	'60-'61	'65-'66	'70-'71
Part-time Day				
1st Year				
2nd Year				
3rd Year				
Graduate				
Other				

PART II   **Instructional Salaries**

Year_____

Instructor:

Gross Salary: Fringe Benefit Factor:

Course Title	Class	Hours	Type	Day/Night	Enrollment	Share

Comments:

PART III   **Instructional Support**

	'55-'56	'60-'61	'65-'66	'70-'71
Salaries				
Supplies/Equip.				
Duplicating				
Telephone & Postage				
Travel				
Other				

PART IV

Administration

Year _____

	Salaries					Supplies Equipment	Duplicating	Telephone & Postage	Travel	Other
	(1)		(2)		(3)					
	No.	Amt.	No.	Amt.	No.	Amt.				
General										
Admissions										
Placement										
Student Activities										
Student Counseling										
Alumni										
Special Projects										
Total										

(1) senior officers, generally defined as the Dean and "top associates";

(2) junior officers, defined as administrative aides, assistants to the dean, executive secretaries and others holding equivalent appointments;

(3) supporting staff, defined as clerical and secretarial and all other personnel.

PART V   **Library**

	'55-'56	'60-'61	'65-'66	'70-'71
Total no. volumes held at end of:				
Total no. volumes added during:				
Total dollars spent during:				
Serials				
Monographs				
Binding & Rebinding				
Other				
Salaries				
Professional Law Librarians				
Full-time Non-Professional				
Part-time Non-Professional				
Other Expenditures				

PART VI   **Student Activities**

	'55-'56	'60-'61	'65-'66	'70-'71
Publications				
Moot Court				
Other:				

PART VII

Financial Aid

Year _____

	Scholarships						Loans			
	No. Students	Allocated Total Amt.	Resources Genl. Inc.	End.	Govt.	Gift	No. Students	Allocated Total Amt.	Resources School	Govt.	Other
1st Yr.											
2nd Yr.											
3rd Yr.											
Graduate											
Other											
Total											

PART VIII   **Special Projects**

Title: Year_____

	Allocated	Resources			
		Genl. Inc.	End.	Gifts	Govt. Aid
Salaries					
Operating Expenses					
Total					

PART IX   **Resources**

Year_____

	Total Amount	General Income	End. Income	Alumni Gifts	Special Gifts	Govt. Aid
Instructional						
Instructional Support						
Administration						
Library						
Student Activities						
Financial Aid						
Special Projects						
Total						

Appendix B

Resource Index

Schools differ depending on the amount of educational resources available to them. Educational resources include faculty members, comprehensiveness of the library, student body and the like. There is a relation, of course, between educational resources and financial resources. Schools with ample financial resources, for instance, are able to pay high faculty salaries and so presumably have among the best teachers on their faculties. We have ranked a preponderance of the schools included in the Totality in accordance with an educational resource index which is called the Resource Index. In establishing the Resource Index the criteria used were: 1) L.S.A.T. median score of entering class in 1963 (this was the only year available to us which had the scores for all the schools),[1] 2) the number of library volumes held in 1970, and 3) the median faculty salary (ex-fringe) in 1970. Of the 135 schools in the Totality sufficient data was available for the inclusion of 105. The classification is extremely rough and presents no more than an approximation of the relative rank of the various schools. It is interesting, however, to note that the classification presented here is extremely similar to the resource classifications set forth in Charles D. Kelso's study of part-time legal education.[2] In fact, in most cases schools held similar positions on our and the Kelso resource indexes.

Each of the 105 qualifying schools was given a rank, highest to lowest, on each criterion, based on the 1963 L.S.A.T. score, the 1970 library volumes and the 1970 median faculty salary. The sum of these three ranks was used as the final score for ranking. The schools were then divided into quartiles, the Fourth (top) Quartile scoring highest, the First Quartile scoring lowest. Each quartile

1. Charles D. Kelso, "The AALS Study of Part Time Legal Education," *1972 Annual Meeting Proceedings*, Part One, Section II (Washington, D.C.: Association of American Law Schools, 1972).
2. The authors recognize that there have been substantial increases in the LSAT median scores of individual law schools since 1963, but assume that the relative position of most schools has generally remained the same.

contains 26 schools except the First Quartile which contains 27. In order to preserve confidentiality the listing below was prepared as follows. For each Quartile, Schools have been sub-divided into groups of five (in a few instances a group comprises six schools) and the average of each criterion is set forth for each group.

	LSAT Median Score 1963	Library Volumes 1970	Median Fac. Salary 1970
Fourth Quartile:			
A	615.4	578,460	27,140
B	581.8	243,920	25,160
C	554.8	200,840	24,260
D	549.6	199,280	22,480
E	538.8	129,550	21,716
Third Quartile:			
A	513.8	120,680	21,840
B	524.4	97,060	20,840
C	510.0	130,360	19,200
D	512.6	102,860	19,580
E	522.2	88,116	18,733
Second Quartile:			
A	475.8	91,320	20,480
B	483.8	88,460	19,280
C	499.4	56,860	17,920
D	467.2	60,780	18,840
E	476.7	57,917	17,050
First Quartile:			
A	454.6	51,180	17,100
B	481.8	53,180	15,020
C	479.8	56,660	15,400
D	469.0	47,200	14,880
E	405.4	37,786	13,414

List of Schools

1. The University of Alabama School of Law
2. Albany Law School, Union University (New York)
3. American University, Washington College of Law (D.C.)
4. University of Arizona College of Law
5. University of Arkansas School of Law (Fayetteville)
6. Baylor University School of Law (Texas)
7. Boston College Law School (Massachusetts)
8. Boston University School of Law (Massachusetts)
9. Brooklyn Law School (New York)
10. University of California School of Law, Berkeley
11. University of California, Hastings College of the Law (San Francisco)
12. University of California School of Law, Los Angeles
13. Capital University Law School (Ohio) (formerly Franklin University)
14. Case Western Reserve University, Franklin T. Backus Law School (Ohio) (formerly Western Reserve University)
15. Catholic University of America School of Law (D.C.)
16. University of Chicago Law School (Illinois)
17. Chicago-Kent College of Law, Illinois Institute of Technology (Illinois)
18. University of Cincinnati College of Law (Ohio)
19. Cleveland State University, Cleveland-Marshall College of Law (Ohio) (formerly Cleveland-Marshall Law School)
20. University of Colorado School of Law
21. Columbia University School of Law (New York)
22. University of Connecticut School of Law
23. Cornell Law School (New York)
24. Creighton University School of Law (Nebraska)
25. Cumberland School of Law of Samford University (Alabama) (formerly

Cumberland University School of Law, Tennessee, formerly Howard College)

26. University of Denver College of Law (Colorado)
27. De Paul University College of Law (Illinois)
28. University of Detroit School of Law (Michigan)
29. Detroit College of Law (Michigan)
30. Dickinson School of Law (Pennsylvania)
31. Drake University Law School (Iowa)
32. Duke University School of Law (North Carolina)
33. Duquesne University School of Law (Pennsylvania)
34. Emory University School of Law (Georgia) (formerly Lamar School of Law)
35. University of Florida, Spessard L. Holland Law Center (formerly College of Law)
36. Florida State University College of Law (formerly Florida A. & M. University)
37. Fordham University School of Law (New York)
38. George Washington University National Law Center (D.C.)
39. Georgetown University Law Center (D.C.)
40. University of Georgia School of Law
41. Golden Gate University School of Law (California)
42. Gonzaga University School of Law (Washington)
43. Harvard University Law School (Massachusetts)
44. University of Houston College of Law (Texas)
45. Howard University School of Law (D.C.)
46. University of Idaho College of Law
47. University of Illinois College of Law
48. Indiana University School of Law, Bloomington
49. Indiana University Indianapolis Law School
50. University of Iowa College of Law (formerly State University of Iowa)
51. John Marshall Law School (Illinois)
52. University of Kansas School of Law
53. University of Kentucky College of Law
54. Lewis and Clark College, Northwestern School of Law (Oregon) (formerly Northwestern College of Law)
55. Louisiana State University Law School
56. University of Louisville School of Law (Kentucky)
57. Loyola University School of Law, Chicago (Illinois)
58. Loyola University School of Law, Los Angeles (California)
59. Loyola University School of Law, New Orleans (Louisiana)
60. McGeorge School of Law, University of the Pacific (California) (formerly McGeorge College of Law)
61. Marquette University Law School (Wisconsin)
62. University of Maryland School of Law
63. Mercer University Law School (formerly Walter F. George School of Law) (Georgia)

64. University of Miami School of Law (Florida)
65. University of Michigan Law School
66. University of Minnesota Law School
67. University of Mississippi School of Law
68. University of Missouri-Columbia, School of Law
69. University of Missouri — Kansas City, School of Law (formerly University of Kansas City, School of Law)
70. University of Montana School of Law (formerly Montana State University)
71. University of Nebraska College of Law
72. University of New Mexico School of Law
73. New York Law School
74. State University of New York at Buffalo School of Law (formerly University of Buffalo School of Law)
75. New York University School of Law
76. University of North Carolina School of Law
77. North Carolina Central University, School of Law (formerly North Carolina College, Law School)
78. University of North Dakota School of Law
79. Northeastern University School of Law (Massachusetts)
80. Northern Kentucky State College, Salmon P. Chase College of Law
81. Northwestern University School of Law (Illinois)
82. Notre Dame Law School (Indiana)
83. Ohio Northern University College of Law
84. Ohio State University College of Law
85. University of Oklahoma College of Law
86. Oklahoma City University Law School
87. University of Oregon School of Law
88. University of Pennsylvania Law School
89. University of Pittsburgh School of Law (Pennsylvania)
90. University of Richmond, The T. C. Williams School of Law (Virginia)
91. Rutgers, The State University School of Law, Camden (New Jersey)
92. Rutgers, The State University School of Law, Newark (New Jersey)
93. St. John's University School of Law (New York)
94. St. Louis University School of Law (Missouri)
95. St. Mary's University of San Antonio School of Law (Texas)
96. University of San Diego School of Law (California)
97. University of San Francisco School of Law (California)
98. University of Santa Clara School of Law (California)
99. Seton Hall University School of Law (New Jersey)
100. Stanford Law School (California)
101. University of South Carolina School of Law
102. University of South Dakota School of Law
103. Southern University School of Law (Louisiana)
104. Southern Methodist University School of Law (Texas)
105. Southwestern University School of Law (California)

106. South Texas College of Law
107. University of Southern California Law Center (formerly Gould School of Law) (California)
108. Stetson University College of Law (Florida) (formerly John B. Stetson University)
109. Suffolk University Law School (Massachusetts)
110. Syracuse University College of Law (New York)
111. Temple University School of Law (Pennsylvania)
112. University of Tennessee College of Law
113. University of Texas School of Law
114. Texas Southern University School of Law
115. University of Toledo College of Law (Ohio)
116. Tulane University School of Law (Louisiana)
117. University of Tulsa College of Law (Oklahoma)
118. University of Utah College of Law
119. Valparaiso University School of Law (Indiana)
120. Vanderbilt University School of Law (Tennessee)
121. Villanova University School of Law (Pennsylvania)
122. University of Virginia School of Law
123. Wake Forest University School of Law (North Carolina)
124. Washburn University School of Law (Kansas) (formerly Washburn University of Topeka)
125. University of Washington School of Law (Seattle)
126. Washington University School of Law (Missouri)
127. Washington and Lee University School of Law (Virginia)
128. Wayne State University Law School (Michigan) (formerly Wayne University)
129. West Virginia University College of Law
130. College of William and Mary, Marshall-Wythe School of Law (Virginia)
131. William Mitchell College of Law (Minnesota) (includes St. Paul College of Law)
132. Willamette University College of Law (Oregon)
133. University of Wisconsin Law School
134. University of Wyoming College of Law
135. Yale Law School

Eight law schools which are included in the Totality were not on the approved list of the A.B.A. in 1955 but were subsequently approved. They are numbers 19, 33, 54, 60, 86, 96, 101 and 104. Two approved schools were not included: the Judge Advocate General's School, because it teaches only graduate students; and the University of Puerto Rico School of Law, because it reported no data in 1955 and 1970.

The main source of data used in analyses of these schools is the 1955, 1960, 1965 and 1970 *Review of Legal Education, Law Schools and Bar Admission Requirements in the United States*, published by The Section of Legal Education and Admissions to the Bar of the American Bar Association, Chicago, Illinois.

Required Credits

Law School of College or University	1955 LL.B. Credit Requirement	1955 First Year Required Credits	1970 J.D. Credit Requirement	1970 First Year Required Credits
1. U. Alabama	82	30	90	30
2. U. Arizona	80	28	85	30
3. Boston College	90	30	90	30
4. Boston University	90	30	84	30
5. Brooklyn Law School	76	24	80	27
6. U. California-Hastings	92	31	90	30
7. Case Western Reserve	80	30	88	32
8. U. Chicago	90*	30*	90*	30*
9. U. Cincinnati	86	32	88	30
10. U. Colorado	90	30	86	31
11. Columbia U.	78	31	82	29
12. U. Connecticut	80	30	86	30
13. Cornell U.	80	30	84	34
14. Creighton U.	82	28	84	29
15. De Paul U.	80	29	84	30
16. U. Detroit	78	26	80	28
17. Dickinson School of Law	87	30	88	31
18. Duke U.	78	30	84	32
19. Emory U.	80	29	87*	32*
20. U. Florida	85	29	84*	31*

Appendix D (continued)

	Law School of College or University	1955		1970	
		LL.B. Credit Requirement	First Year Required Credits	J.D. Credit Requirement	First Year Required Credits
21.	Fordham U.	78	28	82	30
22.	George Washington U.	80	28	84	28
23.	U. Georgia	80*	27*	90*	31*
24.	Harvard U.	78	27	79	27
25.	U. Idaho	82	28	84	30
26.	U. Illinois	92	30	90	30
27.	Illinois Inst. of Tech.	80	28	86	28
28.	Indiana U.–Bloomington	80	32	80	32
29.	U. Iowa	94	30	90	29
30.	U. Kentucky	82	32	83	29
31.	Louisiana State U.	85	30	97	30
32.	U. Louisville	80	30	84	30
33.	Loyola U.–New Orleans	78	28	87	29
34.	U. Maryland	80	29	80	30
35.	Mercer U.	84*	29*	84*	28*
36.	U. Miami	78	28	84	32
37.	U. Michigan	80	30	82	32
38.	U. Mississippi	82	32	90	30
39.	U. Missouri–Columbia	84	30	84	31
40.	U. Nebraska	80	28	88	32
41.	U. New Mexico	83	30	86	34
42.	New York U.	80	29	80	30
43.	U. North Dakota	80	30	84	31
44.	Northwestern U.	90	30	90	30
45.	U. Notre Dame	91	31	91	32
46.	Ohio State U.	87*	30*	85*	31*
47.	Ohio Northern U.	81*	31*	86*	30*
48.	U. Oklahoma	86	29	90	30
49.	U. Oregon	82*	32*	82*	32*
50.	U. Pennsylvania	83	29	85	30
51.	U. Richmond	84	28	84	28
52.	Rutgers U.–Newark	84	30	84	29
53.	Samford U.	82*	27*	84	29
54.	St. John's U.	80	26	82	27
55.	St. Louis U.	80	29	84	28

Appendix D (continued)

Law School of College or University	1955 LL.B. Credit Requirement	1955 First Year Required Credits	1970 J.D. Credit Requirement	1970 First Year Required Credits
56. U. South Dakota	84	28	90	30
57. U. Southern California	86	30	88	30
58. Southwestern U.	80	30	84	30
59. Southern U.	90	30	90	32
60. Southern Methodist U.	84	30	90	29
61. Stanford U.	83*	30*	87	30
62. State U. of New York	90	30	90	31
63. Stetson U.	84	31	86	28
64. Suffolk U.	76	24	90	30
65. Syracuse U.	84	30	86	32
66. Temple U.	78	28	80	28
67. U. Tennessee	80*	31*	84*	30*
68. U. Texas	86	27	88	28
69. Tulane U.	84	30	90	30
70. Union U.	88	30	92	33
71. U. Utah	80*	28*	88	30
72. Valparaiso U.	80	30	85	30
73. Vanderbilt U.	86	30	88	30
74. Villanova U.	86	30	85	30
75. U. Virginia	90	30	90	30
76. Wake Forest U.	80	29	83	29
77. Washburn U.	82	30	85	28
78. U. Washington	88*	30*	90*	31*
79. Washington U.	90	30	86	30
80. West Virginia U.	81	29	85	31
81. U. Wisconsin	90	30	90	30
82. U. Wyoming	80	27	86	30
83. Yale U.	78	28	81	28
Average	83.2	29.3	84	30

* Converted from quarter hour requirement by the following method: quarter hours ÷ 1.5 = credit hours.

Note: Law schools presented are those for which both 1955 and 1970 catalogues are available in Columbia University Law Library. In many instances only the 1969 (or occasionally 1968) catalogue was available and therefore the 1969 figure was used. However, it is improbable that significant changes were made between 1969 and 1970 in credit requirements.

Instructional Cost
Equation

To help analyze increases in instructional cost, we have developed a mathematical method which this Appendix attempts to explicate. The method involves an equation referred to in this study as the Instructional Cost Equation. Section 1 presents our method mathematically in very brief form. For those who are not familiar with mathematical language, the method is explained in section 2.

Section 1

To determine the relationships and effects of the factors causing instructional cost to increase between two periods, we use the following formula:

Instructional Cost Equation

$$\text{Scale factor} \quad \times \quad \text{Student/Faculty Ratio factor} \quad \times \quad \text{Input Cost factor} \quad = \quad \text{Instructional Cost factor}$$

Factors

We define the terms as follows. The earlier year is designated Year 1, and the later is designated Year 2.

$$\text{Scale factor} \quad = \quad \frac{\text{Number of Students in Year 2}}{\text{Number of Students in Year 1}}$$

$$\text{Student/Faculty Ratio factor} \quad = \quad \frac{\dfrac{\text{Number of Students in Year 1}}{\text{Number of Faculty in Year 1}}}{\dfrac{\text{Number of Students in Year 2}}{\text{Number of Faculty in Year 2}}}$$

$$\text{Input Cost factor} = \frac{\dfrac{\text{Instructional Cost}^1 \text{ in Year 2}}{\text{Number of Faculty in Year 2}}}{\dfrac{\text{Instructional Cost in Year 1}}{\text{Number of Faculty in Year 1}}}$$

or

$$\text{Input Cost factor} = \frac{\text{Average Faculty Salary in Year 2}}{\text{Average Faculty Salary in Year 1}}$$

These terms may be expressed as:

$$\text{Scale factor} = \frac{S_2}{S_1}$$

$$\text{Student/Faculty Ratio factor} = \frac{\dfrac{S_1}{F_1}}{\dfrac{S_2}{F_2}} \quad \text{or} \quad \frac{S_1}{S_2} \times \frac{F_2}{F_1}$$

$$\text{Input Cost factor} = \frac{\dfrac{I_2}{F_2}}{\dfrac{I_1}{F_1}} \quad \text{or} \quad \frac{F_1}{F_2} \times \frac{I_2}{I_1}$$

The Instructional Cost Equation may be expressed as:

$$\left(\frac{S_2}{S_1}\right) \times \left(\frac{S_1}{S_2} \times \frac{F_2}{F_1}\right) \times \left(\frac{F_1}{F_2} \times \frac{I_2}{I_1}\right) = \begin{array}{l}\text{Instructional}\\ \text{Cost factor}\end{array}$$

Percent Increase or Decrease from Year 1 to Year 2

The three factors multiplied together in a double-product multiplication, minus 1.00 times 100, produces the percent change in instructional cost between two years.

$$\begin{array}{l}\text{Scale}\\ \text{factor}\end{array} \times \begin{array}{l}\text{Student/Faculty}\\ \text{Ratio factor}\end{array} \times \begin{array}{l}\text{Input Cost}\\ \text{factor}\end{array} = \begin{array}{l}\text{Instructional}\\ \text{Cost factor}\end{array}$$

$$\left(\begin{array}{l}\text{Instructional}\\ \text{Cost factor}\end{array} - 1.00\right) \times 100 = \begin{array}{l}\text{Percent change in}\\ \text{instructional cost}\end{array}$$

Also,

---

1.   Instructional Cost is total salary expenditure for the year.

$$\left(\begin{array}{l}\text{Scale}\\\text{factor}\end{array} - 1.00\right) \times 100 = \begin{array}{l}\text{Percent change in}\\\text{enrollment}\end{array}$$

$$\left(\begin{array}{l}\text{Student/Faculty}\\\text{Ratio factor}\end{array} - 1.00\right) \times 100 = \begin{array}{l}\text{Percent change in}\\\text{student/faculty ratio}\end{array}$$

$$\left(\begin{array}{l}\text{Input Cost}\\\text{factor}\end{array} - 1.00\right) \times 100 = \begin{array}{l}\text{Percent change in}\\\text{average faculty salary}\end{array}$$

Dollar Value and Instructional Cost Equation

$$\begin{array}{l}\text{Dollar value}^2\text{ of}\\\text{instructional}\\\text{cost in Year 1}\end{array} \times \begin{array}{l}\text{Scale}\\\text{factor}\end{array} \times \begin{array}{l}\text{Student/Faculty}\\\text{Ratio factor}\end{array} \times \begin{array}{l}\text{Input Cost}\\\text{factor}\end{array}$$

$$= \begin{array}{l}\text{Dollar value of}\\\text{instructional}\\\text{cost in Year 2}\end{array}$$

Where dollar value of instructional cost in any year is total salary expenditure in that year, or, average faculty salary times number of faculty members.

Allocation of Change in Instructional Cost

In allocating the change in instructional cost between Year 1 and Year 2 among the three factors and their combinations, the following formulae are used:

1. $\begin{array}{l}\text{Year 1}\\\text{instructional}\\\text{cost}\end{array} \times \left(\text{Scale factor} - 1.00\right) =$ Amount of change in instructional cost attributable to change in enrollment alone

2. $\begin{array}{l}\text{Year 1}\\\text{instructional}\\\text{cost}\end{array} \times \left(\begin{array}{l}\text{Student/Faculty}\\\text{Ratio factor}\end{array} - 1.00\right) =$ Amount attributable to change in student/faculty ratio alone

3. $\begin{array}{l}\text{Year 1}\\\text{instructional}\\\text{cost}\end{array} \times \left(\text{Input Cost factor} - 1.00\right) =$ Amount attributable to change in average faculty salary alone

---

2. In order to compare real dollar increases, the dollar value of Year 1 instructional cost should be converted to constant (Year 2) dollars (i.e., Year 1 dollars ÷ Year 1's G.N.P. deflator (or consumer price index factor)), which procedure eliminates increases attributable to inflation and leaves increases attributable only to the three factors.

4. $\text{Year 1 instructional cost} \times \left(\frac{\text{Scale}}{\text{factor}} - 1.00\right) \times \left(\frac{\text{Student/Faculty}}{\text{Ratio factor}} - 1.00\right)$

= Amount attributable to combined effect of change in enrollment and change in student/faculty ratio

5. $\text{Year 1 instructional cost} \times \left(\frac{\text{Scale}}{\text{factor}} - 1.00\right) \times \left(\frac{\text{Input Cost}}{\text{factor}} - 1.00\right)$

= Amount attributable to combined effect of change in enrollment and change in average faculty salary

6. $\text{Year 1 instructional cost} \times \left(\frac{\text{Student/Faculty}}{\text{Ratio factor}} - 1.00\right) \times \left(\frac{\text{Input Cost}}{\text{factor}} - 1.00\right)$

= Amount attributable to combined effect of change in student/faculty ratio and change in average faculty salary

7. $\text{Year 1 instructional cost} \times \left(\frac{\text{Scale}}{\text{factor}} - 1.00\right) \times \left(\frac{\text{Student/Faculty}}{\text{Ratio factor}} - 1.00\right)$

$\times \left(\frac{\text{Input Cost}}{\text{factor}} - 1.00\right)$ = Amount attributable to combined effect of change in enrollment and change in student/faculty ratio and change in average faculty salary

---

NOTE: If no change occurs in a variable from Year 1 to Year 2, the factor equals one. In that case, the factor minus one equals zero, and all equations in which the factor occurs yield zero.

Per-student Instructional Cost Equation

Changes in per-student instructional cost may be analyzed in terms of two of the factors, the Student/Faculty Ratio factor and the Input Cost factor. In this analysis, the following formulae are used:

$\text{Student/Faculty Ratio factor} \times \text{Input Cost factor} = \text{Per-student Instructional Cost factor}$

$\left(\text{Per-student Instructional Cost factor} - 1.00\right) \times 100 = \text{Percent change in per-student instructional cost}$

$\text{Per-student instructional cost in Year 1} \times \left(\text{Per-student Instructional Cost factor} - 1.00\right) = \text{Change in per-student instructional cost from Year 1 to Year 2}$

In allocating the change in per-student instructional cost between Year 1 and Year 2 among the two factors and their combination, the following formulae are used:

1. $\text{Year 1 per-student cost} \times \left(\dfrac{\text{Student/Faculty Ratio factor}} - 1.00 \right) =$ Amount of change in per-student instructional cost attributable to change in student/faculty ratio alone

2. $\text{Year 1 per-student cost} \times \left(\dfrac{\text{Input Cost factor}} - 1.00 \right) =$ Amount attributable to change in average faculty salary alone

3. $\text{Year 1 per-student cost} \times \left(\dfrac{\text{Student/Faculty Ratio factor}} - 1.00 \right) \times \left(\dfrac{\text{Input Cost factor}} - 1.00 \right)$

$=$ Amount attributable to combined effect of change in student/faculty ratio and change in average faculty salary

Two further equations are developed in the text to help analyze changes in instructional cost. The first is called the Faculty Distribution Equation. It is designed to indicate how change in faculty size between two years may be analyzed in terms of the number of faculty members attributable to change in enrollment alone, to change in the student/faculty ratio alone, and to the combined effect of change in both.

The second equation is called the Instructional Dollar Allocation Equation. It is designed to indicate how change in instructional cost between two years may be analyzed in terms of amounts attributable to change in faculty size alone, to change in input cost alone, and to the combined effect of change in both.

Explanations of these equations are not provided in section 2 of this Appendix, but are fully developed in section 5 of chapter 2 in the text. The equations follow.

Faculty Distribution Equation

$\text{Scale factor} \times \text{Student/Faculty Ratio factor} = \text{Faculty Growth factor}$

$\left(\dfrac{\text{Faculty Growth factor}} - 1.00 \right) \times 100 = \text{Percent change in size of faculty}$

$\text{Year 1 faculty size} \times \left(\dfrac{\text{Faculty Growth factor}} - 1.00 \right) =$

Number of faculty members added or subtracted between Year 1 and Year 2

In allocating the increase or decrease in number of faculty members between Year 1 and Year 2 among the two factors and their combination, the following formulae are used:

1. $\text{Year 1 faculty size} \times \left(\text{Scale factor} - 1.00 \right) = $ Number of faculty members added or subtracted attributable to change in enrollment alone

2. $\text{Year 1 faculty size} \times \left(\text{Student/Faculty Ratio factor} - 1.00 \right) = $ Number attributable to change in student/faculty ratio alone

3. $\text{Year 1 faculty size} \times \left(\text{Scale factor} - 1.00 \right) \times \left(\text{Student/Faculty Ratio factor} - 1.00 \right) = $ Number attributable to combined effect of change in enrollment and change in student/faculty ratio

Instructional Dollar Allocation Equation

$$\text{Faculty Growth factor} \times \text{Input Cost factor} = \text{Instructional Cost factor}$$

In allocating the change in instructional cost between Year 1 and Year 2 among the two factors and their combination, the following formulae are used:

1. $\text{Year 1 instructional cost} \times \left(\text{Faculty Growth factor} - 1.00 \right) = $ Amount of change in instructional cost attributable to change in number of faculty members alone

2. $\text{Year 1 instructional cost} \times \left(\text{Input Cost factor} - 1.00 \right) = $ Amount attributable to change in average faculty salary alone

3. $\text{Year 1 instructional cost} \times \left(\text{Faculty Growth factor} - 1.00 \right) \times \left(\text{Input Cost factor} - 1.00 \right) = $ Amount attributable to combined effect of change in number of faculty members and change in average faculty salary

Section 2

In this section, our method is explained in nonmathematical terms. To do so we use a simple example. When the method is grasped from working through the example and explanation, we believe that the more complicated models developed in the text of this study will be understood.

Three critical variables have been selected to which increase in instructional cost over a period of time may be attributed: scale, student/faculty ratio, and input cost. The meaning of these terms is developed as we work through the example. Our method determines how increases in instructional cost may be attributed to the compound effect of these three variables. The earlier year of the time period selected for analysis is designated Year 1, and the later, or more recent year, is Year 2.

Assume in Year 1 a law school with 60 students and 2 professors, each earning $500. Five years later, in Year 2, enrollment has grown to 120 students and the faculty has increased to 6 professors, each earning $1,000. The total instructional cost (total salary expenditures) amounted in Year 1 to $1,000 (2 professors X $500), and in Year 2 to $6,000 (6 professors X $1,000). The increase in instructional cost is $5,000 ($6,000 − $1,000). The objective of our method is to determine how the increase of $5,000 over the five-year period may be broken down into amounts that reflect the impact of the three critical variables: scale, student/faculty ratio, and input cost, both alone and in combination. We shall deal with them one at a time.

The first factor involves the change in the size of student enrollment and is called the *Scale factor*. It indicates the change in enrollment from one year to the next, and is determined by dividing the later year's (Year 2) enrollment by the earlier year's (Year 1). In our example, enrollment grew to 120 students in Year 2 from 60 students in Year 1. The Scale factor is therefore 2 (120 ÷ 60 = 2). The Scale factor can be converted into a percentage which shows the percent change in scale (enrollment). Thus, the Scale factor minus 1.00 times 100 equals the percent change in enrollment. In our example the change is a 100% increase ((2 − 1.00) X 100 = 100 percent). The Scale factor is used to analyze the change in instructional cost resulting from change in faculty size attributable to enrollment change. By considering the Scale factor alone, one can determine the change in instructional cost resulting from change in faculty size attributable to change in enrollment alone.[3] For instance, in our example, in order for the school to maintain in Year 2 the same level of instructional resources that it operated with in Year 1, namely a student/faculty ratio of 30/1, it would be necessary for it to add two instructors to its faculty (60 students ÷ 2 faculty = 30/1). That is, with 120 students in Year 2, in order to have a student/faculty ratio of 30/1 it would be necessary[4] to have 4 teachers (120 students ÷ 4 faculty

---

3.   Initially, we consider only change in faculty size. As an individual faculty member represents the average salary paid to all faculty members, changes in faculty size can easily be converted to changes in instructional cost. This is done below.

4.   In evaluating the effect of Scale factor alone on instructional cost, we assume that the other two factors (Student/Faculty Ratio and Input Cost) remain constant.

= 30/1). This would double the faculty size. Thus, of the four faculty members actually added by Year 2, only two are attributable to the change in scale alone. This brings out a critical assumption made by our method, namely that, in cases where both enrollment and faculty increase, and the faculty increases by at least the same rate as enrollment, part of the faculty increase is deemed to have occurred in order to provide the additional students of Year 2 with the same level of instructional resources that were provided to the students in Year 1; i.e., part of the increase in faculty occurred in order to maintain a constant student/faculty ratio.

The second factor that affects instructional cost is the student/faculty ratio. For purposes of our study, the variable involving a change in this ratio is simply denoted the *Student/Faculty Ratio factor*. This factor indicates the change in a school's student/faulty ratio between two years, and is derived by dividing the student/faculty ratio of Year 1 by the student/faculty ratio of Year 2.[5] In our example, the student/faculty ratio in Year 1 was 30/1 (60 students to 2 faculty members = 30/1) and in Year 2 it decreased to 20/1 (120 students to 6 faculty members = 20/1). Thus the Student/Faculty Ratio factor[6] is 1.5 (30/1 ÷ 20/1 = 1.5). The student/Faculty Ratio factor is used to analyze the change in instructional cost resulting from the change in faculty size attributable to the change in school's student/faculty ratio. By considering the Student/Faculty Ratio factor alone, one can determine the change in instructional cost resulting from change in faculty size attributable to change in student/faculty ratio alone. For instance, in our example,[7] if there had been no change in scale (no enrollment increase) and if the school had operated with the student/faculty ratio that obtained in Year 2, it would be necessary to have three instructors on the school's faculty (60 ÷ 20/1 = 3), and this would result in the faculty's increasing by one instructor, or 50%. Thus, of the four faculty members actually added by Year 2, one instructor is attributable to the change in the student/faculty ratio alone.

So far, we have considered changes in the school's faculty size attributable to enrollment change alone and to student/faculty ratio change alone. These two factors, however, operate in concert, and certain changes in faculty size may be attributable to their combined effect. For instance, in our example, with respect to the additional 60 students enrolled in Year 2 over Year 1, one additional instructor would have to be engaged to provide them with a student/faculty ratio of 20/1,[8] thus (60 ÷ 20/1 =)3 − (60 ÷ 30/1 =)2 = 1. This last result illustrates the joint effect of changes in both scale and student/faculty ratio. Of the four faculty members actually added by Year 2, one is attributable to the combined effect of changes in scale and in student/faculty ratio.

---

5.   Notice that, unlike the other two factors, the Student/Faculty Ratio factor is derived by dividing the quantity in question for Year 1 by that for Year 2. This allows a decrease in the student/faculty ratio to be expressed as a positive number.

6.   The Student/Faculty Ratio factor can be converted into a percentage in the same manner as described above with respect to the Scale factor.

7.   In evaluating the effect of Student/Faculty Ratio factor alone on instructional cost, we assume that the other two factors (Scale and Input Cost) remain constant.

8.   Rather than 30/1 as supposed above in the analysis of the Scale factor alone.

In sum of the four new instructors added to the law school's teaching staff, two are attributable to the Scale factor alone, one to the school's Student/Faculty Ratio factor alone, and one to the combined effect of both factors. The compound (multiplier) effect of these factors is also revealed by noting that the same result is obtained by multiplying the Year 1 figure of two instructors by the Scale factor of 2 (a 100% increase that brings the faculty from two to four members) to take account of enrollment increases, and multiplying this product by the Student/Faculty Ratio factor of 1.5 (a 50% increase that brings the faculty from four to six members) to take account of the decreased student/faculty ratio.[9] In the text, the product of the Scale factor and the Student/Faculty Ratio factor is referred to as the Faculty Growth factor.

The analysis so far has been made only in terms of additional faculty members. These faculty members can be converted into increases in instructional cost by assigning $500, the Year 1 average faculty salary, to each additional faculty member. This is proper, since our analysis so far has not considered increase in average salary or input cost. Thus, of the four faculty members added, two are attributable to the Scale factor alone,[10] 2 × $500 = $1,000; one is attributable to the Student/Faculty Ratio factor alone,[11] 1 × $500 = $500; and one is attributable to the combination of the Scale factor and the Student/Faculty Ratio factor,[12] 1 × $500 = $500. We have thus far accounted for $2,000 of the $5,000 increase in instructional cost.

The third factor that affects instructional cost involves increase in average faculty salary and is called the *Input Cost factor*. It indicates the increase in average faculty salary from one year to the next, and is derived by dividing the average faculty salary of Year 2 by the average faculty salary of Year 1. In our example, the average faculty salary increased from $500 per instructor in Year 1 to $1,000 per instructor in Year 2. The Input Cost factor is thus 2 ($1,000 ÷ $500 = 2).[13] The Input Cost factor is used to analyze the change in instructional cost attributable to change in the average faculty salary. By considering the Input Cost factor alone, one can determine the change in instructional cost attributable to change in average faculty salary alone. For instance, in our example, if there had been no change in scale and no change in student/faculty ratio, the Year 2 instructional cost would have been $2,000, since the Year 1

9. Note that this same result could have been obtained by multiplying the Year 1 figure of two instructors by 1.5 (a 50% increase that brings the faculty from two to three) to take account of the improved student/faculty ratio, and then multiplying this product by 2 (a 100% increase, which brings the faculty from three to six) to take account of increased student enrollment.

10. The increase in instructional cost attributable to change in scale alone can also be calculated by multiplying Year 1 instructional cost by the Scale Factor minus 1.00 ($1,000 × 1 = $1,000).

11. The increase in instructional cost attributable to change in the student/faculty ratio alone can also be calculated by multiplying Year 1 instructional cost by the Student/Faculty Ratio factor minus 1.00 ($1,000 × .5 = $500).

12. The increase in instructional cost attributable to the combined effect of changes in scale and student/faculty ratio can also be calculated by multiplying Year 1 instructional cost by the Scale factor minus 1.00, and the product by the Student/Faculty Ratio factor minus 1.00 ($1,000 × 1 × .5 = $500).

13. The Input Cost factor can be converted into a percentage in the same manner as described above with respect to the Scale factor.

faculty of two members would be paid $2,000 in Year 2 (2 × $1,000).[14] As indicated above, however, the size of the faculty increased between Year 1 and Year 2. Here, again, we observe the combined effect of the several factors. Two of the instructors added to the faculty are attributable to enrollment increase alone (Scale factor). By hypothesis, these two faculty members were paid $2,000 in Year 2. One thousand dollars of this amount has already been accounted for above in considering the Scale factor alone. The second $1,000 received by these instructors is attributable to the joint effect of change in scale (two additional instructors) and change in input cost (the $500 increase in average faculty salary).[15] One instructor added to the faculty is attributable to the reduction in the student/faculty ratio alone (Student/Faculty Ratio factor). By hypothesis, this instructor was paid $1,000 in Year 2. Five Hundred dollars of this amount has already been accounted for above in considering the Student/Faculty Ratio factor alone. The second $500 is attributable to the joint effect of change in the student/faculty ratio (the additional instructor) and change in input cost (the $500 increase in average faculty salary).[16] Finally, one instructor added is attributable to the joint effect of change in scale and change in student/faculty ratio. By hypothesis, this instructor was paid $1,000 in Year 2. Five hundred dollars of this amount has already been accounted for above in considering the joint effect of change in scale and change in student/faculty ratio. The second $500 is attributable to the joint effect of all three factors: Scale increase and Student/Faculty Ratio reduction (the additional instructor), and increased Input Cost (the $500 increase in average salary).[17] We have now accounted for the remaining $3,000 of the $5,000 increase in instructional cost from Year 1 to Year 2.

For the implementation of our method, we utilize the Instructional Cost Equation (I.C. Equation). We first calculate the values of the three critical factors. The product of the three numbers equals the Instructional Cost factor. When 1.00 is subtracted from the Instructional Cost factor and the remainder is multiplied by 100, the result is the percent increase in total instructional cost between Year 1 and Year 2. This is demonstrated in Table 1, using our example.

---

14.   In evaluating the effect of the Input Cost factor alone on instructional cost, we assume that the other two factors (Scale and Student/Faculty Ratio) remain constant. The increase in instructional cost attributable to change in input cost alone can also be calculated by multiplying Year 1 instructional cost by the Input Cost factor minus 1.00 ($1,000 × 1 = $1,000).

15.   The increase in instructional cost attributable to the combined effect of changes in scale and input cost can also be calculated by multiplying Year 1 instructional cost by the Scale factor minus 1.00, and the product by the Input Cost factor minus 1.00 ($1,000 × 1 × 1 = $1,000).

16.   The increase in instructional cost attributable to the combined effect of changes in student/faculty ratio and input cost can also be calculated by multiplying Year 1 instructional cost by the Student/Faculty Ratio factor minus 1.00, and the product by the Input Cost factor minus 1.00 ($1,000 × .5 × 1 = $500).

17.   The increase in instructional cost attributable to the combined effect of changes in scale, student/faculty ratio, and input cost can also be calculated by multiplying Year 1 instructional cost by the Scale factor minus 1.00 and the product by the Student/Faculty Ratio factor minus 1.00 and the product by the Input Cost factor minus 1.00 ($1,000 × 1 × .5 × 1 = $500).

Table 1

Instructional Cost Equation

Scale Factor		Student/ Faculty Ratio Factor		Input Cost Factor		Instruc- tional Cost Factor	Percent Increase in Instructional Cost
2	X	1.5	X	2	=	6	500%

As the analysis above indicates, the total dollar amount of increase in instructional cost between two years may be broken down into seven parts or coefficients, each part representing the effect of one of the factors or the effect of the factors operating together in various combinations. For our example, the breakdown is as follows:

Coefficient	Increase in Instructional Cost
1. Scale (two additional instructors, paid at Year 1's salary level of $500 per instructor, to provide additional 60 students with a student/faculty ratio of 30/1)	$1,000
2. Student/Faculty Ratio (one additional instructor, paid at Year 1's salary level of $500, to provide original 60 students[18] with improved student/faculty ratio of 20/1)	$ 500
3. Input Cost (original two instructors, each receiving an additional $500 over Year 1's salary level, bringing their Year 2 salaries to a level of $1,000)	$1,000
4. Combined effect of Scale and Student/Faculty Ratio (one additional instructor, paid at Year 1's salary level of $500, to provide additional 60 students with a student/faculty ratio of 20/1)	$ 500
5. Combined effect of Scale and Input Cost (two additional instructors, mentioned in item 1, each receiving an additional $500 over Year 1's salary level, bringing their Year 2 salaries to a level of $1,000)	$1,000

18.   Strictly speaking, the 120 students in Year 2 might not contain all the original 60 students of Year 1. The phrase is used figuratively and refers to the number of students equivalent to Year 1's enrollment.

6. Combined effect of Student/Faculty Ratio and Input Cost $ 500
    (one additional instructor, mentioned in item 2,
    receiving an additional $500 over Year 1's salary
    level, bringing his Year 2 salary to a level of $1,000)

7. Combined effect of Scale, Student/Faculty Ratio,
    and Input Cost $ 500
    (one additional instructor, mentioned in item 4,
    receiving an additional $500 over Year 1's salary
    level, bringing his Year 2 salary to a level of $1,000)
                                                          _____
                                                              $5,000

This breakdown demonstrates that it is not possible to divide the entire increase in instructional cost into three parts, one attributable solely to enrollment growth (scale), one attributable solely to change in the student/faculty ratio, and one attributable solely to increase in average salary level (input cost). This is so because much of the increase is attributable to the combined effect of the three factors. In this connection it will be noted that items 4, 5, 6, and 7 totaling $2,500, or half of the entire increase, are attributable to combined effects of the three factors.

One can determine, however, the difference in the increase in instructional cost that would result if any one of the variables had remained constant while the other two changed. For instance, in the above example, if the school's student/faculty ratio had remained constant at 30/1, items 2, 4, 6, and 7 would have been zero. In other words, the increase in instructional cost would have been $3,000 rather than $5,000, that is, $2,000 (or 40%) less. If the average faculty salary had remained constant at $500, items 3, 5, 6, and 7 would have been zero. In these circumstances the increase in instructional cost would have been $2,000 rather than $5,000, that is, $3,000 (or 60%) less. A similar analysis could be made on the assumption that enrollment remained constant at 60 students. Items 1, 4, 5, and 7 would have been zero. The increase in instructional cost would then have been $2,000 rather than $5,000, that is $3,000 (or 60%) less.

In our example, all three factors operated to increase instructional cost. This is not always the case. There are a number of situations that we have studied where input cost and enrollment increase, and during the same period of time, the student/faculty ratio also increases.[19] Let us assume in our simple example that although enrollment doubled, the faculty size remained constant, so that only two faculty members taught 120 students in Year 2. In this case, the school would have a Year 2 student/faculty ratio of 60/1 (120 ÷ 2 = 60/1) and the Student/Faculty Ratio factor would be .5 (30/1 ÷ 60/1 = .5). Table 2 shows the results of working through the I.C. Equation for this example.

---

19. It might also happen that a school's enrollment will decrease or that its average faculty salary will decline. Analyses similar to the one that follows may be made in these cases.

Table 2

Instructional Cost Equation

Scale Factor		Student/ Faculty Ratio Factor		Input Cost Factor		Instruc- tional Cost Fact	Percent Increase in Instructional Cost
2	X	.5	X	2	=	2	100%

This, of course, confirms what simple arithmetic would have revealed. With two faculty members, each being paid $500 in Year 1, the instructional cost was $1,000. With the same two faculty members, each being paid $1,000 in Year 2, the instructional cost was $2,000, an increase of $1,000, or 100%.

The explanation of the I.C. Equation where both enrollment and student/faculty ratio increase involves a number of assumptions. First, it is assumed that the faculty increases to keep pace with scale, so that the new students will be provided with the same student/faculty ratio as the original students.[20] Then it is assumed that the faculty, so increased, is reduced to account for the increased student/faculty ratio. In effect, part of the faculty "reduction" is a reduction of the original (Year 1) faculty effected by increasing the student/faculty ratio provided to the original number of students, and part is a reduction of the additional faculty (assumed to have been added because of enrollment increases) effected by increasing the student/faculty ratio provided to the additional students.[21]

An analysis of the I.C. Equation in Table 2, in terms of the seven coefficients, demonstrates these relationships and shows how they combine with increased input cost.

Coefficient	Change in Instructional Cost
1. Scale (hypothetical addition of two instructors, paid at Year 1's salary level of $500 each, to provide additional 60 students with a student/faculty ratio of 30/1)	$1,000
2. Student/Faculty Ratio (hypothetical reduction of one instructor from original [Year 1] faculty attributable to increased student/faculty ratio so that original 60 students are provided with student/faculty ratio of 60/1,	$ −500

20.   See statement of basic assumption above.
21.   Of course, the analysis can begin with the student/faculty ratio and assume that the original faculty is reduced to account for the increased student/faculty ratio provided to the original students and that the faculty, so reduced, is increased to account for enrollment increases.

resulting in the reduction of $500, the amount which such instructor would be paid at Year 1's salary level of $500)

3. Input Cost

 (two original instructors, each receiving an additional $500 over Year 1's salary level, bringing their Year 2 salary to a level of $1,000 each) $1,000

4. Combined effect of Scale and Student/Faculty Ratio

 (hypothetical reduction of one instructor from two instructors, mentioned in item 1, so that additional 60 students are provided with a student/faculty ratio of 60/1, resulting in a reduction of $500, the amount which such instructor would be paid at Year 1's salary level of $500) $−500

5. Combined effect of Scale and Input Cost

 (two additional instructors, mentioned in item 1, each receiving an additional $500 over Year 1's salary level, bringing their Year 2 salaries to a level of $1,000 each) $1,000

6. Combined effect of Student/Faculty Ratio and Input Cost

 (hypothetical reduction of one instructor, mentioned in item 2, resulting in a reduction of $500, the amount which such instructor would have been paid because of the increase in the level of Year 2's salary) $−500

7. Combined effect of Scale and Student/Faculty Ratio and Input Cost

 (hypothetical reduction of one instructor, mentioned in item 4, resulting in a reduction of $500, the amount which such instructor would have been paid because of the increase in the level of Year 2's salary) $−500

                                                                        $1,000

It is assumed that the faculty doubles because of doubled enrollment: item 1. It is assumed that each instructor receives an additional $500 because of doubled input cost: items 3 and 5. But it is further assumed that the faculty so increased in size is halved because of the increased student/faculty ratio: items 2 and 4.

Finally, because of the assumed reduction in faculty attributable to the increased student/faculty ratio, it is assumed that input-cost increases in items 3 and 5 are reduced: items 6 and 7. It will be noted that if the student/faculty ratio had remained the same in this example, items 2, 4, 6, and 7 would have been zero and instructional cost would have increased by $3,000. Thus, increase in instructional cost was reduced $2,000 because of the increased student/faculty ratio.

In very rough terms, the situation presented by this last example may be analyzed in the following manner. As the school's enrollment increased it might be assumed that its faculty would increase by a like percent; otherwise its students in Year 2 would not be furnished with the same level of instructional resources that were provided to its students in Year 1. Thus, all other things being equal, instructional cost would have increased by an amount equal to the percent increase in enrollment. In this case enrollment increased 100% (from 60 to 120 students); so one might expect that instructional cost would increase 100% (from two to four faculty members at Year 1's salary level). However, the school did not maintain the same level of instructional resources between the two years. In fact, its student/faculty ratio increased enormously. Thus, considerable "savings" were effected, which offset the increase that would have been attributable to enrollment increase. To begin with, $500 was "saved" through a hypothetical 50% reduction of the faculty furnished to the original number of students (i.e., from two members to one) and an additional $500 was "saved," representing the amount that would have been paid by way of salary increase to the original faculty member who, by hypothesis, was eliminated. An additional $500 was "saved" by reducing the additions that would have been made to the faculty to take care of the additional students. Presumably two faculty members should have been added in order to provide the new students with a student/faculty ratio similar to that of Year 1. However, with a reduction in the school's student/faculty ratio, only one faculty member was added on account of the additional students. A final $500 was "saved," representing the amount that would have been paid by way of salary increase to the faculty member who would have been added to the faculty to maintain its Year 1 student/faculty ratio but was not.

Variations in
Instructional Cost

In chapter 2 it is shown that wide variations in the increase in instructional cost between 1955 and 1970 existed for the 115 law schools for which information is available. In this Appendix we attempt to account for these considerable variations among the schools in each Enrollment Group in terms of the three factors that make up the I.C. Equation. Thus, the present inquiry seeks to discover whether these differences in instructional cost increases may be attributed chiefly to differences in enrollment increases, to differences in student/faculty ratio changes, or to differences in input cost increases, or to some particular combination of these factors.

To begin this examination the three Enrollment Groups have been further divided into three subgroups based on increases in instructional cost. Among the schools in each Enrollment Group some bunching occurs. Those schools with the lowest increases in instructional cost are included in a subgroup, which will be designated subgroup L. Those with what might be regarded as medium increases are included in a subgroup designated M, and those with the highest increases are included in a subgroup designated H.

Definite patterns become evident when we examine the three subgroups. The relationships between subgroups within the three Enrollment Groups are similar. Thus, the Small Enrollment Group's subgroup L differs from its subgroup M in the same manner that the Middle Enrollment Group's subgroup L differs from its subgroup M, and the Large Enrollment Group's subgroup L differs from its subgroup M. The same assertion can be made for differences between the three Enrollment Groups' subgroups M and H. First, the differences between subgroups L and M will be examined, then the differences between subgroups M and H.

Figure 1 shows increases in input cost, and Figure 2 shows increases in faculty size of schools included in subgroups L, M, and H of each Enrollment Group. Figure 3 shows enrollment increases and Figure 4 shows student/faculty ratio changes for the Enrollment Groups and their subgroups. It can be seen that the patterns of input cost increases between subgroup L and subgroup M are very similar for all three Enrollment Groups,[1] and that, in contrast, increases in faculty size are dissimilar, the increases for schools in subgroup M being greater than for schools in subgroup L. Consequently, differences in instructional cost increases among schools in subgroups M and L can be attributed to their difference in growth in faculty size rather than to their nearly uniform growth in input cost. Within each Enrollment Group the pattern of subgroup H schools differs from the pattern of subgroup M schools because of *both* somewhat higher increases in input cost and much higher increases in faculty size. These relationships are shown in Figures 1 and 2.

As between faculty increases and input cost increases (the product of which equals instructional cost increases),[2] differences in faculty increases, as indicated, have been the more dominant factor in producing differences in instructional cost increases. (Faculty increases will be discussed below.) Indeed, as indicated above in section 2 of chapter 2, input cost increases have varied less than any of the other factors contributing to increases in instructional cost. Input cost increases for the bulk of the schools in all Groups ranged between 30% to 100%, a difference of 70%. In contrast, the bulk of student/faculty ratio changes ranged from a negative value of −60% to a positive value of 50%, a difference of 110%, and enrollment increases for most schools ranged from 40% to 280%, a difference of 240%.[3]

Thus, it may be concluded that in accounting for the differences in increases of instructional cost between the schools included in each Enrollment Group, input cost increases have had the least impact by reason of the fact that they have been the most uniform. As indicated, however, subgroup H schools have had a somewhat higher increase in input cost than the other two subgroups whose input cost increases were generally similar. For the Large and Middle Enrollment Groups this would appear to be explained by the fact that their H subgroups had a significant number of schools that started with low faculty salaries in 1955. Many of these schools experienced higher than average faculty salary increases (in an apparent attempt to catch up with schools that paid higher salaries). In addition, a number of these schools had average salary increases, but because they started with a relatively low base, they had higher Input Cost factors than schools that paid higher salaries in 1955. Faculty salary increases of Small Enrollment schools did not follow the same pattern as those

1. Input cost increases of subgroups L and M are not exactly similar. Subgroup M's cost increases are, as would be expected, slightly higher than subgroup L's, but, relative to difference in increases in faculty size between subgroups L and M and other differences discussed below, they are very close.
2. In the I.C. Equation format: Scale factor × Student/Faculty Ratio factor = Faculty Growth factor. Faculty Growth factor × Input Cost factor = Instructional Cost factor.
3. Extreme cases have been eliminated for these comparisons.

Figure 1

Input Cost Increases, 1955 to 1970, for Subgroup L,
Subgroup M, and Subgroup H of the Three Enrollment Groups

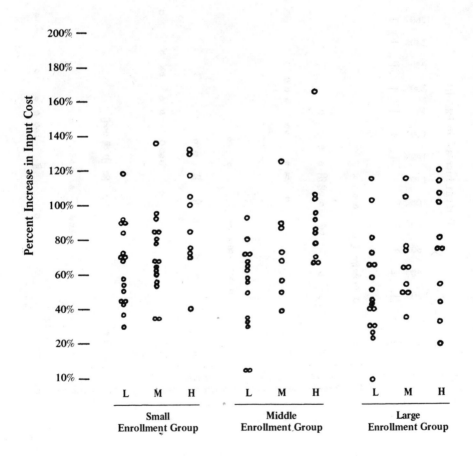

Figure 2

Faculty Increases, 1955 to 1970, for Subgroup L, Subgroup M, and Subgroup H of the Three Enrollment Groups

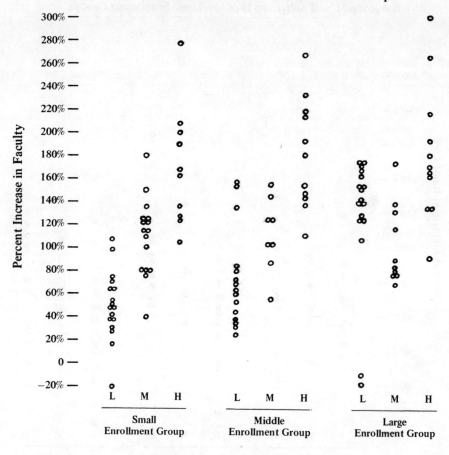

Figure 3

Enrollment Increases, 1955 to 1970, for Subgroup L, Subgroup M, and Subgroup H of the Three Enrollment Groups

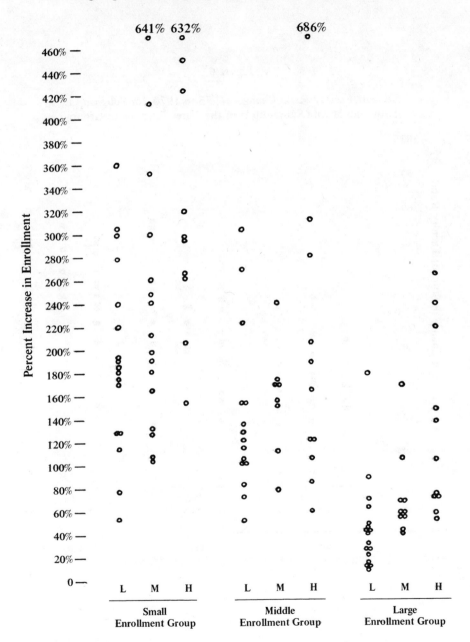

Figure 4

Student/Faculty Ratio Changes, 1955 to 1970, for Subgroup L, Subgroup M, and Subgroup H of the Three Enrollment Groups

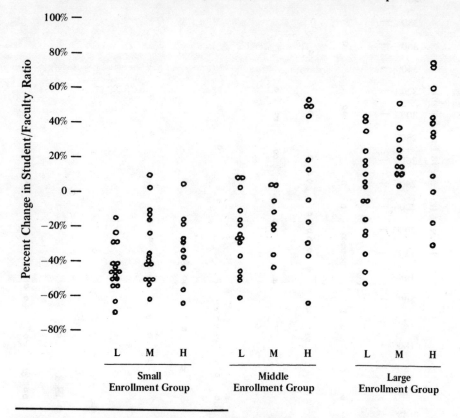

Note: Negative percent figures on the ordinate represent increasing student/faculty ratios and postive percent figures represent decreasing student/faculty ratios.

of the larger schools. Their subgroup H schools did not start in 1955 with lower salaries than subgroups L and M, and their higher input cost increases are due to having only slightly larger absolute increases.

Differences in faculty increases have been significant in defining the three subgroups. (With respect to subgroups L and M, they have been determinative.) It will be recalled that faculty growth in this study is interpreted as a function of enrollment increase and change in a school's student/faculty ratio. Significant differences exist between the manner in which the Scale and Student/Faculty Ratio factors combine in each of the three subgroups, although, as in the cases of increases in input cost and faculty size, the relationships between the three subgroups are similar within all three Enrollment Groups. Thus, for each Enrollment Group, subgroup L and subgroup M scale increases are very similar. Accordingly, the difference in faculty growth between subgroups L and subgroups M may be ascribed to the difference in student/faculty ratio changes between the two subgroups. Figures 2 and 4 indicate these patterns. With respect to the Small and Middle Enrollment schools, it will be observed that student/faculty ratios at schools in subgroup L increased more than at schools in subgroup M.[4] With respect to the Large Enrollment schools, student/faculty ratios at schools in subgroup L decreased less than at schools in subgroup M. Thus, for each Enrollment Group, as between subgroups L and M, scale increases are similar, but student/faculty ratio changes differ. However, the situation reverses itself between subgroups M and H. There scale increases differ (the scale increases of subgroup M being less than those of subgroup H), but student/faculty ratio changes tend to be similar.

In sum, with respect to the factors to which increases in faculty growth are ascribed, subgroup L and subgroup M schools have similar enrollment patterns within each Enrollment Group, but differ because the student/faculty ratio changes of subgroup M schools are more favorable.[5] Subgroup M and subgroup H schools have similar student/faculty ratio patterns, but differ insofar as the enrollment increases of subgroup H schools are larger than those of subgroup M schools.

An explanation of these various patterns of increase in faculty size follows. Theoretically, the different faculty-size increases of the subgroups might be accounted for in three different ways. First, if student/faculty ratio levels were fairly standardized among law schools so that faculty increases to a large extent paralleled enrollment increases, differences in enrollment increase would have been the determining factor in locating schools within the three subgroups. (It should be recalled that although schools were placed in the three subgroups on the basis of increased instructional cost alone, increases in faculty size among the

---

4.   An increase in a student/faculty ratio from 1955 to 1970 is interpreted on the Figure as a negative percentage. A decreased student/faculty ratio is interpreted as a positive percentage.

5.   The word "favorable" assumes that a decreasing student/faculty ratio is a favorable development, or that a student/faculty ratio that increases less than another represents a more favorable student/faculty ratio development. As indicated above, for Small and Middle Enrollment Groups, the student/faculty ratio of subgroups L increased at a faster rate than subgroups M and H and for the Large Enrollment Group, the student/faculty ratio of subgroups M and H decreased at a faster rate than subgroup L.

three subgroups, not surprisingly, were similar to increases in instructional cost.)[6] Second, it might have happened that schools in subgroup L had the lowest enrollment increases and the least favorable student/faculty ratio developments; that schools in subgroup M had moderate enrollment increases and moderately favorable student/faculty ratio developments; and that schools in subgroup H had the highest enrollment increases and the most favorable student/faculty ratio developments.[7] A third possibility would have been for schools to have had similar enrollment increases and differing student/faculty ratio changes. In this case, student/faculty ratio changes would have been the determining factor in locating schools within the three subgroups.

The three patterns suggested above and the pattern that actually developed among the three subgroups are presented schematically below. As Table 1 indicates, the pattern that actually developed followed none of the three general

Table 1

**Patterns of Enrollment and
Student/Faculty Ratio Development by Subgroups**

	Subgroup L	Subgroup M	Subgroup H
First Pattern	Mod S/F r Low Enroll	Mod S/F r Mod Enroll	Mod S/F r High Enroll
Second Pattern	Unfav S/F r Low Enroll	Mod S/F r Mod Enroll	Fav S/F r High Enroll
Third Pattern	Unfav S/F r Mod Enroll	Mod S/F r Mod Enroll	Fav S/F r Mod Enroll
Actual Pattern	Unfav S/F r Mod Enroll	Mod S/F r Mod Enroll	Mod S/F r High Enroll

Note: The symbols "Unfav S/F r," "Mod S/F r," and "Fav S/F r" refer, respectively, to a relatively unfavorable student/faculty ratio development, a relatively moderate student/faculty ratio development, and a relatively favorable student/faculty ratio development. The symbols "Low Enroll," "Mod Enroll" and "High Enroll" refer respectively to relatively low, moderate and high enrollment increases. These terms, of course, are relative to each other as reflecting the different changes of each subgroup within a particular Enrollment Group. Thus, a relatively unfavorable student/faculty ratio development may refer to a quite different phenomenon depending on whether it attaches to the Small, Middle, or Large Enrollment Group.

6.   Thus, subgroup L schools' instructional cost and faculty size increased the least of the three subgroups, subgroup M schools' instructional cost and faculty size increased more than subgroup L and less than subgroup H, and subgroup H schools' instructional cost and faculty size increased the most of the three subgroups.

7.   It may seem somewhat awkward to refer to varying capacities for student/faculty ratio development. In actuality, what we are referring to are differing rates of faculty growth among schools that have had fairly uniform rates of enrollment increase. It might be misleading, however, to discuss different increases in faculty size in terms of increases in enrollment growth. Thus, to avoid a possible confusion, we use the concept of student/faculty ratio development.

possibilities.[8] Rather, schools in subgroups L and M appear to have followed the third pattern suggested, in which schools are supposed to have had similar enrollment increases and differing student/faculty ratio developments. Thus, subgroup L schools had the least favorable student/faculty ratio developments within their own Enrollment Groups and, accordingly, had the smallest faculty increases. On the other hand, schools in subgroups M and H appear to have followed the first pattern suggested, in which schools are supposed to have had similar student/faculty ratio changes and differing enrollment increases. Thus, subgroup H schools had the highest enrollment increases and, accordingly, had the highest faculty increases. In view of the actual changes among the three subgroups, we believe that the most likely over-all interpretation is closest to the third pattern suggested, with a necessary modification to account for the fact that subgroup H schools evidenced only moderate student/faculty ratio developments (similar to those schools in subgroup M) rather than the most favorable student/faculty ratio developments that would otherwise have been expected on the theory underlying the third pattern.

In the context of the analyses suggested above, our interpretation of the differences in faculty increases among the three subgroups is as follows. As a general principle, we believe that there exists a natural inclination on the part of law schools to expand their faculties. Large faculties enable schools to offer a more flexible and fuller educational program. During a time of substantial enrollment growth, such as the period of 1955 to 1970, we assume the normal tendency to expand faculties is reinforced. This would appear to be so for a number of reasons. If a school does not increase its faculty as its enrollment increases, class size tends to increase. Many believe that large classes are pedagogically less effective than small classes. Although there is no consensus as to optimum class size, as classes increase in size, there eventually develops a general inclination to check this growth by expanding the faculty. In addition, increased enrollment usually entails increased tuition income, or larger state subventions, and, accordingly, justifies the hiring of additional professors.

However, although schools in general are prone to increase their faculties as their enrollments increase, some schools are better able than others to increase their faculties relative to their enrollment increases in a manner that brings about a more favorable student/faculty ratio development. Thus, our hypothesis is that the schools in each subgroup had differing faculty increases because of their varying abilities to sustain favorable student/faculty ratio developments. As indicated, this explanation follows that given above for the third pattern. According to this interpretation, however, schools in subgroup H would have had the most favorable student/faculty ratio developments. In fact, they did not,

---

8.   With regard to this analysis, it should be recognized that we are dealing strictly with patterns. Thus, an individual school might be located in one particular subgroup rather than another because of an extreme change in one of its factors. For example, a school with a relatively low enrollment increase might nevertheless be in subgroup H because of an extremely favorable student/faculty ratio development. There are, of course, a number of various combinations of a similar nature and, indeed, a number of schools actually developed in such ways. However, by and large, most schools within each particular subgroup evidenced the general characteristics suggested above by what we refer to as the "actual pattern."

and it is this occurrence that gives rise to the need to modify the theory underlying the third pattern so as to accord with what actually happened. We believe that the schools in subgroup H did not manifest the most favorable student/faculty ratio developments because they had the highest enrollment increases. Thus, although, figuratively speaking, subgroup H schools had a tendency to have their student/faculty ratios develop in the most favorable manner because of their high enrollment increases, this tendency was neutralized. Of course, against this interpretation it may be argued, at least insofar as subgroups M and H are concerned, that the theory underlying the first pattern suggested above is more likely to apply. This theory, it will be recalled, holds that all the schools within each Enrollment Group tended to have their faculties increase at the same rate vis-a-vis their enrollment increases; i.e., they tended to have similar student/faculty ratio changes, and further, this being the case, differences in enrollment increase primarily accounted for differences in faculty increase. We do not subscribe to this hypothesis because we believe that the evidence suggests on balance that no such tendency for similar student/faculty developments existed. In sum, we find it more plausible to suppose that some schools, for whatever reasons, were better able to have their faculties increase in a manner more favorable as against their enrollment increases than other schools. Further, among these schools, a few had extremely high enrollment increases, and, as a result, their student/faculty ratios changed in a way that was somewhat less favorable than what would have been the case if their enrollment increases had been less extreme.

Our thesis interprets changes in faculty size largely in terms of student/faculty ratio changes. In this respect, the patterns of student/faculty ratio changes of schools in the Small and Middle Enrollment Groups were similar to each other but different from the pattern of student/faculty ratio changes in the Large Enrollment Group. The three subgroups of schools in the Small Enrollment Group and in the Middle Enrollment Group had similar enrollment ranges and similar student/faculty ratio ranges in 1955, and, consequently, their student/faculty ratios developed in different manners from similar starting points. In contrast, the three subgroups in the Large Enrollment Group had similar enrollment ranges but differing student/faculty ratio ranges in 1955, and, consequently, their student/faculty ratios developed in different manners from dissimilar starting points. Thus, in 1955, schools in subgroup L of the Large Enrollment Group tended to have low student/faculty ratios, schools in subgroup M tended to have moderate student/faculty ratios, and schools in subgroup H tended to have high student/faculty ratios. With regard to schools in the Large Enrollment Group, it is reasonable that subgroup L schools, having started in a relatively favorable position, should have had the least favorable student/faculty ratio development; that subgroup M schools, having started in a moderate position, should have had a moderately favorable student/faculty ratio development; and that schools in subgroup H, having started in an unfavorable position, should have had the most favorable student/faculty ratio development.

As explained, subgroup H schools had the highest enrollment increases and, therefore, their student/faculty ratio developments were only slightly more favorable than schools in subgroup M.

Attrition

First-year Law Students Who Do Not Return in the Second or Third Years at a Sample of 43 Law Schools for Various Years

The percents of total student enrollment comprised by first-year students and upperclass students are determined in this Appendix by analyzing the enrollments of a sample of 43 law schools over a period of several years. The sample is divided evenly among Small Enrollment Group schools, Middle Enrollment Group schools, and Large Enrollment Group schools, and among schools in the Fourth, Third, Second, and First Quartiles of the Resource Index, plus schools not included in the Index. Pertinent editions of the *Review of Legal Education* are the source of the data.

The number of students in the first-year class is recorded (Year 1); the number of students in the second-year class in the following year (the year after Year 1) is recorded (Year 2); and the number of students in the third-year class in the following year (the year after Year 2) is recorded (Year 3). Thus, in effect, one class is followed through its three years of law school. Enrollment of full-time day students is presented. Note that this calculation is concerned only with enrollment size and makes no attempt to trace the fate of particular students. The enrollment figures are presented in Table 1 for the academic years 1955, 1956, 1957, 1958, and 1968, 1969, 1970, 1971, 1972.

In order to determined the attrition percentage, the following formula is used.

$$(A - (B + C \div 2)) \div A = \text{Attrition percentage}$$

where: A = First-year enrollment in Year 1

B = Second-year enrollment in Year 2

C = Third-year enrollment in Year 3

The attrition percentages for the sample of 43 law schools are presented in Table 2, derived from enrollment figures in Table 1.

In order to interpret the data, the attrition percentage in Table 2 should be located in Table 3. For given attrition percentages, Table 3 gives the percent breakdown between first-year and second-and-third-year students, assuming that the enrollments of these three years add up to 100%. Thus, no drop-outs, or a 0% attrition, would mean that the class reflects the following breakdown: first-year = 33.3% and upperclass = 66.7%. A 32% attrition would mean that the class reflects the following breakdown: first-year = 42% and upperclass = 58%. At the 43 sample schools the entering classes of 1955 averaged an attrition of 30% which can be interpreted as follows: first-year = 41.7%, upperclass = 58.3%. The entering classes of 1970 averaged an attrition of 14% which can be interpreted as first-year = 36.8%, upperclass = 63.2%. It will be noted that the attrition percentage has been declining from the beginning of the fifteen-year period (1955) to the end (1970).

Table 1

Number of First-year, Second-year, and Third-year Students at a Sample of 43 Law Schools, Various Years
(Full-time students)

Law School	Class	1955	1956	1957	1958	1968	1969	1970	1971	1972
1	1st	129	114			139	159	189		
	2nd		67	63			104	136	177	
	3rd			55	63			99	126	175
2	1st	63	53			48	50	124		
	2nd		32	27			33	43	81	
	3rd			28	23			39	38	84
3	1st	147	171			181	172	176		
	2nd		79	97			106	117	207	
	3rd			75	83			81	98	189
4	1st	32	46			78	90	93		
	2nd		19	28			54	66	91	
	3rd			14	27			57	62	92
5	1st	45	49			71	88	173		
	2nd		24	30			53	82	145	
	3rd			24	27			56	74	161
6	1st	103	83			103	183	238		
	2nd		56	64			91	126	193	
	3rd			54	62			84	124	179
7	1st	35	34			178	196	347		
	2nd		21	23			70	79	142	
	3rd			17	26			54	56	101

Table 1 (continued)

Law School	Class	1955	1956	1957	1958	1968	1969	1970	1971	1972
8	1st	59	64			106	153	155		
	2nd		35	44			87	128	145	
	3rd			29	39			77	130	144
9	1st	47	44			50	46	90		
	2nd		30	24			37	37	71	
	3rd			26	23			36	39	70
10	1st	141	144			346	425	458		
	2nd		80	34			221	297	313	
	3rd			85	72			186	303	318
11	1st	28	41			118	238	122		
	2nd		17	24			99	193	130	
	3rd			16	22			81	159	95
12	1st	60	89			198	197	218		
	2nd		44	51			153	188	208	
	3rd			28	38			170	194	235
13	1st	53	60			176	166	176		
	2nd		34	40			134	144	166	
	3rd			30	42			128	149	170
14	1st	16	28			134	135	187		
	2nd		10	18			73	108	157	
	3rd			10	9			72	88	154
15	1st	61	69			91	189	204		
	2nd		39	36			76	143	197	
	3rd			37	38			80	146	205
16	1st	8	9			56	92	138		
	2nd		5	9			29	57	81	
	3rd			5	4			26	40	64
17	1st	51	48			92	87	103		
	2nd		32	35			75	76	93	
	3rd			31	35			68	78	87
18	1st	130	151			167	187	150		
	2nd		82	116			150	172	141	
	3rd			78	109			149	172	148
19	1st	11	15			43	81	128		
	2nd		9	14			43	70	111	
	3rd			5	12			45	86	119

Table 1 (continued)

Law School	Class	1955	1956	1957	1958	1968	1969	1970	1971	1972
20	1st	27	24			46	55	77		
	2nd		20	22			36	44	63	
	3rd			17	17			35	43	56
21	1st	84	81			145	177	318		
	2nd		60	63			124	168	305	
	3rd			57	52			134	166	307
22	1st	60	98			132	136	147		
	2nd		45	58			85	106	80	
	3rd			42	55			72	110	102
23	1st	86	142			185	172	242		
	2nd		63	92			131	130	219	
	3rd			63	87			122	126	206
24	1st	39	54			52	48	72		
	2nd		29	40			35	44	62	
	3rd			28	41			45	46	63
25	1st	154	124			35	88	110		
	2nd		134	106			37	52	90	
	3rd			100	83			24	53	74
26	1st	177	182			170	210	228		
	2nd		134	158			158	209	216	
	3rd			125	158			156	206	212
27	1st	36	43			178	111	168		
	2nd		26	29			132	106	143	
	3rd			29	29			134	104	137
28	1st	26	50			164	164	347		
	2nd		25	22			105	140	225	
	3rd			15	20			94	147	261
29	1st	79	119			139	127	176		
	2nd		59	86			125	118	185	
	3rd			63	92			125	127	182
30	1st	39	43			70	107	154		
	2nd		31	31			81	99	140	
	3rd			30	28			77	91	131
31	1st	181	190			303	344	296		
	2nd		149	159			283	325	304	
	3rd			138	148			278	334	308

Table 1 (continued)

Law School	Class	1955	1956	1957	1958	1968	1969	1970	1971	1972
32	1st	162	176			206	146	273		
	2nd		140	143			185	164	237	
	3rd			124	106			179	158	223
33	1st	44	40			127	135	151		
	2nd		36	33			105	100	127	
	3rd			35	28			101	99	121
34	1st	63	83			209	219	349		
	2nd		53	66			153	141	254	
	3rd			50	64			153	140	249
35	1st	49	47			106	134	174		
	2nd		41	39			90	124	173	
	3rd			39	39			93	127	169
36	1st	52	73			115	119	192		
	2nd		50	50			82	116	173	
	3rd			37	58			77	108	183
37	1st	253	263			320	364	360		
	2nd		237	228			310	335	348	
	3rd			202	217			342	325	341
38	1st	206	178			216	265	395		
	2nd		195	169			186	229	319	
	3rd			171	161			167	200	289
39	1st	123	118			145	168	165		
	2nd		106	114			136	158	167	
	3rd			112	118			139	158	172
40	1st	39	66			136	124	203		
	2nd		30	47			91	96	144	
	3rd			40	37			72	100	129
41	1st	28	28			131	130	128		
	2nd		28	30			95	104	105	
	3rd			25	29			85	99	107
42	1st	170	165			200	241	166		
	2nd		166	163			191	232	169	
	3rd			161	161			174	209	178
43	1st	75	102			201	248	306		
	2nd		69	81			152	224	271	
	3rd			82	76			163	238	278

Table 2

**Attrition Percentage of First-year versus Second-and-third-year
Students at a Sample of 43 Law Schools, Various Years**

Law School	Entering Class				
	1955	1956	1968	1969	1970
1	53%	45%	27%	18%	7%
2	52	53	25	19	33
3	48	47	48	38	*13
4	48	40	29	29	2
5	47	42	23	11	12
6	47	24	15	32	22
7	46	28	65	66	65
8	46	35	23	16	7
9	44	47	27	17	22
10	41	63	41	29	31
11	41	44	24	26	8
12	40	50	18	3	* 2
13	40	32	26	12	5
14	38	52	46	27	17
15	38	46	14	24	1
16	38	28	51	47	47
17	38	27	22	11	13
18	38	25	10	8	4
19	33	13	* 2	4	10
20	31	19	23	21	23
21	30	27	11	6	4
22	28	42	41	21	38
23	27	37	32	26	12
24	27	25	23	6	13
25	27	24	13	40	25
26	27	13	8	1	6
27	24	33	25	5	17
28	23	58	39	13	30
29	23	25	10	4	* 4
30	22	31	*13	11	12
31	21	25	7	4	* 3
32	19	29	12	*10	16
33	19	24	19	26	18
34	18	22	27	36	28
35	18	17	14	6	2
36	16	26	31	6	7
37	13	15	* 2	9	4
38	11	7	18	19	23
39	11	2	5	6	* 3

Table 2 (continued)

Entering Class

Law School	1955	1956	1968	1969	1970
40	10	36	40	21	33
41	5	* 5	31	22	17
42	4	2	9	9	* 5
43	* 1	23	22	7	10
Average of 43 Schools	30%	30%	23%	18%	14%

Note: * indicates that there are more upperclass students than would be expected from the first-year enrollment, i.e., students have been added.

Table 3

The Relationship between First-year and Second-and-third-year Students Based on the Attrition Percentage

Attrition Percentage	Ratio of First-year to Second-and-third-year Students	
	First	Second & Third
0%	33.3% /	66.7%
2	33.8 /	66.2
4	34.2 /	65.8
6	34.7 /	65.3
8	35.2 /	64.8
10	35.7 /	64.3
12	36.2 /	63.8
14	36.8 /	63.2
16	37.3 /	62.7
18	37.9 /	62.1
20	38.5 /	61.5
22	39.0 /	61.0
24	39.7 /	60.3
26	40.3 /	59.7
28	41.0 /	59.0
30	41.7 /	58.3

Table 3 (continued)

Attrition Percentage	Ratio of First-year to Second-and-third-year Students		
	First		Second & Third
32	42.4	/	57.6
34	43.0	/	57.0
36	44.0	/	56.0
38	44.6	/	55.4
40	45.5	/	54.5
42	46.3	/	53.7
44	47.2	/	52.8
46	48.0	/	52.0
48	49.0	/	51.0
50	50.0	/	50.0

Course Groupings

FIRST CATEGORY GROUPING

Corporations

Corporations
Advanced Corporations
Business Organization
Business Associations
Private Corporations
Private and Closed Corporations
Business Planning I
Business Planning II
Corporate Relations
Corporation Problems
Problems of Corporate Practice
Corporation Counseling and Planning
Corporations' Responsibility to
   Society
Counseling in Business Transactions
Business Torts
Corporate Control
Shareholders
Banking Industry
Cooperative Corporate Law
Partnership
Agency

Agency and Partnership
Corporate Reorganization
Corporate Finance
Money and Banking
Accounting for Lawyers
Legal Accounting
Government Regulation of Business
Government Contracts
Regulated Industries
Public Utilities
Government Enterprises
Antitrust
Selected Problems in Antitrust
Unfair Competition
Unfair Trade Practices
Trademarks and Unfair Competition
Law and Competition
Trade Regulations
Securities Act of 1933
Securities and Exchange Commission
Securities Market
Control of Mutual Funds

Commercial Law

Commercial Transactions
Commercial Code
Commercial Paper
Negotiable Instruments
Bills and Notes
Sales
Sales Financing

Checks
Vendor and Purchaser
Creditors' Rights
Bankruptcy
Fraud and Mistake
Contract Remedies
Security Transactions

Procedure

Civil Procedure
Advanced Civil Procedure
Evidence
Equity
Conflicts of Law
Advanced Conflicts
Remedies
Damages
Restitution
Judicial Administration
Administrative Justice Systems
Federal Courts
Federal Jurisdiction

Problems in Federal Practice
State Practice and Procedures
Civil Justice Systems
Trial Techniques
Trial Preparation
Trial Practice
Trial and Appellate Procedure
Trial and Appellate Practice
Medical Legal Problems and
   Trial Practice
Pleading
Pleading Practice

Property

Property
Common Property
Real Estate Transactions
Modern Real Estate Transactions
Real Estate Secured Transactions
Modern Real Estate Law
Land Titles
Mortgages
Trusts and Estates
Trust and Estate Problems
Trust Administration
Descedant Estates

Wills
Wills and Administration
Fiduciary Administration
Future Interest
Suretyships
Conveyances
Public Land Law
Land Use Planning
Mining Law
Oil and Gas Rights
Landlord–Tenant Relations

Taxation

Taxation
Current Problems in Taxation
Tax Policy
Income Tax I
Income Tax II
Federal Taxation

Federal Income Tax
Federal Tax Problems
Tax Distribution
Financing State and Local
   Governments
State and Local Tax

Corporate Taxation
Corporate Income Tax
Taxation of Corporations and
  Shareholders
Taxation of Foreign Income
Taxation of Oil and Gas

Estate and Business Planning
Estate Planning
Estate Tax
Estate and Gift Tax
Taxation of Trusts and
  Estates

SECOND CATEGORY GROUPING

Jurisprudence
This category includes legal history, legal ethics,
and conceives of jurisprudence rather broadly.

Jurisprudence
Modern Legal Philosophy
Legal Theory
Legal Process
Policy Analysis and Jurisprudence
American Legal Method
Civil Law
Legal History
American Legal History
Early American Law
American Legal Thought
Roman Law

Comparative Roman and Modern Law
Legal Ethics
Legal Profession
Lawyer in Modern Society
Law and Social Change
American Slavery
Law and Social Science
Sociology and Law
Law and Behavioral Science
Law and Political Progress
Law and Technology
Law and Economics

Criminal Law

Criminal Law
Advanced Criminal Law
Criminal Law and Administration
Criminal Procedure
Advanced Problems in Criminal
  Procedure
Criminal and Society
Criminal Practice and Procedure
Criminology and Administration of
  Criminal Procedure
Criminal Trial Practice

Urban Criminal Justice
Law Enforcement and Administration
  of Criminal Justice
Responsibility and Punishment
Sociological Study of Law
  Enforcement
Prosecution
Criminal Sanctions
White Collar Crime
Injured Party in Criminal Process
Rights of Inmates

Urban Affairs

This category includes poverty law, race relations and
certain subjects of current interest.

Urban Problems
Urban Legal Problems
Public Law
Consumer Problems
Consumer Protection
Products and Consumers
Food and Drug Law
Drug Law
Social Legislation
Law and Social Welfare
Social Welfare Legislation
Civil Rights and Welfare
Microeconomics and Welfare Economics
Legal Problems of the Poor
Law and the Black Community
Race Relations

American Indian
Equality in Education
Law and Poverty
Law and the Poor
Race and Poverty
Selective Service
Housing
Housing Problems
Urban Renewal
Regional Economic Development
Environmental Management and
  Planning
Environmental Law
Environmental Issues
Natural Resources
Atomic Energy

Labor Law

Labor Law
Labor Relations
Management
Labor and Management
Labor Management Relations Act

Collective Bargaining
Arbitration of Labor Disputes
Employee Rights
Public Employment Relations

Law and the Person

Family Law
Marital Rights
Domestic Relations
Juvenile and the Law

Law and Psychiatry
Medical Legal Issues
Law and Medicine

International and Comparative Law

International Law
Comparative Law
Comparative Civil Law
Public International Law
International Conflict of Laws
International Organizations
International Law and Organizations
International Legal Process
Human Rights and World Order
Development of World Order

Problems in Development of World Order
International Transactions
International Business Transactions
International Trade
Law of International Trade and
  Investment
International Economic Organization
Law and Economic Development
Business Abroad
International Finance

International Monetary Law
Legal Aspects of U.S. Foreign Policy
U.S. Foreign Relations
Inter-American Legal Systems
Common Law of Latin America
Legal Systems of Western Europe
   and Latin America
Laws and Institutions of
   Atlantic Community
European Legal Systems

Common Market
Soviet Public Law
Soviet Civil Law
Asian Law
Chinese Law
Japanese Law
Middle East Problems
African Law
Legal Changes in Africa

Administrative Law

Administrative Law
Government Administration
Government Regulation of Radio

and TV
Administration of Public
   Resources: Public Lands

Constitutional Law

Constitutional Law
American Constitution
American Political Institutions
Supreme Court
History of the Supreme Court
Federal Courts and the
   Federal System

Constitutional Litigation
Political and Civil Rights
Civil Rights
Equal Protection and Civil
   Liberties
Problems in Equal Protection
Church–State Relations

General

Admiralty Law
Advanced Torts
Agricultural Law
Celebrated Cases
Copyright Law
Defamation
Injuries to Relations
Law Review
Legal Aid Clinic
Legal Aid
Clinical Programs
Interviewing and Counseling
Legal Problems
Legal Education

Legislation
Legislative Developments
Legal Writing
Drafting Legislation
State and Local Government
Local Government
Municipal Law
Military Justice
Students' Rights
Insurance
Patent Law
Practice Court
Moot Court